GENETIC ETHICS

A Horizon in Bioethics Series Book from

THE CENTER FOR
BI🌐ETHICS
AND HUMAN DIGNITY

The Horizons in Bioethics Series brings together an array of insightful writers to address important bioethical issues from a forward-looking Christian perspective. The introductory volume, *Bioethics and the Future of Medicine*, covers a broad range of topics and foundational matters. Subsequent volumes focus on a particular set of issues, beginning with the end-of-life theme of *Dignity and Dying* and continuing with the genetics focus of *Genetic Ethics*.

The series is a project of The Center for Bioethics and Human Dignity, an international center located just north of Chicago, Illinois in the United States of America. The Center endeavors to bring Christian perspectives to bear on today's many pressing bioethical challenges. It pursues this task by developing two book series, four audio tape series, four video tape series, numerous conferences in different parts of the world, and a variety of other printed and computer based resources. Through its membership program, the Center networks and provides resources for people interested in bioethical matters all over the world. Members receive the Center's international journal, *Ethics and Medicine*, the Center's newsletter, *Dignity*, the Center's Update Letters, special Worldwide Web access, an Internet News Service and Discussion Forum, and discounts on most bioethics resources in print.

For more information on membership in the Center or its various resources, including present or future books in the Horizons in Bioethics Series, contact the Center at:

The Center for Bioethics and Human Dignity
2065 Half Day Road
Bannockburn, IL 60015 USA
Phone: (847) 317-8180
Fax: (847) 317-8153

Information and ordering is also available through the Center's World Wide Web site on the Internet: http://www.bioethix.org

THE CENTER FOR
BI◉ETHICS
AND HUMAN DIGNITY

presents

Genetic Ethics

Do the Ends Justify the Genes?

Edited by
John F Kilner,
Rebecca D Pentz
and Frank E Young

paternoster press

WILLIAM B EERDMANS PUBLISHING COMPANY
GRAND RAPIDS, MICHIGAN

First published 1997 jointly
in the U.K. by Paternoster Press,
P.O. Box 300, Carlisle, Cumbria CA3 0QS
and in the U.S.A by
Wm. B. Eerdmans Publishing Co.,
255 Jefferson Ave. S.E., Grand Rapids, Michigan 49503

03   02   01   00   99   98   97   7   6   5   4   3   2   1

British Library Cataloguing in Publication Data

A catalogue record for this book is available from the British Library.

ISBN 0-85364-814-x

Library of Congress Cataloging-in-Publication Data

Genetic Ethics : Do the ends justify the genes? / edited by John F. Kilner,
Rebecca D. Pentz and Frank E. Young.
   p. cm. — (Horizon in bioethics series)
Presented by The Center for Bioethics and Human Dignity.
Includes bibliographical references and index.
ISBN 0-8028-4428-6 (paper : alk. paper)
   1.Human genetics—Moral and ethical aspects. 2. Human genetics—
Religious aspects—Christianity. 3. Genetic engineering—Moral and
ethical aspects. 4. Genetic engineering—Religious aspects—
Christianity. I. Kilner, John Frederic. II. Pentz. Rebecca
Davis. III. Young, Frank E. IV. Series
QH438. 7. G43   1997
174' .25—dc21   97-2526
                                                                                                        CIP

Typeset By WestKey Ltd, Falmouth, Cornwall, UK
Printed in the United States of America

Contents

Preface (by the editors)   viii

    John F. Kilner, MDiv, PhD
    (Director, The Center for Bioethics and Human Dignity, Bannockburn, IL, USA)
    Rebecca D. Pentz, PhD
    (Clinical Ethicist and Associate Professor of Clinical Ethics, University of Texas M.D.
    Anderson Cancer Center, USA)
    Frank E. Young, MD, PhD
    (Former Commissioner, U.S. Food and Drug Administration; Director of Adult
    Education, Fourth Presbyterian Church, Washington DC, USA)

Introduction: The Experience of Genetic Challenges

'The Riddle of Suffering'   3
    David B. Biebel, DMin
        (Director of Communications, Christian Medical & Dental Society, USA)

'The Disease of Isolation'   7
    Markie Jackson
        (District Representative, Hemophilia Health Services, USA)

'The Search for Shalom'   13
    Hessel Bouma, III, PhD
        (Professor of Biology, Calvin College, Grand Rapids, MI, USA)

Part I: Genetic Perspective

History

1. 'EUGENICS IN HISTORICAL AND ETHICAL PERSPECTIVE'   25
    Arthur J. Dyck, PhD
        (Saltonstall Professor of Ethics, Harvard University,
        Cambridge/Boston, MA, USA)

2. 'TECHNOLOGY, HISTORY, AND WORLDVIEW'   40
    Nancy R. Pearcey, MA
        (Fellow and Policy Director, The Wilberforce Forum,
        Reston, VA, USA)

Sovereignty
3. 'GOD'S SOVEREIGNTY AND GENETIC ANOMALIES'   49
    Michael S. Beates, STM
       (*Instructor of Biblical Studies, Reformed Theological Seminary,
       Orlando, FL, USA*)

4. 'PLAYING GOD'   60
    Allen D. Verhey, BD, PhD
       (*Blekkink Professor of Religion, Hope College, Holland, MI, USA*)

Humanity
5. 'REDUCING PEOPLE TO GENETICS'   75
    Henk Jochemsen, PhD
       (*Director, Lindeboom Instituut, Ede, The Netherlands*)

6. 'RESISTING REDUCTIONISM BY RESTORING THE CONTEXT'   84
    V. Elving Anderson, PhD
       (*Professor Emeritus of Genetics, University of Minnesota, USA*)

Part II: Genetic Information

The Search
7. 'THE HUMAN GENOME PROJECT'   95
    Francis S. Collins, PhD, MD
       (*Director, The U.S. Human Genome Project*)

8. 'BEHAVIOURAL AND GERM-LINE GENETIC RESEARCH'   104
    Leroy B. Walters, PhD
       (*Professor, Department of Philosophy, Georgetown University,
       Washington, DC, USA*)

9. 'THE INCENTIVE OF PATENTS'   113
    Stephen Sherry, JD
       (*Attorney, Law Firm of McAndrew, Held, & Mallory,
       Chicago, IL, USA*)

The Use
10. 'GENETIC TESTING AND CONFIDENTIALITY'   124
    C. Christopher Hook, MD
       (*Director of Ethics Education, Mayo Graduate School of Medicine,
       Rochester, MN, USA*)

11. 'PRENATAL GENETIC TESTING, ABORTION, AND BEYOND'   136
    Scott B. Rae, PhD
       (*Associate Professor, Biblical Studies and Christian Ethics,
       Talbot School of Theology, Biola University, La Mirada, CA, USA*)

12. 'GENETIC COUNSELLING'   146
    Elizabeth J. Thomson, RN, MA
       (*Acting Branch Chief, ELSI Branch of the National Center for
       Human Genome Research, Bethesda, MD, USA*)

13. 'THE EDUCATIONAL CHALLENGE'   156
     Martha Newsome, DDS
         (*Professor and Program Chair, Department of Biology,
         Tomball College, Houston, TX, USA*)

Part III: Genetic Intervention

Assessment

14. 'GENETIC THERAPY'   171
     Frank E. Young, MD, PhD
         (*Former Commisioner, U.S. Food and Drug Administration, Director of
         Adult Education, Fourth Presbyterian Church, Washington, DC, USA*)

15. 'A THEOLOGICAL BASIS FOR GENETIC INTERVENTION'   183
     John S. Feinberg, ThM, PhD
         (*Professor, Biblical and Systematic Theology, Trinity Evangelical
         Divinity School, Deerfield, IL, USA*)

16. 'ETHICAL STANDARDS FOR GENETIC INTERVENTION'   193
     James C. Peterson, MDiv, PhD
         (*Director, Program in Religion, Ethics, and Technology, Wingate University,
         Wingate, NC, USA*)

17. 'THE CASE OF HUMAN GROWTH HORMONE'   203
     Dónal P. O'Mathúna, PhD
         (*Associate Professor, Mt. Carmel College of Nursing,
         Columbus, OH, USA*)

Engagement

18. 'CONTEMPORARY CHRISTIAN RESPONSIBILITY'   218
     Charles W. Colson, JD
         (*Director, The Wilberforce Forum and Prison Fellowship,
         Reston, VA, USA*)

19. THE CHURCH AND THE NEW GENETICS   230
     C. Ben Mitchell, MDiv, PhD (cand.)
         (*Southern Baptist Human Life Commission, Nashville, TN, USA*)

20. 'THE CHURCH AS A WELCOMING COMMUNITY'   246
     Marsha D. M. Fowler, RN, MDiv, PhD
         (*Professor, Schools of Nursing and Theology, Azusa Pacific University,
         Azusa, CA, USA*)

                                                                   256

Glossary of Genetic Terms

(by Hessel Bouma, III, PhD, *Professor of Biology, Calvin College,
Grand Rapids, MI, USA*)

Preface

A revolution is underway, with profound implications for all spheres of life. It is fuelled by rapid advances in the availability of genetic information and the capability to intervene genetically in response to it.

The ethical issues are glaring. How should parents and society respond when a child, before or after birth, is diagnosed as having a greater-than-average risk for certain genetically influenced diseases? Is a new and troubling wave of eugenics about to break upon us? Should *in utero* genetic therapy be required for known genetic disorders, and should its availability redefine when human life is legally protected? Who should have access to a person's genetic profile? Do companies rightly use it to limit a person's access to employment or health insurance? Should we even be developing expensive genetic technologies at a time when so many people in countries around the world have insufficient access to health care?

Who can or should answer such awesome questions – and on what ethical basis? Do Christian perspectives have anything meaningful to contribute to persons of faith and to societies seeking wisdom for a genetic future? Correcting or enhancing genes may be(come) technically feasible, but in light of the dangers of this enterprise, are the ends in view sufficiently praiseworthy to warrant the risk? Or is it legitimate even to attempt to justify potentially harmful endeavours on the basis of the good that can be achieved? In other words, do the ends justify the genes?

One of the heaviest burdens of genetic knowledge and the capability to intervene is the terrible necessity of personal and social decision-making. This burden alone is no reason to forgo the genetic quest, but it does create a pressing need for assistance in making difficult decisions. This book is designed to provide such assistance. It does so not simply by offering a collection of pragmatic techniques and answers. Rather, it locates such counsel in an exploration of the kind of people and societies we must be, and the ways we must view life and one another, if we are to be able to decide wisely. A Christian perspective has much to offer regarding such matters.

The book begins with an honest look at the life situations in which tough genetic questions arise. David Biebel ponders 'The

Riddle of Suffering,' Markie Jackson laments 'The Disease of Isolation,' and Hessel Bouma, III considers 'The Search for Shalom'. This introduction and Bouma's Glossary of Genetic Terms at the end of the book provide helpful experiential and terminological reference points for the remainder of the book.

Following the book's Introduction, twenty chapters address three dimensions of the genetic challenge: genetic perspective, genetic information, and genetic intervention. Avoiding the temptation to rush immediately to matters of information and intervention, Part I examines three vantage points from which such matters are best addressed: history, sovereignty, and humanity. Arthur Dyck and Nancy Pearcey open Part I with historical investigations into eugenics and technology. Michael Beates and Allen Verhey then examine the place of God by considering how a good and powerful God can co-exist with genetic suffering and by exploring the meaning of 'playing God'. Part I concludes with Henk Jochemsen's and Elving Anderson's investigations into the danger of and alternative to reducing people to their genetics.

In Part II, the book examines the search for genetic information as well as its appropriate use. Francis Collins begins describing the quest by reflecting on the Human Genome Project. Next, Leroy Walters elaborates on the particularly controversial enterprises of behavioural and germ-line research. Stephen Sherry then notes and evaluates the impetus that research efforts receive from the opportunity to patent life forms.

The appropriate use of genetic information involves multiple considerations. Christopher Hook and Scott Rae explore various temptations, including confidentiality breaches and abortion, that are inherent in the enterprise of genetic testing. The effective use of genetic information in genetic counselling is the focus of Elizabeth Thomson's analysis. Martha Newsome then concludes Part II with a challenge to disseminate genetic information as proactively as possible.

The final section of the book is reserved for the controversial subject of genetic intervention. It includes both an assessment of its acceptability and a discussion of how to engage in it responsibly. Frank Young opens Part III with a description and evaluation of the enterprise of genetic therapy. John Feinberg and James Peterson then undertake theological and ethical investigations of how to distinguish acceptable genetic interventions – for example, those that can correct harmful genetic deficiencies – from other interventions that should be opposed. Donal O'Mathuna employs the example of Human Growth Hormone to illustrate the distinction.

The last three chapters address the theme of engagement in complementary ways. Charles Colson examines the responsibility of Christians to be informed about and actively involved in the extraordinarily important issues surrounding genetic intervention. Ben Mitchell considers the role that the institutional church should play. Marsha Fowler then concludes with a discussion of what ministry among people with genetic challenges should look like.

We are reminded again and again throughout this book that to be concerned about those touched by genetic challenges is not to narrow our focus to a small group of people. Every one of us is afflicted by genetic limitations to a degree that not one of us knows. Yet, at the same time, genetic limitations can be among the greatest of disadvantages for particular individuals and families. Whether motivated by stewardship of our own bodies or by concern for others, genetic ethics must be high on the agenda of us all.

John F. Kilner
Rebecca D. Pentz
Frank E. Young

[INTRODUCTION:]

The Experience of Genetic Challenges

The Riddle of Suffering

David B. Biebel, DMin

In 1978 my wife and I lost a three year old son, Jonathan, to a genetic disorder called infantile bilateral striatal necrosis. Eight years later we nearly lost a second son, Christopher, to the same disease, which causes brain damage and may lead to death. For me as a Christian, these experiences have had both natural human components and spiritual results.

On a purely human level, to experience genetic disease in one's children is to be immersed in a boiling cauldron of almost pure pain, with a generous helping of surprise, confusion, disappointment, anger, and guilt thrown in. In the beginning, this experience may act like glue, uniting a couple or a family against something beyond their control. In the end, it often becomes a wedge, driving people apart. That almost happened to my wife and me, but by God's grace we survived (and things continue to get better every year).

People grappling with genetic illness need help. For a Christian who happens to be a doctor, or a nurse, or an ethicist, or a pastor or chaplain who wants to help such people, I have a few suggestions.

First, we must keep our focus on the *people* involved, both the patient and his or her family. It is all too easy to think of the person before us as another *case* of cystic fibrosis, or infantile bilateral striatal necrosis, or whatever the disease may be. We so readily focus on the disease itself. However, the only way to help people affected by genetic disease is to remember that they are people who once had hopes and dreams much like our own – people who need understanding, support, encouragement, and compassion. Compassion entails holding their pain in our hearts. Even when there is nothing we can do in terms of 'treatment', our hearts can share their pain.

Christians who happen to be doctors, or nurses, or ethicists, or pastors, or chaplains, or whatever, would do well to ask themselves, as they try to help families grappling with genetic illness, 'What would Jesus do?'

I believe that:

- He would validate the pain, for he was a man of sorrows. He would not say, 'You shouldn't feel this way.' He would say, 'I'm sorry.'
- He would weep with those who weep. One of our fondest memories of the whole ordeal with Jonathan was hearing that the neurologist who had taken care of him in Milwaukee had wept upon hearing of our son's death.
- He would comfort those who mourn by being with them, for he is 'Immanuel', God with us.
- He would carry the pain: a sorrow shared is a sorrow diminished. He would say: 'This is our pain, our challenge. I am with you, you don't need to be afraid.'
- He would bind up the hurt, fill the void with himself, and nurture the hurting child in us toward maturity, showing us how to use the pain for good, as he did.
- He would not scold, judge, give a lot of advice, or offer pious platitudes or pat answers to questions nobody is asking.
- In my case, because he is the good shepherd, he went out into the wilderness and found this lost lamb, picked me up, and carried me home.

There is one other essential observation regarding the human side of the suffering that comes with genetic disease. I hate what this disease has done to our sons and our family through their suffering (and ours, with them). So if the genetic disorder could be dealt with for future generations through genetic therapy, I would rejoice. Had I known ahead of time the agony that genetic illness would bring us, I would have preferred to avoid it. So I understand why people who approach this issue on a purely human level using secular values and reasoning may choose to kill unborn, genetically deficient children in an effort to avoid the kind of pain I have just described. But there is more than a purely human dimension to life.

Spiritually speaking, when I ask myself would I rather that Jonathan and Christopher had never been born, the answer is: absolutely not. Though it broke my heart twice to share their sufferings, through them I know a lot more about love and faithfulness, kindness, gentleness, and humility than I could possibly otherwise have known. Through them I have learned what is important and what is not. People are important; things are not.

As Peter Kreeft writes in *Making Sense Out of Suffering*: 'Love somehow goes with suffering. Truth, wisdom, knowledge of reality, go with suffering. It seems that everything that has intrinsic value, everything that cannot be bought or negotiated or compromised or relativised or reduced, goes with suffering.'

Looking back, I can see that the experience with all its wondering and wandering has made me:

- stronger because it showed me my weakness,
- wiser because it showed the foolishness of centring life on anything other than God,
- more dependent because as the master of my own destiny I utterly failed;
- closer to God, whom I love today more than I ever did before, whom I know today better than I ever could have known him without these experiences, and whom I serve today more wholeheartedly than ever before.

I have come to see both the experiences and what I have learned through them as a trust, a gift. In his grace he has called me to share this trust with others who have their own unique struggles and who desperately need to know the reason for the hope that is in us.

A few weeks after Christopher became ill, although he seemed to be improving slowly, we could not rouse him for his late-night medication. 'Is it another attack?' we wondered. 'The beginning of the end? Will he ever wake again?'

I climbed into bed with him, resolving that if another son of mine had to die, he would not die alone. Before I fell asleep that night, with Chris cradled in my arm, I talked to him as he slept: 'Daddy loves you. We all love you. Jesus loves you. You don't have to be afraid. If you don't wake up, you'll go to be with him . . . and we'll see you again . . . and then we'll all be happy, we'll be healthy, and we'll understand.'

I still do not understand, nearly ten years later, why the Lord allowed my sons to be afflicted with infantile bilateral striatal necrosis. I cannot understand why Jonathan died or why Christopher survived. Today Christopher is almost totally recovered.

However, I do understand this: life is a riddle, which God wants me to experience, but not necessarily solve. When I was struggling to solve it, I found 1 Corinthians 13:12, which makes sense only in the original Greek. Paul basically says, 'Now we see (or understand) through a mirror, *in a riddle*, but then face to face.'

Modern Christians sometimes rush to put God's truth into little boxes, neatly systematized, categorized, organized, and principalized, when God's perspective on suffering is too big for any of that. While for some people 'spirituality' is defined by what we know, God may be more concerned with how we handle what we *cannot* know.

A riddle loses its mystery and its power, even perhaps its significance, once it is solved. By keeping us in our riddle (everyone's riddle is unique), God is helping us to learn about walking by faith, and not by sight.

That is what I intend to do, and what we can help others do, until we see him face to face. That eternal meeting is when the meaning of everything, including our suffering with genetic illness, will suddenly and absolutely come clear . . . when (see Rev. 21:4) he wipes away every tear from our eyes; and there is no longer any genetic illness, suffering, or death; when there is no longer any mourning, or crying, or pain; for the first things will have passed away . . . and he will make everything new.

The Disease of Isolation

Markie Jackson

I work with families in their homes, primarily one-on-one with several groups of people who are in need of special assistance. These groups include young parents of newborn babies with a genetic condition called hemophilia, as well as HIV infected children and HIV infected adults who are dying because of complications. Most of what I do is very private – nothing like telling my own story publicly, which I find hard to do. It has always been a story that my family has held close. It has been a long journey. It has been a journey that we started twenty-one years ago.

Picture in your minds a beautiful, healthy, baby boy. With red curls and big green eyes, he would have been any parent's joy. Three days after this baby was circumcised, his skin turned black and blue, he became swollen, and he continued to bleed. Because the physicians could not discover what was causing these problems and because this baby was really bruised and looked so bad, they hid him in the back of the nursery. Fearing that the medical staff had utterly failed in the care of this child, they would not bring him to me – his mother. They hid him and kept me sedated. When the physicians in the hospital decided that they must have clipped a vessel during the circumcision, they started putting in what turned out to be a long series of stitches. This infant, when I brought him home, had twenty-one stitches altogether. But because his problem was *not* due to a clipped blood vessel, he almost bled to death. Three days later the physicians finally realized that the situation was beyond them and that they needed to call someone else in for assistance.

They called in a physician who took one look at my child and knew immediately – because she had seen this condition one other time in her life while doing mission work overseas – that my child was suffering from hemophilia. What a God-send! She ordered the testing. She gave him his clotting factor. I took my child home.

When I took my son home, I knew virtually nothing about his disease or how to care for him. No one taught us anything. This child was sent home with inexperienced parents who were told merely, 'This child is not normal. He has hemophilia. He won't grow up like other children. He won't play sports. And by the time he's ten, he'll have damaged joints.' That is what I knew. I was terrified when I took this child home.

Before we left the hospital, they told us to return in eight weeks for some genetic testing. I did not have a clue what that was; nor did I know how hemophilia was transmitted. We were not able to wait eight weeks, though, before returning. Six weeks later we were in the emergency room. My child had sustained a traumatic bleed. It took seventeen attempts at giving him his clotting factor before his bleeding stopped. Still, he was simply handed back to us with the words, 'Take him home.'

This happened again and again and again. No one educated us. We did not know the questions to ask. Young, scared parents do not know where to start in learning about their child's affliction. One cannot assume that someone else down the line is giving them information. Physicians must not assume that the social worker is. Social workers must not assume that the physician is. Parents do not know what to ask, or to whom to go. It is an amazing thing that my child is still alive today, because we were totally inexperienced.

When our son was three years old, we were told definitely not to have any more children. Because I was a carrier for hemophilia, we were advised that future children should be out of the question. But if we decided to have children, we could abort all male children; these were the options we were given. With our Christian backgrounds, abortion was not an option. In fact, I could not believe that a physician would even suggest such an option to young parents.

We wrestled with our decision whether or not to have more children. When our son was four years old, we adopted a child. She is the light of our life. This was our way of avoiding the prospect of having another child who might also be afflicted with the hereditary disease from which our son suffered. We wanted other children. We wanted to have a complete and whole family. For us, adoption was the perfect answer. It was the very thing that we needed to make our family whole. So, there are options out there that young parents may not think about. Fortunately, a good Christian friend of mine brought adoption to my attention. For us, it was the perfect solution. Without both our son and our daughter, our family would not have been complete.

However, the adoption could not have taken place without the help of certain individuals. Many agencies would not allow us to adopt because we had hemophilia in our family. Hemophilia is not contagious, so it was hard to understand why they did not want us to have a child. We opted to pursue a private (legal) adoption, because that was the only means we had. Adoption is one of the most blessed events that can possibly happen to a family. Helping someone to go through with an adoption is one of the greatest gifts we can give.

At five years old, my son started kindergarten. For some reason, he started having spontaneous nose bleeds that year. He was having gushing nose bleeds seven to eight times a day. He would wake at night, with his bed and hair soaked with blood. This was something that we had to cope with every single day. I cannot tell you the endless trips that we took to physicians. They cauterized his nose. They packed his nose. They scratched their heads. They paced up and down the hall. No one could tell us anything. This was his first year in school, so it was really traumatic. We had a little boy running around who was constantly bleeding all over everything. The school got concerned; his parents got more concerned. However, his kindergarten teacher was a Christian woman who came by one afternoon and decided to educate herself about hemophilia. She decided to learn what she could do to make the whole experience as simple and non-traumatic as possible for him. She, too, was a God-send. Our son was the only child in kindergarten who actually learned to do laundry that year.

At six years old, my son went to hemophilia camp. Going to hemophilia camp means so much to boys with this disease. It was the first time in my son's life that he was with other individuals who had the same disorder and he did not feel isolated. They understood everything. If he had a nose bleed, it was not a big deal. If he could not walk, that too was fine. They would sit and play with him. He made friends that year that were to last a lifetime. People who shared his disease gave him what society could not provide. They gave him what an extended family would not give him because they were afraid. It is really a shame that he had to go three states away to find the support he needed, instead of having it in his own local environment. He had a stable home, but his social world was very cruel. People did not know what hemophilia was, so they did not want to be near him. I had to stop work because no one wanted to keep my child in day care. Perhaps they thought hemophilia was contagious. We live in a really uneducated world.

My son, who was told he would never play sports and that he would be in a wheelchair by the time he was ten, excelled in T-ball, little league, water skiing; this child has tried everything. He has not only tried everything, but he has done well because he was taught that the disease does not limit him – he limits himself. He has to get out there and try. Other individuals, though, tried to limit him. In gym class, for instance, he was placed in a chair. He was never allowed to participate. He was confined to a corner and told to write reports and watch the other children play. In his own home environment, however, he was out there excelling in everything he wanted to do because he was not afraid to try. Family members were willing to let him try and not hold him back.

My child had learned to manage his hemophilia. It did not manage him. We were coping with life as we knew it, though it was not normal by any means. Two weeks before my child's thirteenth birthday in 1987, I took him to the clinic. While we were at the clinic, I was asked to come into the next room and to visit with some physicians. I went into the room and, for two hours, was bombarded with statistics. My child had contracted HIV because some of the blood products that I had been giving him for the past thirteen years to control his bleeding had been contaminated with the virus. I cannot tell you what this news did to us. I had to tell his sister because she needed to be protected. It was his responsibility to protect society. His nose bleeds had continued off and on. So upon this thirteen-year-old child I placed a burden that should not have to be put on any child. It was the most heart-wrenching day I can ever remember when I had to tell my child that the five friends he had seen buried that year had died from a disease caused by a virus with which he had been infected.

I had taught my child that God is the One who gives us the circumstances of our lives – that each experience is for a reason. We do not know those reasons. Sometimes it is not for us to know, but it is for how we use our experiences that we will answer some day. That is what I truly believe. It was extremely difficult to tell my child this at that point of his life. As a young teenager, he was just coming to terms with death. He should not have had to worry about so much. His faith was really tested – and mine as well. I was questioning the things I had told my child for years. So we went into counselling. It takes a lot of courage to begin counselling. It takes even more courage to tell the truth once you get there. In this case, counselling provided just the assistance we needed.

During 1988 my son lost his best friend. This friend had been with my son at camp since he was six years old, and his death really took a hard toll on him. They were going to graduate from high school together, but in the November before they were to graduate in May, his friend died. This was one too many deaths for a young child to face. It was very traumatic. He went through such a rebellious stage that more counselling was needed – for me. But through it all, he has managed to pull himself back together. He has managed to recognize that, somehow, every experience no matter how bad, is something God wants to use to help someone else. When we were reflecting on his life's experiences recently, I asked him what he would want others to know about them. His answer was simple. We are all on this journey of life together; our paths may be different, but God has put us all here, and it is only by God's grace that others are not on the same path.

God's grace and design is in each of our lives. This is a reality that has kept my child going. My child is doing *very* well. People have studied him repeatedly because they cannot make out why he is doing so well. Other children who have been infected with the HIV virus are not doing well. Other adults are dying. For some reason, however, my son actually has an immunity system that seems stronger than mine. I believe the reason is that he has entrusted his life to the Lord. My son works in the hemophilia community. He gives of himself wholly, as I do. It is God's blessings alone that are keeping us going.

My message to carers of hemophiliac and/or HIV patients is that they must educate patients and their families. Carers should not assume that patients and their families know anything but should empower them with knowledge. An empowered patient is a much healthier patient. The provision of knowledge will relieve so much stress, just as the absence of such knowledge caused us years of anxiety. It caused us marital problems as well. If only someone had taken the time to sit down with us at the very beginning and tell us what was normal, what to expect, and where we could go for help when we needed it. For instance, emotions such as anger and fear are normal feelings for parents of children with hemophilia and/or HIV. We did not know that. We certainly did not know how to handle our emotions when we experienced them. It caused our family a lot of grief. Fortunately, we were able to pull our family back together through counselling, through prayer, and through the help of a lot of friends.

The worst harm done to us early on was failing to provide us with the knowledge that we needed about my son's condition. For thirteen years, no one bothered to educate our family about hemophilia. My child could have been much healthier. As it turned out, my child was one of the ones that did not have to become HIV-infected. Blood-clotting factor that had been heat-treated to ensure the absence of the HIV virus was available beginning in 1985. My child was infected in 1987 – two years after this factor was available. We had a physician who did not give us information and who chose to keep my son on a product that was not safe. In order for people to have faith in them, physicians must give patients and their families the information they need to evaluate all of the available options.

My child has continued to excel. He became a father this past year, against all odds. We have the most beautiful grandchild, who is the joy of my son's life. This child is totally healthy and his mother is not HIV-infected. When my son was a little boy, he always said he wanted to be a father. So among the things that I am most thankful for is that God has blessed him with a son who is healthy.

I will lose my child due to AIDS. I know that. It is something that is in the future. I need people's prayers; yet some of the cruellest places I have been are churches. As a Christian, I cannot tell you how that breaks my heart.

We have told a handful of friends about my son's condition. You can count those that remain as our friends on two fingers now. I am not sure what their problem is – maybe it is fear – but most of those we have told have not been able to handle it. They have run. We have told some family members, and we have not seen them now in years. Persons afflicted with hemophilia and/or HIV and their families so desperately need people who will simply be there for them.

Last year I was with a man dying from AIDS in Memphis. I had known him for years. He asked a pastor to please come to pray with him. That is all he wanted. The pastor did not come for days. Eventually, I had to go and find a chaplain from a nearby hospital and plead with him to come. I said, 'All this person needs is for someone to go in and pray with him. Please let him die in peace. You don't have to touch anything. Don't even breathe if you don't want to. Just pray with him.' We need to be there for these people. They are not contagious. We must not be afraid to reach out to them. They need us so badly. Isolation is a disease worse than the hemophilia or AIDS. These people are not their disease. They are people just like us.

The Search for Shalom [1]

Hessel Bouma, III, PhD

It is 1983. Mr. and Mrs. White are school teachers with two children, a 4-year-old daughter and a 3-year-old son, and are members of the local Lutheran church. Very ill as an infant, their son has been hospitalized twice, and tested for many things but without any definitive diagnosis. At wit's end and shooting in the dark, their pediatrician suggests, 'You know, I think we ought to test your son for CF (cystic fibrosis). [2] Just to rule it out, because I'm sure he doesn't have it.' The very next day the Whites travel with their children to the nearest large city where their son is tested. He tests positive! Before the news even sinks in, the clinicians suggest their daughter be tested also. She tests positive too! Years later, Mrs. White recalls that day as 'the worst day of our lives' and that the only initial information given them was, 'Your children are going to die'.

Educated and resourceful, the Whites seek second opinions. Different tests confirm the CF diagnoses. Again, the results are presented coldly and negatively, though with a caveat, 'There are degrees of severity. We do not know how your children will do.' For the impending school year, Mr. and Mrs. White continue their teaching jobs but take their children out of pre-school and arrange for Mrs. White's parents to care for them. At the end of the year, Mrs. White leaves her job to care for her children full-time; Mr. White frets that he may never be able to change jobs lest they lose their health insurance coverage of the children. With the encouragement of a hospital social worker, they try out a CF support group but do not join since most of the group consists of people with similar, recently-diagnosed cases and a dominant woman whose daughter was so ill she never attended public school, was hospitalized regularly, and died at the age of seventeen. Their search for information in textbooks is similarly depressing – badly dated and showing CF patients with 'grotesque looking children'. One notable exception, however, is some very educational material from the Cystic Fibrosis Foundation. Ultimately they are referred to an elderly pulmonary specialist. Knowledgeable, patient, openly honest, the doctor restores their confidence, gives them realistic hope, and places them in contact with a group doing genetic research on cystic fibrosis. Within the year the children are participating in an enzyme study.

With strong parental support and good medical attention, both children are doing quite well. Mrs. White begins to see herself as a 'CF Mom', packing enzyme pills and medications in her children's lunches, writing notes to teachers about special concerns, filling out insurance forms *ad infinitum*, and patiently biting her lip as well-intentioned relatives and friends tell her, 'Maybe the doctors are wrong' or '[T]hey're going to outgrow it'. She continues to mull over the admonition of her pediatrician, 'Don't plan to have any more children'.

As the Whites' children continue to do well, Mr. and Mrs. White decide to try to have additional children, though only with prenatal diagnosis, to avoid having another child with cystic fibrosis. When Mrs. White becomes pregnant, CVS (chorionic villus sampling) at nine weeks reveals the fetus will have cystic fibrosis, and they abort the pregnancy. But two more pregnancies result in two healthy children after similar testing with CVS indicates that the fetuses will be carriers but not affected.

The White's children are now 17, 15, 9, and 7. The parents continue to ponder whether to tell the younger children they were tested for CF. Would their older children then ask, 'What if testing had been available with us? Would you have not allowed us to be born?' Asked whether they ever shared any of the initial diagnoses, thoughts of having additional children, or prenatal testing with their Lutheran pastor or congregation, the Whites respond, 'No'.

*   *   *   *   *   *   *

We join a second family in 1990. Mr. and Mrs. Smith are in their late twenties and run their own paint contracting company. Self-employed, they are uninsured. Having been raised in a dysfunctional family, Mrs. Smith left the church as a child, took drugs, and had an abortion as a sixteen-year-old. Ultimately committing her life to God, she is also committed to avoiding her family's previous mistakes. Shortly after their marriage, Mr. and Mrs. Smith become members of a large, full gospel, non-denominational church.

Mrs. Smith did not want a large family but always envisaged herself with one, maybe two children – boys. It turns out she has two daughters, now aged five and two. When she becomes pregnant again, she is devastated. Thoughts of putting three kids to bed at night and going grocery shopping with three children depress her. She does not want this baby and privately prays that she will lose it.

In the fourth month of her pregnancy, she agrees when her obstetrician suggests she have a maternal serum test. The test indicates she may have a 'problem pregnancy', perhaps a Down's syndrome baby. She and her husband are referred to a nearby hospital for an ultrasound. The friendly, outgoing technician performing the sonogram suddenly becomes really quiet, stops the procedure prematurely, and leaves the room. A few minutes later, the head of radiology enters, tells her to get dressed, and indicates that her doctor wants to see her. As she dresses, the radiologist takes Mr. Smith aside, telling him that the baby's head is four times larger than it should be and the stomach is outside the abdomen. Later, in the doctor's office, the doctor tells them the baby does not have a chance but has a serious disorder (later identified as Trisomy 18³). He urges them to abort immediately, giving Mrs. Smith vaginal suppositories to take that same night in preparation for labour the next day.

However, Mrs. Smith responds, '[We] go to a church where we believe in miracles. We believe God's still alive and he still cares about his people and he does things for them. He's active in their lives. [So] we thought we'd just pray and trust God and ask for a miracle'. From the doctor's office they go to her mother's home and tell her the news. Then they call their pastor who says, 'It's not my place to make this decision for you. You need to pray about it'. So the Smiths wait and ask their congregation to pray for them too.

When the Smiths inform the doctor and his staff of their decision not to end the pregnancy, they sense the staff are disapproving, curt, even full of ugly feelings and hate. But as the pregnancy progresses, the staff soften, begrudgingly appreciating the Smith's commitment to their unborn child even at considerable inconvenience, expense, and substantial risk to Mrs. Smith's health.

Mrs. Smith struggles with guilt. A year later she explains:

> I felt guilty, because I thought, 'I didn't even want him, and now he's sick and he's dying'. I was desperate. I loved him and I wanted him. I can't explain it. I thought, 'He's gotta live. He's just gotta live'. Then, too, it was the boy that I always wanted and didn't have. We're still not over it.

Through it all, the members of their church pray for them and support them, assuring that whatever happens, they will support them. The Smiths tentatively decide that they will abort if her life is in danger.

In her seventh month, on Christmas eve, Mrs. Smith goes into labour. When relatives and friends – including four associate ministers – from church hear, they come to the hospital and briefly visit throughout labour. As the time for delivery comes, the doctor arrives – the same doctor who had urged them to end the pregnancy – and the room is cleared. Through his own tears, the doctor delivers their son and lays him on his mother's chest. In the ensuing hour, relatives and friends gather with them and their dying son, looking at him, holding his hand, touching his face. He lives one hour. (No extraordinary or ordinary medical treatments were provided.) God has answered one of her most fervent prayers: he was born alive.

It is Mrs. Smith's mother who staunchly insists on a viewing and funeral. Through many tears, shared with many relatives and friends both within and outside the Christian community, the healing begins.

In retrospect, Mr. and Mrs. Smith remain grateful for a prenatal diagnosis which enabled them to prepare for the birth and death of their son. They are also profoundly grateful to their supporting church community, led by a senior pastor whose wife had experienced several miscarriages and had reluctantly ended another pregnancy under exceptional circumstances.

*   *   *   *   *   *   *

We again turn back the clock to 1990. A third set of parents, Mr. and Mrs. MacDonald, are both college educated. He is employed in the oil and gas industry, she as a sales representative for a major international business firm. When his firm fell on hard times, it ceased providing any health care benefits; so they are grateful for family health coverage through her employment. They are members of the local Catholic parish, though a recent change in priests has diminished their connections and commitments. They have one son who will be turning five shortly and Mrs. MacDonald is expecting their second child – a boy as identified on an otherwise uneventful ultrasound test. In March, Mrs. MacDonald goes into premature labour, which her doctor successfully stops. An amniocentesis the next day indicates that the fetus's lungs are insufficiently developed, so she takes ritodrine for four weeks. Upon C-section delivery, the obstetrician immediately notes Matthew has a partial cleft lip and club foot. Their pediatrician assures them, 'These are everyday problems. This is nothing'.

In ensuing weeks, Matthew has difficulty eating and gains no weight until put on cereal. At four months, a plastic surgeon operates to repair the cleft palate and an orthopedic surgeon corrects the right leg. But when Matthew is taken off the anesthetic, he ceases breathing and needs to be resuscitated and intubated. He is discharged after a ten-day hospitalization. By the age of six months, Matthew is still not sitting up. When therapists cannot explain his developmental delay and therapy produces minimal advances, the pediatrician suspects cerebral palsy. An MRI and an EEG over a three-week period rule out cerebral palsy but do show inadequate myelination. The specialist muses, 'We just have to hope he catches up'.

By Matthew's first birthday, Mrs. MacDonald is depressed at the thought of giving him a birthday party, since he will not even know it. In desperation, she asks her pediatrician to initiate some chromosome tests. Three weeks later, when the results indicate there may be a problem with chromosome #5,[4] the pediatrician laments that he really does not trust that lab. They repeat the test. Three weeks later, the doctor informs them that Matthew has a piece missing from the middle portion of chromosome #5. It is extremely rare, it happens at conception, and, explains the doctor, he has never seen a little child with this particular problem. He says he does not know what prognosis to offer except that Mr. and Mrs. MacDonald are looking at severe handicaps, severe retardation, and severe hypotonia. Mr. MacDonald passes out.

Gradually the MacDonalds' lives change. Dad takes responsibility for their oldest son, mother for Matthew. Mrs. MacDonald undertakes to educate herself about chromosomal deletions. Matthew's health necessitates that he stay at home, so Mrs. MacDonald rarely ventures out except to work and to the medical library where the frequency of her visits necessitates monthly parking passes. By August, 1991, when she develops stomach pains, she is sure it is a well-earned ulcer. On the contrary, it turns out that she is pregnant despite being on the pill.

Her mother says, 'Pregnancy is always a cause for joy'. Mrs. MacDonald returns to her obstetrician and insists, 'Schedule a chromosome test'. Though chromosome tests had shown that neither she nor her husband have a chromosomal deletion, they feel they cannot have another child like Matthew. So a sample of chorionic villi are taken and sent for chromosomal analysis. Three weeks later the test results are in. Of twenty duplicate samples, nineteen show no problem, one is unclear. Unsatisfied that the risk is low enough, she insists on an early amniocentesis two weeks later. Three weeks later they are informed the chromosomes look fine and that they have a little girl, whom they decide to name Christina.

As time passes, Mrs. MacDonald continues to bear the principal burden of caring for Matthew. Her amount of sleep decreases as her worries increase. Can she care for Matthew as well as Christina and her older son? She explores alternatives for Matthew. Finally a woman in the state capital who does placements for the state refers her – because they are Catholic – to a place in an adjacent state. It is a home called 'Holy Angels' run by an order of nuns known as 'Our Lady of Sorrows'. They provide continuous care for fifteen babies as well as teenagers and adults who, developmentally, are like one-to-four-year-old children. Very ambivalent about whether institutionalizing Matthew is the appropriate thing to do, the MacDonalds are greatly encouraged by an afternoon visit to 'Holy Angels'. Two weeks later, after reviewing Matthew's foot-thick medical files, the Catholic sisters promise to accept him several weeks before Christina is to be born.

*   *   *   *   *   *   *

The experiences of the Whites, Smiths, and MacDonalds illustrate a host of issues facing persons with genetic conditions today.[5] *To what extent will we allow our genetic heritage to determine who we fundamentally are?* Are the Whites who are carriers or affected with cystic fibrosis, is baby Smith with Trisomy 18, or is Matthew MacDonald with a deletion of part of chromosome #5 fundamentally different from other human beings in any way that can possibly justify the stigmatization and ostracization associated with genetic conditions? What are the impacts of labelling on persons with genetic conditions or parents and relatives of someone with a genetic condition? How can the stigmatization and ostracization be eliminated, the labelling minimized, and the dignity of all persons, regardless of genetic identity, affirmed?

Should the presence of a genetic condition in a person affect the health care coverage, insurability, or employment of that individual? Mr. White and Mrs. MacDonald perceive themselves as locked into their present jobs so that health care coverage for their children will continue. Would losing or changing their jobs prevent them from obtaining group health insurance coverage with their new employers because their children have 'pre-existing conditions', or is current legislation now sufficient to protect them from this problem? Are the Whites' healthy children less likely to be considered for employment because they are identified as carriers of a genetic condition? Did the Smiths' lack of health insurance preclude diagnostic or treatment options for them? Could a health insurance carrier legitimately tell the Whites it will cover the CVS prenatal testing only if they agree to abort any fetus who will be affected with cystic fibrosis? On the average, persons like the two White children with cystic fibrosis average two weeks per year of hospitalization and annual medical care costs of $10–15,000. Institutionalized care such as Matthew MacDonald receives at 'Holy Angels' currently runs between $250–300 per day, or around $90–100,000 annually, paid for by Medicaid, state and federal funds, and Catholic charities (including vows of poverty taken by the Catholic sisters who run the home).

While some states (eleven at the last count) have enacted legislation to eliminate genetic discrimination, it is too soon to tell how effective these efforts are. Furthermore, the majority of states have yet to address these issues. There is a two-fold challenge to society and religious communities here: to support health care reform and efforts to end discrimination in employment aimed at eradicating injustices and to contribute to organizations and individuals providing care for persons with genetic conditions.

For what purposes should genetic tests be developed and used? For example, should the Whites' oldest daughter have been tested pre-symptomatically? Should the potential spouses of all the White children be tested before marriage? Should the Smiths have undergone maternal serum testing if they were opposed to pregnancy termination? Should Mrs. MacDonald be permitted to insist on amniocentesis, with its slight risks, just because the CVS results were 95% rather than 100% conclusive?

Given the rapid pace of developments in genetics and the Human Genome Project, what is the prognosis for persons with genetic conditions? Genetic conditions may be quite variable. For example, CF may be characterized as sub-mild, mild, moderate, or severe. Can we accurately narrow the range of prognoses given to families with a genetic condition? Is it realistic for the Whites to hope for a cure for cystic fibrosis in the next few years? Do we pursue means of curing baby Smith's Trisomy 18 by removing the additional genetic material or curing Matthew MacDonald's partial deletion of chromosome #5 by adding the missing genes? Or do our best hopes lie in identifying and developing better treatments for symptoms and in delaying the development and progression of symptoms? Experience to date indicates that true cures for genetic conditions are years to decades away. For single-gene conditions, the development of new, innovative therapies is a realistic possibility but will require considerable time and resources. They are, therefore, more likely to be achieved for common genetic conditions than for rare ones. For many conditions, compassionate care and symptom management remain the most realistic hope.

Should genetic testing and counselling be regulated? Are there circumstances in which society should forbid genetic testing, e.g., for sex determination? May anyone do genetic testing and counselling, or should some measure of certification and quality control be required? The Whites, Smiths, and MacDonalds were all initially counselled by health care professionals untrained in genetic counselling; their initial experiences were deplorable and regrettable. In contrast, each is highly appreciative of the counselling they ultimately received from trained genetic counsellors. Are there genetics laboratories of dubious quality such as the MacDonalds apparently encountered? Or was their physician 'buying time' for a confirmation test from a second laboratory in light of the grim prognosis? May genetic counsellors, other health care practitioners, or religious leaders be directive (rather than non-directive) in their counselling? The Whites experienced directive counselling in both the testing of their oldest daughter and their pediatrician's admonition not to have more children. The Smiths experienced directive counselling from their obstetrician urging pregnancy termination almost immediately upon diagnosis.

Should the reproductive choices of persons who are carriers of or affected by a genetic condition be limited? If so, should these limits be placed by society, by one's religious tradition, voluntarily by the individual? Should the choice of whether or not to have another child by a couple at risk for a genetic condition be limited to pre-conception choices? Should the Whites be told, 'No more children'? Should they have to bear special penalties if they have another child with cystic fibrosis either intentionally as a result of taking the 25% risk of having another affected child or as a consequence of contraceptive failure? Is it morally irresponsible knowingly to bring into this world a child with significant genetic deficiencies?

Should pregnancy termination following maternal serum screening, sonograms, CVS, and/or amniocentesis be a regulated option? If pregnancy termination is not an allowable option, will society at large or a religious community in particular support a woman and her family in caring for an affected child? The Smiths found such support in their church; the MacDonalds found such support in 'Holy Angels'. If pregnancy termination is accepted, will society cease to care or in some ways curtail the treatments available for individuals already afflicted with a genetic disease? Will society limit its search for better treatments and cures for genetic diseases? Will women be coerced, subtly or overtly, to abort their unborn with certain genetic conditions, thereby causing women to become tentative about their pregnancies until everything is seen to be 'right'? If pregnancy termination were to be limited to severe genetic conditions, can a meaningful line be drawn between severe and less severe genetic conditions?[6]

Finally, virtually everyone with a genetic condition at one time or another wonders, 'Why me? What did I do to deserve this?' For members of religious traditions, the questions reflect a crisis of theodicy. If God is good, if God is omnipotent, then why am I suffering from this condition?[7]

How can religious traditions better address the issues of theodicy and assist members in their individual struggles with genetic conditions? The 'new genetics' poses difficult questions necessitating deeply personal and moral decisions. Unfortunately, most families appear to be like the Whites and the MacDonalds – very hesitant to involve members of their religious communities in their decisions, perhaps fearing superficial answers, rash judgment, and a lack of support. But there also are remarkable examples of religious communities such as the Smiths', who support people through their difficult decisions. There are other models as well, such as the 'Holy Angels', who provide exemplary, compassionate care.

This chapter represents a concerted effort on the part of many people both to appreciate genetic challenges and to appraise genetic possibilities. It emerges from a commitment

to promote life, not death; health, not sickness,
to suffer and counsel with those who suffer,
to care compassionately when one cannot cure, and
to be a part of God's presence in the valley of the shadow of
death. . . .
in short to search for shalom.

NOTES

1. This essay draws upon interviews of actual families published in Hessel Bouma, III and B. Andrew Lustig, eds., *Case Study Interviews*, (Houston, TX: The Institute of Religion, 1992). The three accounts are all from the perspective of the families; only the names have been changed to provide a measure of anonymity. The interviews were conducted with Mrs. White, Mr. and Mrs. Smith, and Mrs. MacDonald and her mother. Readers should resist the temptation to generalize from these accounts about either specific genetic conditions or the responses by particular religious traditions.

2. Cystic fibrosis (CF) is the most common, fatal (current median life expectancy in late 20s), autosomal recessive disease in Caucasian populations. Approximately 1 in 25 Caucasians are carriers; between 1 in 2,000 and 1 in 3,000 are affected. The disease is characterized by a sodium and chloride salt imbalance, and thick mucus which contributes to chronic lung infections and pancreatic and digestive tract deficiencies. After decades of research, the CF gene was mapped to chromosome 7q31.2, cloned, and sequenced in 1989. Between 70 and 80% of persons with CF have a 3-base pair deletion which causes the cystic fibrosis transmembrane conductance regulator (the primary gene product) to lack one amino acid, phenylalanine, in the 508th position of 1,480 amino acids. Another approximately 500 different mutations in this gene have also now been described. Treatments consist of 'clap therapy' to loosen thick mucus, antibiotics, dietary enzymes, and psychosocial support. On the average, persons with CF spend two weeks/year hospitalized with average annual healthcare costs in the $10,000-15,000 range. For further information: Welsh, Michael J., Lap-Chee, Tsui, Boat, Thomas F. and Beaudet, Arthur L., 'Cystic fibrosis', In Scriver et al., eds., *The Metabolic and Molecular Basis of Inherited Disease*, (New York, McGraw-Hill, Inc. 1995), pp. 3799–3876; U.S. Congress, Office of Technology Assessment, 'Cystic Fibrosis and DNA Tests: Implications of Carrier Screening', OTA-BA-532 (Washington, DC, U.S. Government Printing Office, August 1992); *On-line Mendelian Inheritance in Man* (http:www3.ncbi.nlm.nih.gov/Omim/); (Cystic Fibrosis Foundation, 6931 Arlington Road, No. 200, Bethesda, MD, 20814).

3. Trisomy 18 is a genetic condition due to the presence of an abnormal number of chromosomes: three copies of chromosome #18 rather than the normal pair. It is due to a failure of the chromosomes to migrate appropriately (nondisjunction) to separate daughter cells during the formation of gametes. It appears to occur more frequently in the formation of eggs, correlates with increasing maternal age, and occurs approximately once in 5,000 liveborn infants. It is characterized by an abnormally small jaw, multiple malformations, severe failure to thrive, and an average life expectancy of approximately 6 months. For further information: Beaudet, Arthur L., Scriver, Charles R., Sly, William S. and Valie, David, 'Genetics, Biochemistry, and Molecular Basis of Variant Human Phenotypes', in *The Metabolic and Molecular Bases of Inherited Disease*, (New York, McGraw-Hill, Inc. 1995), pp. 66–68; Support Organization for Trisomy (SOFT) 18/13, c/o Barb Van Herreweghe, 2982 S. Union Street, Rochester, NY, 14624.

4. The deletion of a piece of a chromosome is usually quite rare and occurs randomly (unless it occurs in the formation of one parent's reproductive organs). The severity of any deletion is dependent upon the number of genes lost and how essential the lost genes are for normal functioning. Relatively simple diagnostic tests can identify gross deletions, but until the human genome map is completed, assessing how many genes are missing is difficult at best. Establishing any accurate prognosis is similarly problematical. For further information: Ledbetter, David H., and Ballabio, Andrea, 'Molecular cytogenetics of contiguous gene syndromes: Mechanisms and consequences of gene dosage imbalance', in *The Metabolic and Molecular Bases of Inherited Disease*, (New York, McGraw-Hill, Inc. 1995), pp. 811–839; National Organization for Rare Disorders, P.O. Box 8923, New Fairfield, CT, 06812-8923.

5. Many of these issues have been identified as part of the Ethical, Legal, and Social Issues (ELSI) initiative of the Human Genome Project. See U.S. Department of Health and Human Services and U.S. Department of Energy, *Understanding Our Genetic Inheritance. The U.S. Human Genome Project: The First Five Years, 1991–1995*. (available from the National Technical Information Service, U.S. Department of Commerce, Springfield, Virginia, 22161). *Cf.* Genetics, Religion and Ethics Project, 'Summary Reflection Statement', *Human Gene Therapy* 3:525–527, (1992).

6. Several Christians have attempted to develop relevant criteria. For example, Bouma III Hessel, Diekema Douglas, Langerak Edward, Rottman Theodore and Verhey, Allen, *Christian Faith, Health, and Medical Practice*, (Grand Rapids, Eerdmans 1989), p. 227 discuss cases like Trisomy 18 and Tay-Sachs (in which the infant experiences a period of unrelenting pain and then dies). Cf. Jones, D. Gareth, *Brave New People*, (Downers Grove [IL], InterVarsity 1984), p. 178; and Wennberg, Robert, *Life in the Distance*, (Grand Rapids, Eerdmans 1985), pp. 142–143.

7. In the complete series of interviews from which the cases of the Whites, Smiths, and MacDonalds are taken, most families candidly described the struggles of their crisis. If families had a strong, good relationship with their religious community, they were far more willing to seek and accept advice and support from them. Some turned to biblically unsound writings such as Rabbi Harold Kushner's *When Bad Things Happen to Good People* (see Michael Beates' discussion of Kusher's approach in Chapter 3). Christians, for example, commonly consult Smedes, Lewis B, *How Can It be All Right When Everything is All Wrong?*, (San Francisco, CA: Harper & Row, 1982); Biebel, David B., *If God is So Good, Why Do I Hurt So Bad?*, (Colorado Springs, CO, NavPress, 1989); Hauerwas, Stanley, *Naming the Silences: God, Medicine, and the Problem of Suffering*, (Grand Rapids, MI: Eerdmans, 1990).

PART I

Genetic Perspective

[1]

Eugenics in Historical and Ethical Perspective

Arthur J. Dyck, PhD

The term 'eugenics' was introduced by the British biologist Sir Francis Galton in 1883. He defined the science of eugenics as 'the study of the agencies under social control which may improve or impair the racial qualities of future generations physically or mentally'.[1] Galton, a cousin of Charles Darwin, explicitly hoped to improve the human stock by gaining knowledge and instituting public policies that would help 'the more suitable races' prevail over 'the less suitable races'. Current definitions of eugenics do not refer to races or racial qualities but to biological welfare or an improved genetic constitution for the human species. Indeed, geneticists generally do not use the term eugenics to describe any of their work, even when it is designed to cure diseases or prevent the inheritance of them. The tendencies within eugenics to view some races as superior, and the atrocities defended on eugenic grounds in Nazi Germany, have combined to make eugenics a word with persisting ugly connotations.

It comes as no surprise, therefore, that in 1990, James D. Watson, then Director of the Genome Project, sounded this warning:

> The power of the information to be gained from mapping and sequencing projects raises concerns about how it will be used. There is no avoiding the fact that arguments drawn in part from genetics have been politically misused in the past, most egregiously by the Nazis but also elsewhere in Europe and North America. Indeed, the specter of coercive government eugenics programs persists even today in statutes still on the books in several nations. . . . The only way to ensure that history does not repeat itself is for the scientific and medical communities to remain constantly vigilant for abuses of genetics.[2]

Watson's warning sounds right: Of course scientists and physicians should be vigilant so that history does not repeat itself in the form of misuses of genetic findings, coercive governmental eugenic programmes, and atrocities of the Nazi variety. But Watson's warning is couched in a view of history and of the science of genetics that misleads him with respect to what the 'specter' of eugenics is all about. And his view is all too widely shared. The view I refer to fails to grasp (1) that science and medicine willingly provided the

25

information, rationale and technical knowledge for Nazi policies and coercive policies in other countries; (2) that science, medicine and law at present willingly provide the information, rationale, and technical know-how for current eugenic practices in the United States, some of them quite coercive and arguably unethical; and (3) that certain premises assumed by the science of genetics sanction eugenic practices, some of them clearly unethical, some even attacking the very requisites of communal life.

EUGENICS AS A SCIENCE AND POLICY: HISTORIC ABUSES

To begin, let us examine the origins and nature of eugenics as a science, and see how it was related to governmental policies, particularly in Nazi Germany.

Eugenics as a modern science begins with Galton. He used statistical correlations to study the inheritance of intelligence, publishing *Hereditary Genius* in 1869. His aim was to maximize intelligence and prevent feeblemindedness. To achieve those aims, he advocated marital arrangements to breed a highly intelligent group of men for a number of generations.

The impact of Charles Darwin's *The Origin of Species* was enormous. The theory of evolution undermined earlier notions of natural equality and gave impetus to the prospect of biology as a science of human development and progress. To the extent that Social Darwinists stressed the survival of the fittest, they saw eugenics as unnecessary. But some social Darwinists were alarmed because educated and successful individuals were having far fewer children than the poor, feebleminded, and otherwise unfit, and also alarmed because medical care for the 'weak' was interfering with the natural struggle in which the fit survived and the unfit perished.

It is noteworthy that German eugenics, or racial hygiene, emerged as a direct response to the rapid increase of the poor and the assistance provided for the poor and weak by medical intervention and welfare policies. In 1895, the German Social Darwinist Alfred Ploetz wrote the founding document of racial hygiene, the term he coined. Racial hygiene was an attack on medical practice that helps the individual but endangers the race by allowing individuals, who would not have otherwise survived, to live and reproduce themselves. Some in Britain spoke of certain diseases as 'our racial friends' because they attacked those with a weak constitution. In the United States, Margaret Sanger, a leader in the movement for birth control worldwide, advocated 'more children for the fit, less from the unfit – that is the chief issue of birth control'.[3] She joined with many others in the eugenics and racial hygiene movements in seeking government intervention to prevent the feebleminded from procreating. Sterilization was instituted in many nations with the support of Sanger and many other eugenicists.

Eugenics movements grew rapidly in the early 20th century. Ploetz founded a journal of racial and social biology in 1904, and in 1905 a Society for Racial Hygiene. In 1907, it went 'international'. The American Eugenics Society began in 1923.

In 1931, the German Society for Racial Hygiene added 'eugenics' to its title. By doing this its leaders successfully brought back those who had broken away to form their own organizations in order to dissociate themselves from the Nordic supremacist and Nazi movements. But a number of leaders in the field of racial hygiene continued to believe in Nordic supremacy and increasingly expressed positive regard for Hitler's willingness to put race at the centre of his policies, and to implement programmes aimed at ending racial deterioration. The idea that some races are superior to others was not limited to Germany. In Britain and the United States, for example, as well as in Germany, there were leading figures in the early twentieth century who regarded blacks as inferior. Lower IQ scores were often cited to bolster the argument, even though, then as now, the comparative weight of heredity and environment in determining mental ability was widely debated.

Policies within the eugenics movements in the early decades of the 20th century included *positive eugenics*, which sought to foster more breeding among those deemed to be socially meritorious; and *negative eugenics*, which sought to discourage breeding among those deemed to be socially disadvantageous. The primary targets of negative eugenics were the so-called feebleminded, but criminals and the 'incurably mentally ill' were targeted as well. The major method for preventing procreation in these groups was sterilization. The United States led the way. In 1907, Indiana passed the first laws allowing sterilization of the mentally ill and criminally insane; by the late 1920s, similar laws had been passed in 28 states. As a result, 15,000 individuals were sterilized before 1930, many of them against their will and most while incarcerated in prisons or homes for the mentally ill.

Switzerland had the first European sterilization law that permitted public health officials to have the mentally ill and the feebleminded sterilized, if they were regarded as incurable and likely to produce 'degenerate offspring'. A number of other European countries did the same.

When Germany passed its own sterilization law in 1933, the Nazis simply changed the voluntary one proposed by the Weimar Republic to allow for compulsory sterilization. The purpose was explicitly eugenic. An estimated 400,000 sterilizations took place in Germany, mostly from 1934 to 1937. By comparison, 30,000 people had been sterilized on eugenic grounds in the United States by 1939.

In October of 1939, designated as the year of 'the duty to be healthy', Hitler began a euthanasia programme. He secretly permitted doctors to grant a merciful death to patients judged to be incurably ill. By August 24, 1941, more than 70,000 patients had been killed. A key justification was afforded by a book *Release and Destruction of Lives Not Worth Living* (1920), by Hoche, a professor of medicine, and Binding, a professor of law. The book advocated 'that the principle of allowable killing' should be extended to the incurably sick, including the mentally ill and handicapped'.[4] The book was widely discussed because, for some, mercy killing would solve economic problems and help meet eugenic aims at the same time.[5] Once more, Germany was not alone in the push for euthanasia. British physicians founded a Euthanasia Legalization Society in 1935 and submitted a bill to allow voluntary euthanasia before the House of Lords. The *British Medical Journal* carried on a lively debate on this subject from 1936 to 1941. One view which kept surfacing was that euthanasia should be an option for those who were mentally retarded, though otherwise healthy. Debate over euthanasia policy peaked during this same period in the Untied States. As in Germany, saving money on medical costs was argued by many who favoured euthanasia.

Germany was alone, however, in sanctioning the compulsory killing of patients, and in applying this practice to those regarded as members of inferior races. There are those who completely separate these killings from the science of eugenics and its aims. But there were those in Germany among its leading biologists, most of them physicians, who welcomed Hitler and his policies precisely because he put race at the centre of building a new state. As many as 50 percent of German physicians joined the Nazi party; a number did genetic research in the concentration camps which was later judged to be a criminal act at the Nuremberg trials.[6] These facts are necessary to help account for the opposition, not just to the Nazis, but to eugenics itself, and to certain of its ideas and policies.

In his encyclical *Casti Connubii* (1930), Pope Pius XI condemned eugenics. Criticisms from scientists were much slower in coming. The revelations of Nazi atrocities did provoke a powerful reaction. In the United States, enforcement of sterilization laws dropped sharply in the 40s and was practically non-existent by the 50s. Sterilization was attacked by geneticists as relatively useless, but also as discriminatory, having been applied mainly to immigrants and the poor, and disproportionately to blacks. The tools used to classify individuals as mentally deficient, IQ tests, came under increased scrutiny: what these tests measured was more and more viewed as reflecting the level of one's education and one's social and cultural environment. 'Feebleness' was not stable; it changed with changes in environmental conditions. Indeed, the statistics on mental deficiency in England and the United States came to be viewed as class biased. Furthermore, the English physician Lionel Penrose, who uncovered PKU (phenylketonuria), showed that mental deficiencies were complex in causation – not simply hereditary, or environmental, or pathological.

Scientists began to shun the term 'eugenics'; the 'American Eugenic Society' became 'the Society for the Study of Social Biology'. Eugenics had come to be associated with racism. The Annals of Eugenics changed from 'the scientific study of racial problems' to 'the genetic study of human populations'. By 1950, the American Society of Human Genetics was established, and by 1954, the *American Journal of Human Genetics*. There were those who believed that too little was known to lay down guidelines for human breeding. But, along with the post-World War II emphasis on gaining new knowledge in genetics, new eugenic impulses came to the fore. For example, twenty-three geneticists signed the 'Geneticists Manifesto' to encourage a scientific and social attitude toward reproduction. One method advocated was that of setting up clinics to offer artificial insemination using sperm donated by 'superior' persons. One such 'Repository for Germinal Choice' was established in California using sperm from male scientists. The biases are evident. The aim was to decrease the 'genetic load', the total number of potentially lethal genes in the human gene pool: Galton revisited!

One of the major ways in which the concerns of negative eugenics were and are being pursued is through centres for genetic counselling. These multiplied rapidly between the 1950s and 1980s; there were 500 such centres in the United States; by 1984, every National Health Region in Britain provided genetic counseling at such centres. Individuals who observed patterns of diseases among their kin or who had a diseased child, could come to find out what the probabilities were that future offspring would suffer from an inherited affliction.

Given the history and nature of eugenics as a science and movement, it is surely misleading to say, as Watson did, that the Nazis were misusing arguments drawn from genetics. Hitler and the Nazi party implemented policies advocated and practised by scientists, mostly physicians. What the Nazis did was advocated in leading textbooks in use at the time not only in Germany but in many other countries. One of the most highly acclaimed, not only in Germany but extensively in the USA, was read by Hitler while he was serving time in Landsberg prison for his role in the Munich Beer-Hall Putsch of 1923.[7] One of its co-authors was Fritz Lenz. The first issue of the neo-Nazi *Neue Anthropologie* honoured him in 1972, 'as the grandfather of racial hygiene in Germany'.[8] For Hitler to put the finding and theories of this and other similar scientific texts into practice required only that he permit physicians, leading biologists and eugenicists, and those taught by them, to carry out the policies they advocated. As indicated earlier, thousands of sterilizations and deaths resulted.

The historical record, then, documents that physicians imbued with eugenics as a science willingly, and out of their convictions, sterilized and killed many thousands of people. In this light, what shall we say about Watson's claim that vigilance by the scientific and medical communities is the *only way* to ensure that history does not repeat itself? What Watson is calling for is akin to insisting that the best bet for avoiding atrocities is to have the foxes alone watch out for what happens to the chickens!

Now, to be sure, not all geneticists should be considered foxes. And scientists should indeed be vigilant as many today surely are. Nevertheless, the need for genuine watchdogs has been demonstrated. In 1966, the late Henry K. Beecher, then a professor at Harvard Medical School, published twenty-two examples of unethical experiments carried out in the United States, each of them in violation of the Nuremberg Code.[9] The United States government responded by creating Institutional Review Boards to monitor research conducted in any institutions receiving federal funds. These boards must include members who are not scientists, such as professionals representing law and ethics. Thought should be given to the kind of oversight that would be most effective and ethically sound with respect to such activities as genetic counselling and screening done outside the context of research.

EUGENICS IN CURRENT GENETIC POLICIES: POTENTIAL AND ACTUAL ABUSES

But what about the dangers of coercive government programmes alluded to by Watson? Watson is surely correct to warn against any repeat of compulsory sterilization, abortion, and euthanasia for eugenic purposes or for any other purpose. However, in this regard also, Watson may not recognize where the true danger lies.

Currently, and in the future, eugenics in the United States is, and will be, voluntarily carried out by physicians and genetic counsellors. Eugenics takes place in what are regarded as autonomous choices on the part of willing individuals. Without government interference, abuses and coercion occur and will continue to occur unless the ethical and legal climate changes markedly.

Consider the existence of a test to determine one's status with regard to Huntington's disease. Huntington's is a severely crippling neurological disorder. Afflicted individuals experience a gradual loss of control over their muscles, body, and mind. The average age at onset is thirty-eight, but it can strike at age two or age seventy. Individuals generally live for sixteen years after onset of the disease.

There is no cure. For many, much of these sixteen years will be spent in a state of dependence in a nursing home.

In 1986, there were two centres that tested people for the probability of suffering from Huntington's disease. By 1991, there were twenty-three such centres in the United States. From nine to sixteen percent of those eligible have been coming to these centres.

Kimberly A. Quaid, director of such a testing programme and an assistant clinical professor of medical and molecular genetics and psychiatry at Indiana University School of Medicine, has noted that:

> What can be most disturbing about genetic information is that the risks of finding out that you are a gene carrier for a specific disease may be not only psychological, that is, anxiety, depression, or family discord, but social. These social risks can include desertion, stigmatization, discrimination, and potential loss of insurance or employment. These are terrible risks for currently healthy individuals to run for the sake of self-knowledge, no matter how important that information might be either for themselves or for other family members.[10]

Quaid observes also that the risk of adverse reactions on the part of individuals who have been tested or who are presumed to be potential candidates for Huntington's is heightened by the attitudes of many, certainly not all, health professionals. 'Primary physicians sometimes convey an attitude of hopelessness' with respect to conditions regarded as genetic in origin.[11] One can see the effects of such an attitude on a young woman, who finally had the courage to see a neurologist after her father had been diagnosed as having Huntington's disease; she describes these effects as follows:

> I sat in horror as he relayed to me the details of the disease. He painted a bleak, hopeless picture and told me that I should consider having my tubes tied to avoid having children. He did not bother to refer me to any self-help groups, genetic counseling, or the Huntington Disease Society of America. The doctor left me feeling hopeless and of little value to myself or others. I was certain that I was damaged and defective and that no one would ever love me. Looking back, it is not surprising that I sank into a depression which became progressively deeper from that day on, culminating several years later in two attempts to take my life.[12]

Later, this woman did discover self-help groups and the National Hereditary Disease Foundation. She also read about the disease and advances in treating and managing the behaviour associated with it. She also experienced some genetic counselling with a doctor and a counsellor who helped her regain some hope and self-confidence. She also found out about predictive tests. But as someone in her mid-twenties she considered the gap between knowing and the onset of the disease too great, and she also wanted children. In her own words, 'I decided that persons at risk for other diseases –

cancer, heart disease, diabetes – are not generally discouraged by the medical establishment, nor by society, from having children, and neither should I be so discouraged'.[13]

At this point in her thinking, this young woman has clearly discerned the premise inherent in the eugenic advice she has been receiving: Someone who has Huntington's disease does not have a life worthy of life! Again, she expresses this so well in her own words:

> There is no treatment or cure for H.D. What good would it do me to know one way or the other? Would I really modify my behavior or lead my life any differently? A yes answer to that question would surely nullify the meaning of my present life. I decided to live life to the fullest, with hope for the future.[14]

Not only do many medical professionals implicitly repudiate her worth and the worth of individuals with Huntington's disease, but many, though not all, also seek to change what for her is a positive, hopeful attitude toward her life now and in the future. Once more, let us hear her eloquent voice:

> My personal philosophy has not been one generally accepted by the majority of medical practitioners that I have known in the past ten years. I have been told that I live in denial because I do not wish to have the test. I have even been told that I am ignorant because I wish to have children! One gynecologist even called me at home without invitation after a routine office visit to try to advise me about alternatives to having my own children. I have begun to feel that these doctors believe that with enough genetic counselling I will eventually make the 'right' decision in my life (that is, not to have children).[15]

Contrary to the official policy, these genetic counsellors are not 'value neutral' by any stretch of the imagination. Indeed, they are zealously seeking a convert to their own version of the genetic gospel realized through negative eugenic measures. All of this is happening without any certainty that this woman either has Huntington's or will ever pass it on to her offspring. It is not a case of compulsion, governmental or otherwise. But by any definition, their pressure on this woman is coercive and involves a severe degree of stigmatization, severe enough to induce two attempts at suicide from a woman who devoutly wishes to live life to the fullest and have children! Those professionals who strive with her convinced her for a time to regard her life as unworthy to be lived, healthy though she is so far. Furthermore, these same professionals treat her as a threat to others who are assumed to be at risk of having a life unworthy of life, namely, her future children should she have any.

Quaid speaks also of the difficulties encountered by those who, because of the new predictive test, live in the expectation that they will have Huntington's disease and will some day suffer from its symptoms. Some of these individuals have told her of their inability to know how to describe themselves to others. In response, Quaid tells them and us that they belong in a 'new category', one that 'we need to think about how to handle'.[16]

Think about Quaid's response. She is a genetic counsellor, critical of those who would rob their clients of hope, or in any way portray them as 'tainted'. Yet, she herself does not know what to say to persons whom she can describe only as being in a 'new category'. There surely is a way to describe such individuals in a way that inspires hope and does not taint. We can say they are 'worthy of life'; they are 'loved by God'; they are our neighbours whom we love; they are our neighbours who can love us and can have the high privilege of loving God. And for those who seek God, there is a gospel beyond any genetic gospel, freely offered, without coercion, of a new life in Christ now, and, beyond all diseases and corruptions of our mortal bodies, forever. No genetic counsellor need be empty or speechless when it comes to inspiring hope.

Coercion can and does come, as we have noted, by way of discrimination by employers, insurance companies, and genetic counsellors. Coercion need not come from governments but from the very concepts that geneticists, physicians, and health professionals tend to share as they implicitly or explicitly practise negative eugenics. Coercion also stems from cost-benefit analyses as it did in Germany before and during the Nazi period.

There is yet another source of coercion, namely the fear of liability. In 1985, the Department of Professional Liability of the American College of Obstetricians and Gynecologists issued an alert to all of its members: inform all pregnant patients of the availability of maternal serum alpha-fetoprotein screening for a variety of defects. The alert instructed all physicians that it is 'imperative that every prenatal patient be advised of the advisability of this test and that your discussion about the test and the patient's decision with respect to the test be documented in the patient's chart'.[17] This imperative to treat this test for defects as advisable for all pregnant patients flew in the face of the College's official position at the time that such screening is of dubious value. Among the serious reasons for cautioning against routine screening of this kind are that too many false negatives and false positives are associated with the test in question and appropriate counselling is often not available. Testing should not occur in the absence of appropriate counselling. The rationale for the alert was not medical, however, but legal. It was to be able to offer 'the best possible defense in a medical malpractice suit' in the case of a baby born 'with a neural tube defect'.[18] Given the variety of ways that coercion

can and does arise in the context of genetic screening and counselling, Diane Paul, an historian of eugenics takes the view that:

> In the absence of public policy designed to prevent it, reproductive decisions
> will often be driven by the conjoined interest of powerful nonstate entities,
> such as physicians, lawyers, insurers, and biotechnology firms. These are
> entities over which the public has limited control – precisely because they
> are private. . . . 'It is when left to the free market that the fruits of genome
> research are most assuredly rotten'.[19]

Some are inclined to respond to these cautionary analyses of a free
market for the products of genetic research by emphasizing that
genetic testing and counselling should be held to the standards of
informed, voluntary, and confidential choices on the part of those
who are tested and counselled. But that has not prevented discrimination by insurers and employers nor will it prevent marketing that
would, as Wilfond and Fost have noted, 'easily generate fear and
anxiety so that many people would demand screening'.[20]

But 'autonomous choices', to the extent they are absolutized,
open the door to a whole range of eugenic demands. If and when
the knowledge is available, what will prevent socio-economic inequality with regard to who requests and who can obtain a whole
range of alleged desirable characteristics for their children? Diane
Paul, contemplating this possibility, comments that:

> This is not a future many critics of the new genetic technologies would
> welcome. But it seems to be the path down which we are headed –
> unfortunately by default, rather than as the result of reasonable debate.[21]

One major reason for the lack of debate is that Watson is not alone
in misunderstanding eugenic abuses: how those happened in the
past; how they happen now; and what will help to make them
happen in the future.

That brings us to the most important misunderstanding of how
and why genetics perpetrates unethical practices – even atrocities.
Watson speaks of the need to prevent the misuse of genetic
information that results from genetic research. That is important
to be sure. But the greater actual and potential danger to individual
well being, and to the very existence of human communities as we
know them, comes from some of the governing assumptions about
human beings typically embedded in genetic science and shared by
many genetic scientists.

COMPARING NAZI PRINCIPLES OF EUGENICS AND CERTAIN ASSUMPTIONS ABOUT GENETICS

Certain assumptions within genetics (then called eugenics or racial
hygiene) shaped Nazi thinking and policy. Indeed, leading German

geneticists regarded National Socialism as applied biology. Gerhard Wagner, then leader of the German medical profession, asserted that:

> Knowledge of racial hygiene and genetics has become a purely scientific path, the knowledge of an extraordinary number of German doctors. It has influenced to a substantial degree the basic world view of the State, and indeed may even be said to embody the very formulations of the present state. . . .[22]

Now what ideas or principles exist in genetics that provide the formulations of a state like Nazi Germany? The biologist, Theobald Lang, enunciated three, and one can find parallels to these in a leading founder of socio-biology, E.O. Wilson of Harvard, in his Pulitzer prize winning book *On Human Nature*. Lang asserted that National Socialism, as applied biology, affirmed the following:

1) Inequality;
2) The deeply enduring nature of genetic traits;
3) The necessity to change economic orders and conceptions of civilization that exert a negative selection on future generations.[23]

1. INEQUALITY AND LIFE UNWORTHY OF LIFE.

As we have noted earlier, Darwin's theory of evolution undermined the notion of natural equality. Wilson, like many geneticists, accepts the Darwinian understanding of evolution. However, he takes the theory much further. Wilson argues that the Darwinian myth is superior to the Creation myth, and scientific materialism is superior to any belief in a personal God.[24] Scientific materialism, according to Wilson, is based on the quest for knowledge, not the pure desire to believe that is responsible for the belief in a personal God. Scientific materialism asserts that life and mind have a physical basis; that it is the mind that creates moralities; that the mind is constructed to pursue truth.

We have discussed earlier the contemporary tendencies to view some lives as unworthy of life. Wilson does not completely support this view but he does say that when our genetic knowledge is more complete, we will then have the option of a 'democratically contrived eugenics'.[25] He does not say what that would look like. However, we do know this much. He rules out the idea of worth attributed to human beings from any external or transcendental source. Being loved by God is not, for him, a basis for assessing human worth. Once religion is explained as a product of the brain's evolution, Wilson exclaims, 'its power as an external source of morality will be gone forever. . . .'[26] The evolutionary epic and scientific materialism will replace existing religion; and theology will cease to be an independent discipline as genetic knowledge grows.

In adopting the 'religion' of scientific materialism as Wilson describes it, he has abandoned two essential pillars of democracy and of communal governance as such. The first pillar is that human beings are 'born equal' and naturally have the capacity to know right and wrong, good and evil. Within Judaism and Christianity these truths are anchored in the notions of the law written on the heart, and of everyone created as bearers of the image of God. Because human beings naturally know right and wrong they can form communities and governments. As equals, all human beings should, as a matter of principle, be afforded the opportunity to vote and to participate in governmental and communal activities.

The second pillar of democracy is the human proclivity to sin. Humans are prone to evil as well as to good, and none is entirely free of these tendencies. Wilson provides no account of the mind's tendency to deny and distort truth. The idea of our sinfulness undergirds the concepts of a loyal opposition, the necessity of contending parties, and the separation of powers. Everyone and every group, requires correction, and no individual or group has the whole truth on what policies are best. Knowledge of what is right makes voting and representative government possible; sinful tendencies make voting and multiple parties necessary.

Wilson attacks these pillars of democracy without replacing them. This he does in the name of genetics and the superiority of what he regards as scientifically derived truth. He takes science as he understands it to be the one source of truth. We would do well to remember that the appeal to pure science helped silence opposition to the Nazi party and helped gain support for Nazi policies.[27]

2. THE ABIDING NATURE OF EVOLUTIONARY GENETIC FORCES.

Consider now the second Nazi principle and its parallel in E.O. Wilson. As Wilson flatly declares, 'the genes hold culture on a leash'. That is why Wilson believes that 'the cultural evolution of higher ethical values' cannot 'gain a direction and momentum of its own'.[28] In short, cultural evolution cannot replace genetic evolution: Human behaviour cannot progress beyond genetic determinants. Though the desire to be religious is an ineradicable part of human nature, it is the Darwinian myth and scientific materialism that will fill the need to be religious as genetic knowledge grows.

3. ALTERING CONCEPTS OF CIVILIZATION THAT STAND IN THE WAY OF GENETIC EVOLUTION.

We turn now to the third principle of Naziism. Wilson is concerned to change conceptions of human nature and of culture in so far as they stand in the way of, or do not make sense of, evolutionary processes that ensure our survival as a species. For him that means substituting the Darwinian myth for a belief in a personal God and Creator. It also means practising eugenics based on genetic knowledge.

The foregoing analysis leads me to one final set of observations. It is misleading to speak of the dangers of repeating the history of eugenics. Eugenics is not simply a matter of history. Eugenics is practised today. Though theoretically voluntary, unethical and ethically questionable practices persist. Indeed, they multiply with the prospect of multiplying even more rapidly. Above all, the very ideas and concepts that informed and motivated German physicians and the Nazi state are in place. Someone like Wilson even 'ups the ante' with his ideas that are subversive of human community and democratic institutions. We dare not go that way! The assumptions of modern genetics need to be analyzed for their theological and moral assumptions; the views of geneticists also need to be studied and aired. That is my research proposal for concerned scholars. In this struggle, ignorance is not bliss.

Wilson ends his book by praising the Promethean spirit of science for its knowledge but also for constructing 'the mythology of scientific materialism, guided by the corrective devices of the scientific method, [appealing] to the deepest needs of human nature, and kept strong by the blind hopes that the journey on which we are now embarked will be farther and better than the one just completed'.[29] I agree with Wilson on one thing: these hopes of his are blind. We cannot get something from nothing; we can get life only from life. These truths are among the bases for a belief in an eternally living Creator.[30] And being endowed with life in all its glory and mystery, I know I am loved by that Creator. Wilson's scientific materialism is not based on complete knowledge; and it does not and cannot satisfy our deepest human needs. We need truth and we need to be loved by the very source of our lives.

Being loved by God is our only realistic hope for continued life in the fullest sense. Being loved by God is also our only realistic hope that our lives will be regarded as lives, worthy of life, and all of us equally worthy of life. And as for scientific materialism: reliable witnesses met with the resurrected Jesus who promised us that we can join him in life eternal. So, like Job, I can say, and every human being has a chance to say, 'though . . . worms destroy this body, yet in my flesh shall I see God'.[31]

NOTES

1. Kevles, Daniel J., *In the Name of Eugenics: Genetics and the Uses of Heredity* (Berkeley, University of California Press 1985), p. ix.

2. Watson, James D. and Cook-Deegan, Robert Mullan, 'The Human Genome Project and International Health', *JAMA* (June 27 1990) 263:24, p. 3324.

3. Kevles, Daniel J., op. cit., p. 90.

4. Proctor, Robert N., *Racial Hygiene: Medicine Under the Nazis* (Cambridge, Harvard University Press 1988), p. 178.

5. For a very thorough discussion of the extensive involvement of large sectors of German society, professional and ordinary working class people, committed to these ideas and their implementation, see Burleigh, Michael, *Death and Deliverance: 'Euthanasia' In Germany 1900–1945* (New York, Cambridge University Press 1994).

6. German medicine served the Nazi party and its policies in a great many ways. (See Proctor, Robert N., op. cit., especially Chapter 3, 'Political Biology: Doctors in the Nazi Cause'.)

7. Proctor, Robert N., op. cit., p. 60. Proctor footnotes this textbook on p. 50 (see footnote 15 on p. 350).

8. Proctor, Robert N., op. cit., p. 48. For a full account of Fritz Lenz, consult the whole chapter on him by Proctor, pp. 46–63.

9. Beecher, Henry K., 'Ethics and Clinical Research', *New England Journal of Medicine* (1966) v. 274, 1354–1360.

10. Quaid, Kimberly A., 'A Few Words from a "Wise" Woman', in Weir, Robert F., Lawrence, Susan C. and Fales, Evan (eds.), *Genes and Human Self-Knowledge* (Iowa City, University of Iowa Press 1994), p. 9. As for the risks of various kinds of discrimination, see Billings, P.R., Kohn, M.A., De Cuevas, M., Beckwith, J., Alper, J.S. and Natowicz, M.R., 'Discrimination as a Consequence of Genetic Testing', *American Journal Human Genetics* (1992) v. 50, 476–482.

11. Ibid.

12. Ibid., pp. 9–10.

13. Ibid., pp. 10–11.

14. Ibid., p. 11.

15. Ibid.

16. Ibid., pp. 15–16.

17. Cited in Paul, Diane B., 'Is Human Genetics Disguised Eugenics?', in Weir, Lawrence, and Fales, Evan (eds.), op. cit., pp. 77–78.

18. Ibid., p. 78.

19. Ibid.

20. Ibid.

21. Ibid., p. 79.

22. Proctor, Robert N. op. cit., p. 45.

23. Ibid., p. 30.

24. Wilson, Edward O., *On Human Nature* (Cambridge, Harvard University Press 1978). The argument permeates the whole book but see particularly Chapter 8, 'Religion' and Chapter 9, 'Hope'.

25. Ibid., p. 206. See also p. 216. (Page references are to the Bantam edition of the book; 1979, a complete edition of the original hardcover edition).

26. Ibid., p. 208.

27. Proctor, Robert N., op. cit. This is one of the central arguments of his book.

28. Wilson, Edward O., op. cit., p. 175.

29. Ibid., p. 217.

30. For a much fuller discussion of arguments for the existence of God, and of my agreements and disagreements with E.O. Wilson, see Dyck, Arthur J., *Rethinking Rights and Responsibilities: The Moral Bonds of Community* (Cleveland, Pilgrim Press 1994), Chapter 6.

31. Job 19:26, King James Version.

[2]

Technology, History, and Worldview

Nancy R. Pearcey, MA

At a recent conference on gene patenting, Princeton University professor Robert George described an ethics class where his students were discussing a host of contentious social issues. Included among them were whether we should allow surrogate motherhood or the sale of children. To his surprise, the students in his class all voted solidly against these possibilities. As he put it, 'This was pretty much an anything-goes crowd, yet every one of them was opposed to surrogate motherhood and a market in children'. But when he pressed the students to give reasons to support what they felt, Dr George said, they stuttered and mumbled and could not come up with any. In other words, they had a visceral sense that certain ways of treating human beings are simply wrong, but they did not have the principles to support their views or argue for them.

Dr George's classroom is reflective of American culture as a whole. To some degree people sense instinctively what is right and what is wrong. They sense instinctively, for example, that genetic technologies are potentially a great good but are also potentially a great danger. Certain uses of genetic technology, many Americans would insist, are morally wrong. But if you were to ask them to articulate *reasons* for that visceral sense of moral boundaries, they could not do it. As Robert Bellah shows so poignantly in his book *Habits of the Heart,*[1] most Americans' vocabulary does not even give them the language to express an objective morality.

What does this mean for Christians striving to be salt and light in the culture? It means that there is, as the saying goes, good news and bad news. The good news is that on moral issues believers can often find common ground with non-believers. On the level of basic human experience – that visceral sense of right and wrong – Christians can often find a point of contact with non-Christians as both engage in what has been dubbed the culture war, which is spreading rapidly to the issues of life and death.

The bad news is that on a conceptual level, most Americans today have no rational grounds for their moral intuitions – no matter how sound those intuitions themselves may be. They lack a vocabulary even to speak of an objective morality. In fact, the vocabulary that is available to them is often antithetical to the very idea of an objective moral framework. If we are to fight the culture war effectively, we must realize that the contemporary secular mindset has no resources within itself to generate moral guidelines, to set moral boundaries on the potentially dangerous uses of genetic technologies.

This means that before we discuss specific ethical problems, we must grasp the contemporary mindset itself, which we will call 'liberalism', with its aspiration to be 'free' from biblical and other constraints. We cannot simply lift moral precepts from one context – from a Christian worldview – and inject them into another context – into modern liberalism. We must understand liberalism as a comprehensive worldview and analyze how it differs from a biblical worldview.

IT DID NOT HAVE TO BE

Consider first a biblical picture of reality as it applies to technology, especially the relation between technology and moral principles. Historically, modern science and technology have their roots firmly in a Christian worldview. This has been noted by several historians, both Christian and secular.[2] Modern science rests on certain foundational assumptions that were provided by Christian belief, such as the assumption that the world has a rational, intelligible order because it is created by a rational God, coupled with the assumption that we can discover that order because we are created in God's image. The next step, however – the application of science to practical problems through technology – depended on three additional principles.

The first principle is that the universe is contingent and can be changed. To understand what contingency means and how important it was historically, we must go back to the ancient Greeks. The Greeks taught that nature is teleological, that it is imbued with inherent rational purposes. These purposes were thought of as logically necessary. Once you understood the purpose of a tree or a rock, you could logically deduce what its essential properties must be.

The teleological view of nature has been regarded by many Christians throughout western history as compatible with biblical faith. In some extreme forms, however, it was not compatible, for it seemed to imply that an object's inherent nature and purpose place limits on God himself. For example, in the late Middle Ages some Christian Aristotelians argued that the nature of the heavens demanded circular motion by an inner law of rational necessity. Not only was this later discovered to be empirically mistaken, but even at the time some theologians protested that it seemed to imply that

God could not have made the planets' orbits anything but circular, that his hand was constrained by some inherent necessity in the structure of things. As historian A. C. Crombie explains, Christian Aristotelianism held that

> the ultimate rational causes of things in God's mind could be discovered by the human reason; and that Aristotle had in fact discovered those causes, so that the universe *must necessarily* be constituted as he had described it, and *could not* be otherwise.[3]

This suggestion that matter had prescribed properties that God himself could not change gave rise in the thirteenth century to a reaction known as voluntarism. Voluntarism emphasized God's freedom to create the world according to his own will and purposes. Natural laws were not rational purposes *within* nature, voluntarists argued; they were divine commands imposed from *outside* nature by a transcendent God. The order of the universe is not intrinsic, it is bestowed by God; and if he wants to, he can change that order. He could even have created a world with a different order from the one that exists. The structure and existence of the universe are not rationally necessary, they are contingent upon the free and transcendent will of God.

The idea of contingency proved to be a powerful impetus to the development of technology. The Greek view had led to passivity in the face of nature: Nature could be contemplated but not manipulated. But contingency implied an active role for human beings. Historian Christopher Kaiser in his book *Creation and the History of Science* puts it this way: 'Things do not have to continue as they now are because their existence depends on a God who created them beginning with nothing, who can therefore transform them as he will.'[4] This conviction opened the door to a new level of creative manipulation of natural objects. Whereas the Greeks looked for purposes inherent in nature, the early modern scientists asked how they could impose their own purposes on nature. They set out to analyse the properties of the wood in a tree or the minerals in a rock, and then creatively think up new ways in which people might make use of those properties. To cite simple illustrations, when we grind up trees to make paper or extract minerals from rocks and smelt them down to make cars and trucks, these are not purposes found anywhere in nature. They are human purposes imposed on nature.

The idea of contingency allowed the human mind to conceive the possibility of radical change. History was not cyclical, the endless return of the same thing. Instead history was linear. In the course of time God can create things that are genuinely new, and so can human beings, who are made in his image. They can invent, innovate, and discover new uses for natural forces.

KNOWLEDGE IN ACTION

A second principle necessary for the development of technology was epistemological, and it likewise emerged from Christian belief. In many religious traditions, divinity is immanent in the universe. It may be conceived of either as several deities inhabiting the rivers and woods (animism) or as a single spirit permeating all things (pantheism). Either way, divinity is a quality of something *within* the universe; the universe itself is the sole all-encompassing reality.

In this context, human beings are also completely immanent in nature. This idea is typically expressed through totems and idols, where humans are connected to the creatures of the natural world in a bond of spiritual kinship. This immanent form of spirituality generates an intellectual stance that is passive vis-a-vis nature. The human mind is embedded in nature and cannot transcend it as subject over against object. The goal of knowledge is merely to adapt and conform to nature. There is no concept of harnessing nature's forces for practical ends.

But the Bible begins with a transcendent God and with humans created in his image. Here humans find their essential kinship not with nature but with God. We are his representatives, extending his 'dominion' over creation, in the words of Genesis. As a result, the human mind is capable of transcending nature and confronting it as subject against object. The human mind is active vis-a-vis nature. We do not seek knowledge merely to conform to nature; instead we are free to manipulate nature, both conceptually in mathematical formulas and practically in experiments. This intellectual stance enabled people to conceive the idea of active intervention into natural processes to advance human purposes.

DUTY AND DOMINION

We now have two principles in place: the concept of a world susceptible to change, and of human beings capable of changing it. The third precondition for modern technology was moral sanction. Once again, that came from Christianity.

From the time of the early church, Christians stressed the practical arts as means of reversing the destructive effects of humanity's fall into sin and the curse on nature, recorded in Genesis 3. Knowledge was considered a gift of God to alleviate toil and suffering.

For example, in the fourth century, Basil, Bishop of Caesarea, founded history's first hospital open to the public on a regular basis. He also organized relief for famine victims. Basil's theological rationale was twofold: First, because God created the world, there is a possibility of radical change – the God who created can also restore, overcoming the effects of the Fall. This, according to Basil, is the lesson of the biblical miracles of healing. Second, God's people are called to carry on this ministry of help and healing, not necessarily in miracles but in acts of charity and service.

In other words, even before the scientific revolution, Christian scholars were giving the technical arts a theological justification and a positive value they did not have in either ancient Greek or ancient Jewish culture.[5] During the scientific revolution, this theme was, if anything, intensified. The writings of the early modern scientists are permeated with religious concern for the poor and the sick. The application of science to the improvement of the human condition was considered a religious duty, an act of obedience to God and of Christian charity. Cotton Mather wrote in 1654 that 'to study the nature and course and use of all God's works is a duty imposed by God'. In the words of historian P.M. Rattansi, Christianity 'imposed a religious obligation' to make science 'serve the twin ends of glorifying God and benefiting fellow-men'.[6] In short, technology was regarded as a servant of moral and charitable purposes.

Consider the example of Paracelsus, a 16th-century physician who pioneered the use of chemistry in medicine. Paracelsus was a devout Christian and derived his medical calling from two biblical principles. First, he believed that Christ's victory over death meant that all illnesses could eventually be healed. (In our own day of miracle drugs that idea may not sound novel, but in Paracelsus's day it was revolutionary.) The impetus for scientific research, then, was to fulfil the ministry of healing and restoration ordained by Christ. Second, Paracelsus argued that loving our neighbours as ourselves means doing everything we can to help them, by cultivating all the creative and technical arts.[7]

The Reformers stood in the same tradition. Martin Luther viewed the human arts as means of restoring, at least in part, Adam's dominion over creation. He saw scientists as co-workers with God in his creative activity. In fact, Luther anticipated that religious reformation would lead to a new era of scientific and technological progress. Both Luther and Calvin applied the Christian ideal of charity and service to the arts and sciences, arguing that they should be used not for personal ambition but to promote the public good.[8]

One man often credited – or blamed, as the case may be – with being a prime mover in the development of technology was Francis Bacon. His writings stress repeatedly the theme of mastery over nature. What we hear about less often, however, is that Bacon believed that the purpose of science was to restore Adam's original dominion over nature, a restoration he saw foreshadowed in Jesus' miracles of healing diseases and subduing the forces of nature. As a result, Bacon urged that the arts and sciences are dependent on the grace of God, and that prayer must be an important part of any effort to advance science.[9]

To sum up, Christianity provided both intellectual and moral presuppositions necessary for the great explosion of science and technology since the beginning of the Scientific Revolution. Modern Christians can learn much from the insights of historical figures and their explications of biblical principles. The ethical issues we face today are new, of course, yet many of them echo problems that technology has raised from the beginning of the Christian era. We have, as the letter to Hebrews puts it, a cloud of witnesses to encourage us.

NOTHING BUT HISTORY

Yet as we trace these ideas over time, we also see them becoming secularized until they reach their current form in contemporary liberalism. Ironically, in many ways liberalism is a child – a step-child, if you will – of Christianity, in the sense that it adopted Christian ideas and employed them out of context.

For example, the idea of contingency – that nature is malleable and can be changed – degenerated within liberalism into a philosophy of unrestricted human mastery. The universe was reduced to an endless chain of contingent events, with no objective order, no meaning, no final truth. A recent book by David Roberts of the University of Georgia is called *Nothing But History*, and the title alone is a succinct summary of the book's theme. In postmodern philosophy, Roberts says, there is nothing but history: 'The world is ever provisional . . . we are caught up in endless history'.[10] In postmodernism, contingency is understood to mean there is no objective moral order to which we must submit. There is only a constant flux of uninterpreted events, of history, which we are free to master according to our own purposes.

This notion of radical contingency was first applied to the natural sciences, and later extended to the social sciences. The late George Grant, a Canadian philosopher and a Christian, wrote that if science is about the conquest and mastery of nature, then the human sciences are about the mastery of *human* nature. Human nature came to be seen as something to be conquered, controlled, and changed. Values came to be seen as something we freely create in our attempts to master our personal and social world. Even the term 'value' has a subjective connotation, compared with the older term 'goodness'. Value is something I confer on something, not a quality it has objectively; it is something I create, not something I discover. As a result, Grant warned, liberalism is impotent to provide any moral direction to modern technology because both grow from the same soil – from a secular ideal of creative mastery that acknowledges no given cosmic or moral order but opens vistas of constant creating and recreating of both our world and ourselves.[11]

The decoupling of technology from moral guidelines meant that in fact technologies began to be developed that were inhumane and destructive, leading to a profound pessimism. One of the earliest signs of an emerging disenchantment with science and technology was *Gulliver's Travels*, where Jonathan Swift parodied the Royal Society (England's scientific association). Later, in *Rasselas*, Samuel Johnson portrayed the desire to control nature as a madness that puts the self in the place of God. William Blake described the effects of technology in a poem using his famous phrase about 'dark Satanic mills'. Later generations of critics also portrayed their concerns about technology in literature and poetry, up to Aldous Huxley's *Brave New World* and beyond.

A CROWD OF WITNESSES

Today we seem to stand at the threshold of that Brave New World, and the only way to tackle the tough ethical issues we face is to stop treating them in isolation and start placing them within an overall philosophical framework – an understanding of two worldviews in conflict. Doing so is important for two reasons.

First, Christians often make the mistake of taking individual moral principles (such as 'abortion is wrong'), abstracting these principles from the biblical worldview that makes sense of them, and then proclaiming them in the public sphere. These principles appear to be arbitrary, and Christians come across as moralists trying to impose private preferences by coercion. We need to find ways to communicate moral principles within an overall, integrated system of beliefs about the world. In doing this, we can learn much from our historical forebears, who often had a more holistic understanding of their faith as a story encompassing all of life, a story that tells us where we came from and what our purpose is.

Second, Christians can develop a new apologetic by pointing out that much of what is attractive and beneficial in modernity has blossomed in Christian soil. The concept of the contingency of nature is a good example. In a Christian framework, contingency simply means that the order of the world is open to *re*-ordering – both by God and by human beings, who have the power to inject new events into chains of cause and effect. But torn from its Christian roots, contingency has come to mean there is no enduring or stable order in the world. Everything is in evolutionary flux. Even nature's stable patterns – the 'laws' of nature – are regarded as merely handles for manipulating natural objects.

Today, with the possibility of manipulating human genes, this secular notion of contingency will inevitably lead to the conclusion that there is no core human nature that is part of the moral order and that we are obligated to respect. There is no restraint on our urge to tinker and change. When people recognize the dangers in such unrestricted freedom, we can call them back to a Christian concept of contingency. The positive benefits of the idea of contingency – the creative freedom it has unleashed in science and technology – will flourish only within a framework that also places ethical limits on that creativity. Otherwise, contingency will lead eventually not to freedom but, ironically, to control, as some people develop the technology to subject other people to genetic control and manipulation.

Similarly, consider the concept of Christian charity, healing, and restoration. As Charles Taylor shows in his book *Sources of the Self*[12], the Christian teaching on charity has been secularized to an ideal of universal benevolence. Yet when torn from its biblical roots, benevolence dissolves into a vague and formless ideal. To quote the late moral philosopher Alasdair MacIntyre: 'Unlike charity, benevolence as a virtue became a license for almost any kind of manipulative intervention in the affairs of others.'[13] Whereas many speak in ominous terms of a Brave New World, the geneticists and medical researchers who are busy developing the technology that could create that world are absolutely convinced that they are acting out of pure benevolence.

Consider a second story from the gene patenting conference described at the outset of this chapter. Among the participants were a handful of presidents and CEOs of major companies that are conducting gene research for commercial use. Listening to these captains of industry was quite enlightening. They were utterly convinced that everything they are doing is for benevolent purposes. Some of the Christian theologians and ethicists around the table tried to get them to consider the possibility that certain technologies could lead to undesirable effects: to the commercialization of the human body, or genetic determinism, or the reduction of human life to consumerist values. But such concerns fell on deaf ears. The company representatives seemed totally convinced that if genetic tinkering helps people to feel better and be happier, that is by definition benevolent, and immune from criticism.

We are not besieged by cartoon-style mad scientists who are out to create Frankensteins. If the genetic revolution gives birth to a nightmare, it will be the work of committed researchers who are wholly sincere, wholly convinced that they are doing good. Only if we stand firm on the biblical meaning of charity, buttressed by an awareness of historic Christian thought, will we be able to discern the difference between true scientific progress and well-meaning totalitarianism. Only by God's grace will we be enabled to defend the one while decrying the other.

NOTES

1. Bellah, Robert, Madsen, Richard, Sullivan, William, Swidler, Ann, Tipton Steven, *Habits of the Heart: Individualism and Commitment in American Life* (Berkeley, University of California Press 1985).

2. For an extended discussion see Pearcey, Nancy R. and Thaxton, Charles B., *The Soul of Science: Christian Faith and Natural Philosophy* (Wheaton, Illinois, Crossway Books 1994), chapter 1.

3. Cited in Pearcey and Thaxton, pp. 31–32, emphasis added.

4. Kaiser, Christopher, *Creation and the History of Science* (Grand Rapids, Eerdmans 1991), p. 36.

5. Kaiser, pp. 34–51.

6. Cited in Pearcey and Thaxton, pp. 35–36.

7. Kaiser, pp. 116–120.

8. Kaiser, pp. 139–150.

9. Kaiser, pp. 146–149.

10. Roberts, David D., *Nothing But History: Reconstruction and Extremity after Metaphysics* (Berkeley, University of California Press 1995), p. 129.

11. Grant, George, *Technology and Empire* (Toronto, House of Anansi 1969). See also his *Time As History*, ed. and intro. by William Christian (Toronto: University of Toronto Press).

This is not to say that the Greek view of necessary order has been given up completely. Postmodernism still vies with the remaining vestiges of modernism, which represents a continuation of the Greek heritage. A historical link connects the ancient Pythagorean view of mathematics to the mathematical physics of the early modern scientists, such as Copernicus, Kepler, Galileo, and Newton. The Pythagorean influence led them to conflate mathematical order and natural order, producing various forms of determinism and reductionism characteristic of Enlightenment thinking. (See Pearcey and Thaxton, *The Soul of Science*, chapters 6 and 7.) The academic world today is split between those (mostly in the hard sciences) who still champion Enlightenment objectivism and those (in literature, history, and the social sciences) who embrace postmodernist subjectivism.

12. Taylor, Charles, *Sources of the Self: The Making of the Modern Identity* (Cambridge, Harvard University Press 1989).

13. MacIntyre, Alisdair, *After Virtue: A Study in Moral Theory* (Notre Dame, Notre Dame Press 1981, 1984), p. 232.

[3]

God's Sovereignty and Genetic Anomalies

Michael S. Beates, STM

What is the connection between God's sovereignty in creation and the presence of acutely grotesque or at least mysterious genetic 'accidents'? Did God purpose to make these, or did he start the biological machine we call humanity and then step back to watch it run, leaving the entry of sin to wreak the havoc we see in 'malformations'? Are genetic anomalies strictly related to sin and the Fall, freeing God from any responsibility regarding them? If God has no part in such debilitating human physical conditions, then what hope does the Christian faith offer those who are afflicted or those who care for or treat these afflicted?

In the midst of a technical ethnographic study of the profession of genetic counselling, provocatively entitled *All God's Mistakes: Genetic Counseling in a Pediatric Hospital*, a strikingly personal and honest statement appears:

> There is one final burden that parents also have to face: their own impotence and powerlessness to change the situation. This requires accepting the limits on their children's development, despite finding the best infant stimulation programs, procuring the best support services, and providing the best parenting. It requires accepting the limits of the possible. . . .
>
> In the end, this impotence overwhelms some parents; their children become a source of 'Chronic Sorrow', their original loss is reexperienced as each developmental milestone fails to be reached. For the genetic counselors' part, their own impotence to fix what cannot be fixed often overwhelms them.
>
> Finally, watching all this as a witness, being asked to help and not knowing how, overwhelmed me as well. . . . I felt some sort of cosmic anger that there was so much random and contingent pain and suffering. I was overwhelmed and then paralyzed by the limits of rational understanding.[1]

From the secular perspective of this book, such frustration is inevitable and not surprising. All too often, however, even people who profess a Christian worldview capitulate to such an existential position. The capitulation may be quite subtle (and perhaps unintended), as when we refer to 'reproductive mishaps'.[2] Yet to speak of 'mishaps' is to dismiss the notion of God's sovereignty. Some

49

may be willing to do just that, but as this essay will show, we cannot do so without doing violence to Scripture. God's sovereignty, human responsibility, and evil must all be accounted for in a genuinely biblical outlook.

If God is sovereign and 'ordains whatsoever comes to pass' (Westminster Confession of Faith), then what do we make of seemingly tragic or grotesque genetic anomalies? We commonly call such anomalies 'malformations' or 'defects'. But can we at once affirm God's sovereignty over creation and refer to products of his creative work as 'defective' or 'malformed'? That in short is the subject of this chapter.

We will consider briefly the Bible's teaching about God's sovereignty and then discuss how such a biblical perspective may bring comfort to the afflicted, encouragement and strength to those who care for them, and direction to those who guide their treatment.

THE SOVEREIGNTY OF GOD

While virtually all Christians profess belief in God's sovereignty, as soon as we begin to discuss the depth of that sovereignty, we find many Christians hold to an oxymoronic version of limited sovereignty. 'God is sovereign except when . . .' we hear many say.[3] R.C. Sproul has often said there is precious little sovereignty left in many people's idea of God's sovereignty. A.W. Tozer, in his classic work *Knowledge of the Holy*, writes: 'And were God lacking one infinitesimal modicum of power, that lack would end His reign and undo His kingdom; that one stray atom of power would belong to someone else and God would be a limited ruler and hence not sovereign.'[4] When we say with the Westminster Confession of Faith that 'God from all eternity, did, by the most wise and holy counsel of His own will, freely, and unchangeably ordain whatsoever comes to pass;'[5] we are affirming not one thin brand of Reformed Christianity but the theological premise undergirding all of theism, including Judaism, Islam, and Christianity. More importantly, such a statement of God's sovereignty is faithful to the teaching of Scripture.

Genesis 1–3. From the creation accounts in Genesis we may assume that people were created with a perfect genetic makeup. The Fall caused fallenness throughout our entire being right down to our genes, our DNA, and our very souls. But this Fall was no surprise to God, and his plan of redemption was not a 'Plan B'. Indeed, even our fallenness must somehow eventually glorify him because he has determined that all things will give glory to him. How aspects of fallenness like genetic anomalies glorify him is the difficult question.

Psalm 115:1-3. 'Not to us O LORD, not to us, but to your name be the glory, because of your love and faithfulness. Why do the nations say, "Where is their God?" Our God is in heaven; he does whatever pleases him.'[6]

Daniel 4:35. 'He does as he pleases with the powers of heaven and the peoples of the earth. No one can hold back his hand or say to him, "What have you done?" ' These two texts, among many others, affirm that God is all powerful in his character and reign. In his omnipotence he is able to do whatever he chooses to do according to his nature.

Deuteronomy 32:4. 'He is the Rock, his works are perfect, and all his ways are just. A faithful God who does no wrong, upright and just is he.' This text adds the affirmation that God is also perfectly good, upright and just.[7] We know by God's character that he does not sin. If he does not sin and has created and ordained all things, then in some sense, all that he creates is good.

It is at this point that the classic problem arises: if God exists and yet difficulties like genetic anomalies also exist, then God is either all powerful or all good, but not both. If he were beneficent and powerful, he would not permit such difficulties, we think. The alternatives are that he is omnipotent but cold, heartless, or tyrannical in the exercise of this power, or that he is good but not powerful enough to prevent evil and tragedy like genetic anomalies.

However, these texts affirm both that God is good and that he is all powerful. Consequently, we are left with the difficult conclusion that in so far as God decides not to prevent anomalies, in some sense he therefore ordains them, deciding that they should happen. If it is according to his good will to let genetic anomalies happen, in some sense it is good that they happen even if we cannot fathom what that good may be.[8]

Other biblical texts, in fact, affirm in a straightforward manner this difficult (and for many unacceptable) conclusion that God is sovereignly involved in all things, even things we consider bad or wrong.

Exodus 4:11. 'The LORD said to him [Moses], "Who gave man his mouth? Who makes him deaf or mute? Who gives him sight or makes him blind? Is it not I, the LORD?" '

Isaiah 45:5-9. 'I am the LORD, and there is no other; apart from me there is no God. . . . I form the light and create darkness, I bring prosperity and create disaster; I the LORD do all these things. . . . Does the clay say to the potter, "What are you making?" Does your work say "He has no hands"?'[9]

In these two difficult texts we see God not denying complicity with things we call bad, but, to our surprise, taking the credit. Commenting on this passage, Walter Kaiser makes a careful distinction between moral evil and physical evil, reminding us that God, by his nature, cannot be involved in moral evil. He then comments on the Isaiah passage saying, 'According to the Hebrew way of speaking, which ignores secondary causation in a way Western thought would never do, whatever God permits must be directly attributed to him, often without noting that secondary and sinful parties were the immediate causes of physical disaster.'[10]

One further passage, **Romans 11:36**, provides an overall perspective: 'For from him and through him and to him are all things. To him be glory forever! Amen.' All things have their origin in him, are sustained by him, and will give glory to him. Charles Hodge said it as well as anyone when he wrote:

> The authority of God is limited by nothing out of Himself, but it is controlled, in all its manifestations, by his infinite perfections. . . . This sovereignty of God is the ground of peace and confidence to all his people. They rejoice that the Lord God omnipotent reigneth; that neither necessity, nor chance, nor the folly of man, nor the malice of Satan controls the sequence of events and all their issues. Infinite wisdom, love, and power, belong to Him, our great God and Savior, into whose hands all power in heaven and earth has been committed.[11]

God's ultimate purpose in all things is to bring glory to himself. So every act of providence, the good and the bad, the sweet and the bitter, reveals some aspect of his glory, some new measure of his marvellous perfection and his awesome majesty. He does this not only that his glory may be revealed but also, secondarily, so that his creatures, especially his chosen children, may bask in the glory of his greatness and with increasing devotion worship him, honour him, and delight in him for all the glory that he has chosen to reveal through the good and the bad.

IF GOD IS SOVEREIGN, WHY. . . ?

God, then, is both all powerful and all good. As Creator and Sustainer of all that is, he is ultimately responsible for the presence of genetic anomalies. Yet, when considering the reason for such anomalies, we must bear in mind the broader teaching of Scripture, that 'neither is God the author of sin, nor is violence offered to the will of the creatures.'[12] If God is not up in heaven wringing his hands at his inability to prevent diseases or genetic anomalies that take the lives of children,[13] if he did not slip up and let a few design flaws somehow escape quality control while he was dealing with a more urgent situation in Eastern Europe, then what is his purpose in creating some people with Down's syndrome, DeLang's syndrome, trisomy 18, trisomy 13, or any of the many other radical genetic anomalies that are incompatible with life? While our understanding of God's purposes is far from complete, at least four possible reasons warrant consideration.

First, as previously noted, God creates some people with genetic anomalies simply for the sake of his glory. Scripture teaches that all things are made by him (Jn. 1:3) and for his glory (Isa. 48:10-11; Rom. 11:33).

Many people are not willing to bear the truth that everything God makes and does he uses to glorify himself. It is too much for many to believe that all that happens to them is for the sake of the glory of God's name. That is a hard teaching, but in it there is great comfort, and by our very affirmation of it, we further glorify our awesome sovereign God. The comfort is that when we embrace the truth that God will glorify himself through everything that happens, we know that in the providence of God nothing is lost or in vain. Nothing we experience is meaningless; everything is significant, the bitter and sweet. We may not see the sweet side of it in this life. We may not be able to say at the time of the death of loved ones that their death glorifies God. However, we can rest absolutely certain that such things are not mistakes nor do they happen by chance. We can also be certain that even such awful things will glorify God, because he has said so, and he keeps his promise.

Second, God creates some people with genetic anomalies not only for the sake of his own glory, but also to show us our own brokenness and our need of his grace. The disabled among us, whether genetically disabled or otherwise, remind us of our own inherent disabilities. When we see them with their limitations, we can begin to see ourselves in a new, more honest manner as broken men and women before God in need of redemption, body and soul.

Michael Card, in his song 'When a Window is a Mirror', sings about a boy in his church born with Down's syndrome: 'Each time I gaze upon this boy, there's something moves inside. I see my own deformities, no longer need to hide'.[14] Such children help us to clarify our vision of ourselves. I speak from personal experience and not just from biblical teaching. My eldest daughter, now 14, was born with a genetic anomaly termed 8p + . She is profoundly disabled and will require lifelong care. Her condition is so rare that we do not even know what her life expectancy is. Though life with our daughter has been extremely difficult (and expensive) at times, we have learned important lessons about life and the value of life from her.

We recently received a letter from a friend that captures well this idea of seeing our own brokenness in those with genetic disabilities. In the course of her letter, Nancy Jensen writes the following:

> As a daughter of the King, I am of worth beyond my capacity to perform. I am measured in worth by God's love for me, not by my love toward Him. There is nothing I could perform that would fill a service to Him, nothing. Yet He loves me. . . .

Then I thought of Jessica. She is loved by your family and given a worth beyond her capacity to perform. Her place in your home is ensured by your love for her, not by her ability to be loving, or helpful, or to achieve anything. I realized with humility that I am just like her in God's family, only far more handicapped. In the spiritual realm, I can't move right – much less walk or anything wonderful, can't feed myself or dress myself. . . . And I don't even see how handicapped I am, thinking I'm fine and strong and competent. Still, God loves me, His crippled child, His own chosen special treasure. Just like you two have built your house to accommodate Jessica's needs, so God has ordered all of creation and redemption to accommodate us.

So the Lord used your precious Jessica to show me who I really am to Him. It's humbling, true, but still a great comfort, because it's right.[15]

Healthy 'normal' people (one author has insightfully referred to this broad class of people as 'the temporarily able-bodied'[16]) tend to avoid people with disabilities and to feel uncomfortable around them when avoidance is not possible. This reaction is due primarily to the hubris of our day that sees ourselves as beautiful, whole, perfect people. When we encounter someone who is broken in body, it reminds us that we are much more like this disabled person than we would like to admit. Our differences are not differences of kind, only differences of degree. Such a realization humbles us, and humility is not a virtue cultivated in the contemporary western world. As one writer recently put it, 'Humility has a dank and shameful smell to the worldly, the scent of failure, lowliness, and obscurity.'[17]

Third, God creates some people with genetic anomalies not only for his own glory and to show us our own brokenness, but also because such disabled people present the church with the gift of allowing followers of Christ to serve them unconditionally, with no expectation of receiving back. In this way they help us to mirror God and to experience giving grace to another as God does to us. 'The one worth of the "worthless," ' writes C. Everett Koop, 'is that they prove whether or not we are worthy to care for them. The very existence of the handicapped and imperfect, and the love bestowed on them by those who care, stands as a testimony to the sacredness of human life and to our contention that this sacredness far outweighs any ethic concerned with the *quality* of human life.'[18]

In an age characterized largely by the desire for and the exercise of power and personal autonomy, the genetically disabled unmask the weakness of our power struggles. Henri Nouwen has said, 'Maybe it is that power offers an easy substitute for the hard task of love. It seems easier to be God than to love God, easier to control people than to love people, easier to own life than to love life.'[19] We must be committed to loving all humans as people born *imago Dei*, in the image of God. While the *imago Dei* is most clearly displayed in our ability to reason, communicate, exercise dominion, and so forth, the *imago* in biblical perspective is first ontological – intrinsically part of who we are as people apart from any ability we may by God's grace have and use. That image may be more physically and visibly twisted and marred in some, as with anencephalic children or children with radical genetic anomalies. However, such disfigurement of their *imago Dei* is no more severe than our own when it comes to the immaterial aspect of our souls. We must affirm that they, like us all, are made in God's image and need his redemptive work to be wrought in them body and soul – as do we all.

Fourth, God creates some people with genetic anomalies to increase our desire for heaven. Revelation 21:3-4 says, 'And I heard a loud voice from the throne saying, "Now the dwelling of God is with men, and he will live with them. They will be his people, and God himself will be with them and be their God. He will wipe every tear from their eyes. There will be no more death or mourning or crying or pain, for the old order of things has passed away."' In that final state God promises to redeem all things, making all things new and perfect. In our twentieth century western society, we are healthy, whole, happy, and satisfied (or so we believe from the TV commercials and so we tell ourselves). Indeed, we are comfortable to the point that we seem to lose the sense of desiring heaven. But things like genetic anomalies serve as sign posts, reminding us that we are on a journey and that this world is not our home. They draw us back to the truth that this life is not as good as we like to think and that the prospect of heaven is real and inviting.[20]

When we are faced with excruciatingly painful life situations brought on by genetic anomalies, we ask (and rightfully so), 'If this is from God, how can this be good?' But if such a hardship causes the believer to long more deeply for God's presence and to look forward to his making all things new, then it has meaning and purpose. If such trials beckon followers of Christ to love the Lord our God rather than this world, then he is glorified in such circumstances. We see radical examples of such an outlook in the book of Hebrews. According to Hebrews 10:32–34, early believers accepted *joyfully* the plundering of their homes and property because they knew they had 'a better possession and an abiding one'. Just a few verses later in Hebrews 11:24–26 we are reminded that Moses refused to be called the son of Pharaoh's daughter but chose to endure ill treatment with God's people 'rather than to enjoy the pleasures of sin for a short time.' It says, 'He regarded disgrace for the sake of Christ as of greater value than the treasures of Egypt, because he was looking ahead to his reward'. Luther said it well in his hymn 'A Mighty Fortress':

Let goods and kindred go, this mortal life also.
The body they may kill, God's truth abideth still.
His kingdom is forever.

The Puritans endured difficult, often painful, lives due to afflictions that we often cure with just a pill or an injection. They did not need people with genetic anomalies to survive to remind them of their brokenness and need for heaven – their own lives testified to that truth quite well. But God's providence is ironic in a way. He has given us knowledge and technological advances that save many of us from formerly fatal sicknesses and medical conditions. At the same time, this technology also preserves life for many with genetic anomalies and disabilities who just a generation or two ago would not have survived. So though we have gained comfort, God still reminds us of our brokenness and our need of heaven by the genetically afflicted among us.

THE COMFORT OF GOD'S SOVEREIGNTY

The church does not have a strong record when it comes to dealing with strange and awesome breakthroughs such as those that genetic research is making possible. Christians have too often missed the point altogether, becoming side tracked by peripheral issues, often because of fear. The same response to people with disabilities and people with genetic anomalies has been all too common. Martin Luther is a good example. Never one to leave others wondering exactly what he thought on an issue, Luther was quoted as saying that a particular 12-year-old mentally retarded boy was 'merely a lump of flesh without a soul' and recommended killing the boy. Paul Althaus says Luther 'referred to malformed infants as change-lings not created by God, but made by the devil. They either had no soul, or the devil was their soul.'[21]

Such a narrow vision and erroneous thinking may shock us in our self-perceived enlightenment, but many in our pews are probably closer to Luther's medieval perspective than we would care to believe. Particularly in light of the secular discussion about and consequent assault on 'personhood', followers of Christ must respect God's creation of all people and see them not as problems to be disposed of or hidden away. Rather we must see them as mirrors of our own human brokenness and as divine vehicles of his grace. We must do whatever we can to respect God's image in even the most broken and twisted lives, whether already born or still in the womb.[22] Even the least carry intrinsic dignity and worth.

When confronted by the harsh reality of a newborn child displaying radical abnormalities, the truth of God's sovereignty must be a comfort. The alternative, the prospect that he is not responsible nor in control, is utterly frightening. There is hope in the midst of bitter providences and severe mercies. Charles Spurgeon, in his inimitable way, said this about bitter and sweet providence:

> I believe that every particle of dust that dances in the sunbeam does not move an atom more or less than God wishes; that every particle of spray that dashes against a steam boat has its orbit as well as the sun in the heavens; that the chaff from the hand of the winnower is steered as the stars in their courses, and the creeping of an aphid over the rose bud is as much fixed as the march of the devastating pestilence; the fall of leaves from a poplar is as fully ordained as the tumbling of an avalanche. What is fate? Fate is this: whatever is, must be. But there is a difference between that and providence. Providence says whatever God ordains must be. But the wisdom of God never ordains anything without purpose. Everything in this world is working for some great end. Fate does not say that. There is all the difference between fate and providence that there is between a man with good eyes and a blind man. He who has faith is better than the stoic. The stoical philosopher bore it because he believed it must be. The Christian bears it because he believes it is working for his good.[23]

Such a viewpoint turns worldly thinking on its head, but the gospel has a way of doing that. God has always been choosing the losers and the rejected rather than the winners and the insiders to carry and show forth his truth. In his wonderfully poignant book about the value of people and the grace of God, Christopher de Vinck quotes his mother writing about his profoundly retarded brother who died at age 33: 'Oliver was always a "hopeless" case, yet he was such a precious gift for our whole family. 'God has chosen the foolish things of the world to confound the wise; and God has chosen the weak things of the world to confound the things which are mighty' (1 Cor. 1:27 KJV). This child had no apparent usefulness or meaning, and the world would reject him as an unproductive burden. But he was a holy innocent, a child of light.'[24]

Though the truth of Scripture cannot dull the pain caused by the occurrence of genetic anomalies, when we grasp the truth of God's sovereignty we begin to understand that pain and suffering are never wasted in God's plan. Indeed, his most important lessons are taught in the wilderness and through affliction and tribulation. Our very redemption was purchased by pain and with infinite suffering by our Saviour Christ Jesus on the Via Dolorosa and the mount of Calvary.

One of the most frequently-quoted but least-believed verses of Scripture is Romans 8:28. 'And we know that in all things God works for the good of those who love him, who have been called according to his purpose.' If we really believed that verse, if we really believed it to be true, we could rest in peace even in the midst of painful realities of life, such as children born with genetic anomalies. Scripture does not teach here that all things in and of themselves *are* good. Genetic anomalies like my daughter's are not good in an *absolute* sense. Rather, for believers they are good in an *ultimate* sense. God works through the fallenness of this world, a fallenness for which humanity has genuine responsibility, to bring about ultimate good. Meanwhile, in genetic anomalies we have an opportunity to experience the truth of Jesus' words to Paul: 'My grace is sufficient for you, for my power is made perfect in weakness' (2 Cor. 12:9).

NOTES

1. Bosk, Charles, *All God's Mistakes: Genetic Counseling in a Pediatric Hospital* (Chicago, University of Chicago Press 1992), pp. 55–56.

2. E.g., see Shelp, Earl E., *Born to Die? Deciding the Fate of Critically Ill Newborns* (New York, The Free Press 1986), introduction.

3. Some scholars have recently posited the concept of a self-limiting God. Though creative, such constructions do not appear to me to address adequately the complete range of teachings about God in Scripture, which is the primary source for our understanding about God.

4. Tozer, A.W. *The Knowledge of the Holy* (New York, Harper 1961), p. 115.

5. Westminster Confession of Faith, III.1a

6. NIV is used throughout unless otherwise noted.

7. See also Gen. 18:25; Num. 23:19; Ps. 89:14; 100:5; 136:1; Jer. 33:11.

8. For extended discussions of the question of God's power versus God's goodness, see two messages by R.C. Sproul – 'The Goodness of God' and 'The Sovereignty of God' (Lake, Mary, Fla: Ligonier Ministries, 1990), audio tapes SD90.8,9 – and Jerry Bridges, *Trusting God Even When Life Hurts* (Colorado Springs, Colo.: NavPress 1988), pp.23–53.

9. See also Job 2:9-10; Eccl. 7:13-14; Lam. 3:37-38; 1 Tim. 6:15-16; 1 Pet. 4:19.

10. Kaiser, Walter, *Hard Saying of the Old Testament* (Downers Grove, Ill., InterVarsity Press 1988), pp. 194–195.

11. Hodge, Charles, *Systematic Theology* (Grand Rapids, Mich., Eerdmans, n.d.), I:441.

12. Westminster Confession of Faith, III.1b.

13. This is the position taken by Rabbi Harold Kushner in his popular but biblically unsound book, *When Bad Things Happen to Good People* (New York, Schocken 1981).

14. Card, Michael, 'When a Window is a Mirror', *Come to the Cradle*, (Sparrow 1993).

15. from personal correspondence to Mary Beates, April 28, 1996.

16. Eiesland, Nancy L., *The Disabled God: Toward a Liberatory Theology of Disability* (Nashville, Abingdon Press 1994), p. 25 and throughout the book.

17. Eberstadt, Fernanda, *Isaac and His Devils* (Warner Books, 1992), as quoted by George Grant in 'Fear and Humility', *Tabletalk* (vol. 20, no. 10), October, 1996, p.58. See also 2 Cor. 2:15–16, which corroborates this spiritual truth.

18. Schaeffer, Francis, Koop, C. Everett, et al., *Plan For Action; An Action Alternative Handbook for 'Whatever Happened to the Human Race?'* (Old Tappan, N.J., Revell 1980), p. 79 (emphasis in the original).

19. Nouwen, Henri, *In the Name of Jesus: Reflections on Christian Leadership* (New York, Crossroads 1994), p. 59.

20. On these thoughts I recommend Marshall Shelley's two articles in *Christianity Today* which poignantly recount the circumstances of two of his children who lived brief lives

and died with genetic anomalies. See 'The Sightless, Wordless, Helpless Theologian' (April 26, 1993) and 'Two Minutes to Eternity' (May 16, 1994).

21. Althaus, Paul, *The Ethics of Martin Luther* (Philadelphia, Fortress 1972), pp. 37–38, 99–100.

22. Even though a Trisomy 18, an encephalic, or Tay-Sach's syndrome child is doomed to a short and even possibly painful life, it is not our place to subvert God's sovereign creative act by destroying such a life. When we do, we add two human injustices to our usurpation of God's authority: We deprive the child of the privilege of being held in the loving arms of the parents; and we deprive the parents of the opportunity to hold – however briefly – their child as a vital part of their grieving process.

23. Spurgeon Charles, in a sermon on Ezekiel 1 ('Wheels Within a Wheel') quoted by John Piper at a Ligonier Ministries Conference in Grand Rapids, Mich., October 1995 (Ligonier audio tape GR95.4).

24. de Vink, Christopher, *The Power of the Powerless* (Grand Rapids, Mich, Zondervan Publishing House 1995), p. 95.

4

Playing God

Allen D. Verhey, BD, PhD

Should human beings play God? It is a question frequently asked in discussions of genetics. We are sometimes invited to play God, and we are sometimes warned against it, but before we decide whether to accept the invitation or to heed the warning, it would be good to know what it means to 'play God'.

When my daughter, Kate, was very young, she once invited the rest of the family to play '52-semi'. She was holding a deck of cards, obviously eager to play. But when we asked for an explanation of this game, she would give none, only repeating her invitation to play '52-semi'. Finally we said, 'OK, Katie, let's play "52-semi."' She threw the cards up into the air and, when they had fallen back to the floor, commanded triumphantly, 'Now pick 'em up'. She had got mixed up, confusing '52-semi' with '52 pick-up', but suddenly – too late – we knew what she meant. Should human beings 'play God'? It depends, you see, on what it means to 'play God'. The phrase means different things to different people, and it is used not so much to state a principle as to invoke a perspective – *different* perspectives, in fact, by different people.

This chapter will examine the report of the President's Commission on genetics called *Splicing Life*, the lament of some religious people about other people 'playing God', the invitation of Joseph Fletcher, 'Come, let us play God', and the warnings of Paul Ramsey. We must be ever attentive not only to particular moral problems raised by genetic knowledge and power but also to the perspective from which we examine and evaluate these new powers and problems. If, in the end, we are to 'play God', it must be in the context of a perspective in which 'God' is taken seriously and 'play' playfully.

The President's Commission report on *Splicing Life* is a good place to begin. The Commission noted the concerns voiced about 'playing God' in genetics and undertook to make some sense of the phrase. It decided that the phrase 'playing God' does not have 'a specific religious meaning'. If the Commission had meant by that only that the phrase does not simply mean one thing, then one could hardly object. However, the Commission proceeded to assert that 'at its heart' the phrase is 'an expression of a sense of awe [in response to extraordinary *human* powers] – and concern [about the possible consequences of these vast new powers]'[1] It simply translated the warnings against 'playing god' into a concern about the consequences of exercising great human powers.[2]

The Commission reduced the meaning of the phrase to secular terms and made 'God' superfluous. 'At its heart', according to the Commission, the phrase 'playing God' has nothing to do with 'God'. Moreover, there is nothing very playful about 'playing God' either. The human powers in genetics and their possible consequences are too serious for playfulness.

'Playing God' might mean what the Commission understood it to mean, something like, 'Human powers are awesome. Let's not play around!' It evidently does mean something like that to many who use the phrase. Such an interpretation is hardly trivial, but neither is it very useful in the guiding or limiting of human powers. It is worth asking, however, whether the President's Commission interpreted the phrase from a particular perspective. I think the answer to that question is yes – and that the perspective invoked was the Baconian perspective.

The President's Commission highlighted one very important feature of contemporary culture, the hegemony of scientific knowledge. 'Since the Enlightenment', it said, 'Western societies have exalted the search for greater knowledge'. Scientific knowledge, beginning with Copernicus, has both 'dethroned human beings as the unique center of the world' and delivered 'vast powers for action' into their hands.[3]

Science has taught us the hard lesson that human beings and their earth are not 'the center of the universe', but it is now placing in human hands powers and responsibilities 'to make decisions which we formerly left to God'.[4] This is, to borrow the phrase of Dietrich Bonhoeffer, humanity's 'coming of age'.[5] Where such is the context for talk of 'playing God', it is not surprising that 'God' is superfluous, that 'God' is not taken seriously when we try to make sense of the phrase. Bonhoeffer, after all, described humanity's 'coming of age' as an effort to think of the world *etsi deus non daretur*, ('as though God were not a given').[6] Science has no need of God 'as a working hypothesis'[7]; in fact it is not even permitted for science qua science to make use of 'God'. There are assumptions operative in this perspective, however, not only about 'God' but about humanity, knowledge, and nature as well.

With respect to humanity, science has taught us that we are not 'the center of the universe'. However, science has not taught us where we do belong. As Nietzsche aptly put it, 'since Copernicus man has been rolling from the center into x'.[8] Once human beings and their earth were at the centre. They did not put themselves there; God put them there, and it was simply accepted as a matter

of course that they *were* there. After Copernicus had shown that
they were not there, not at the centre, humanity was left to fend
for itself (or simply continue 'rolling'). This *positionlessness* was the
new assumption, and it meant that humanity had to attempt to
secure (if somewhat anxiously) a place for itself – and what better
place than at the centre.

After Copernicus, humanity had to *put* itself at the centre, *make*
itself *into* the centre. The very science, moreover, that destroyed the
illusion that humanity was at the centre gave to humanity power in
the world and over the world. Such mastery, however, has not
eliminated human insecurity and anxiety; in fact, the new powers
and their unintended consequences evoke new anxieties. In this
context, 'playing God' might well be interpreted as 'an expression
of a sense of awe [before human powers] – and concern [about
unanticipated consequences]'.[9]

There are assumptions in the Baconian perspective concerning
knowledge, too. The comment of the President's Commission that
'[s]ince the Enlightenment, Western societies have exalted the
search for greater knowledge'[10] requires a gloss. They have exalted
a particular kind of knowledge, the knowledge for which they
reserve the honorific term 'science'. It is simply not true that the
search for knowledge began to be exalted only as a result of the
Enlightenment. Thomas Aquinas, for example, had exalted the
search for knowledge long before the Enlightenment, affirming 'all
knowledge' as 'good'. He distinguished, however, 'practical' from
'speculative' (or theoretical) sciences. The difference was that the
practical sciences were for the sake of some work to be done, while
the speculative sciences were for their own sake.[11]

That classical account (and celebration) of knowledge must be
contrasted with the modern account epitomized in Francis Bacon's
The Great Instauration and 'exalted' in western societies. In Bacon all
knowledge is sought for its utility, 'for the benefit and use of life'.[12]
The knowledge to be sought is 'no mere felicity of speculation',[13]
which is but the 'boyhood of knowledge' and 'barren of works'.[14]
The knowledge to be sought is the practical knowledge that will
make humanity 'capable of overcoming the difficulties and obscu-
rities of nature',[15] able to subdue and overcome its vexations and
miseries. 'And so those twin objects, human knowledge and human
power, do really meet in one.'[16] The knowledge 'exalted' in western
societies is this power over nature which presumably brings human
well-being in its train.

In the classical account, theory (or the speculative sciences)
provided the wisdom to use the practical sciences appropriately.
The modern account may admit, as Bacon did, that for knowledge
to be beneficial humanity must 'perfect and govern it in charity',[17]
but science is 'not self-sufficiently the source of that human quality

that makes it beneficial'.[18] Moreover, the compassion (or 'charity') that responds viscerally to the vexations and miseries of humanity will urge us to do something to relieve those miseries, but it will not tell us what to do. Bacon's account of knowledge arms compassion simply with artifice, not with wisdom.[19] For the charity to 'perfect and govern' human powers and for the wisdom to guide charity, science must call upon something else. But upon what? And how can humanity have 'knowledge' of it?

Knowledge of that which transcends 'use' has no place in Bacon's theory.[20] Knowledge of that which might guide and limit the human use of human powers was the subject of classical theory, but not of the Enlightenment 'search for greater knowledge'. In this context there is no place for either 'play' (because play is not 'useful'[21]) or 'God' (because God is transcendent and will not be used).

With the different assumptions concerning knowledge come also different assumptions concerning nature. The Baconian project sets humanity not only over nature but against it. The natural order and natural processes have no dignity of their own; their value is reduced to their usefulness to humanity – and nature does not serve humanity 'naturally'. In Bacon's perspective nature threatens to rule and to ruin humanity; against the powers of nature knowledge promises the power to relieve humanity's miseries and 'to endow the human family with new mercies'.[22] The fault that runs through our world and through our lives is, according to Bacon, finally to be located in nature. Nature may be – and must be – mastered.[23]

This, I think, is the perspective invoked by the President's Commission, and it is from this perspective that it understands 'playing God' as having nothing to do with either 'play' or 'God', but as having rather to do with human scientific knowledge and power over nature even when (or especially when) the faith that human well-being will come in the train of technology is a creed ripe for doubt.

Religious people have sometimes celebrated this Baconian perspective and its quest for scientific knowledge and technical power – and have sometimes lamented it. Some who have lamented it have raised their voices in protest against almost every new scientific hypothesis and against almost all technological developments (for example, anaesthesia during childbirth, or vaccinations). Such persons evidently regard scientific inquiry as a threat to faith in God and technical innovation as an offence to God. These lament a 'humanity come of age' and long to go back to a former time, a time of our childhood (if only we knew the way!). They want to preserve the necessity of 'God' in human ignorance and powerlessness. But such a 'God' can only ever be a 'God of the Gaps' and can only ever be in retreat to the margins.

It is an old and unhappy story in Christian apologetics that locates

God's presence and power where human knowledge and strength have reached their (temporary) limit. Newton, for example, saw certain irregularities in the motion of the planets, movements which he could not explain by his theory of gravity, and in those irregularities he saw, he said, the direct intervention of God. When later astronomers and physicists provided a natural explanation for what had puzzled Newton, 'God' was no longer necessary. And there is the old story of the patient who, when told that the only thing left to do was to pray, said, 'Oh, my! And I didn't even think it was serious'. The God of the Gaps is invoked, after all, only where doctors are powerless.

In the context of such a piety, a defensive faith in the God of the Gaps, 'playing God' means to encroach on those areas of human life where human beings have been ignorant or powerless, for there God rules, there only God has the authority to act. In this context 'playing God' means to seize God's place at the boundaries of human knowledge and power, to usurp God's authority and dominion there. In this context it is understandable that humanity should be warned, 'Thou shalt not play God'.

Once again the phrase is used not so much to state a principle as to invoke a perspective. To be sure, such warnings serve to remind humanity of its fallibility and finitude, and such warnings are good. There are, however, at least three problems with this perspective and with such warnings against 'playing God'.

The first and fundamental problem with this perspective is that the God of the Gaps is not the God who is made known in creation and in Scripture. The God of creation and Scripture made and sustains the order we observe and rely upon. To describe that order in terms of scientific understanding does not explain God away; it is to give an account of the way God orders God's world. The order of the world comes to us no less from the gracious hand of God than from the extraordinary events humans call 'miracles'. 'Nature' is no less the work of God than 'grace'. Moreover, to understand the earth and its order as God's is not to understand it in a way that prohibits 'natural scientific' explanations. It is to be called to serve God's cause, to be responsible to God in the midst of it.

The second problem with this perspective and with such warnings against 'playing God' is that they are indiscriminate; they do not permit discriminating judgments. There are some things which we already know how to do which we surely ought never to do. And there are some things (including some things in genetics) which we cannot yet do but which we must make an effort to learn to do if God is God and we are called to 'follow' one who heals the sick and feeds the hungry. The warning against 'playing God' in this perspective is reduced to the slogan 'It's not nice to fool with Mother Nature (at least not any more than we are currently comfortable with)'. Ironically, then, the warning enthrones 'nature' as god rather than the One who transcends it and our knowledge of it.

The third problem is a corollary of these other problems. By its failure to make discriminating judgments, and by its confusion of God with natural process, this perspective nurtures irresponsibility. It does not take all our human powers to be part of our human response-ability to God, part of our answer-ability to serve God's cause in the midst of the world.

It is little wonder, then, that some other religious people have reacted against this God of the Gaps and against this warning, 'Thou shalt not play God'. These people have sometimes celebrated the advances of science and the innovations of technology, urging humanity to go forward bravely, uttering a priestly benediction over the Baconian project. They sometimes also use the phrase 'playing God', but usually to invite humanity to 'play God'. Joseph Fletcher, for example, responded provocatively to the charge that his enthusiasm for genetic technology amounted to a license to 'play God' by admitting the charge and by making the invitation explicit; 'Let's play God', he said.[24]

For Fletcher, however, the God of the Gaps 'that old, primitive God is dead'.[25] Dead also are the 'taboos' which prohibited trespass on the territory of that God's rule,[26] the 'fatalism' that passively accepted the will of that God,[27] and the 'obsolete theodicy'[28] that attempted to defend that God.[29] 'What we need', he said, 'is a new God.'[30] However, Fletcher's 'new God' bore a striking resemblance to the God of the eighteenth century deist, and indifference to a God so conceived is inevitable. Life may proceed as though God were not a given.

Although Fletcher said little more about this 'new God', he did say that 'any God worth believing in wills the best possible well-being for human beings'.[31] Fletcher's 'new God' turns out to be a heavenly utilitarian, and this God, too, humanity must 'play'.

So, Fletcher's invitation to 'play God' comes to this: humanity should use its new powers to achieve the greatest good for the greatest number of people (not intimidated by 'taboos'), to take control over 'nature' (not enervated by 'fatalism'), to take responsibility, to design and make a new and better world, to substitute for an absent God. 'It was *easier* in the old days', Fletcher said,[32]

> to attribute at least some of what happened to God's will – we could say with a moral shrug that we weren't responsible. Now we have to shoulder it all. The moral tab is ours and we have to pick it up. The excuses of ignorance and helplessness are growing thin.

Notice what has happened to responsibility here. Fletcher underscores human responsibility, but we are responsible not so much *to*

God as *instead* of God.[33] That shift puts an enormous (and messianic) burden on genetics, a burden which leaves little time for 'play'.

The phrase 'playing God' does here state a principle, namely, utility, but it also does more than that – it invokes a perspective, a perspective in which God is superfluous, in which humanity is maker and designer, in which knowledge is power, and in which nature must be mastered to maximize human well-being. Such a perspective makes the invitation to 'play God' – and much else in Fletcher's discussion of genetics – meaningful. Christians may welcome Fletcher's burial of the God of the Gaps, but they still wait and watch and pray not for the invention of some 'new God' but for the appearance of the one God who continues to create, preserve, and redeem humanity and the earth. Moreover, Fletcher's invitation to 'play God' need not seem blasphemous to those trained to 'imitate God', to 'follow God', to be disciples of one who made God present among us. But to map the path of discipleship and imitation as 'the utilitarian way' must seem strange to those who know the law and the prophets, the gospels and the gospel.

It seemed strange, at least, to Paul Ramsey. In Ramsey's usage, although we are usually warned against 'playing God', we are sometimes encouraged to 'play God in the correct way'[34] or to 'play God as God plays God'[35] – and God is no utilitarian. 'God', Ramsey said[36],

> is not a rationalist whose care is a function of indicators of our personhood, or of our achievement within those capacities. He makes his rain to fall upon the just and the unjust alike, and his sun to rise on the abnormal as well as the normal. Indeed, he has special care for the weak and the vulnerable among us earth people. He cares according to need, not capacity or merit.

These divine patterns and images are, according to Ramsey, at 'the foundation of Western medical care'.[37]

One might expect Ramsey, then, simply to echo Fletcher's invitation to 'play God' while engaging him and others in conversation concerning who this God is whom we are invited to 'play'. However, he also (and more frequently) warned against 'playing God'. The phrase itself, he admitted, is 'not [a] very helpful characterization',[38] but he used it to name – and to warn against – the Baconian project,[39] and to invite a different perspective on the world.

The fundamental premise of the perspective Ramsey warns against is that 'God' is superfluous. 'Where there is no God . . .', he said,[40] there humanity is creator, maker, the engineer of the future, and there nature, even human nature, may be and must be controlled and managed with messianic ambition. Where 'God' is superfluous and human beings cast in this role of 'the maker', there morality is reduced to the consideration of consequences, knowledge is construed simply as power, and nature – including the human nature given to humanity as embodied and communal – is left with no dignity of its own.

Ramsey's warnings against 'playing God' are not immediately identified with a particular moral rule or principle; rather, they challenge the wisdom and the sufficiency of the assumptions too much at work in western culture. It is not that some 'God of the Gaps' is threatened. It is not simply that human powers are awesome or that the consequences of 'interfering with nature' are worrying, as the President's Commission suggested. It is rather that the fundamental perspective from which we interpret our responsibilities is critically important in our assessment of what those responsibilities are.[41]

The fundamental perspective which Ramsey recommends and with which he contrasts 'playing God' is 'to view the world as a Christian or as a Jew',[42] i.e., as if God were a given – and not just any old god (nor Fletcher's 'new God') but the God who creates and keeps a world and a covenant. That means, among other things, that the end of all things may be left to God. Where God is God and not us, there can be a certain eschatological nonchalance. From this perspective, our responsibilities, while great, will not be regarded as being of messianic proportion. There will be some room, then, for an ethics of means as well as the consideration of consequences,[43] for reflection about the kind of behaviour which is worthy of human nature as created by God, as embodied and interdependent, for example.

When joined with such reflection, Ramsey's warnings that we should not 'play God' do provide some prohibitions. When joined with an interpretation of human procreation, for example, the warning against 'playing God' carries the prohibition against putting 'entirely asunder what God joined together', against separating 'in principle' the unitive and procreative goods of human sexuality, against reducing human procreation either to biology or to contract. That prohibition supports, in turn, a series of more particular prohibitions, for example, a prohibition against artificial insemination using the sperm of a donor.[44]

When joined with an interpretation of the patient as 'a sacredness in the natural, biological order',[45] the 'edification' drawn from the warning against 'playing God' includes prohibitions against deliberately killing patients, including very little patients, for the sake of relieving their (or another's) suffering. It is unacceptable to use one, even a very little one, even one created in a petri dish, without consent, to learn to help others.

Ramsey warns against 'playing God', against trying to substitute for an absent God, against trying to 'be' God. Yet as we have seen, Ramsey can also invite people to 'play God in the correct way'. Such 'playing' is not to substitute for an absent God, not to 'be' God, but to 'imitate' God,[46] to follow in God's way like a child 'playing' a parent.

In both the warning and the invitation a perspective is invoked, an outlook which assumes that God is God and not us, that humanity is called to honour and to nurture the nature God gave, that knowledge of something transcending the useful is possible, and that the fault that runs through our lives and our world is not simply located in nature but in human pride or sloth.

Those of us who share this perspective will make sense of the phrase 'playing God' in the light of it and find it appropriate sometimes to sound a warning against 'playing God' and sometimes to issue an invitation to 'play God' in imitation of God's care and grace.

Permit me to focus on the invitation to 'play God' – and first to underscore the invitation to 'play'.[47] Many have complained that 'playing God' is serious stuff and regretted the implication of 'playfulness' in the phrase.[48] Some 'play', however, can be very serious indeed – as anyone who plays noon-hour basketball knows quite well. It is quite possible for playfulness to be serious, but it is not possible for it to be purely serviceable.

When Teilhard de Chardin said that 'in the great game that is being played, we are the players as well as . . . the stakes',[49] he created a powerful image to call attention both to the extraordinary powers of human beings and to the awesome consequences of exercising those powers. No wonder playfulness seems inappropriate. Precisely because the stakes are high, however, it may be apt to set alongside de Chardin's image a Dutch proverb, 'It is not the marbles that matter but the game'.[50] When the stakes are high, or even when the stakes alone are taken seriously, then one is tempted to cheat in order to win. And when one cheats, then one only pretends to play; the cheat plays neither fairly nor seriously.

Play, even marbles, can be serious, but it cannot be purely serviceable; it cannot allow attention to be monopolized by the stakes, by the consequences of winning or losing. When our attention is riveted by de Chardin's image that we are 'the stakes', it may well be important to allow our imagination to be captured by his image that we are 'the players', too. Then we may be able to avoid reducing the moral life to a concern about consequences, even where the stakes are high. We may be able to avoid reducing ourselves to makers and designers and our existence to joyless and incessant work. We may see that we are at stake, not just in the sense of some plastic destiny our powers may make but already in the imagination, in the image of ourselves with which human creativity begins.[51]

The invitation is an invitation to 'play', but it is more specifically

an invitation to 'play God', and that invitation requires attention to
the God whom we are invited to play. In the foreword to a book
entitled *Should Doctors Play God?* Mrs. Billy Graham wrote,[52]

> If I were an actress who was going to play, let's say, Joan of Arc, I would
> learn all there is to learn about Joan of Arc. And, if I were a doctor or anyone
> else trying to play God, I would learn all I could about God.

That seems a prudent strategy for an actress – and good advice for
people called to imitate God. The invitation to 'play God', to cast
ourselves playfully in the role of God, invites theological reflection;
it invites reflection about 'God'.

Permit me, then, simply to select a few images of God in the
Christian tradition and to suggest something of their relevance to
'playing God' in genetics. Two of these images are regularly invoked
in these discussions: creator and healer, and the third is often
overlooked: God is the one who takes the side of the poor.

First, then, what might it mean playfully to cast ourselves in the
role of the creator? This, of course, has been the topic of much
discussion. Nevertheless, the biblical story suggests that to cast
ourselves in the role of the creator might mean something too often
overlooked. It might mean that we look at the creation and at its
genetics and say to ourselves, 'God, that's good'. It might mean,
that is, first of all, to wonder, to stand in awe, to delight in the
elegant structure of the creation and its DNA. It would mean a
celebration of knowledge which was not simply mastery. It would
mean an appreciation of nature – and of human nature – as given,
rather than a suspicion of it as threatening and requiring human
mastery.

The story also suggests a second meaning too often overlooked.
It might mean to take a day off, to rest, to play. But we have already
talked of that.

To playfully cast ourselves in the role of the creator also means
a third thing, a thing seldom overlooked in these discussions: that
human creativity is given with the creation. Human beings are
created and called to exercise dominion in the world – and there is
no apparent reason to suppose that such creativity and control does
not extend to genetics. It is not 'Mother Nature' who is God, after
all, in the Christian story. Human creativity and control, however,
are to be exercised in response to God, in imitation of God's ways,
and in service to God's cause. That is a part of the Christian story,
too, a part of the story usually captured when we describe ourselves
as stewards and our responsibility as stewardship.

We can discover something of God's cause, the cause stewards
serve, in a second feature of the story. God is the healer. Jesus, the
one in whom God and the cause of God were made known, was a
healer. We discover there that the plan of God is life, not death;

the plan of God is human flourishing, including the human flourishing we call health, not disease.

What does it mean to cast ourselves playfully in the role of God the healer? It means to promote life and its flourishing, not death or human suffering. Therefore, genetic therapy, like other therapeutic interventions which aim at health, may be celebrated. Healing is 'playing God' the way God plays God. Genetic therapies, however, are still mostly (but not completely) a distant hope. The more immediate contributions of genetics to medicine are in genetic diagnosis. And where there are therapeutic options, these too may be celebrated. However, genetic diagnoses without therapeutic options are sometimes deeply ambiguous.

Prenatal diagnoses, for example, are frequently ambiguous. Already we can diagnose a number of genetic conditions in a fetus, and the number is constantly growing. For most of these there is no therapy. The tests allow parents to make a decision about whether to give birth or to abort. How shall we 'play God' here in ways responsible to God? If God's purpose is life rather than death, then those who would 'play God' in imitation of God will not be disposed to abort; they will not celebrate abortion as a 'therapeutic option'.

Some Christians, it should be noted, give (reluctant) approval to abortions under highly unusual, tragic conditions.[53] But no Christian who 'plays God' the way God plays God will celebrate any abortion, and the attitude of heart and mind which accepts rather than rejects children will not be easily overridden. Moreover, when some children with Down's syndrome are aborted because they have that disorder or some girls are aborted because they are girls, then prenatal diagnoses have been – and will be – used irresponsibly. When the slogan about 'preventing birth defects' is taken to justify preventing the birth of 'defectives' – those who do not measure up to the standards or match the preferences of parents – then there is reason to worry that the 'good parent' will no longer be disposed to give the sort of uncalculating nurture that can evoke and sustain trust from children but, instead, the sort of calculating nurture that is prepared to abandon or abort the offspring who do not match specifications. Those who would 'play God' the way God plays God – or, if you will, the way God 'plays parent' – would sustain care for the weak and the helpless, and for the little ones who do not measure up.

Consider, finally, this third image: God is one who takes the side of the poor. What would it mean to cast ourselves in the role of one who takes the side of the poor? It would mean, at the very least, a concern for social justice. It would mean, for example, asking about the allocation of resources to the human genome project. When cities are crumbling, when schools are deteriorating, when we complain about not having sufficient resources to help the poor or the homeless, when we do not have the resources to provide care for all the sick, is this a just and fair use of our society's resources? Is it an allocation of social resources that can claim to imitate God's care and concern for the poor?

Having raised that question, let me focus instead on the sharing of the burdens and benefits of the human genome project itself. Who bears the burdens? Who will benefit? And is the distribution fair? Does it fit the story of one who takes the side of the poor and powerless? If we cast ourselves in this role, if we attempt to mirror God's justice and care for the poor and powerless, we will not create human life in order to learn from it with the intention of destroying it after we have learned what we can from it. We will not put the unborn at risk in experiments to learn some things that would benefit others, even if it were a great benefit, even if it would benefit a great number of others. And we would be cautious about stigmatizing some as diseased and others as carriers.

But consider also the sharing of benefits. Who stands to benefit from the human genome initiative? Will genetic powers be marketed? Presumably they will, since the patenting of micro-organisms is now protected by law. Will the poor have access to the health-care and other genetic benefits that their taxes helped develop? Will the genetically-poor be able to obtain health insurance, or will insurance companies use genetic information to screen them out? Will the category of 'pre-existing condition' be redefined to make it easier for insurance companies to make a still larger profit? Will corporations use genetic information to screen applicants in order to hire those with greatest promise of long-term productivity? The point of these questions is not simply to lament our failure to accomplish health care reform. It is to suggest that 'playing God' as God plays God will be attentive not only to intriguing questions about the frontiers of technology and science but also to mundane questions about fairness, about the effect of such innovations on the poor. If we are to 'play God' as God plays God, then we have a pattern for imitation in God's hospitality to the poor and to the stranger, to the powerless and to the voiceless, to one who is different from both us and the norm, including some genetic norm. If we are to 'play God' as God plays God, then we will work for a society where human beings – each of them, even the least of them – is treated as worthy of God's care and affection.

There is space here for only a selection of images of God, and I admit that the connections to claims about genetic interventions are developed far too briefly. Hopefully, enough has been said to suggest the importance of the perspective in terms of which we think about genetics and in terms of which we make sense not only of our powers but of the phrase 'playing God'.

We must, in stewardship and service, resist the power of the Baconian perspective in the culture and in the academy. We must, in stewardship and in service, resist the temptation to worship some God of the Gaps instead of the God of Scripture and creation. We must, in faith, refuse to pretend to substitute for an absent God – *etsi deus non daretur.* We must, in faithfulness, respond with all our powers and with all human powers to the cause of God made known in Christ. We must 'play God' as God plays God. God is God, and not us, but God has called us to follow where God leads, to imitate God's works, to serve God's cause.[54]

NOTES

1. President's Commission for the Study of Ethical Problems in Medicine and Biomedical and Behavioral Research, *Splicing Life: A Report on the Social and Ethical Issues of Genetic Engineering with Human Beings,* (US Government Printing Office, Washington D.C. 1982), p. 54.

2. Lebacqz, Karen, 'The Ghosts Are On the Wall: A Parable for Manipulating Life', in Esbjornson Robert, (ed.), *The Manipulation of Life,* (Harper and Row, San Francisco 1984), p. 33.

3. President's Commission for the Study of Ethical Problems in Medicine and Biomedical and Behavioral Research, *Splicing Life: A Report on the Social and Ethical Issues of Genetic Engineering with Human Beings,* (US Government Printing Office, Washington D.C. 1982), p. 54.

4. Augenstein, Leroy, *Come Let Us Play God,* (Harper and Row, New York 1962), p. 11.

5. Ibid., p. 143.

6. Bonhoeffer, Dietrich, *Letters and Papers from Prison* (edited by Eberhard Bethge, translated by Reginald H. Fuller), (New York, Macmillan Company 1953), p. 218.

7. Ibid.

8. Cited in Jungel, Eberhard, *God as the Mystery of the World* (translated by Darrell Guder), (Grand Rapids, William B. Eerdmans Publishing Company 1983), p. 15.

9. President's Commission for the Study of Ethical Problems in Medicine and Biomedical and Behavioral Research, *Splicing Life: A Report on the Social and Ethical Issues of Genetic Engineering with Human Beings,* (US Government Printing Office, Washington D.C. 1982), p. 54.

10. Ibid.

11. Aquinas, Commentary on Aristotle's *On the Soul,* I, 3; cited in Jonas Hans, *The Phenomenon of Life: Toward a Philosophical Biology,* (Dell Publishing Co., New York 1966), p. 188.

12. Bacon, Francis, *The New Organon and Related Writings* (edited by Fulton H. Anderson), (The Liberal Arts Press, Bobbs-Merrill Co., Indianapolis [1620] 1960), p. 15.

13. Ibid., p. 29.

13. Ibid., p. 8.

15. Ibid., p. 19.

16. Ibid., p. 29.

17. Ibid., p. 15.

18. Jonas, op cit., p. 195.

19. O'Donovan, Oliver, *Begotten or Made?,* (Oxford, Oxford University Press 1984), pp. 10–12.

20. To be sure, Bacon recommended his 'great instauration' as a form of obedience to God, as a restoration to humanity of the power over nature which was given at creation but lost through the fall. Indeed, he prays 'that things human may not interfere with things divine, and that . . . there may arise in our minds no incredulity or darkness with regard to the divine mysteries' (Bacon, op cit., pp. 14–15). Even so, such mysteries have no theoretical place in Bacon's account of knowledge.

21. Jonas (op cit., p. 194) contrasts the relations of leisure to theory in the classical and modern traditions. In the classical account leisure was an antecedent condition for speculative knowledge, for contemplation; in modern theory leisure is an effect of knowledge (as power), one of the benefits of that knowledge that provides relief from the miseries of humanity, including toil. 'Wherefore', Bacon says (op cit., p. 29), 'if we labour in thy works with the sweat of our brows, thou wilt make us partakers of . . . thy sabbath.'

22. Bacon, op cit., p. 29.

23. Jonas, op cit., p. 192.

24. Fletcher, Joseph, 'Technological Devices in Medical Care', in Vaux, Kenneth, (ed.), *Who Shall Live? Medicine, Technology, Ethics*, (Philadelphia, Fortress Press 1970), p. 126.

25. Ibid., p. 132, and Fletcher, Joseph, *The Ethics of Genetic Control: Ending Reproductive Roulette*, (Anchor Books, Garden City, New York), 1974, p. 200.

26. Fletcher, *The Ethics of Genetic Control: Ending Reproductive Roulette*, p. 127.

27. Ibid., p. 128.

28. Theodicy absolves God from the origin of sin and places responsibility clearly on mankind.

29. Fletcher, 'Technological Devices in Medical Care', p. 132.

30. Ibid., p. 132.

31. Fletcher, *The Ethics of Genetic Control: Ending Reproductive Roulette*, p. xix.

32. Ibid., p. 200.

33. On the shift from theodicy to 'anthropodicy' see Hauerwas, Stanley, *Naming the Silences: God, Medicine, and the Problem of Suffering*, (Grand Rapids, Eerdmans, Michigan), pp. 59–64.

34. Ramsey, Paul, *The Patient as Person: Explorations in Medical Ethics*, (New Haven, Yale University Press 1970), p. 256.

35. Ramsey, Paul, *Ethics at the Edges of Life: Medical and Legal Intersections*, (New Haven, Yale University Press 1978), p. 203.

36. Ibid., p. 205.

37. Ibid.

38. Ramsey, Paul, *Fabricated Man: The Ethics of Genetic Control*, (New Haven, Yale University Press 1970), p. 90.

39. Ibid., p. 91.

40. Ibid., p. 91-96.

41. Ibid., pp. 28, 143.

42. Ibid., p. 22.

43. Ibid., pp. 23–32.

44. Ibid., pp. 32–33, 47–52.

45. Ramsey, *The Patient as Person: Explorations in Medical Ethics*, p. xiii.

46. Ibid., p. 259.

47. A delightful essay by van Eys, Jan, 'Should Doctors Play God?' *Perspectives in Biology and Medicine*, 25:481–485 (1982), also underscores the invitation to 'play' in the phrase 'play God'.

48. Lebacqz, op cit., n. 19.

49. de Chardin, Teilhard, *The Phenomenon of Man* (translated by Bernard Wall), (New York, Harper and Row 1961), p. 230.

50. Quoted in Huizenga, Johan, *HomoLudens: A Study of the Play-Element in Culture*, (Boston, Beacon Press 1950), p. 49.

51. Hartt, Julian, *The Restless Quest*, (Philadelphia, United Church Press 1975), pp. 117, 134.

52. Graham, Ruth, 'Foreword', in Frazier Claude E., (ed.), *Should Doctors Play God?* (Nashville, Broadman 1971), p. vii.

53. See for example, the Calvin Center book – Bouma III, Hessel, Diekema, Douglas, Langerak, Edward, Rottman, Theodore and Verhey, Allen, *Christian Faith, Health, and Medical Practice*, (Grand Rapids, Eerdmans 1989), pp. 205–233, 245–251 – which discusses cases like Trisomy 18 and Tay-Sachs (in which the infant experiences a period of unrelenting pain and then dies).

54. This essay is adapted from material in ' "Playing God" and Invoking a Perspective', *Journal of Medicine and Philosophy* 20:347–364, (1995).

5

Reducing People to Genetics

Henk Jochemsen, MSc, PhD

'Our genetic blueprint has made believing in an Infinite Absolute part of our nature'. This quotation from the June 24, 1996 issue of *Time* Magazine, drawn from the book *Timeless Healing*, is a succinct but eloquent expression of the recent tendency to reduce people to genetics, i.e., to their genes.[1] Even the seemingly innate religiosity of the human being is ascribed to the genes in this statement, and the 'genetic blueprint' is presented as determinitive. One author defines this 'geneticization' as: 'an ongoing process by which differences between individuals are reduced to their DNA code, with most disorders, behaviours and physiological variations defined, at least in part, as genetic in origin. It refers as well to the process by which interventions employing genetic technologies are adopted to manage problems of health'.[2] Hubbard and Wald, among others, have provided a number of examples of these processes.[3] It is hard to tell exactly how widespread such thinking is among the general public or among scientists and physicians, though it seems prevalent. Moreover, it is likely to be encouraged, explicitly or implicitly, by the Human Genome Project, whose very existence draws attention to the importance of genetics.

In order to avoid the pitfalls of genetic reductionism, it is necessary to examine its backgrounds and understand why it is incorrect and dangerous. Such are the aims of this chapter.

THE BACKGROUND OF GENETIC REDUCTIONISM

Medical genetics, like medicine in general, is based primarily on the principles and findings of the natural sciences. Modern science is characterized by a specific way of investigating the reality in which we live. It tries to explain phenomena on the basis of empirical functional relationships. In this explanatory process, it engages in abstraction, including the reduction of reality, objectivization of what is investigated, quantification of what is observed, establishment of causal relations between observations, and the formulation of models and theories.[4,5,6] The scientific approach to reality implies a reduction of the real entity or creature under study to an impersonal object (objectivization), thereby taking it out of the context in which it naturally or normally is situated. Only what can be perceived by the senses, directly or indirectly, is taken into consideration. The search for the origin of things is transformed into a question about the material causes; reflections on the essence and meaning of things are replaced by querying their function and usage.[7]

As long as we recognize the specific and limited nature of scientific knowledge, it can be quite valuable and useful. However, in the course of modern western history there has been a tendency to overestimate scientific and technological knowledge and to consider that which is presented in scientific models as the real or really important world. It is one thing to use a certain methodology to study reality, to set up models of certain phenomena, and to have specific questions answered in a way that allows some intervention. It is quite another to consider these abstract models as true representations of reality itself, thereby conveniently omitting the fact that the models are reductions of reality. Dealing with reality only on the basis of these reduced representations leads to a violation of reality. Unfortunately this is what has happpened in various aspects of mainstream modern medicine.

In much of mainstream modern medicine, the explanatory strategy includes reductionism, dualism, and determinism.[8] *Reductionism* manifests itself in the way that the machine has become the main metaphor for the human body (now seen as a genetic-neurological-hormonal information processing machine) and in the understanding of disease as physiology gone astray.[9] As a consequence, basic sciences like physics, biochemistry, and molecular biology are considered the basis for the applied sciences that make up medical science: anatomy, physiology, pathology etc. *Determinism* appears in the modern 'medical gaze' in which the human being is reduced to genetic, physiological, and mental processes that in principle could give a causal explanation of diseases and disorders at the material level.[10] The mind-matter *dualism* of modern science manifests itself in medicine in three forms:[11] the mind-body dualism (the so-called Cartesian image of humanity[12]) and the dualisms between the human being and its natural and social environments.[13,14] In such a model, disease is a deviation in the body's structure or processes that in principle can be localized and treated on a material basis.

In medical genetics, the predominant 'medical model' finds expression in the so-called central dogma of molecular biology.[15] This dogma states that the hereditary information is stored in DNA in the form of a code, and that this information is expressed by two sequential processes: transcription into RNA and then translation into specific proteins that are essential for the expression of individual traits (see fig. 1). In other words, the genetic information encoded in DNA determines the phenotypic traits of an organism by directing the synthesis of proteins. The flow of information occurs in one direction: from DNA via RNA and proteins to traits. A gene is defined as a unit of heredity containing the information for one protein.

Fig. 1. The central dogma of molecular biology.

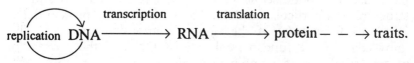

This model clearly implies a rather deterministic view of human beings. The genes determine how the individual will be, or at least how that individual can be. The natural and social environment influences the extent to which certain traits will be expressed, but not the character of the traits themselves as fixed entities.[16,17] This model clearly invites understanding genes and gene defects as the most fundamental causes of disease. At the Ciba Symposium in June 1989, Sydney Brenner, a leading scientist involved in the mapping and sequencing of the human genome, expressed the prevailing view of genetics as follows: 'Genetics investigates the plan of the organism. This plan is embodied in a collection of genes that is handed down in the germ-line to specify the construction of the organism. . . . The manifesto – if not the programme – of molecular genetics must remain the computation of organisms from their DNA sequences.'[18]

A CRITIQUE OF GENETIC REDUCTIONISM

The prevailing approach in modern medicine has been very successful at elucidating the functioning of the human body and discovering causes of many diseases at the material level. Many possibilities for therapeutic and palliative interventions have resulted – to the great and ongoing benefit of many people. To date, the benefits of medical genetics have mainly related to diagnosis and counselling; genetic therapies are in their infancy.

Meanwhile, we are becoming increasingly aware of the limits and insufficiencies of the prevailing reductionistic understanding of medical genetics (and medicine in general). Its *theoretical framework*, though effective in certain respects, is inadequate in others. Furthermore, the very character of contemporary medical genetics, because of its inadequate theory, constitutes a *danger to medical practice*. Both concerns warrant elaboration.

INADEQUATE THEORY.

As stated above, the so-called central dogma of molecular biology is still a leading model in molecular-biological and human-genetics research. This model, however, over-simplifies and over-emphasizes the role of the genes in organisms, especially in humans. Correctly understood, this model simply presents an account of the biophysical and biochemical relationship that exists between a particular nucleotide sequence of some stretch of DNA and the structure of a particular protein. The structure of a protein determines its function(s), if the right conditions are present. This knowledge of the fundamental role of DNA in the process of protein synthesis, in combination with recombinant-DNA techniques, has made possible the economical production of important human proteins, such as insulin and interferon. The production process involves manipulating micro-organisms, which have been cultivated in special growth media to synthesize these proteins. However, the relationship between a specific protein and the expression of a particular trait of an organism under normal conditions is mostly unknown, even for micro-organisms (not to mention the human being). The relation between the biochemical structure of proteins and the structure of organs or an entire organism is probably only indirect.[19] Leading scientist Francois Jacob has formulated this observation as follows: '. . . during the development of the embryo, the world is no longer merely linear. The one-dimensional sequence of bases in the genes determines in some way the production of two-dimensional tissues and organs that give the organism its shape, its properties, and . . . its four-dimensional behavior. How this occurs is a mystery.'[20] In other words, to postulate a straightforward relationship between genetic information and traits is unfounded.

At this point an important epistemological objection arises against the prevailing view of the role of genes in living organisms, including human beings. According to the prevailing view, a rather direct causal relation exists between the genes and the traits of an organism. So one refers to genes not only for physical traits like colour of eyes or hair, or of genes for well-known monogenic 'genetic' diseases like sickle cell anemia, or phenylketonuria (PKU).[21] One also speaks of genes for such complex conditions as obesity, Alzheimer's Disease, manic-depression, schizophrenia and even alcoholism and homosexuality.[22] In some cases, the claim of having identified the gene for one of these conditions withstands the test of criticism for only a short time. But people are constantly making similar claims. Such claims do not sufficiently distinguish between two kinds of knowledge:[23] Molecular biological knowledge of DNA sequences in a certain individual differs fundamentally from the knowledge involved in a clinical diagnosis of an individual patient.[24,25] The former concerns scientific knowledge marked by the abstractions of the scientific method, whereas the latter relates to the health conditions of a unique individual. In the process of making a particular diagnosis, general scientific knowledge is not just applied, but included in a cognitive process that is marked not so much by reduction and objectivization, as by recognition and judgment. Scientific knowledge is integrated and interpreted in a wider framework of data, insights and meaning.[26] The two forms of knowledge presuppose two different epistemic attitudes and cannot, therefore, be equated.[27] Observing that specific genetic defects are sometimes highly correlated with certain clinical pictures does not contradict this objection. Such an observation does not prove that genes are causally related to traits. It proves only that gene *defects* can disturb the development of the organism. The gene or gene defect acquires meaning only in the context of the existence and functioning of the entire organism. In other words, the observation that concrete genetic information is a necessary precondition does not make that information a *sufficient* precondition for a 'normal' development.[28] Much more is needed for such development.

Moreover, DNA arguably cannot be the 'cause' or origin of biological life. Speaking of the genetic code or of the genetic message, as geneticists do, in itself presupposes that there is someone or something that can read and interpret the code or message. In fact, the word 'message' implies that there is a meaning to be interpreted. The DNA sequence contains a message for the organism, and the organism contains the 'mechanism' that can translate the DNA sequence into meaningful activities. The meaning of the DNA sequence is not generated by the mechanism; this mechanism presupposes the meaning of a genetic message. In fact, the DNA has not even generated the translation mechanism. Such generation would be impossible, since for the expression of the meaning the DNA precisely needs this mechanism.[29,30] So the genetic message cannot give a sufficient explanation of the development of the organism; the genetic code as a meaningful message itself needs an explanation, both a final and a causal one.[31,32] Christians know that the source of all meaning, including the meaningfulness of genetic information for the living organism, resides in the creative work of God. God not only created the DNA, he imbued it with meaning.

A DANGER TO PRACTICE.

To a great extent, medical science is characterized by abstract scientific models about the functioning of the human body and the deviations of normal functioning that constitute, or correspond to, diseases. Yet when dealing with actual people in practice, we can so easily forget the limitations of the models. In modern medicine there is a constant danger that the objectivization so characteristic of the scientific attitude comes to dominate the physician-patient relationship as well. Physicians begin to treat patients as abstractions and thereby exert a control over them.[33] The danger of this occurring is only increased by the high expectations people have of modern science and technology. To a certain extent, science and technology have even become the interpretative and meaning-giving framework for many.[34,35,36,37,38] In other words, the medical model has been internalized by many people, not just by medical scientists and physicians. People want to control their bodies and minds, and they see medicine as the best instrument to those ends. As the more general medical model gives way to a more specifically genetic model, people begin to understand themselves as their genes. This can lead to an evasion of responsiblity and, therefore, a dehumanization of human social life. A striking example is a recently-attempted legal defence that an accused murderer was innocent because he came from a family that has a gene predisposing its members to violence. (The defence was rejected.[39]) While some measure of mitigated legal responsibility is not out of the question when clearly established genetic factors are at work (see LeRoy Walters' chapter in this volume), the leap to dismiss moral responsibility completely based on any genetic influence whatsoever is alarming. In situations of alcoholism, obesity, homosexuality, etc., we can similarly expect that people will erroneously think they can be excused by their genes.

Genetic explanations may also be employed in society as a convenient way to address – though actually exacerbate – difficult social problems. The model of the gene as a blueprint, as determining factor and a source of good and evil, nicely fits into our pursuit for control over life and health and security. Genetic intervention augments the possibilities for manipulation of human beings. Gene technology, like technology in general, is not just a value-neutral instrument to achieve ethically valuable goals. It is a value-laden power that influences the self-understanding of people and social relationships. 'In that sense all technology is a new organism that insinuates itself into living cultures through altering them irrevocably.'[40] The machine metaphor of the human body and the central dogma of the role of genes in the body have such formative power. Nevertheless, they are theoretically insufficient and dangerous for medical practice.

An alternative understanding of medicine and genetics is required. The details of such an understanding are beyond the scope of this chapter. However, suffice it to say here that we should understand genes in the context of the whole human being, and not the other way around. (For more on restoring the proper context, see V. Elving Anderson's chapter that follows.) Embodiment and its brokenness – the relatedness, the spirituality and the responsibility of the human being – all should be taken into account.

––––––––––

Today in biomedicine we often hear: Genes are the answer! But what exactly is the question? No doubt many researchers and doctors sincerely try to find therapies for people with congenital diseases. Hopefully they will find them. However, the whole genetic enterprise seems to be permeated by another question – or should we say quest – to which genes are considered to be the answer. This is the quest for Paradise Restored through human technology. In the book *Bioethics in Europe* the authors maintain: 'Once the basics of genetic engineering have been mastered, almost anything is possible in terms of manipulating materials to achieve a desired effect. Fish can be altered to enable them to tolerate low temperatures. Plant breeders can produce crop resistance to drought or disease. Already fruit and vegetables that stay fresh longer or ripen more slowly are appearing on supermarket shelves.'[41] French molecular biologist Daniel Cohen also enthuses in his book, *Genes of Hope*, about the promises of the new gene technology: 'First, . . . it [will make it possible] to cure sick people. The physically and mentally sick people.' Later on, he says, we will be able to 'produce a human being that is more complex and complicated, more subtle, more distinguished from the animal that lives today'. He also writes: 'Away with the dictatorship of natural selection, long live the lordship of mankind over everything alive.'[42] These statements sound like an echo of the words of the Father of Salomon's House in Francis Bacon's utopia 'New Atlantis'.

Recognizing the Christian duty to provide help and healing for ill and marginalized people, Christian eschatology teaches us not to expect a Utopia as a creation of human science and technology, but to expect God's recreation of heaven and earth. Wild pretensions can easily turn new genetic technologies into weapons against true humanity in our society. An adequate and effective ethics of genetics will require an anthropology encompassing genetic information, a philosophy of technology, and a holistic understanding of (medical) genetics.

NOTES

1. Hubbard, R. and Wald, E., *Exploding the Gene Myth* (Boston, Beacon Press 1993).
2. Lippman, A., 'Prenatal Testing and Screening', in Clark, A., (ed.), *Genetic Counselling – Practice and Principles* (London, Routledge 1994), p. 144.

3. See note 1.

4. Eibach, U., *Gentechnik – Der Griff nach dem Leben* (Wuppertal, Brockhaus Verlag 1986), p. 54.

5. Blokhuis, P., *Kennis en abstractie,* Thesis (Amsterdam, VU-uitgeverij 1985).

6. Schuurman, E., *Tussen technische onmacht en menselijke overmacht* (Kampen, Kok 1985), esp. ch. 2.

7. Staudinger, H. and Behler, W., *Chance und Risiko der Gegenwart* (Paderborn, F Schöningh 1976).

8. Foss, F., 'The challenge to Biomedicine: A Foundation Perspective', *J Med Philosophy* 14 (1989), pp. 165–91.

9. See note 8, p. 170.

10. Finkenstein, J.L., 'Biomedicine and Technocratic Power', *Hastings Center Report* 20 (No. 4, July/August 1990), pp. 13–6.

11. Levin, D.M. and Solomon, G.F., 'The Discursive Formation of the Body in the History of Medicine', *J Med Philosophy* 15 (1990), p. 533.

12. ten Have, H., 'Medicine and the Cartesian Image of Man', *Theoretical Medicine* 8 (1987) pp. 235–46.

13. Belau, H., 'Oekologie – Gesundheit – Medizin – oekologische Gesundheitsstrategie', *Gesundh.-wesen* 54 (1992), pp. 284–96.

14. de Vries, M.J., *Choosing Life – A New Perspective on Illness and Healing,* Publications of the Helen Dowling Institute for Biopsychosocial Medicine 4 (Lisse: Swets & Zeitlinger 1993).

15. Suzuki, D. and Knudtson,P., *Genethics* (Cambridge (MA), Harvard University Press 1989), p. 52 ff.

16. van der Weele, C., 'De plicht met onze talenten te woekeren', *Filosofie & Praktijk* 9 (No. 2, 1988), pp. 57–71.

17. Hubbard, R., 'The Theory and Practice of Genetic Reductionism. From Mendel's Laws to Genetic Engineering', in Rose, S., (ed.), *Towards a liberatory biology* (London, Allison & Busby 1982).

18. Brenner, S., 'The Human Genome: The Nature of the Enterprise' in *Human Genetic Information: Science, Law and Ethics.* Ciba Foundation Symposium 149 (Chichester, Wiley 1990) pp. 7,12.

19. Tauber, A.I. and Sarkar, S., 'The Human Genome Project: Has Blind Reductionism Gone Too Far?' *Persp Biol Med* 35 (No. 2, winter 1992), pp. 220–35.

20. Jacob, F., quotation taken from Suzuki, D. and Knudtson, P., *Genethics* (Cambridge (MA), Harvard University Press 1989), p. 339.

21. *GenEthics News* (July/Aug 1995), p. 9.

22. See note 1, pp. 37, 66, 94–103 resp.

23. Kütemeyer, W., 'Wissenschaft, Methode und Mensch von der Medizin aus gesehen' in *Menschenzüchtung. Das Problem der genetischen Manipulierung der Menschen* (München, Beck, 19702), pp. 113–33.

24. Elzasser, W.M., *The Chief Abstractions of Biology* (Amsterdam/ Oxford, North-Holland Publishing Cy 1975), pp. 45–73.

25. See note 1.

26. ten Have, H., 'Ziekte als wijsgerig probleem', *Wijsgerig Perspectief* 25 (No. 1, 1984), pp. 5–12.

27. Glas, G., 'Clinical Practice and the Complexity of Medical Knowledge', Paper presented at the First World Congress organised by the European Society for the Philosophy of Medicine and Health Care, and Association Descartes (Paris, 30 May–4 June 1994).

28. Weiss, P.A., 'The Living System: Determinism Stratified' in A Koestler and JR Smythies (eds.), *The Alpbach Symposium Beyond Reductionism* (London, Hutchinson & Co Ltd 1972, first edition 1969), pp. 33–7.

29. Commoner, B., 'Failure of the Watson-Crick Theory as a Chemical Explanation for Inheritance', *Nature* 220 (1968), pp. 334–40.

30. Jochemsen, H., 'Selective Binding between Protein and Nucleic Acid, and Information Transfer', *Mededelingen Landbouwhogeschool Wageningen* 16 (1975).

31. Polanyi, M., 'Life's Irreducible Structure', *Science* 160 (1968), pp. 1308–12.

32. Seifert, J., 'Genetischer Code und Teleologie', *Arzt und Christ* 34 (1988), pp. 185–200.

33. Porto, E.M., 'Social Context and Historical Emergence: The Underlying Dimension of Medical Ethics', *Theoretical Medicine* 11 (1990), pp. 145–56. Admittedly, the danger of treating patients as objects is much more acute in some specialties, e.g. transplantation surgery, than in others, e.g. general practice. Furthermore, the point here is not that medical geneticists have a subjective motivation to obtain control over their patients. Rather, the ethos of control is structurally present in modern medicine insofar as it is (practised as) applied science.

34. See note 4.

35. Jaspers, K., 'The Physician in the Technological Age', *Theoretical Medicine* 10 (1989), pp. 261.

36. See note 6.

37. See note 7.

38. Jochemsen et al., 'The Medical Profession in Modern Society: The Importance of Defining Limits', in Kilner, J.F. et al., *Bioethics and the future of medicine* (Carlisle, UK, Paternoster Press 1995), ch. 2.

39. *GenEthics News* (No.6, 1995), p. 9.

40. Bloom, Keith C., 'Bad Axioms in Genetic Engineering', *Hastings Center report* (Aug/Sept. 1988), p. 13.

41. Rogers, A. and de Bousingen, Denis D., *Bioethics in Europe* (Council of Europe Press 1995), p. 87.

42. Quoted from a book review by L. Fittkau in *Gen-ethischer Informations Dienst* 111 (April 1996), pp. 44–5.

6

Resisting Reductionism by Restoring the Context

V. Elving Anderson, PhD

Every day, it seems, the newspapers report the discovery of a new gene. We hear about the 'obesity' gene, 'alcoholic' gene, 'happiness' gene, 'criminal' gene', 'breast cancer' gene, 'novelty seeking' gene, and 'allergy' gene. Some of these represent what we would like to be or become, but others reflect our fears.

It is not long before one of these descriptions fits too closely, and then the questions arise within us. Is this the way others look at us? Do they see us personally, or are we just the embodiment of the genes that we carry? When we go to our doctors for annual physical exams, do they remember us as persons or as gene carriers? For that matter, how do we view others?

Occasionally we may even hear about a gene that people claim can predict our fate and constrain our future. Does this reflect a loss of personal freedom? Has genetic research produced a new demonism?

Finally we wonder: *Are Genes Us?*[1] As the Human Genome Project identifies more and more genes, will each of us receive, at least figuratively, an extended 'bar code' like those used to show the cost of grocery items? At a party such identifiers would provide a way to start a conversation with one person or, alternatively, reason to avoid someone else. All of these thoughts and fears reflect the possibility that a gene label will be stuck on to our life, thereby reducing us to a biochemical entity.

Are there any ways to resist this reductionism? One possible strategy is suggested by Troy Duster's description of reductionism as 'stripping away the context'.[2] If loss of context is a key factor in reductionism, we should try to *restore that context*. With Duster's perceptive phrase in mind, the rest of this chapter will attempt to address three questions:

1) What has recent research told us about the complexities of genetic systems?
2) What opportunities do we have for trying to restore the context?
3) What guidance can biblical perspectives provide?

RECENT DEVELOPMENTS IN GENETIC RESEARCH

In some ways the DNA story is surprisingly simple, but it must not be interpreted simplistically. The genetic code is formed from four basic nucleotides (abbreviated as A, C, G, and T). The further fact that these nucleotides form pairs (A-T and C-G) has greatly facilitated research and has made genetic engineering and gene therapy possible. At the same time, recent research has challenged some of the commonly held views about genetics and has revealed levels of complexity that can counteract reductionism. Some of the most important elements in our present understanding are as follows.

Genes never act alone. A new human life starts as a single cell formed by the joining of an ovum and a sperm cell; but these provide much more than DNA. The ovum brings an initial source of energy and numerous mitochondria that can produce more. Then there are the various enzymes that are needed for replication of the DNA and for making gene products. Other factors are needed for initiating and controlling the early cell divisions.

As development proceeds, the genes from the mother and the father begin to enter into the picture, although the growing embryo continues to be dependent on the nutrition provided by the mother. Soon the action of a given gene becomes modified by the products of other genes. As a result many human traits are described as *multifactorial,* representing the joint effect of a number of genes together with internal and external environmental factors. This interaction, often complex, is part of the context that must be restored in order to make explanations adequate.

Gene action is indirect. People sometimes say that genes provide the 'blueprint' for development. However, this analogy can be quite misleading. A blueprint on a work table has important information about the design of a specific building, but it has no power to construct it. Someone must read and interpret the plans. The building materials and the workers must be made available. A sequence must be established—first the foundation, then the rough framing, followed by closing in the structure, and then the finer details. Some pages of the blueprint are for the basement and others for the kitchen. A supervisor or architect continually checks the progress to make certain the plans are followed, and even alters the plans if necessary to meet unexpected circumstances.

Genes, on the other hand, are involved in the construction. A simplified view of gene action would look like the following:

Gene Protein Cellular Whole
Sequence → Structure → Functions → Organism → Phenotype

The primary function of the DNA sequence is to provide the information for arranging amino acids into a one-dimensional strand that is able to fold into a three-dimensional protein. Some proteins serve as building components, some form enzymes, and others have a variety of functions. The chain of events finally leads to the expressed phenotype – the features that can be observed. Each of the intervening arrows is subject to internal or external environmental factors. Without the genes nothing would happen, but the final effects are more or less modifiable.

Genes are turned on and off. There may be as many as 80,000 genes in the human genome, but only a small fraction (perhaps less than 5%) are functioning in any single cell. Thus gene action must be regulated, often by promoters or enhancers in the DNA at either end of the gene itself or by circulating hormones. Some genes are active in the liver, others in the brain. Life experiences (such as repeated seizures) can turn on specific genes, at first temporarily but sometimes permanently. Identical twins start out with the same sets of genes, but as adults their functioning genes may no longer be completely identical. The importance of this gene regulation is demonstrated by some medical treatments that act by turning up the expression of some genes or turning down others.

Genes act at different times during development. Genes in the early embryo lay out the basic body pattern, from head to feet, and from front to back. The parts of the brain are established first, and then neurons migrate out from the brain stem. As development proceeds, the neuronal extensions are guided less by their genes and more by variation in the internal environment. Many neurons make synaptic connections, but those that fail to do so are programmed to die.

Genetic traits are often described as 'inborn', but this does not mean that all genetic effects are observable at birth. Consider conditions as different as diabetes, schizophrenia, and Alzheimer's disease. While each is partly affected by genetic factors, each can appear at any point throughout life.

Genes and environment are both important. No human characteristic is absolutely genetically determined, and none is completely environmentally controlled. The role of environment may be stronger for infectious diseases, but there are still genetic differences in susceptibility. Genes are more important for enzyme problems such as phenylketonuria (PKU), but most of the harmful effects of PKU can be controlled by diet.

It turns out that the first efforts at treating medical problems are often environmental, such as altering lifestyle. Studies of cholesterol level, for example, have shown quite clearly that the variability in human populations is about half genetic and half environmental. We can control the level in part by alterations of diet. If more intervention is required, we can use several different types of medication, some of which work by altering the cellular environment so as to regulate gene action. In other medical conditions the relative contribution of genes and environment must be determined by careful study.

A genotype (the sum total of an individual's genes) 'does not determine a particular phenotype; instead it sets limits, a "range of reaction", on the range of possible phenotypes from that genotype. . . . [T]he behavioral repertoire of a developing individual results from the interplay between its genes and the environment it encounters as it travels along the strip map of its life.'[3] One must never underestimate the importance of this interplay. Humans are not simply the product of their genes nor mere creatures of their environment.

Genes function within their own context. Because genes never act alone but instead act indirectly, are turned on and off, act differently during development, and interact with the environment, their context is essential to their function. Accordingly, one important step in resisting reductionism is to recognize this context and make every effort to restore it.

RESTORING THE CONTEXT

There are three dimensions within which the context needs to be restored. (a) Genetics differs from other disciplines in that it cuts across all levels of biological study, from cells to populations[4] (Figure 1). Findings from cells, individuals, or populations can provide clues for DNA research, but interpretations of DNA findings are incomplete until we consider the biological implications for the other levels as well. (b) Disciplines outside of the sciences

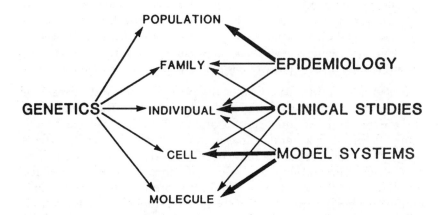

Fig. 1. Genetics as a collaborative and integrative research perspective.

are also part of the story. Biology lies midway in the traditional scheme for levels of knowledge:

Sociology
Psychology
Biology
Chemistry
Physics

Chemistry and physics are manifestly involved in medical research, but we must further recognize that human traits and medical problems (particularly those affecting behavior) are *biopsychosocial* in nature. Thus, a complete understanding of biology depends upon all levels of knowledge. (c) The third important dimension within which the context needs to be restored – the overarching religious dimension (specifically, a biblical frame of reference)—will be the focus of the concluding section of this chapter. These various dimensions offer special challenges and opportunities for researchers, caregivers, and people in general.

Researchers. Reductionism (in one sense at least) can be quite appropriate as a research strategy. When faced with a complex problem it may be necessary to focus initially on a few of the more important factors. Such studies, however, should always be initiated, carried out, and interpreted within a broader context. A research paper begins by explaining why the study is needed and concludes by outlining the implications for future research planning. Thus it is good science to show how one piece of evidence fits into the larger puzzle, as Savageau has explained:[5]

> Any respectable reductionist is also a reconstructionist. If you ask a reductionist what his or her directive is, you will find that it is to reduce complex systems to their elemental units in order to characterize them and, once this is accomplished, to use this knowledge for reconstructing an understanding of the intact entity with which the investigation started. The problem is that the reconstructionist phase of this program is seldom carried out.

It is also good ethics to consider the possible uses and misuses of the research. This consideration should start with the initial plans for the research design. Careful attention to the welfare of the human subjects is a standard requirement, but the potential effects upon the broader public may need consideration as well. The controversy surrounding discussions of genes and intelligence,[6] for example, could have been reduced by more careful planning and contextualized interpretation of the genetic studies. In fact, research in human behavioural genetics should always recognize that behavioural traits are biopsychosocial in principle.

Caregivers. Recent developments in genetics have led to a sharp increase in the number and sophistication of tests for the predisposition to a number of medical problems. At the same time the need to keep medical costs down is leading to miniaturization of tests so that minute amounts of blood or other body fluids can be used. Some of these tests can even be automated for home use, with results phoned in to the medical centre. Yet the more sophisticated the test, the greater the need for interpretation by an expert. Who will be available to explore the social, psychological, and medical context for the individual?

In the opinion of Méhes, a pediatrician from Hungary:[7]

> This progress in molecular genetics undoubtedly is a beneficent advance. However, its overestimation and the neglect of classical methods of clinical genetics will result in adverse effects. Most importantly this will affect the adequate evaluation of the clinical picture . . . This may lead to incorrect selection of patients for more sophisticated and often wasteful investigations with immense expenses, whereas patients and families in urgent need of molecular analyses may miss the necessary investigations. Without referring to further examples from Hungary, I assume that the hazards of isolating the patient from the examiner of his or her molecules have also been recognized in other parts of the world.

Genetic counsellors are playing a central role in limiting the reductionism that otherwise might occur. They are trained to gain information about the family setting, and thus are in a good position to interpret the test results back to the individual and wider family. Nurses, therapists, and other professionals have similar opportunities to restore the context for genetic information in other facets of patient care.

People in general. Each individual bears part of the responsibility for recognizing the context within which a genetic concern should be viewed. What can we do when confronted with a problem in ourselves or a loved one?

To begin with, we need a realistic view of the effects of genes. The unstable fascination and fear that the general public has about genetics needs to be replaced by a more balanced understanding. To this end, a simple description of the major themes in the first section of this chapter may be of help.

We should also seek information about the availability of appropriate methods for treatment of genetic conditions. In less severe problems, modification of aspects of lifestyle may deserve first attention. Specific medications may be directed toward the major cause or toward symptoms. Molecular tests may help to make a more accurate diagnosis, which in turn can indicate a more precise method of treatment. Experimental gene insertion therapy is available for only a few conditions, however, because of the stringent safeguards for safety and effectiveness.

Family, friends, and church provide a final and essential part of the 'context', although each of these human resources may need some update about the ways that genes work. In any case, no individual with a genetic problem or question should be left to feel isolated or deserted.

One family's story. Jessica was diagnosed with cleidocranial dysplasia, which had caused serious problems in her back, hips, spine, and teeth.[8] She had been shuffled from one doctor to another, and no one had recognized the big picture. Jessica and her mother were referred to Dr. Robin (a geneticist and pediatrician in Cleveland), who explained how all of her problems had been caused by a single gene that had become nonfunctional. Blood samples from the family helped his lab to make important discoveries, but that is not what Dr. Robin remembers most or is most proud of:

> Rather, it is that afternoon I spent with Jessica and her mother. They left that day with a new outlook on their lives: Jessica was freed from the burden of 'being cursed' with a host of medical ailments, and her mother was relieved from the guilt that she had caused her daughter's problems. . . . I did not cure or fix any of Jessica's physical ailments, but I did give her and her mother something else that day: information, which gave them some peace of mind.

BIBLICAL PERSPECTIVES

Although we cannot expect guidance about the details of medical genetics from the Bible, there are some broad principles that can be translated into modern terms. In particular, there are three themes from Genesis 1 and 2 which, if taken together, provide the foundation for a life of stewardship. People who apply the concept of stewardship to scientific problems usually restrict it to care for the environment. However, the ideas are much more broadly applicable, providing guidance for all areas of biology as well as for the conduct of scientific research itself.

> So God created man in his own image, in the image of God he created him; male and female he created them. God blessed them and said to them, 'Be fruitful and increase in number, fill the earth and subdue it. Rule over the fish of the sea and the birds of the air and over every living creature that moves on the ground. . . . The Lord God took the man and put him in the Garden of Eden, to work it and *take care* of it.[9] (emphasis added.)

At this point we can consider briefly the relevance of the three components of the 'Genesis mandate' as the *context* for the application and interpretation of findings from molecular genetics.[10]

Fill. This command can be understood in a quantitative or qualitative sense. Recognizing the historical tendency to understand it quantitatively, some have held it responsible for increases in

human population size and consumption of environmental resources. It is now urgent, however, to pay more attention to its
qualitative meaning. Since one of the goals of genetics is to help
individuals reach their human potential, we should give priority to
treatment of diagnosable problems through modification of the
environment or the expression of genes. To go further and strive
for a genetically ideal or perfect human, however, would reflect a
gross misunderstanding of genetics and of human nature. Even in
our therapeutic efforts, we must remember that 'when we fill the
earth we bring about changes in it, and in doing so we assume moral
responsibility for the quality of those changes',[11]

Rule over. The command to master or rule over does not, as some
have claimed, mean that humans are free to exploit nature in a
selfish manner for their own ends. As stewards, 'we are not pre-
tending to be God, but rather acting as his representatives on earth.
Made like God, we stand in his place, to help fill it, to occupy his
territories by subduing and ruling what he has made, and ultimately
to care for it'.[12] We have an obligation to change the world for the
better, but in this we are accountable to the Lord.

Take care of. Many of the other chapters in this book address key
ethical issues involved in genetic research and its applications. For
example, efforts to maintain the confidentiality of genetic information and to avoid the discrimination that can result from genetic
labelling of individuals and groups are essential (see Christopher
Hook's chapter). To be lastingly effective, however, these efforts
require that we restore the context for genetic understanding in its
several dimensions. We resist reductionism first by realizing the
dimensions of the context ourselves, and then by helping others to
do so.

Any one of these three themes from Genesis, if taken by itself,
can be used to justify unwarranted conclusions. Taken together,
they form the basis for a view of stewardship that is relevant for
the doing of genetic research as well as for its application.

> In all our scientific endeavors, we must not ignore the fact that those whom
> we study or treat are human beings who must be viewed holistically, as
> embodied persons. Neither can we overlook the fact that those who do the
> study, interpret the results, implement the conclusions in patient treatment,
> and report them to others are, first and foremost, human beings who
> themselves contribute to their findings through their personal knowledge
> and choices.[13]

Many who are fascinated by recent developments in genetics are
also wisely fearful lest our humanity be reduced to biochemistry.
DNA and genes carry out their function in a broad and complex
context. Restoring that context will provide an essential safeguard
against a simplistic reductionism. Scientists who carry out genetic

research, as well as others who care for those with genetic problems, must play key roles here by recognizing the context for their work. In this effort a biblical view of stewardship provides incentive and guidance.

NOTES

1. This is the title of a book that explores some of the reactions to recent developments in genetics (Cranor, C.F., editor, *Are Genes Us? The Social Consequences of the New Genetics* (New Brunswick, NJ:Rutgers University Press 1994). Another treatment of the topic can be found in: Nelkin, D. and Lindee, M.S., *The DNA Mystique. The Gene as a Cultural Icon* (New York, WH Freeman 1995).

2. This is from a personal conversation, but a more complete view can be found in: Duster, T., *Backdoor to Eugenics* (New York, Routledge 1990).

3. From Merrell, D.J., *The Adaptive Seascape* (Minneapolis, University of Minnesota Press 1994), p.205

4. Anderson, V.E., 'Prospects for Future Research', in *Genetic Basis of the Epilepsies*, edited by Anderson, V.E., Hauser, W.A., Penry, J.K. and Sing, C.F., (New York, Raven Press 1982), p.352.

5. Savageau, M.A., 'Reconstructionist Molecular Biology', *The New Biologist*, vol.3 (Febuary 1991), pp.190–197.

6. Allen, A., Anderson, B., Andrews, L. et al. [20 more], '*The Bell Curve:* Statement by the NIH-DOE Joint Working Group on the Ethical, Legal, and Social Implications of Human Genome Research', *The American Journal of Human Genetics* vol.59 (August 1996), pp.487–488.

7. Méhes, K., 'Classical Genetics in the Era of Molecular Genetics', *American Journal of Medical Genetics*, vol.61 (Febuary 2,1996), pp.394–395.

8. Robin, N.H., 'The Good that We Do', *American Journal of Medical Genetics*, vol.65 (November 11, 1996), pp.257–258.

9. Genesis 1:27,28;2:15 NIV

10. See chapters 7 and 9 in: Reichenbach, B.R. and Anderson, V.E., *On Behalf of God: A Christian Ethic for Biology* (Grand Rapids, William B. Eerdmans 1995)

11. Op. cit., p.184.

12. Op. cit., p.55.

13. Op. cit., p.295.

PART II

Genetic Information

7

The Human Genome Project

Francis S. Collins, MD, PhD

'Jesus went through all the towns and villages, teaching in their synagogues, preaching the good news of the kingdom, and healing every disease and sickness' (Matt. 9:35). If healing is something which Jesus Christ in his short time on this earth spent so much time on, it is something that those who would follow him should also consider especially important. Such is the theological justification for the Human Genome Project – an initiative to map the entire genetic make-up of human beings. This initiative is a natural extension of our commitment to heal the sick.

There are, however, plenty of precedents for potentially beneficial medical advances being used in unethical ways. People's propensity to sin is ever present. That potential for misuse requires all of us to take responsibility for making sure that medical advances are used in ways that benefit rather than injure people.

Genetics has traditionally been viewed as a branch of medicine that is devoted to the study of relatively rare disorders. Only in the last ten years or so have we begun to have the confidence that these same strategies might usefully be applied to understanding hereditary components that contribute to many other diseases that are not inherited in simple ways. Virtually every disease, except perhaps trauma, has a genetic component. This does not mean that every disease is predetermined on the basis of genetics but rather that every disease has a hereditary contribution. For cystic fibrosis, the disease comes about because a child has inherited a misspelled copy of the responsible gene from each parent.[1] If the misspellings are the severe type, the child will almost certainly develop cystic fibrosis. But the severity of the disease may not be identical between children who have the same genetic constitution, because the environment also plays a role in determining exactly how the disease develops. For many common diseases that afflict us, including heart disease, hypertension, breast cancer, prostate cancer, and schizophrenia, a genetic contribution is evident since these diseases tend to run in families.[2]

Yet, these diseases cannot be understood in a simple one-gene fashion. There will not be 'a gene' for any of these complex diseases.

There may be a long list of genes for complex disorders like diabetes, each one of which makes a rather modest contribution. Understanding the genes that play a predictive role in diseases like diabetes will, however, allow a better understanding of the disease and facilitate the development of new treatments. It is part of our mandate as Christians to pursue such medical advances, attempting to emulate Christ in his healing role.

Genetics and the environment are always both at work – sometimes together, sometimes not together, to prevent or contribute to a disease. We are probably treading on thin ice to neglect one in order to emphasize the other. Understanding the environmental contributions to disease has proved very difficult. We are at a point of time, however, when understanding the genetic component is very rapidly becoming possible. Interestingly, one of the consequences of this genetic revolution will be the ability to understand the environmental contributions better, once genetic variables are defined.

If something is genetic, then somewhere in the DNA molecule there is a difference in the sequence between the people who are susceptible and the people who are not. DNA is the information-carrying molecule of all living things. We know that 3 billion base pairs of DNA is all that is needed to specify all the instructions that the human body needs. The Human Genome Project is based on the notion that this number is knowable and that we will have, some seven or eight years from now, that entire instruction set written down and in a publicly available database so that anybody who wants to try to understand it can do so.[3] Having this opportunity to look at our own instruction book is a phenomenally significant event in human history.

The work of a scientist involved in this project, particularly a scientist who has the joy of also being a Christian, is a work of discovery which can also be a form of worship. As a scientist, one of the most exhilarating experiences is to learn something, to understand something, that no human has understood before. To have a chance to see the glory of creation, the intricacy of it, the beauty of it, is really an experience not to be matched. Scientists who do not have a personal faith in God also undoubtedly experience the exhilaration of discovery. But to have that joy of discovery, mixed together with the joy of worship, is truly a powerful moment for a Christian who is also a scientist.

THE GENETIC QUEST

DNA is not arranged in a chaotic mass inside the nucleus. It is organized into genes, which are simply packets of information, stretches of DNA that code for particular bodily operations. These genes, about 100,000 of them, are organized into chromosomes. Human cells – other than the reproductive (egg and sperm) cells – typically have 23 pairs of chromosomes; extra or less genetic material can cause serious problems. One of the challenges to the geneticist is to try to work out which gene goes with which disease. A major reason for the Human Genome Project is to make this task easier. Consider the example of cystic fibrosis (CF). Boomer Esiason, the football quarterback, was recently featured on the cover of *Sports Illustrated* with his young son sitting on his shoulders. Boomer Esiason's son, Gunner, has CF, the most common potentially fatal recessive disorder of northern European Caucasians.[4] One in 2500 newborns have the disease. Esiason must be a carrier because CF is a recessive disease. In order for the child to be affected, both parents must carry an altered copy of the gene, and they must both pass on that copy to the child.

Curing this disease would be wonderful. CF is a terrible disease for children and young adults to endure. The problems associated with it are largely in the lungs. The mucus that normally is smoothly cleared out of the lungs, carrying with it inhaled bacteria and dust, is thick and sticky in CF. The result is recurrent infections and, eventually, destruction of lung tissue. The current average age of death for people with CF is thirty. To try to find new clues about the cause of this devastating disease that might help lead to new treatments, a group of scientists including myself set out some years ago to identify the CF gene. Since there are three billion base pairs, how does one find the right gene? First, we had to discover the specific part of one of the 23 chromosomes where the gene is located. To do this, we needed families with CF and a collection of 'genetic markers'. A genetic marker is a bit of DNA that varies from one person to the other and therefore can be used to track inheritance in a family. For example, if the marker and the CF gene are on different chromosomes, and one tests these families, the marker will have absolutely no predictive ability to indicate which children develop CF and which do not. But if enough genetic markers are tested, eventually by chance one will locate a marker that is next door to the cystic fibrosis gene. When that occurs, one will notice that this marker tends to predict which children have CF and which do not.

Once we identified the right chromosome, we narrowed the region down by trying to pick other markers in the vicinity. The idea is to locate a manageable interval of, say, a couple of million base pairs and then to sift through that interval looking for the right gene.

It is actually rather simple in principle to pinpoint this gene. For a gene to be responsible for a disease, there has to be a misspelling in the gene in people with the disease. For CF what we found was a very subtle change. After ten years of work, it all came down to three base pairs. The sequence CTT, which is normally present in people who do not have cystic fibrosis, was deleted in about 70 percent of the cystic fibrosis chromosomes. Finding this alteration, then, proved that we had the right gene.[5]

But finding the gene is just the end of the beginning.[6] The discovery provides diagnostic capability. It becomes possible to go out and try to identify individuals who have misspellings in the gene. However, what one really wants is to use the gene to identify a strategy that will make it possible to do more to help people with the disease than could be done previously. That may involve developing a gene therapy or perhaps a drug therapy, as long as it works and does not have unacceptable side effects. There has been a lot of excitement about gene therapy for cystic fibrosis, because one should, theoretically, be able to correct the disease by putting the normal gene back in the lungs. All that is required is one normal copy of the gene. Yet gene therapy has turned out to be quite a technical challenge.[7] While more than 100 cystic fibrosis patients have gone through clinical trials of gene therapy for this disease, none has been cured as a result.[8] In fact, the outcomes have been unexpectedly disappointing. The vehicle that is being used to deliver that normal gene to the patient's lung turns out to produce such an immune reaction that the effect is very short-lived. Realistically, it will be several years before we can tell whether or not gene therapy is going to pay off for CF in the short term. Meanwhile, drug therapy is an alternative. The media, at least in the past, have been so positive about gene therapy that they have tended to overlook the other benefits that come from gene discovery. For many diseases, the pathway to effective treatments and therapy will be based upon having the gene in hand, which will allow sufficient understanding of the disease to be able to design a drug that is much more specific and effective than would otherwise be possible.

Diagnostic testing, on the other hand, becomes available much more quickly than therapies. For a disease like cystic fibrosis, people imagine that diagnostic testing occurs primarily in the prenatal setting, so that couples may receive a warning of the birth of a child with CF and terminate the pregnancy. In fact, most of the CF testing that has been done has led to continuation of a pregnancy.[9] Moreover, with the identification of the CF gene, it is now possible to determine whether or not a husband and wife are carriers for this condition even before they initiate a pregnancy.[10] Most often, the outcome will be that they are not at risk.

The Human Genome Project was designed in part to make this process of discovery achievable for the thousands of diseases that afflict us. Finding the gene for cystic fibrosis was, in many ways, easy, compared to, say, diabetes.[11] Without the kind of maps and sequence information provided by this Project, we would never understand the genetics of most diseases. The Human Genome

Project has three very simple goals. We want a genetic map. We want a physical map. We want the DNA sequence. First, the genetic map consists of the markers needed to localize the disease gene. There must be a lot of markers; otherwise, if one is looking for a disease gene and there is not a marker near it, one might miss it. When the Genome Project started in 1990, we reckoned we needed about 1500 markers, scattered over all the chromosomes.[12] We aimed to have those markers by the end of 1995. This goal was completed by the middle of 1993, and now we have over 10,000 markers, a truly terrific genetic map.

The second goal of the Human Genome Project was to create physical maps. A physical map is a collection of ordered, overlapping, purified (cloned) fragments of DNA that cover a particular region. We aimed originally to finish the physical maps by the end of 1998 but we have already completed 96 percent.[13]

The really difficult part of the Human Genome Project is to sequence the entire three billion base pairs. Until recently, most of our sequencing efforts have been devoted to studying the sequence of simpler organisms like bacteria, yeast, fruit flies and roundworms because their genomes are much more manageable. We began only in this year in earnest the business of sequencing human DNA. The expectation is that the original goal of getting all of the sequence by the year 2005 will be met.

As a consequence of the maps created by the Human Genome Project, a dizzying number of genes are being discovered.[14] Hardly a week goes by when there is not a new gene discovery. The medical consequences of that are now emerging rapidly.

Breast cancer is a very powerful paradigm for what is happening in molecular medicine.[15] A gene for breast cancer called BRCA1 was mapped in 1990 and identified precisely in 1994.[16] A woman with a misspelled copy of BRCA1 from a family with a high incidence of breast cancer has a 50% risk of getting breast cancer by the age of fifty – with a lifelong risk of about 85 percent. In the general population, about one in 200 women have a hereditary susceptibility to early onset breast cancer.[17] In the Jewish population, it is one in 40.[18]

PRESSING ETHICAL ISSUES

Should we mount a crash programme to identify those women and warn them of the risk of developing cancer? The answer to that depends on whether or not it would help them to know. Would the information be useful? Are there interventions that could be offered, drastic or otherwise, that would improve chances of survival for somebody in this very high-risk category? We do not yet know. We are in an early stage of learning the appropriate use of this kind of presymptomatic testing. Until we really understand the benefits and the risks, many people feel that it is inappropriate to offer this testing outside of a research protocol.[19] They identify with the writer of Ecclesiastes who mused in a rather different context, 'For with much wisdom comes much sorrow; the more knowledge, the more grief' (Eccl. 1:18).

The Ethical, Legal, and Social Implications (ELSI) programme of the Human Genome Project is devoted to wrestling with these issues. While the Human Genome Project does not introduce any completely new ethical dilemmas, the project does accelerate the rate at which genetic discoveries are occurring and, therefore, the number of people whose lives are going to be affected.

We are all walking around with four or five genes that are really spoiled, and another ten or twenty or more that are moderately altered in a way that is not good for us. There are no perfect genetic specimens. Therefore, if we do not have a set of protections in place so that genetic information cannot be used against people, we are all at risk. None of us can afford to turn our heads and assume that this will not have an impact on us.

The story of Monica (not her real name) whom we recently saw at the National Institutes of Health will help illustrate this point. She has an aunt with ovarian cancer and a cousin with breast cancer. The aunt and cousin have been found to have a mutation in BRCA1. So Monica came to see us in the research clinic at the NIH, seeking information about whether or not she should also be tested in order to decide whether or not she should go through some intense surveillance or even consider surgery. After hearing all of the reasons for and against testing, she decided not to be tested for one reason only. Monica was a federal employee who was getting ready to leave government employment in order to run her own consulting business, and she would need to get her own health insurance. She was quite concerned that if she had this test and it was positive – and that information fell into the hands of her insurance company – she would be uninsurable.

Monica is right to be concerned. Is this just? Is it ethical? Should DNA sequences that people have no control over be used against them to take away their health care coverage? For some people, losing insurance is a lethal event. If a woman needs mammograms on a regular basis, but cannot afford them, and her health insurance company has dropped her because of genetic information, the outcome can be fatal. Yet we are at present allowing this predicament by failing to correct a system that discriminates against people on this basis. Christians cannot be silent about such discrimination. If health care is not something that should be reserved for a privileged few who have wealth and resources, but rather something which should be available to anyone with health needs, then access to health care should not depend on happening to have the 'right' DNA sequence.

Some progress is occurring on this critical issue.[20] Several states have passed legislation to make it illegal for health insurance companies to use genetic information to deny coverage. However, most of those do not prevent the setting of exorbitant premiums – effectively the equivalent of denying coverage.[21] On the federal level, The Health Insurance Portability and Accountability Act of 1996 has been enacted to provide limited protection against genetic discrimination by health insurers. As these legislative initiatives suggest, this issue is winnable but not yet won. Christians need to stand up and speak about this health care discrimination in a passionate way, out of their commitments to justice and meeting the needs of the weak.

Employment discrimination is another serious issue.[22] Employers can use genetic information to deny people jobs or to pass them over for promotion. There is currently nothing to prevent such practices. While the Equal Employment Opportunities Commission has ruled that using genetic information to deny somebody a job is illegal, this ruling is plagued by various loopholes and problems. So employment discrimination also continues to be an appropriate issue for Christian concern and action.

Genetic patenting is an even more complicated arena. The patenting of intellectual property and life forms is a complex matter that involves ethics, law, and various practical and technical matters, as the chapter on patenting in this book explains. The church must be much more careful than it has been not to react indiscriminately against new genetic possibilities, but rather to consider each innovation on its own merits.[23] The church has so much to contribute to the meaningful dialogue about the interface between faith and genetic science. Those opportunities must not be squandered in making ill-considered statements which sound righteous in their indignation, but underneath are based on unsupported premises.

CHALLENGES FOR THE CHURCH

There are, in fact, five challenges facing the church today. The first challenge is to become informed. Proverbs 19:2 reads, 'It is not good to have zeal without knowledge'. The church is a place where zeal is often expressed very effectively, but it must be backed up with that depth of knowledge that allows zeal to have credibility. While 'Genome' is not a word found in the Bible, the Bible has much to say about the pursuit of new knowledge and capabilities. An accurate understanding of the scientific facts is not an obstacle to understanding how the Bible speaks to the world in which we live – it is an aid.

The second challenge is to resist the temptation to take emotional cheap shots. Passion is great; distortion is not. When we have an opportunity to talk about genetics, we should talk about the issues that are real rather than always gravitating toward Frankenstein scenarios. Such scenarios are easy to construct and get everyone stirred up; but they rarely yield insight for today's most pressing ethical issues.

Third, we should resist the temptation simply to (try to) close the door on all genetic research. When the hopes of many individuals-perhaps all of us, in some way-of escaping from some significant medical illness depend on this kind of research, we must be careful not to react against more than is warranted by careful ethical reflection. On the contrary, we must take responsibility for how the genetic information we are obtaining should be used.

The fourth challenge is to move beyond simply describing the dilemmas that genetics poses. We have had those discussions now for four or five years, and we know fairly precisely what the issues are. It is time to take positions on the ethical issues and develop ways of implementing those positions. It is not enough to describe theoretical scenarios that make everybody uncomfortable. We have to consider what to do.

Finally, the fifth challenge for the church is for us to remember that we are representing God Almighty. To the extent that we speak with reason and with love, God is glorified. If we do not, he is not. Unfortunately, these standards have not always guided our conversation when it comes to very emotional issues.

My prayer for all of us is that we find wisdom. James 1:5 reads: 'All who lack wisdom, let them ask of God, who gives to all freely and without reproach, and it will be given to them.' I claim that promise for all of us.

NOTES

1. Welsh, M.J., Tsui, L-C., Boat, J.F., Beaudet, A.L.: 'Cystic Fibrosis' in *The Metabolic And Molecular Bases of Inherited Disease*, eds. Scriver, C.R., Beaudet, A.L., Sly, W.S. and Valle, D., (New York, McGraw-Hill 1995), pp. 3799–3876.

2. Lander, E.S. and Schork, N.J., 'Genetic Dissection of Complex Traits', *Science* 265:2037–48 1994.

3. Collins, F.S., 'Ahead of Schedule and Under Budget: The Genome Project Passes its Fifth Birthday', *Proc. Natl. Acad. Sci. U.S.A.* 92:10821–10823 (1995).

4. Welsh, M.J. et al.

5. Ibid.

6. Collins, F.S., 'Positional Cloning Moves from Perditional to Traditional', *Nature Genetics* 9:347–350 (1995).

7. Wilson, J.M., 'Gene Therapy for Cystic Fibrosis: Challenges and Future Directions', *J. Clin. Invest.* 96:2547–2554 (1995).

8. Sorelle, Ruth, 'The Gene Doctors', *The Houston Chronicle Sunday* (April 1995) Special Report.

9. Welsh, M.J. et al.

10. Ibid.

11. Lander and Schork.

12. Collins, F.S. and Galas, D., 'A New Five-Year Plan for the U.S. Human Genome Project (Policy Forum)', *Science 262*:43–46 (1993).

13. Hudson, T.J. et al., 'An STS-Based Map of the Human Genome', *Science 270*:1945–1954 (1995).

14. Collins, F.S., 'Positional Cloning Moves from Perditional to Traditional', *Nature Genetics 9*:347–350 (1995).

15. Collins, F.S., 'BRCA1–Lots of Mutations, Lots of Dilemmas', *N. Engl. J. Med. 334*:186–188 (1996).

16. Miki, Y. et al., 'A Strong Candidate for the Breast and Ovarian Cancer Susceptibility Gene BRCA1', *Science 266*:66–71 (1994).

17. Regarding breast cancer generally, cf. Hoskins, K.F. Stopfer, J.E., Calzone K.A. et al., 'Assessment and Counseling for Women With a Family History of Breast Cancer: A Guide for Clinicians', *JAMA 273*:577–85 (1996). The figure of 1 in 200 represents 5% or 1 in 20 women with breast cancer. (About 10% of women eventually get breast cancer.)

18. Muto, M.G. et al., 'Frequency of the BRCA1 185delAG Mutation Among Jewish Women with Ovarian Cancer and Matched Population Controls', *Cancer Research 56*:1250–1252 (1996).

19. Collins, F.S., 'BRCA1–Lots of Mutations, Lots of Dilemmas'. *N. Engl. J. Med. 334*:186–188 (1996).

20. Hudson, K.L. et al., 'Genetic Discrimination and Health Insurance: An Urgent Need for Reform', *Science 270*:391–393 (1995).

21. Rothenberg, Karen H., 'Genetic Information and Health Insurance: State Legislative Approaches', *Journal of Law, Medicine and Ethics 23*:312–19 (1995).

22. Brown, Steven R., Marshall, Karen, eds., *Advances in Genetic Information: A Guide for State Policy Makers*, (Lexington, Kentucky, The Council of State Governments 1993).

23. In May, 1995, Jeremy Rifkin succeeded in convincing a group of religious leaders to sign a document objecting broadly to patenting of organisms, life forms, organs, tissues, genes, and cells. Because these entities were lumped together as if they were all the same, the statement was essentially meaningless. As a Christian, it was a black day for me when the church that I care so much about supported a statement that was considered ludicrous in the scientific community. It became an excuse for many to consider the church irrelevant: If the people in the church could not respond to this issue in a more sophisticated way than this, then what credibility should be given to church statements?

8

Behavioural and Germ-Line Genetic Research

LeRoy B. Walters, PhD

Two fascinating areas of genetic research have particularly important implications for Christian theology and ethics. The first area is research on *behavioural genetics*, or genetic influences on human and animal behaviour. Research on behavioural genetics is directly related to the Christian understanding of the human person and to Christian ethics more broadly. The second area of genetic research is somewhat more difficult to capture in one or two words: it is research on deliberately changing specific genes in our descendants. The technical term for this effort is *germ-line genetic intervention*. Research on transmitting genetic changes to future generations raises important questions at both the micro and the macro levels. At the micro level, we can ask: What are the ethical responsibilities of people of faith in their reproduction? At the macro level, we can consider a more ambitious, and in some ways more frightening, question: What role, if any, should Christian believers have in guiding the genetic future of humanity.

BEHAVIOURAL GENETICS

Heredity plays at least some role in the development of human personality traits and human behaviour. Most families are characterized by certain personality traits. While it is difficult to disentangle the genetic and environmental factors that contribute to these obvious patterns, social scientists and molecular biologists are devising rather sophisticated techniques for distinguishing between nature and nurture. In this effort, the study of identical twins who are reared in different environments has been immensely helpful.[1]

We should not assume that research on genetics and behaviour is solely a twentieth-century phenomenon. In his nineteenth century book, *The Descent of Man*, Charles Darwin wrote the following comments:

> I have elsewhere so fully discussed the subject of Inheritance, that I need here add hardly anything. A greater number of facts have been collected with respect to the transmission of the most trifling, as well as of the most important characters in man, than in any of the lower animals; though the

facts are copious enough with respect to the latter. So in regard to mental qualities, their transmission is manifest in our dogs, horses, and other domestic animals. Besides special tastes and habits, general intelligence, courage, bad and good temper, &c. are certainly transmitted. With man we see similar facts in almost every family . . .[2]

In his earlier book, *On the Origin of Species*, Darwin had discussed the inheritance of behavioural traits in a chapter on instinct (Chapter VII). Always an astute observer of nature, Darwin was especially intrigued by the traits that seemed to have been inherited by one domesticated species, the dog.

But let us look to the familiar case of several breeds of dogs: it cannot be doubted that young pointers (I have myself seen a striking instance) will sometimes point and even back other dogs the very first time that they are taken out; retrieving is certainly in some degree inherited by retrievers; and a tendency to run round, instead of at, a flock of sheep, by shepherd-dogs. I cannot see that these actions, performed without experience by the young, and in nearly the same manner by each individual, performed with eager delight by each breed, and without the end being known, – for the young pointer can no more know that he points to aid his master, than the white butterfly knows why she lays her eggs on the leaf of the cabbage, – I cannot see that these actions differ essentially from true [that is, natural] instincts.[3]

If Darwin had been writing in the era that followed the rediscovery of Gregor Mendel's work, he would surely have tied his discussion of instincts to genes.

Three aspects of behaviour have been of special interest to behavioural geneticists: (1) personality traits; (2) general intellectual ability (sometimes called 'intelligence'); and (3) tendencies toward violently-aggressive behaviour. We turn first to personality traits. Five broad traits or 'super factors' capture the most important aspects of personality. The first trait is *extraversion* or *introversion*. In other words, how outgoing or retiring is a particular person? The second factor is *neuroticism*. Researchers ask: How anxious is this person? How quickly can he or she recover from upsetting experiences? The third factor is *conscientiousness*. Here researchers try to determine whether a person is relatively organized and dependable or relatively impulsive and careless. A fourth personality factor is *agreeableness*. In this case researchers seek to measure whether people are, on balance, sympathetic, warm, and good-natured or quarrelsome, aggressive, and unfriendly. The fifth and final super factor is *openness*. In assessing this factor, researchers ask: Is this person curious and open to new experiences and stimuli, or is the person narrow, shallow, and unreflective?

Assuming that these categories capture at least some important dimensions of personality, we can then ask the question: To what extent are these personality factors influenced by heredity? The two largest studies of genetics and personality traits suggest that the genetic influence on these five major personality traits is between 42% and 46%.[4] The underlying assumption of this research is that comparative studies of identical and fraternal twins can indicate the extent to which genetics governs particular traits in the general population. To the degree that these studies and the underlying assumption are valid, the best current research suggests that genetic influences may constitute almost half of the total set of influences shaping our personalities. Other important influences measured to date include the environments that we share with our siblings and the environments that are unique to ourselves.[5]

A second behavioural characteristic that has been intensively studied by genetic researchers is general intellectual ability. This is an enormously controversial topic, and rational discussion of this topic has not been furthered by the racial fixation of books like *The Bell Curve*.[6] Admittedly, the measurement of general intellectual ability is a daunting task, even with sophisticated neuropsychological tests that analyse how the brain processes various kinds of information.[7] However, it appears that at least *part* of the ability to do well in elementary and secondary school classwork, as well as in higher education, is inborn.

To what extent is our general intellectual ability influenced by genetic factors? The best available evidence is based on the same twin study measures and underlying assumption employed with regard to personality traits. It suggests that in pre-adolescent children, between 40% and 50% of general intellectual ability is closely correlated with inheritance.[8] One recent study of 332 identical twin pairs and 242 fraternal twin pairs aged 7–16 reached the following conclusions about specific components of intellectual performance: the heritability (h^2) of verbal comprehension is 0.44; the heritability of perceptual organization is 0.50; and the heritability of freedom from distractibility is 0.49.[9]

A third topic that has been studied by several behavioural geneticists is the inborn tendency toward violently-aggressive behaviour. Like the discussion of general intellectual ability, this discussion has sometimes had racial – and indeed racist – overtones.[10] The focus of attention could just as easily have been the male gender, especially males in their teens and twenties.[11]

Much remains unclear about the extent to which violently-aggressive behaviour is genetically influenced. However, one reported case from a Dutch extended family seems instructive. Consider the following excerpt from an article in the *American Journal of Human Genetics*:

Behavioural problems were reported for all eight affected males. Abnormal behaviour was documented for affected males in at least four different sibships living in different parts of the country at different times. Most striking were repeated episodes of aggressive, sometimes, violent behaviour, occurring in all eight affected males. Aggressive behaviour was usually triggered by anger and was often out of proportion to the provocation. Aggressive behaviour tended to cluster in periods of 1–3 d[ays], during which the affected male would sleep very little and would experience frequent night terrors. . . . In one instance, an affected male was convicted of the rape of his sister, at 23 years. He was transferred to an institution for psychopaths, where he was described as quiet and easy to handle. In spite of this, fights occurred with other inmates, and he was repeatedly transferred to a different pavilion. At the age of 35 years, while working in the fields, he stabbed one of the wardens in the chest with a pitchfork, after having been told to get on with his work. Another affected male tried to run over his boss with a car at the sheltered workshop where he was employed after having been told that his work was not up to par. A third affected male would enter his sisters' bedrooms at night, armed with a knife, and force them to undress. At least two affected males in this family are known arsonists. This latter behaviour appears linked to stressful circumstances, such as the death of a relative.[12]

Through laboratory analyses the researchers who were studying this extended family were able to detect a mutation in a gene on the X-chromosome that produces an enzyme called monoamine oxidase A. This mutation was present in all five of the males who were available for testing. In three of the males there were also abnormalities in two brain chemicals.[13] The high levels of one chemical, norepinephrine, and the low levels of the other chemical, serotonin, have been associated with increased aggression in both human and animal studies.[14]

How does this research in behavioural genetics relate to Christian theology and Christian ethics? The case history of the Dutch extended family suggests that certain people may not be fully 'responsible' for their behaviour.

The genetic predispositions and environmental stresses of these young Dutch men appear sometimes to have overwhelmed their good intentions and their inhibitions. It is of course possible to go too far in the direction of absolving people of responsibility for their actions. However, in marginal cases like these, at least, we may need a notion of diminished responsibility in our ethical analyses.

The case of the Dutch extended family may be only the tip of the iceberg. Even for more 'normal' people like ourselves, between 42% and 46% of our major personality characteristics may be strongly influenced by genetic factors. Some of these factors seem quite unrelated to morality. Whether we are more extraverted or introverted seems to be a matter of indifference, ethically speaking. On the other hand, terms like 'conscientious', 'careless', 'warm', and 'quarrelsome' are closely related to a person's character. If current research results stand the test of time, they will suggest that these characteristics are genetically influenced.

Here again the notion of diminished moral responsibility may be important. Through practice and with proper social support people can overcome inborn tendencies to be careless or quarrelsome. The point remains, however, that some of us have been dealt a better hand, genetically speaking, than others. Stark differences in early childhood environments may exacerbate these inborn differences, or they may begin to ameliorate the less desirable tendencies.

At a deeper level, the research on major personality factors has implications for our doctrine of the human person. If the behavioural geneticists are correct, our personalities are partially determined and partially indeterminate and therefore free. In the free space that exists, we have the opportunity to develop our positive tendencies, to compensate for our negative tendencies, and to become engaged with others in their quest to do the same. Divine grace is often mediated through such constructive engagement, first in the home, but also in the workplace and in the wider society.

The discovery that 40–50% of general intellectual ability may be genetically based also has important implications. Our intellectual capacities are a gift, most obviously from our parents, but ultimately from God. The biblical mandate to care for the weak suggests that this gift is best used not to foster an intellectual elite, but rather to help those less fortunate to have the best education possible and to develop creative ways of compensating for their inherited weaknesses or disabilities. This educational ministry includes reaching out to the people who have fared worst in this natural lottery – namely, people who are classified as mentally retarded.

Behavioural genetics also reveals new forms of natural evil. Theologians have always known that hurricanes, tornadoes, and earthquakes are natural evils, and they have sought to come to terms with such evils in their theological systems. Now we can also see that monoamine oxidase A deficiency, and mental retardation, and even an inborn tendency to be quarrelsome are genetic natural evils. Why these particular evils are present we do not know. Whether they can gradually be diminished, either in individuals or in populations, we also do not know. These evils are aspects of human existence as we encounter it. We can hope that, in the long run, in part through the constructive, healing engagement of people of faith, the pervasiveness of at least some types of genetic natural evil can be reduced.

GERM-LINE GENETIC INTERVENTION

We turn now to our second major topic, the attempt to transmit specific genetic changes to future generations. Here the focus will be primarily on physical health and disease rather than on behavioural traits. However, the analysis in principle is applicable to the kinds of behaviour issues that we have just considered.

How could specific genetic changes be passed on to future generations from a technical standpoint? One possibility would be to use *in vitro* fertilization to create one or more early embryos and then to introduce the desired genetic change into the embryo at a very early stage. The new gene could be inserted into the preimplantation embryo with a fine needle, or a virus could be used to carry the gene into the embryo. The other possibility would be to modify sperm or egg cells before fertilization occurs. This modification could be performed in one of two ways. The reproductive cells could be removed from the bodies of the prospective parents in the laboratory. Alternatively, and more ambitiously, genes with very smart guidance systems could be administered to the prospective parents – perhaps by injection – and these genes would then find their way to the reproductive cells in the parents' bodies.

One technical note is necessary at this point. Precisely because the genetic changes would be passed on to future generations, genetic researchers will want to have a method for repairing, or more accurately, replacing the malfunctioning target genes with properly functioning genes. The current method of simply adding properly functioning gene to a cell while leaving the malfunctioning gene in place undisturbed will not be satisfactory.

An analogy from word processing may prove helpful here. If one thinks of a cell as a ten-page document, a mutation is like a misspelled word in the document. Current techniques simply add a properly-spelled word to the document – anywhere in the text. In other words, one simply uses the 'insert' function and adds the properly-spelled word, leaving the misspelled word undisturbed. Because cells are more dynamic than documents, gene addition works. As long as the properly functioning gene is there somewhere in the cell and it performs its function, the cell is, in effect, corrected.

Gene replacement would be much more like the 'global-search-and-replace' function in word processing. In a document, for example, the word IOWA might be misspelled as WIAO. To correct this error, one could direct a word processing program to find WIAO wherever it occurs and to replace it with IOWA. In an analogous way, researchers hope to insert a properly functioning gene into embryonic cells or reproductive cells and to replace the malfunctioning gene in the process. In this way researchers will be able to ensure that a specific, identifiable gene is not transmitted to future generations of a family.

So powerful a technique as transmitting genetic changes might well be considered in a number of situations. One would involve a married couple in which both prospective parents are carriers of similar mutations in the gene that causes cystic fibrosis (CF). The couple decides to have children with the aid of *in vitro* fertilization. Preimplantation diagnosis is performed on the four resulting embryos at the eight-cell stage. One of the four embryos is found to be free of the CF gene, two are discovered to be carriers, while the fourth will be affected with CF. Rather than discarding the carrier and affected embryos, the couple decides to have the gene-replacement technique employed.

Two other situations in which germ-line gene replacement would appear particularly attractive involve conditions that would be difficult if not impossible to treat by means of gene therapy after the embryonic stage of development. In one such scenario, the embryo has a malfunctioning tumour suppressor gene that will be present in all of its cells when it is fully developed and born. It would be difficult to reach all of the individual's cells with a gene therapy treatment after birth. The only known way to reach all of the biological individual's cells is to intervene either before or shortly after fertilization. In the other scenario, a mutation causes severe damage to many brain cells in developing embryos and fetuses – damage that cannot be reversed by gene therapy after birth. The only way to prevent this brain damage is to intervene before the brain begins to develop.

Whether or not the deliberate transmission of genetic changes to future generations will be morally justifiable, if and when gene replacement techniques are quite reliable, is a debatable issue. One argument in favour of germ-line genetic intervention to prevent disease is that it is more efficient than repeating somatic-cell gene therapy generation after generation in at-risk families. A second argument is that the repair of human embryos is more compatible with the health professional's healing role than is preimplantation and selective abortion. Third, parents exercise appropriate parental responsibility by preventing a specific disease from affecting their children and grandchildren. Finally, researchers should be free to develop new methods for treating and preventing disease, even if potential abuses of the techniques they develop can be imagined.

On the other hand, critics of germ-line intervention raise a different set of considerations. One is that alternatives are available for at-risk couples, including adoption, preimplantation diagnosis and selective discard, and prenatal diagnosis and selective abortion. A second argument is that a failed attempt to replace a malfunctioning gene may make the overall condition of a future person worse than it otherwise would have been; in addition, this genetic 'mistake' may not be able to be removed and therefore may be transmitted to multiple future generations. Third, germ-line genetic intervention could be misused by overly ambitious parents to enhance their future children's capabilities; such enhancements may not be in the best interests of the children. Finally, this powerful technique could be employed by politicians, researchers, or others to produce genetically engineered human beings according to their own blueprints.

What will be the implications of germ-line genetic intervention for the Christian faith? At the micro level new questions of responsible parenthood will need to be faced. The Human Genome Project will surely enable the diagnosis of many more genetic diseases, traits, and even predispositions at the prenatal and preimplantation stages of life. We will need to exercise moral discernment both in diagnosing and in responding to the results of these newly available diagnostic tests.

At the macro level, the possibility of passing specific, targeted changes to future generations raises breathtaking possibilities. We should choose our words carefully in describing the new situation that our descendants will face when germ-line techniques are more fully developed. Human beings will not be able to 'control evolution'. Our descendants will, however, be able to reduce the incidence of specific genetic diseases like cystic fibrosis during the course of many generations. In that sense, they will have a direct and deliberate effect on the future course of the human race.

People of faith should not draw back from this awesome possibility. As long as we remember that we are stewards of the divine creation, we can employ even germ-line genetic intervention as a remedy for certain natural evils and as a way to enhance the quality of human life.

NOTES

1. See, for example, the helpful overview by Plomin, Robert, Owen, Michael J. and McGuffin, Peter, 'The Genetic Basis of Complex behaviours', *Science*, vol. 264 (June 17, 1994), pp. 1733–1739.

2. *The Descent of Man and Selection in Relation to Sex* revised ed.; (New York, D. Appleton and Company 1896), Part I, Chapter II (pp. 27–28).

3. London, Murray 1859, p. 213.

4. Bouchard, Thomas J., 'Genes, Environment, and Personality', *Science*, vol. 264 (June 17, 1994), pp. 1700–1701.

5. See Bouchard, op. cit., p. 1700.

6. Herrnstein, Richard J. and Murray, Charles, *The Bell Curve: Intelligence and Class Structure in American Life* (New York, Free Press 1994).

7. On the Wechsler Intelligence Scale, a test that seeks to measure various types of cognitive functioning, see Frank, George, *The Wechsler Enterprise: An Assessment of the*

Development, Structure and Use of the Wechsler Tests of Intelligence (New York, Pergamon Press 1983).

8. See, for example, Plomin et al., op. cit., p. 1734, and Castro, Stephanie D., DeFries, J.C. and Fulker, David W. 'Multivariate Genetic Analysis of Wechsler Intelligence Scale for Children – Revised (WISC–R) Factors', *Behavior Genetics*, vol. 25 (January 1995), 25–32.

9. Castro et al., op. cit.

10. See, for example, the debate that surrounded a conference on genetic factors in violent behaviour that was funded by the National Institutes of Health and convened by the Center for Philosophy and Public Policy at the University of Maryland (Laurie Goodman, 'Crime and Genetics Conference Breeds Further Controversy', *Nature* vol. 377 (September 28, 1995), p. 276).

11. Engelhardt, H. Tristram, Jr., 'Human Nature Technologically Revisited', *Social Philosophy and Policy*, vol 8 (Autumn 1990), p. 188.

12. Brunner, H.G., et al., 'X-Linked Borderline Mental Retardation with Prominent behavioural Disturbance: Phenotype, Genetic Localization, and Evidence for Disturbed Monoamine Metabolism', *American Journal of Human Genetics*, vol 52 (June 1993), p. 1035.

13. Brunner, H.G. et al., 'Abnormal behaviour Associated with a Point Mutation in the Structural Gene for Monoamine Oxidase A', *Science*, vol. 262 (October 22, 1993), p. 579.

14. Eichelman, Burr, 'Bridges from the Animal Laboratory to the Study of Violent or Criminal Individuals', in Hodgins Sheilagh., ed., *Mental Disorder and Crime* (Newbury Park, CA, Sage Publications 1993), pp. 198–200.

15. See Nelson, J. Robert, *On the New Frontiers of Genetics and Religion* (Grand Rapids, MI, Eerdmans 1994), esp. pp110–114, and Cole-Turner, Ronald, *The New Genesis: Theology and the Genetic Revolution* (Louisville, Westminster/John Knox Press 1993).

[9]

The Incentive of Patents

Stephen F. Sherry, JD

Under present US law, whatever people can engineer, including living material – can be patented. Literally 'anything under the sun made by man' is included, according to the US Supreme Court (June 16, 1980) in *Diamond v. Chakrabarty*. History shows that the prospect of obtaining patent rights can have a tremendous impact on the scope and direction of technological development. As Abraham Lincoln observed, 'Patents add fuel to the fire of genius'.[1]

Patents can drive the investment of millions of dollars of private money into the enterprise of technological development. When that happens, those with a substantial investment at stake may exert tremendous influence on decisions about what research to pursue and what applications to develop. The outcome of those decisions cannot help but be affected by the investor's ultimate objective – profit. The question is whether or to what extent the patent system should be permitted to exert that kind of profound influence in the area of biotechnology research and genetic engineering.

PATENTING AS AN INCENTIVE

The founders of America considered the prospect of patent rights so important that they made specific provision for that incentive in the United States Constitution. Congress has been granted broad power to create laws that:

> Promote the Progress of Science and useful Arts, by securing for limited Times to Authors and Inventors the exclusive Right to their respective Writings and Discoveries[2]

Pursuant to that Constitutional mandate, Congress has enacted patent laws that grant a patent holder:

> the right to exclude all others from making, using or selling the patented invention in the United States, without license, for a period of 20 years.[3]

The first patent statute was enacted on April 10, 1790.

Being able to secure exclusive rights for an invention generates an enormous incentive that encourages inventiveness and research

113

efforts. Indeed, some economic experts believe that the availability of patent protection is critical to fostering the development of commercially important inventions. Professor F.M. Scherer of Harvard University's John F. Kennedy School of Government wrote:

> Developing an invention to the point of commercial applicability is costly. The risks of development, while often exaggerated, are also appreciable. To be willing to bear these costs and risks, potential innovators must have some hope of being able to sell their product at a price which exceeds the cost of production, so that they will recoup their development costs plus a premium for risk. But if imitators can swarm in to copy the invention as soon as it has been introduced, post-innovation prices will fall rapidly to the level of production cost, wiping out supra-normal profits for innovators and imitators alike. One would have to be a fool or a philanthropist to invest heavily in invention and development when the imitative steamroller is expected to eliminate profits so quickly and relentlessly. The fundamental argument for a patent system is that patent protection permits the innovator (or inventor) to retard competitive imitation, and hence to anticipate earning supra-normal profits if its contribution in fact proves technically and commercially successful.[4]

This consequent economic power associated with patents is no doubt a driving factor in technological development. Since the issuance of the first patent in the United States, there have been over 5 million patents granted by the federal government.

Technological development and research programmes in the biotechnology industry are subject to the same influences.[5] Perhaps the biotechnology industry is especially sensitive to the impact of potential patent rights because of the usual need for long-term cash commitments to finance protracted development cycles. For example, one US company spent $900,000 over several years to develop a more durable and productive maize hybrid and $600,000 for a similar soybean variety.[6] Genentech and Amgen have each spent millions of dollars researching and developing pharmaceuticals using recombinant DNA technology. The cost and development times are vastly greater for biotech inventions with medical applications.

The Supreme Court's decision in *Diamond v. Chakrabarty*[7] marked the beginning of a dramatic expansion of patent rights available for biotech inventions. The resultant impact of this new economic incentive on the scope and pace of development in biotechnology and genetic engineering is undeniable. Just four months after the Supreme Court's decision, Genentech raised $36 million in one day with its stock offering. A 1984 National Academy of Sciences study estimated that a potential yearly business of between $40 billion and $100 billion lies in the biotechnology industry.[8] In 1988, the American biotech industry reported revenues of $762 million with export sales of $215 million. Those revenues were about double what had been earned in 1987 and quadruple earnings in 1986.[9]

By April 8, 1990 (ten years after the *Chakrabarty* decision), over 7800 patent applications involving genetically engineered life forms were on file in the United States Patent and Trademark Office.[10] During the first quarter of 1991, American biotech companies raised $1 billion through public stock offerings.[11] The growth of the biotech industry has been projected at $40 billion dollars for the next ten years.[12]

Certainly patent protection has stimulated innovation, growth, and competitiveness in the American biotechnology industry. Patent incentives no doubt have accelerated the pace of genetic engineering research. There is, however, a danger lurking beneath the surface of this seeming prosperity, advancement of scientific knowledge, and expanding human ability to shape the world. That danger is complacency and lack of vigilance. Pragmatic concerns focusing on investment opportunities in biotech firms and the promise of deliverance from disease and suffering may have diverted the attention of the American public from exploring the ethical implications of gene manipulation and other aspects of biotechnology as fastidiously as would otherwise have been the case.

If the patent system is providing a powerful encouragement and incentive for development of technology that could be questionable on ethical grounds, who will say so? Who will articulate what restraints or limitations should be imposed on the availability of patent rights for the fruit of research in certain areas of biotechnology. So far, the US Congress and the general American public have simply watched while these matters have been determined by the judicial system. In the absence of public debate and legislative action, the courts will continue to be called upon to make decisions about the extent to which life is patentable. Inevitably, those judicial determinations will profoundly impact the scope and direction of biotech research and, as a consequence, the world our children will inherit. Do we want them to inherit a whirlwind?

PATENTABILITY OF LIFE BEFORE CHAKRABARTY

Following the creation of the patent system, the courts generated a body of judicial precedents which identified certain subject matter as being beyond the scope of patent protection. Such subject matter comprised scientific principles, laws of nature, physical phenomena, abstract ideas, and products of nature.[13]

The products of nature doctrine stated that something which existed previously in nature could not be patented. Using this doctrine, the Patent Office long enforced a policy denying patents for any form of living matter.

That policy was so well established and taken for granted that Congress enacted special legislation to recognize rights for plant breeders who would not otherwise have qualified for protections under the patent laws.[14] That legislation became known as the Plant Patent Act of 1930. Later, Congress enacted further special legislation to permit patents on certain forms of plants – the Plant Variety Protection Act of 1970. However, Congress left inventions relating to life forms based upon micro-organisms, animals, and humans totally unprotected by legislation.

PATENTS FOR MICRO-ORGANISMS – CHAKRABARTY

The *Chakrabarty* case began when the Patent Office denied patent protection for a genetically engineered strain of bacteria capable of breaking down multiple components of crude oil.[15] The invention was a process for introducing specific plasmids capable of breaking down four different oil components into a host Pseudomonas bacteria. The unaltered, naturally occurring Pseudomonas had no ability to degrade oil. When the case reached the United States Supreme Court in 1980, the Court overruled the Patent Office and held that the genetically engineered micro-organism was patentable even though it constituted living matter.

Seven years later, another inventor submitted an application to the Patent Office dealing with living matter. This time, the invention involved a higher life form, a polyploid oyster.[16] The Patent Office Examiner denied the application because it involved an attempt to patent living material.

Appeal was made to the Patent Office Board of Appeals. Although the Board of Appeals denied the inventor a patent on the polyploid oyster, it did expressly recognize that a complex living organism beyond the microscopic world of bacteria was legally subject to patent protection. In response to the decision by the Board of Appeals, the Patent Office issued a policy statement in which it announced that non-naturally occurring non-human multi-cellular living organisms, including animals, would be considered patentable subject matter.[17]

ONE YEAR LATER – THE HARVARD MOUSE

One year after the Patent Office issued its policy decision, it granted United States Patent No. 4,736,866 to Harvard University for an invention in a 'transgenic non-human mammal'. More particularly, the patent was directed to a genetically engineered mouse made to be highly susceptible to cancer. This was the first actual granting of a United States patent on a multi-cellular living organism – a living mammal.[18]

In response to the Harvard Mouse patent, animal rights activists and other groups of concerned citizens attempted to arouse public debate regarding biotech research. They sought legislation that would curtail all patents for living materials.

The general public, however, showed little negative reaction to the Harvard mouse patent.

The ever-expanding scope of patent protection being recognized for living organisms failed to cause a groundswell of concern. As a matter of last resort, the activists sought relief through the judicial route.[19]

In the case of *Animal Legal Defense Fund v. Quigg,* the Patent Office policy of recognizing the patentability of complex, non-human life forms was challenged.[20] The case eventually was tossed out of court on the ground that the Animal Legal Defense Fund had no standing to contest the Patent Office policy. Although avoiding the specific issue raised by the lawsuit, the court took the opportunity to re-affirm the liberal definition that a patent can be granted on living matter provided there is inventive manipulation and the subject matter is not found identically in nature.[21] A year and a half later, the Patent Office issued patents for three more genetically engineered strains of mice.[22]

PATENTING LIVING HUMAN MATERIALS?

The risks associated with manipulating the genetic make-up of complex animal life and, more particularly, human life are not yet well-understood. Nevertheless, the US patent system continues to fuel the fire of private, commercially-based biotechnology research. The judicial system has exerted the only real influence on the issue of patenting life. As we have seen, the courts liberally construe the patent law to encompass 'anything under the sun made by man'.

Congress has remained content to accept the expansive definition of patentable subject matter crafted by the courts. Under such circumstances, there is reason to be concerned about how far the courts may be willing to expand the scope of patentability for living matter. Concern is especially warranted with regard to the question of patenting living human materials.

Since expanding the scope of patent protection encourages research, one could reasonably expect that expanding the scope of patentability to include living human materials will encourage and accelerate genetic engineering research with that focus. The incentive must be balanced by adequate consideration of potential abuses and dangers that might be posed by research directed to manipulating human materials.

At present, no real prohibitions or exclusions exist with respect to patenting living human materials that have been altered by genetic engineering.[23] It may not be possible today to manipulate human genetic material to produce 'enhanced' human beings. It may not yet be possible to create humanoid creatures (animals with human traits). However, now is the appropriate time to explore circumscribing the reach of the patent laws, rather than waiting until we are faced with the arrival of scientific reality – and the vested interest of a biotech industry eager to generate profit from the commercial application of genetically engineered inventions.

Under the present state of US patent law, processes and products related to human germ-line gene therapy could be protected by patents.[24] That research could produce a genetically altered human embryo. A particularly novel and useful embryo could then be patented, cloned and sold. Conceivably, patentable human gene therapy could be the basis for generating patented transgenic humans or transgenic embryos. Indeed, the present patent laws may create an incentive for research directed to altering the human germ line and developing genetically altered human materials.

The United States Patent Office attempted to eliminate this concern by recognizing, as a matter of its own policy, only patent applications for 'non-human' organisms.[25] The problem is that the Patent Office policy directly contradicts the plain language of the Supreme Court's *Chakrabarty* decision. Humans made by 'man' were not excluded by the Supreme Court from the scope of patent protection.

The Patent Office stated that transgenic humans could not be patentable because the 13th Amendment to the United States Constitution, which prohibits slavery and involuntary servitude, would be violated. If this were true, then the Patent Office statement limiting patents to 'non-human' organisms is superfluous and unnecessary. In fact, the patent right is only an exclusionary right. A patent gives its owner the right to exclude others from using the invention without permission, but it does not operate to grant the owner any affirmative rights to use the invention. Thus, the 13th Amendment would not be implicated by the mere granting of the patent right.[26]

In any event, the Patent Office has already granted patents for some human biologics, such as hybridomas and immortalized cell lines.[27] Therefore, the Patent Office exclusion of human organisms would not seem to extend to the cellular level or even the level of tissues. Further, the Patent Office policy statement does not mention anything about processes.

An inventor could potentially control the market for transgenic humans or transgenic embryos by patenting the method of gene transfer, rather than by attempting to patent the product of the gene transfer itself. Patents covering a method of creating human organisms grant *de facto* rights to the organisms themselves, unless someone invents a different route to produce the same product. Because genes themselves may be patentable, an inventor might be able to patent both a given gene and the method of using it in gene therapy. That would create yet another avenue for controlling and exploiting the creation of transgenic humans or transgenic embryos without necessarily patenting the end product itself.

Consistent with the current law, a genetically altered human being would not be considered a human being. The patent law has already recognized that a genetically altered mouse is distinct from a naturally occurring, non-altered mouse. That same distinction may be sufficient for opening the door to the granting of a patent on genetically altered human life.

One commentator posited the hypothetical 'near-human' which has been genetically engineered so there is no brain.[28] Such an organism could be a source for harvesting organs for transplantation. 'Near-humans' could become a preferred vehicle for medical research on drugs and surgical techniques because they would not feel pain and animal subjects would no longer be needed. Additionally, a 'near-human' would be the ideal surrogate womb.[29]

Obviously, the hypothetical is an extreme example of what biotechnology research may be capable of in the future. Yet, it serves as a useful basis for pointing out that a central difficulty in discussing this area is definitional – we have no workable definition of the term 'human being'. Unless the term 'human being' is defined, great discretion is left in the hands of the Patent Office, researchers and the courts to make that determination. As research progresses, ultimately the definition will be provided. It would seem that any creation short of a 'full human being' is patentable subject matter.

In trying to define what a 'full human being' is, we run the risk of being over-inclusive or under-inclusive. The former would cause the term 'human being' to encompass creatures we may now consider higher animals. Being under-inclusive could result in excluding sentient altered creatures who may morally and humanely deserve to have legal protection to live as a person.

One option could be to start from the premise that a creature born to human parents is necessarily a human being. However, this requires a definition that establishes the parents first as humans and is ultimately circular. A second option might use the benchmark of rational deliberation and choice to identify a human being. That does not really get us very far, since many animal behaviours suggest rational deliberation and reasoned choice.[30] Furthermore, a severely retarded person might not have the ability to make rational choices, yet we have not questioned his or her right to full legal protection under the law and the right to live as a human being in our society. One might suggest using genetic make up as a definition of a human organism, but how much genetic material must a creature possess to be considered human?

Even if we were able to produce an acceptable definition of a 'full human being', we would still need to confront the issue of whether some limitations should be placed on the availability of patents for human-related biotech inventions. The patent laws should not contribute to the encouragement of research in areas where ethical concerns would mandate imposing restraints. The pursuit of knowledge and the encouragement of that effort through the patent law is not excused from the operation of conscience. As Francois Rabelais observed long ago, 'Knowledge without conscience is the ruination of the soul'.[31]

History has shown that the judicial system is unlikely to step in and wrestle with the ethical questions regarding the placing of limits on the patenting of human living material.[32] Even if the courts were willing to step in, we should not ignore our responsibility to address these issues.

God is righteous[33] and throughout the Bible, God calls men and women to righteousness. That call is applicable at all levels of society and is relevant to every area of civil and personal life.

For law to be righteous, it must operate in civil affairs so that it conforms with God's standards of justice and enhances the welfare of the community. Laws must not be wicked, evil or wrong – nor should they promote wicked, evil or wrong outcomes. Patent laws cannot be an exception.

God gives people the responsibility to order society so that God's divine order is maintained and people are encouraged to do God's will. We, like Solomon, should pray for righteousness that we might govern righteously through the law.[34] We cannot act as if we are just animals with bigger brains, denying the image of God stamped on us.

> Our humanity were a poor thing were it not for the divinity which stirs within us.
>
> – Francis Bacon (1561–1626)

We have a responsibility to ensure that the patent laws are not used to foster means of oppression and injustice. God will judge us for how we use the law and whether we permit others to be mistreated, or creation to be corrupted.[35]

Some are willing to worship science and technology and place their faith and hope in what humankind can create. They adhere to the presupposition that advances in science are essentially neutral and only the application of science poses a threat. However, history suggests a more nuanced perspective: that major advances in the technological competence of humankind typically lead to revolutionary changes in the economic and political structure of society. The advancement of biotechnology, encouraged by the economic incentive of the patent laws, will probably do the same. Strict ethical parameters are essential. Let us hope that in the future, we will not be echoing the lament of Charles Lindbergh:

> But I have seen the science I worshiped and the aircraft I loved destroying the civilization I expected them to serve.

The issue is what is wise. We need wisdom in deciding what should and should not be encouraged in the area of genetic research through the incentive of the patent laws. At what point does human manipulation and patenting of living organisms appropriate to humanity a sovereignty over the created order that is properly reserved to God alone? Do human beings really have the moral standing and wisdom to design their own genetic makeup? Is human ingenuity really capable of controlling the forces it may unleash through such an enterprise?

Dr. Marshall Nirenberg, who won the Nobel Prize for his work in genetics, wrote:

> When man becomes capable of instructing his own cells, he must refrain from doing so until he has sufficient wisdom to use this knowledge for the benefit of mankind.[36]

Ethical considerations should inform and control the application of the patent laws.

Patents are by definition a utilitarian legal construct with an economic purpose. That which falls within the scope of patent protection cannot escape the inevitable effect of commodification. As a society, should we resist the commodification of certain subject matter? If so, then we may need to impose appropriate limits on the availability of patent rights for such subject matter. Presently, the patent laws are adrift on a sea of pragmatism where seemingly the only voice being heard is the one of economic necessity. That voice is motivated by pecuniary considerations and the need for industrial protection and preservation. The real question is not simply whether the 'cost' in ethical terms of an invention's use warrants offering an incentive for its development. Rather, we must address whether the social 'price' of offering the incentive is already so high that further cost assessment is unnecessary.

NOTES

1. Lincoln was the only president of the United States ever to be granted a patent.
2. United States Constitution, Article I, Section 8.
3. Title 35 of the United States Code at Section 154.
4. Industrial Market Structure and Economic Performance (Chicago: Rand McNally, 1970).
5. Scalise, David G. and Nugent, Daniel, 'Patenting Living Matter In The European Community: Diriment Of The Draft Directive', *Fordham International Law Journal*, vol.16 (1992–1993), pp.990–1032. For example,

'By early 1985, Europe's biotechnology industry found itself at a competitive disadvantage vis-a-vis its international rivals in a deficit that was fast approaching perilous dimensions. Its predicament was attributable to the woefully deficient patent rights recognized by most European nations pertaining to the protection of industrial property. For many of Europe's biotechnology companies the solution was to relocate outside the European Community ("EC") into countries that fostered innovation with liberal patent laws' (p. 991).

6. Whaite, Robin & Jones, Nigel, 'Biotechnological Patents in Europe – The Draft Directive', *European Intellectual Property Review*, vol.11 (1989), p.146.

7. 447 U.S. 330 (1980).

8. Sellers, Michael E., 'Patenting Nonnaturally Occurring, Man-Made Life: A Practical Look at the Economic, Environmental, and Ethical Challenges Facing "Animal Patents" ', *Arkansas Law Review*, vol.47 (1994), p.284.

9. Jones, Terri A., 'Patenting Transgenic Animals: When The Cat's Away, The Mice Will Play', *Vermont Law Review*, vol.17 (1993), p.884.

10. 'Technology Lets Gene Out of Bottle', *Chicago Tribune*, (April 8, 1990), p.1.

11. Crawford, Mark, 'Wall Street Takes Stock of Biotechnology', *New Scientist*, vol.132 (November 23, 1991), p.36.

12. *Coordinated Framework for Regulation of Biotechnology: Hearing Before the Subcommittee on Investigations and Oversight and the Subcommittee on Natural Resources, Agriculture Research and Environment and the Subcommittee on Science, Research and Technology of the House Committee on Science and Technology, 99th Cong., 2nd Sess. 6 (1986) (statement by Rep. Schneider, R.I.).*

13. Chaucer, Bradford, 'Life, The Patent Office And Everything: Patentability Of Lifeforms Created Through Bioengineering Techniques', *Bridgeport Law Review*, vol.9 (1988), pp.413–447.

14. Czarnetzky, John M., 'Altering Nature's Blueprints For Profit: Patenting Multicellular Animals', *Virginia Law Review*, vol.74, (1988), pp.1327–1362.

15. Darr, Frank P., 'Expanding Patent Coverage: Policy Implications of Diamond v. Chakrabarty', *Ohio State Law Journal*, vol.42, (1981), pp.1061–1083.

16. Tropper, Matthew B., 'Patentability of Genetically Engineered Life-Forms: Legal Issues and Solutions', *The John Marshall Law Review*, vol.25, (1991), pp.119–142.

17. King, Robert L., 'The Modern Industrial Revolution: Transgenic Animals and the Patent Law', *Washington University Law Quarterly*, vol.67, (1989), pp.653–659.

18. Landau, Michael B., 'Multicellular Vertebrate Mammals as "Patentable Subject Matter" Under 35 U.S.C. § 101: Promotion of Science and the Useful Arts or an Open Invitation for Abuse?', *Dickinson Law Review*, vol.97 (Winter 1993), pp.203–226.

19. Hecht, Elizabeth Joy, 'Beyond *Animal Legal Defense Fund v. Quigg*: The Controversy Over Transgenic Animal Patents Continues', *The American University Law Review*, vol.41 (1992), pp.1023–1074.

20. Bateman, Rand, '*Animal Legal Defense Fund v. Quigg*: The Illogical Climax to the Animal Patenting Debate', *Journal of Contemporary Law*, vol.19, no.1 (1993), pp.115–141.

21. Animal Legal Defense Fund v. Quigg, 932 F.2d 920 (Fed.Cir.1991).

22. Sellers, Michael E., 'Patenting Nonnaturally Occurring, Man-Made Life: A Practical Look at the Economic, Environmental, and Ethical Challenges Facing "Animal Patents" ', *Arkansas Law Review*, vol.47 (1994), pp.269–297.

23. O'Connor, Kevin W., 'Patenting Animals and Other Living Things', *Southern California Law Review*, vol.65 (1991), pp.597–621.

24. Burk, Dan L., 'Patenting Transgenic Human Embryos: A Nonuse Cost Perspective', *Houston Law Review*, vol.30 (1993), pp.1597–1669.

25. In April of 1987, the United States Patent and Trademark Office promulgated a rule allowing for the patenting of animals. That rule is printed at vol.1077 of the Official Gazette of the Patent Office, p.24 (April 21, 1987).

26. Fishman, Rachel E., 'Patenting Human Beings: Do Sub-Human Creatures Deserve Constitutional Protection?', *American Journal of Law & Medicine*, vol.XV, no.4, pp.461–482.

27. *See, e.g.*, Moore v. Regents of Univ. Of Cal., 793 P.2d 479 (Cal.1990), cert. denied, 499 U.S. 936 (1991).

28. Walker, Russell H., 'Patent Law – Should Genetically Engineered Human Beings Be Patentable?', *Memphis State University Law Review*, vol.22 (1991), pp.101–117.

29. *Id.* at 108–9.

30. Orangutans have limited mode of speaking and are monogamous. Therefore, one might argue for the existence of rational deliberation and choice in their behaviour. If so, the definition of 'human being' could apply to orangutans.

31. Compare with Merges, Robert P., 'Intellectual Property In Higher Life Forms: The Patent System And Controversial Technologies', *Maryland Law Review*, vol.47 (1988), pp.1051–1075. For example,

> But avenues of scientific research must not be closed off in fear of what we will find out. Technology is neither inherently good nor inherently bad it just is, until it is applied in a specific context. Patents on new technology should be granted, reserving the right to regulate specific applications. This is the only sensible course (p. 1075).

Id. at 1075.

32. Consider for example, Judge Richard A. Posner, who is the chief judge of the United States Court of Appeals for the Seventh Circuit. In an article on Judge Posner in the National Law Journal dated June 17, 1996, he is reported to have confirmed his comfort 'with the idea that people are just "monkeys with big brains" '. I would expect Judge Posner to construe the Supreme Court's decision in *Chakrabarty* as endorsing the patentability of genetically engineered human life.

33. See 2 Chr. 12:6; Ps. 7:9; 103:17; Zep. 3:5; and Zec. 8:8.

34. See Ps. 72.

35. Amos 2:4–16.

36. Manspeizer, David, 'The Cheshire Cat, the March Hare, and the Harvard Mouse: Animal Patents Open Up a New, Genetically-Engineered Wonderland', *Rutgers Law Review*, vol.43 (1991), p.438.

10

Genetic Testing and Confidentiality

C. Christopher Hook, MD

'Declare the past, diagnose the present, foretell the future: Practise these acts. As to diseases, make a habit of two things – to help, or at least do no harm.' So wrote Hippocrates in *The Epidemics*.[1] Foretell the future. Prognostication is part of the work and duty of the healer. The explosion in genetic information provides us with an opportunity not just to diagnose a present malady, but also as never before to discern the risks for the future development of disease.

Like all medical knowledge genetic information can be quite beneficial. It can empower the patient and the healer. The individual who has been found not to possess a gene for a terrible disorder such as Huntington's Disease, or a cancer gene such as the breast and ovarian cancer gene BRCA1, may gain release from anxiety or the freedom to engage in career and family planning. To those who possess so-called cancer genes, genetic knowledge may provide an important impetus to reduce other risk factors for subsequent cancer development through increased medical surveillance, avoidance of environmental carcinogens, the employment of chemoprevention, or the use of prophylactic measures such as prophylactic mastectomy.

GENETIC TESTING

This potential for doing good by preventing harm provides genetic testing with its moral justification. As God affirms in Ezekiel 33:6, 'If the watchman sees the sword coming and does not blow the trumpet to warn the people, and the sword comes and takes the life of one of them, that man will be taken away because of his sin, but I will hold the watchman accountable for his blood.' We must reduce harm and injury whenever possible.

In spite of genetic information's potential for good, in a fallen world that which is beneficial can also cause harm. While genetic information may be helpful, it can become an instrument of discrimination and prejudice, a source of fear and anxiety.

Before proceeding further in examining this potential for good and harm, we should clarify some terms. Genetic tests examine whether or not certain individuals or groups of individuals have particular abnormalities in their genetic code. While 'testing' can therefore be carried out on specific individuals or larger groups, sometimes people use 'testing' to refer to individuals, in contrast with 'screening' to refer to larger groups or populations. When an individual is tested there is usually a family history to suggest that the individual is at increased risk of a disorder. When a population is screened, the hope is to reduce the impact or incidence of an illness on a large scale. The individuals in the population screening may have no family history suggesting increased risk. While many of the concerns about the use of genetic information pertain to both testing and screening, the approaches are also different in important ways.

A genetic test must be evaluated like any other medical test. Its sensitivity and specificity, that is, its ability to detect the abnormal state when present and to confirm the normal state when disease is absent, is crucial. When one is attempting to predict the potential risks of developing a serious or life-threatening illness, accuracy is critical. With regard to a known genetic mutation, direct testing will eventually be able to produce complete accuracy. However, many genes carry multiple mutations. There are over 300 known mutations in the Factor IX gene which may lead to abnormal clotting function[2]. Recent studies have shown over 100 mutations in the breast and ovarian cancer susceptibility gene, BRCA1[3]. Some mutations, however, may be neutral polymorphisms, that is, mutations that have no clinical significance. With such a large number of mutations possible, the testing may not detect every case that could have clinical significance. For example, consider the inherited disorder Activated Protein C Resistance, which predisposes patients to form blood clots. In the majority of cases, this disorder is caused by a specific abnormality in the Factor V molecule. Molecular genetic analysis looking for this specific mutation picks up the majority of cases. But if one of the other mutations is present, the genetic test may be falsely negative. In other words, the patient may have a negative test but also have the disorder because he or she possesses one of the other mutations.[4].

A test's lack of complete accuracy does not completely invalidate its potential use for an individual, but it does underscore the importance of a patient's understanding the limitations of a test and giving a truly informed consent prior to its use. However, when such tests are employed as screening tools for a larger population, there is additional cause for concern as the following scenario illustrates. Assume a breast cancer gene is present in 1 out of every 200 members of the population. At the present time the sensitivity of the test for this gene – that is, its ability to detect those patients with the abnormal gene – is 90%. The specificity (accuracy) in identifying the absence of the gene is also 90%. If we tested 10,000 individuals, according to the prevalence of the gene in the population, there would be 50 true carriers. However, with 90% sensitivity, only 45 of those carriers would test positive and 5 would falsely test negative. In light of the 90% specificity, out of the 9,950 who did not have the gene, 8,955 would be correctly identified as negative. However, of that same population, 995 patients would falsely be identified as carriers. Tremendous anxiety and inappropriate management would probably result. For a test to be appropriately used as a population screening tool, therefore, it must be as close to 100% sensitive and specific as possible.

Another issue, the penetrance of the gene, can also confound the reliability of this type of testing. Penetrance is the rate of actual expression of the gene. Not all genes are expressed 100% of the time. Accordingly, patients can have an abnormal gene, but if that gene is not expressed, they will not suffer the disorder associated with it. We are still in the process of learning the rates of penetrance of some of the mutations that can now be detected. For all of the above reasons, tests for the breast cancer gene and most other cancer-associated genes should be considered experimental at the present time rather than ready for use in wide-spread testing or screening[5].

Before a patient undergoes a test with potential ambiguities, he or she should be informed and be able to provide voluntary consent to the testing. Included in the consent process should be information on how the test is performed. Is there a requirement for other family members to be tested, as necessary in linkage studies? If so, what are the chances of the results and/or identity of the patient being disclosed to family members? What are the sensitivity and specificity of the test? What is the potential to make other discoveries such as the fact that one is not the genetic parent of one's child? What are the implications of the testing? Can we do anything about a positive result? Will undesirable decisions have to be made based upon the information, such as to proceed with an abortion? What are the other implications, such as the potential for insurance or employment discrimination?

PROTECTING CONFIDENTIALITY

One of the most important questions that arises regarding genetic information is: Who should have access to this information? In addition to the patient, should other at-risk family members be notified of the results of testing? What about a potential mate? Should parents have the right to obtain this information about their children? Since employers need to hire employees who can best perform the required tasks, should an employer have access to such information if the employee's behaviour or reliability is involved? Insurers have long been in the business of assessing risk in order to identify who is eligible for insurance and what it should cost. Genetic information could be an extremely important factor in identifying future risk. Should insurers therefore have access to such information? When insurers pay for the test, do they automatically have a right to the information? Does the government have the right to test potential employees, particularly those seeking positions in the Armed Forces or public office, to identify possible deficiencies that could affect their performance on the job? Or in the final analysis should only the patient and his or her primary physician have access to this information? In other words, is confidentiality an absolute principle? Can it realistically be maintained?

Protecting the confidentiality of a patient's medical history is a longstanding tradition in medicine. In The Oath, Hippocrates stated, 'And whatever I shall see or hear in the course of my profession,. . .if it be what should not be published abroad, I will never divulge, holding such things to be holy secrets.'[6] This obligation may be even more important with regard to genetic information. Such information has already been used for discriminatory purposes. When screening for sickle cell disease was initiated in the 1970s, many African-Americans with sickle cell trait lost their jobs or health insurance or were dismissed from the military when they were healthy and at no risk of developing problems[7]. Billings *et al.* reported the results of a survey performed to assess the incidence and types of genetic discrimination that patients were experiencing[8]. A mailing was sent to solicit cases from 1119 professionals working in the fields of clinical genetics, genetics counselling, disability medicine, pediatrics, and social services in the New England area. The investigators received 42 responses of which 29 met sufficient criteria for further analysis. Of those 29 responses, 41 separate incidents of discrimination were reported; 32 incidents involved insurance including application or coverages for health, life, disability, mortgage and auto insurance and 7 involved employment. Many of the individuals involved had undergone testing only because another family member had been affected with a genetic condition; they themselves were still healthy. One patient with hereditary hemochromatosis, a disease of iron absorption and storage which can be well managed, was denied insurance. He stated: 'I might as well have had AIDS'. Another case involved the brother of an individual who had Gaucher's disease[9]. This brother was screened and the results suggested that he was an asymptomatic carrier. When he applied for a governmental job and included the history of his testing in the application, he was denied the job because he was 'a carrier like sickle cell'.

In April, 1996 a study from Stanford and Harvard Universities was published documenting 206 cases of genetic discrimination by businesses, insurance agencies, schools, blood banks, and the military. Included among the cases was a situation in which a woman's HMO would pay for an abortion of the woman's fetus that carried a gene for cystic fibrosis, but would not pay for the birth and care of the child if it were born. Another involved a social worker who was fired when her employer learned that Huntington's Disease affected a member of her family. Previously the worker had received excellent reviews and had gone through three promotions. The authors suggest that nearly 50% of people who have a known gene that could predispose them to disease have experienced adverse discrimination. The study was sharply criticized by insurance groups, who claimed that it was anecdotal and based on stories from members of support groups for genetic diseases.[10]

One approach to preventing discrimination and protecting confidentiality has been to consider genetic information to be different from other medical information. It therefore is kept separate from the patient's medical record, sometimes in secondary or sham histories. Strict confidentiality, however, is very difficult to maintain. If the results of genetic testing are to be of benefit to the patient, they will generally affect patient behaviour or influence the course of care. Heightened surveillance procedures or prophylactic interventions may be employed, and these will be reported in the patient's medical history. Once they are reported, maintaining confidentiality from insurers, other health care providers, etc., will not be possible. Even if the reasons for various aspects of the patient's care are not explicitly stated, the astute observer will surmise what they are. More fundamentally, it is not good policy to exclude certain aspects of the patient's health status from the medical record. All individuals who are charged with making health decisions for the patient should have access to that material. If no record is formally kept in the patient's history, then the information may be transmitted inaccurately to other care providers by word of the patient. What will not be communicated may be the limits of the testing that was employed and cautions involved in its interpretation. If such information could be recorded openly in the patient's record, then there would be far less opportunity for misunderstanding and miscommunication during the course of treatment.

Mehlman *et al.* have proposed that genetic counselling and testing be done on an anonymous basis[11]. This approach is flawed for the same reasons as having a sham history. In general, if genetic testing has advanced to the point of producing a result that will be shared with the patient, this result must be included in the patient's regular medical record. Eleven states have anti-genetic discrimination laws of some kind regarding insurance and/or employment[12]. Strict across-the-board legislation of this type passed for the entire United States is the only realistic solution to the problem of discrimination. Patients and physicians should not have to adopt dishonest or secretive behaviours which cannot succeed and are counterproductive to the overall care of the patient.

There are other major challenges to confidentiality as well. For example, should a potential spouse have a right to information about his or her future partner's genetic status? As procreation is a significant feature of many, if not most, marriages, should the risk to the potential offspring be known prior to engaging in the commitment of matrimony? Certainly the type of disorder and the mode of inheritance will have an influence on potential solutions to this problem.

For those disorders that are transmitted in on autosomal recessive fashion, such as cystic fibrosis or Tay-Sachs disease, one potential model is the Chevre Dor Yeshorim programme created by The Committee for Prevention of Jewish Genetic Diseases[13]. In an autosomal recessive process the abnormality is not clinically manifest unless the individual has two abnormal genes. If a person has only one abnormal gene, that individual is a carrier of the gene but may not experience the abnormal condition. However, if that person marries another carrier, each of their children has a one in four chance of inheriting two abnormal genes and manifesting the disease. One in 25 Ashkenazi Jews is a carrier of the Tay-Sachs gene and one in 25 is a carrier of the cystic fibrosis gene. In the Dor Yeshorim programme, young men and women of maritable age are assigned a number. Their blood is then tested, with the only identifier being that number; names are not recorded. When a match is proposed, a prospective couple can call and give their numbers. The couple is then informed whether the marriage can proceed safely or if their children would have a one in four risk of having either Tay-Sachs or cystic fibrosis.

To a close community such as the Orthodox Jews, this programme has been helpful in preventing the labelling of 'tainted blood' that could stigmatize young men and women. Only if both members of the proposed couple are carriers is the genetic status revealed, and then only to the couple. If the couple receives word of the risk and calls off the proposed marriage, no specific explanation must be given. While anonymous testing is usually problematic, this type of anonymous testing can be acceptable because the carrier status has no influence on the remainder of the patients' health care – only on their decisions regarding marriage and procreation. The programme has been extremely well received by the Jewish population it serves, and many tragic family situations have been averted. This approach has the added advantage of not relying on disease status after a child has been conceived. There is no temptation to terminate the child's life before birth, and consequently this type of a programme is consistent with the Jewish and Christian reverence for life.

Consider, however, a somewhat different scenario. What if the patient has several family members with Huntington's Disease, an autosomal dominant disorder, and testing shows that the patient has a high probability of contracting Huntington's Disease herself?[16] She is going to get married soon. In discussions you learn that the patient has not shared with her fiancé the family history of Huntington's Disease, nor her likelihood of suffering from the disease later in life. The patient states that she does not want the fiancé to know this information, for fear he would no longer want to get married. A similar challenge to the requirement of confidentiality could be envisioned where an individual refuses to allow other family members to be notified of their potential risk and need for testing after the patient has tested positive for some serious genetic disorder. Is there an obligation to maintain strict confidentiality in these circumstances, or is the caregiver obligated to warn others of potential risk?

George Annas and his colleagues have proposed a Genetic Privacy Act according to which no such duty to breach confidentiality exists legally; and they would strictly prohibit any disclosure of genetic information to relatives over a patient's refusal[15]. Annas writes, 'This "no exception rule" also maximizes the privacy between individuals, who receive services that result in private genetic information, and their health care providers. It also places the responsibility for informing relatives of their potential genetic risks on the family member who has such knowledge, which is where we believe it morally belongs. Further, we think it is reasonable to assume that with proper counseling and guidance from supportive and informed practitioners, family members will act in a protective manner toward other family members[16].' Lori Andrews adds that trying to protect other individuals will have serious downstream effects. It will transform a right to disclose into a duty to disclose – a duty that will be hard to limit legally. Any relative who had not been contacted could potentially sue the caregiver. Accordingly, Andrews maintains, it is best to maintain a strict wall and not allow any disclosure to occur without the patient's consent[17].

BREACHING CONFIDENTIALITY

While these arguments are strong and total confidentiality has a certain practical appeal, confidentiality without exceptions poses ethical problems. People do at times choose to conceal vital genetic information from a relative who needs it, and no amount of counselling will induce the patient to do the right thing. The motivations for withholding such information usually include self-ishness, spitefulness, anger, and/or some interpersonal conflict within the family. None of these reasons overrides the moral requirement of preventing major suffering or preserving life. Re-member Ezekiel 33:6. Family members do have a moral obligation to inform their affected relatives, but caregivers must also be 'on watch' to prevent harm and illness.

The difficulty of establishing legal limits to a potential duty to inform is insufficient moral justification for prohibiting the rightful sharing of this information to protect known individuals at risk. Physicians have a higher moral calling than minimizing legal risk. Confidentiality is an important principle; but it is not absolute. In some situations there are competing obligations, some of which are greater than confidentiality. One of these is the duty to protect and preserve life. In Jewish moral theology only three laws are more important than the obligation to heal or save life: the prohibitions against idolatry, adultery, and murder[18]. This reverence for life is also characteristic of Christian ethics, as discussed in the final three chapters of this book. Such reverence challenges us to act when confronted by a patient's irresponsibility.

Two groups, the President's Commission for the Study of Ethical Problems in Medicine and Biomedical and Behavioral Research in 1983[19] and the Committee on Genetic Risks of the Institute of Medicine in 1994[20], have identified conditions under which confidentiality could ethically be breached and relatives informed about genetic risks. In their view, relatives could be informed if: 1) all attempts to elicit voluntary disclosure from the patient have failed; 2) there is a high probability of irreversible or fatal harm to the relative without disclosure; 3) the disclosure of the information will prevent the harm; 4) the disclosure is limited to the information necessary for the diagnosis and/or treatment of the relative.

Admittedly, the question of whom to inform could generate a never-ending list, but parents, siblings, and offspring constitute the primary people in view. This group comprises those individuals that are most likely to be affected. If subsequent testing of a relative is positive, then those in a similar familial relationship to that individ-ual could be informed, and so on. Legislation could be crafted that would explicitly allow the disclosure of protective information to these individuals while barring disclosure to others except under unusual specified conditions. Such legislation would safeguard both physicians and patients from unwarranted expectations or requests for information.

The finding of a genetic predisposition to a serious illness such as Huntington's Disease or cancer can produce a tremendous change in a person's life and evoke significant emotional responses. While we all know that we are going to die, we nevertheless are very concerned about how we will die. The thought of being transformed by a severely dementing illness or enduring the ravages of metastatic cancer is frightening, even to those of us who know our eternal future is secure in Christ's hands. Studies have investigated the psychological and social consequences of being tested for Huntington's Disease. In one survey, 11% said they would consider suicide if they were found to be positive for the Huntington's gene. 5% said they would commit suicide. 40% of patients who test positive for the Huntington's gene develop severe depression. Others develop sexual promiscuity and impulsiveness[21]. Patients who know they have a high susceptibility to cancer either through familial risk factors or through genetic testing experience strong emotional consequences as well. Lehrman found that of a group of 121 patients with first degree relatives with ovarian cancer, 80% felt that they would become depressed if they tested positive for the BRCA1 gene. 32% thought that this information would impair their quality of life[22]. Kash *et al.* found that 27% of women at a high risk for breast cancer experience psychological distress and are in need of counselling[23].

Negative results of genetic testing can also induce emotional/psychological problems. 10 to 20% of patients found to be negative for the Huntington's gene experience significant difficulties. Some of these problems are the result of needing to confront consequences of decisions made when patients assumed they were going to contract Huntington's Disease. Survivor guilt has also been a significant factor[24]. Lehrman found that 25% of women with a mother, sister, and/or daughter who had a history of ovarian cancer indicated they would feel guilty if they themselves were found to be negative for the BRCA1 gene[25]. Because of the potential emotional consequences, such genetic testing should be voluntary and informed. In addition, providers of genetic testing have an obligation to ensure that patients receive adequate counselling before and after the testing and that later counselling is available to help patients deal with negative consequences should they occur.

Two further questions arise at this point. First, what are our obligations to act upon the results of genetic testing? Is there an obligation to forgo procreation? Linus Pauling, the Nobel Prize laureate, has stated that carriers of cystic fibrosis who have children 'add to the amount of human suffering and should feel guilty for their actions'.[26] Bentley Glass, one of the past presidents of the American Association for the Advancement of Science, has maintained, 'No parent will have the right to burden society with a malformed or mentally incompetent child.'[27] As Christians we can reply that every life is precious regardless of its genetic constitution or physical affliction or impairment. Accordingly, there is no strict obligation to refrain from procreation. It is between the individual and God to determine if having genetically-related children is a good idea. For the Christian there is no such concept as 'wrongful life', and we should resist policies of forced or coerced testing, sterilization or abortion. Testing and the decision not to bear offspring may be wise or desirable but it should not be mandated.

A second question that arises at this point is whether or not parents should be able to have their children tested for genetic predisposition to various diseases. Can parents have their child submit a specimen for linkage analysis to assist other family members in diagnosis? If the testing will lead to interventions that can benefit the child prior to the age of majority, such testing is permissible and can be encouraged. However, if the testing is presymptomatic testing, e.g., for a late onset malignancy or Huntington's Disease, testing should be prohibited until children reach the age of majority or reproductive activity and can give their own informed consent. If information gained through testing may influence a child's sexual activity, then it is appropriate to consider testing as long as the child's informed consent is obtained (to the extent that the child is able to provide it). In the case of collecting a specimen for linkage analysis to benefit another family member, testing is permissible with parental consent as long as no results of that child's studies are shared with the parents, additional family members, or the child until he or she can provide informed consent.

Parents may also wish to test their unborn children through prenatal testing. If the testing is to assist the family in knowing how to prepare to care for a child, it may well be morally acceptable. The presence of a genetic disease, however, is not sufficient grounds for the termination of an innocent life through abortion, as Scott Rae explains in the chapter that follows. But what of blastomere separation and genetic testing in conjunction with *in vitro* fertilization? If some of the embryos have a genetic anomaly and others do not, should we implant only those embryos without the genetic problem? A full discussion of the ethical questions raised by *in vitro* fertilization is beyond the scope of this chapter, except to affirm that there is a parental obligation for the implantation of all of the viable embryos created. As such, genetic discrimination between embryos becomes moot. That there are often more embryos created than can be reasonably implanted is not sufficient reason to condone preimplantation testing; rather it raises serious concerns about the moral acceptability of *in vitro* fertilization procedures.

Genetic testing presents us with amazing diagnostic resources and the potential to alter the natural history of some diseases for some patients. In other cases our new knowledge may predict the future but not enable us to do anything about it. As Tiresias confronted Oedipus the King in Sophocles' tragedy, 'It is but sorrow to be wise when wisdom profits not.'[28] Let us humbly go before the Almighty, seeking God's wisdom and guidance, which in contrast to our own is true and always profitable.

NOTES

1. Hippocrates, *Epidemics 1, XI. Hippocrates, Volume I* trans. WHS Jones. (Cambridge, Harvard University Press 1964.) p. 165.

2. Mosher, Deane F. 'Disorders of Coagulation', in Bennett, J. Claude and Plum, F. (ed) Cecil Textbook of Medicine, 20th Edition. (Philadelphia, W.B. Saunders Company 1996.)

3. Collins, Francis S., 'BRCA1 – Lots of Mutations, Lots of Dilemmas.' *N. Engl. J. Med.* 334:186–188, (1996).

4. Dahlback, Bjorn, 'New Molecular Insights into the Genetics of Thrombophilia', *Thrombosis and Hemostasis* 74:139–148, (1995).

5. Collins, Francis S., 'BRCA1 – Lots of Mutations, Lots of Dilemmas', *N. Engl. J. Med.* 334:186–188, (1996).

6. Hippocrates, 'The Oath', in *Hippocrates, Volume 1*, trans. W.H.S. Jones. (Cambridge, Harvard University Press 1964), p. 301.

7. Kenen, Regina H. and Schmidt, Robert M, 'Stigmatization of Carrier Status: Social Implications of Heterozygote Genetic Screening Programs', *Am. J. Public Health* 68:1116–1120, (1978).

8. Billings, Paul R., Kohn, Mel A., deCuevas, Margaret, et al., 'Discrimination as a Consequence of Genetic Testing', *Am. J. Hum. Genet.* 50:476–482, (1992).

9. Gaucher's Disease is an enzyme deficiency resulting in the accumulation of a material in some of the white blood cells that can manifest as enlargement of the spleen and liver and create other problems. 10. *AP on-line. Pentagon Yields on DNA samples.* (Associated Press April 11 1996).

11. Mehlman, Maxwell J., Kodish, Eric D., Whitehouse, Peter, Zin, Arthur B., et. al., 'The Need for Anonymous Genetic Counseling and Testing', *Am. J. Hum. Genetic.* 58:393–397, (1996).

12. Hudson, Cathy L., Rothenberg, Karen H., Andrews, Lorie B., Ellis Kahn, Mary Jo, and Collins, Francis S., 'Genetic Discrimination and Health Insurance: An Urgent Need for Reform', *Science* 270:391–393, (1995).

13. Rosner, Fred. 'Screening for Tay-Sachs Disease: A Note of Caution', *J. Clin. Ethics* 2:251–252, (1991).

14. Huntington's Disease is an incurable late onset disease of the central nervous system. It leads to a devastating dementia and involuntary movements. Its symptoms usually begin to appear in the fourth or fifth decade.

15. Annas, George J., Glantz, Leonard H., and Roche, Patricia A., *The Genetic Privacy Act and Commentary*. Copies may be obtained by contacting Dr. Annas at Health Law Department, Boston University School of Public Health, 80 East Concorde Street, Boston, MA 02118.

16. Annas, George J., Glantz, Leonard H., and Roche, Patricia A., 'Drafting the Genetic Privacy Act: Science, Policy, and Practical Considerations', *J. Law, Med, and Ethics* 23:360–366, (1995).

17. Andrews, Lori B., 'Legal Aspects of Genetic Information', *Yale J. Biol. and Med.* 64:29–40, (1991).

18. Rosner, Fred. *Modern Medicine in Jewish Ethics*, second revised and augmented edition. Also, David M. Feldman, *Health and Medicine in the Jewish Tradition.* (New York, Crossroad Publishing Company 1986), p. 24. (Hoboken, KTAV Publishing House, Inc. 1991), p. 10.

19. President's Commission for the Study of Ethical Problems in Medicine and Biomedical and Behavioral Research. Screening and Counseling for Genetic Conditions: A Report on the Ethical, Social, and Legal Implications for Genetic Screening, Counseling and Education Program. (Washington, U.S. Government Printing Office.)

20. Andrews, Lori B., Fullerton, Jane E., Hotzman, Neil A., and Motulski, Arno G., eds., Committee on Assessing Genetic Risks: Division of Health Sciences Policy-Institute of Medicine. *Assessing Genetic Risks: Implications for Health and Social Policy.* (Washington, National Academy Press 1994), pp. 278–279.

21. Kessler, Seymore, Field, Tracy, Worth, Laurel, Mosbarger, Heidi, 'Attitudes of Persons at Risk for Huntington's Disease Toward Predictive Testing', *Amer. J. Med. Genet.* 26:259–270, (1987).

22. Lerman, Karyn, Daly, Mary, Mesny, Agnes, Balsham, Andrew, 'Attitudes About Genetic Testing for Breast-Ovarian Cancer Susceptibility', *J. Clin. Oncol.* 12:843–850, (1994).

23. Kash, Catherine M., Holland, Jimmie C., Halper, Marilyn S., Miller, Daniel G., 'Psychological Distress and Surveillance Behaviors of Women with a Family History of Breast Cancer', *J. Nat. Can. Instit.* 84:24–30, (1992).

24. Huggins, Marlene, Block, Maurice, Wiggins, Sandy, Shelan, Adam, et. al., 'Productive Testing for Huntington's Disease in Canada: Adverse Effects and Unexpected Results in Those Receiving a Decreased Risk', *Amer. J. Med. Genet.* 42:508–515, (1992).

25. Lehrman, Karyn, Daly, Mary, Mesny, Agnes, Balsham, Andrew, 'Attitudes about Genetic Testing for Breast/Ovarian Cancer Susceptibility', *J. Clin. Oncol.* 12:843–850, (1994).

26. Pauling, Linus, *Our Hope for the Future in Birth Defects,* ed. Fishbein, M. (Philadelphia, Lippincott, 1263). As quoted in Nelkin, Dorothy and Tancredi, Laurence, *Dangerous Diagnostics: The Social Consequences of Biological Information* (Chicago, University of Chicago Press, 1994), p. 12.

27. Glass, Bentley, 'Science: Endless Horizon or Golden Age?' *Science* 171:23–29, (1971). As quoted in Nelkin, Dorothy and Tancredi Laurence, *Dangerous Diagnostics: The Social Consequences of Biological Information* (Chicago, University of Chicago Press 1994), p. 12.

28. Sophocles, *Oedipus Etiphus the King and Eight Great Tragedies* (New York, Mentor Books, 1957), pp. 65–66. As quoted in Wexler, Nancy S., 'The Tiresias Complex: Huntington's Disease as a Paradigm of Testing for Late Onset Disorders', *FASEB J.* 6:2820–2825, (1992).

11

Prenatal Genetic Testing, Abortion, and Beyond

Scott B Rae, PhD

Dave and Diane are about to have their first experience with prenatal genetic testing. Dave's family medical history includes some individuals who have suffered from Huntington's disease. Since Dave carries the gene, there is a chance that any children he and Diane have will inherit the gene and end up with the disease. Understandably they are very concerned about the welfare of any children that they might have. Dave knows about the ravages of the disease from his own research into its symptoms, and both he and Diane are fairly sure that they do not want to subject a child to the horrors of Huntington's disease. They want children very badly, though, and so far they are not comfortable with adoption. They are even less comfortable with using a sperm donor in order to bypass Dave's genes and yet still have 'their own' children. They consider prenatal genetic testing to be non-negotiable, and they will definitely have whatever tests are necessary to determine if their child will suffer from Huntington's disease. Though they admit that ending a pregnancy would be difficult, both of them would do so if they discovered through testing that their baby would be born destined to endure Huntington's disease.

We could even take Dave's and Diane's predicament one step further. In order to insure the best probability of a child without the gene for Huntington's disease, they decide to do a much more sophisticated form of prenatal genetic testing. They are going to test for the gene before Diane even becomes pregnant. The way they can do this is by using *in vitro* fertilization instead of natural conception. Even though they do not have an infertility problem, they think that it would make sense to have conception occur outside the womb. They will test the embryos in the lab to see which ones do not have the gene. They will implant several of the embryos that do not have the defective gene and discard the ones that do have it. This way they insure that the child that develops in Diane's womb will not have to grow up to be afflicted with Huntington's disease. It will help them to have a number of embryos from which to choose, since some will probably have the gene and others will probably be damaged or destroyed in the process of testing them for the gene.

The predicament of Jim and Lori is somewhat different. They have three boys, and they very much want a girl. In fact, the only reason that they are trying to have a fourth child is that they might have a girl. They do not particularly want a larger family, but they anticipate that all the additional expense and effort of a four-child family would be worth it in order to have a girl. They are interested in prenatal genetic testing to determine if the child Lori is carrying is a girl. If it is not, then they admit that they would be faced with a very difficult decision. They acknowledge that they might consider ending the pregnancy if they found out that the child was a boy.

Testing for gender selection is normally opposed by most if not all bioethics scholars, but in clinics across the United States it occurs more frequently than one might suppose. A couple rarely acknowledges that they are ending a pregnancy for that reason. However, it does happen in the United States and other parts of the West. It occurs even more frequently in countries where women's rights are not as respected as they are in the West. For example, in India, where male children are valued much more highly than female children, physicians and genetic counsellors are in a difficult situation – wanting to offer the testing but fully aware that some couples will routinely end the pregnancy if testing reveals that the child is a girl. Similarly in China, where access to such testing is available, the government's restrictive population policies put pressure on couples to end pregnancies when the fetus is female. Many developing areas do not have widespread access to prenatal diagnostic technology. Instead of aborting female fetuses there, some people practise infanticide of female newborns.

THE HUMAN GENOME PROJECT

One of the primary reasons prenatal genetic testing is becoming more widespread is that the amount of genetic information available to couples has increased exponentially in the past few years. Once genetic research links a disease to a specific gene, a prenatal diagnostic test can usually be developed without much difficulty. The Human Genome Project (see earlier chapter by Francis Collins) promises to produce an abundance of genetic information that can be used by couples who wish to know what genetic predispositions their child has inherited. While a number of conditions, such as Down's syndrome and Huntington's disease, have well known genetic links, the number of conditions for which a fetus can be tested will dramatically increase in the next decade.

Although the Human Genome Project raises the long-term prospect of genetic engineering for genetic enhancement, the more immediate promise of the project is the information it will provide. Some conditions can even be treated *in utero* through the exciting field of fetal therapy. In many cases, the information available to a couple will help them prepare for their child. Sometimes what a couple finds out about their child will result in their terminating the pregnancy. Overall, the Human Genome Project will probably make genetic testing more routine as the number of conditions which are detectable in the womb steadily increase.

In general, medical technology that improves the lot of the human race and helps to alleviate effects of the entrance of sin into the world is linked to God's general revelation. The ability of human beings to look into the womb and examine the genetic structure of tiny fetuses and even smaller embryos ultimately comes from God. His wisdom revealed outside of Scripture has enabled human beings to develop the technology that identifies the results of sin in various forms, including that of genetic diseases.[1] Thus prenatal genetic testing *per se* does not appear to be wrong – though couples are not morally obligated to use it. Rather, it is important that couples acknowledge that the womb is still 'the secret place' over which God alone ultimately has control (Ps. 139:15). Further, they should realize that these tests are not infallible (all have a margin of error) and some do involve a degree of risk both to the mother and the fetus. If the benefit of obtaining the information is greater or proportionate to the risk incurred in the test, then utilizing genetic testing technology is morally appropriate.

THE ABORTION ASSUMPTION

What couples do with the information gleaned from prenatal genetic testing is quite another matter. Most genetic counsellors will say that they operate with the presumption of objectivity. Their role is to give information and maximize reproductive choice for the couple.[2] Yet when public health officials talk about the benefits of prenatal screening in reducing the incidence of genetic diseases, they typically assume that couples will end their pregnancy if they receive bad news from their testing.[3] In fact, some of the medical literature employs the term 'amniocentesis' to refer not only to the testing but also the abortion that the authors assume a couple will authorize if their fetus is discovered to have some genetic defect.[4] Public health authorities sometimes suggest that prenatal testing is a great help in eliminating the incidence of genetic diseases. But the only way it can be helpful in that way is if couples end their pregnancies. The genetic disease is thereby eliminated, but at the expense of the child who has the disease. Needless to say, the incidence of every disease would decrease dramatically if medicine had the liberty to do away with the people who have it.

This abortion assumption is certainly understandable. Couples who discover that their child has a genetic abnormality often experience a desire to end their pregnancy. After the anticipation of conception and the excitement of pregnancy, to find out that the child one is carrying has genetic defects can be a crushing disappointment that many couples wish to put behind them by ending the pregnancy. In addition, couples want to avoid the difficult scenario of raising a handicapped child with all the physical, emotional and financial demands.

However, going through with an abortion of a genetically deformed fetus is also a difficult process. Most genetic anomalies are detected by amniocentesis and the results are not available until the second term of pregnancy. By this time the fetus resembles a baby in many ways and its features are becoming visible by ultrasound. This is not to say that the appearance of humanness is a valid criterion for the right to life, but rather, that the more the fetus resembles a baby, the more emotionally difficult it is in many cases for the parents to authorize the abortion. Many couples experience profound grief, loss and guilt when abortion for deformity is performed. This experience reflects a (perhaps vague) perception that the fetus may well be a person like the rest of us, after all. Indeed, if it is true that the fetus is a 'substance' and the result of a continuous process of development that begins at conception, in which there is no metaphysically relevant decisive moment, then the fetus, at whatever stage of development, is a fully human person with a right to life.[5] The problematic element in prenatal genetic testing, then, is the decision to end a pregnancy because of the information that the testing reveals.

People often invoke the presence of a genetically deformed child in the womb to justify abortion. While learning that one's child *in utero* is not healthy is difficult, the ethical justification for ending the child's life under such circumstances requires careful consideration. The most frequent justification is a quality of life argument. The child born with such abnormalities is deemed incapable of having a life worth living. The child will never grow up to be what a normal child would be in terms of mental capacity and/or bodily functions. In many cases the child may have a life filled with suffering. For example, children with severe Down's syndrome or spina bifida often have very difficult lives.

Preempting a child's life on quality-of-life grounds, however, is objectionable for a number of reasons. First, the couple must realize that prenatal genetic tests have a margin of error. The AFP test is notorious for both false positives and negatives, often requiring involved follow-up testing and substantial anxiety to the couple awaiting the results. Even amniocentesis is not 100% reliable, and couples should be very careful about terminating a pregnancy based on tests that can be in error.

Second, even were the tests to be entirely accurate, the degree of deformity that the child will experience is difficult to predict. For example, there are varying degrees of abnormality with Down's syndrome. Some cases are very severe and others are quite mild. Individuals with mild cases often lead relatively normal lives and are virtually indistinguishable to the casual observer. A recent network television series entitled 'Life Goes On' was about a high school student with Down's syndrome. His case was mild and he attended school with his friends and did most things that his peers did. Some genetic diseases such as Huntington's disease do not appear until later in life.

Third, even if the degree of deformity to be experienced could be predicted with certainty, it is presumptuous to suggest that the lives of the genetically or otherwise disabled persons are not worth living. That is a value judgment, not a medical fact, and no one has the right to impose that kind of value judgment upon other people, especially when doing so results in their death. Not even parents should have the right to set the standard of a 'life worth living' for their child. It is all too easy for the parents to confuse the burden of life for the child with the burden on the parents of caring for the child. The notion of a life not worth living should not be used to disguise the wish of parents to avoid a great burden themselves. Though society should not underestimate the challenge of a lifetime of caring for these children (and the church should lead the way in helping parents to meet this challenge), the hardship on the parents does not justify ending the pregnancy any more than the financial hardship of a poor woman justifies her ending her pregnancy.

Suggesting that the life of a genetically handicapped fetus is not worth living is further presumptuous because there is no inherent connection between disability and unhappiness or personal fulfilment. It is illuminating to ask handicapped individuals if, on account of their disability, they view their lives as not worth living and would prefer never to have been born at all. One learns that unhappiness does not necessarily follow from possession of a disability. Some of the most fulfilled and happy people are those who have succeeded in overcoming their disabilities, and they would probably be offended at the suggestion that their lives are unhappy, not to mention not worth living.

The fourth and most important reason that disability does not justify ending a pregnancy is that the entity in the womb, however genetically deformed, is still a human person. Those who defend the moral right of parents to abort genetically defective children assume, whether they acknowledge it or not, that the fetus is less than a full human person. Unless one assumes that the handicapped unborn is not a person, there is no inherent moral difference between abortion for reasons of genetic deformity and executing adults who are genetically handicapped. Yet very few consider executing handicapped adults simply on the basis of their handicap, because society acknowledges that they are persons with a right to life. In fact, persons with disabilities are deemed more worthy of protection from discrimination, not less, because of their vulnerability due to the physical and mental challenges they face. Suffering the tragedy of having a child with genetic abnormalities can be horrendous, but inflicting the tragedy of death on another person by abortion is worse.[6]

If couples do not accept the abortion assumption implicit in most prenatal genetic testing, then the use of this technology can be ethically justifiable. However, if a couple is committed to continuing the pregnancy regardless of the results of the tests, then one might well wonder what the purpose is for having the testing done in the first place. It would seem pointless and perhaps even foolish to submit to the risks of prenatal tests when the results will not affect the decision about continuing the pregnancy. Admittedly, in many cases that is true and it would be unwise to undergo particularly the riskier tests without a compelling reason to do so. Nevertheless, it is legitimate to use prenatal genetic testing to prepare for the arrival of a child who will end up having a genetic defect – particularly tests that carry little risk and are not invasive, such as ultrasound imaging and the AFP blood test.[7] In fact, for most couples, seeing their child on the ultrasound monitor for the first time is one of the most thrilling experiences a person can have. The ultrasound image can usually identify the gender of the child if the parents desire to know that prior to birth. If there are good reasons for further genetic testing, such as a family history of genetic disease or advanced age of the mother, then further testing may also be legitimate to reassure the parents that their child is healthy or to prepare them for the emotional and perhaps financial rigours of raising a handicapped child. Even couples who have a strong preference for one gender over another for whatever reason may be well served by ultrasound and disclosure of the child's gender. If the child is not of the desired gender, then the parents have time to work through the disappointment prior to the delivery date. By the time of the child's birth, they are emotionally prepared to bond properly with that newborn child – a process which is crucial to that child's development.

Furthermore, some genetic anomalies can be treated if care is initiated before or shortly after birth. For example, in the case of spina bifida, physicians can close the sac surrounding the spinal column after birth. However, the child must go immediately from the delivery room to the operating room in order to minimize the exposure to the spinal column. Accordingly, it is very helpful if this condition is known prior to birth.[8] The field of fetal therapy is also developing some exciting technologies that enable physicians to treat some conditions and even perform limited fetal surgery on developing fetuses in the womb. As this field continues to grow, more conditions will probably be treatable *in utero*, increasing the legitimate need for prenatal testing.

PREIMPLANTATION EMBRYOS

Technology has recently made even earlier prenatal genetic testing possible: testing embryos prior to implantation. Embryo testing is possible only when conception occurs via *in vitro* fertilization (IVF). Accordingly, for the foreseeable future, testing of embryos will probably not become widespread or routine for couples who do not need technological assistance in conception. Since couples who use IVF or other sophisticated reproductive technologies often have amniocentesis or CVS testing done, some people recommend embryo testing as a routine part of IVF. Such a practice would make it possible for defective embryos to be discarded instead of implanted, thereby providing the couple with greater assurance that their fetus would not carry any deleterious genes. Some researchers see embryo testing as a means to move toward eliminating certain types of genetic diseases.

However, embryo research in general and embryo testing for individual couples pose the same moral problem. If personhood begins at conception, then there is no moral difference between aborting a fetus and discarding an embryo. If the results of genetic testing indicate that certain embryos have genetic defects, then there is no moral difference between discarding them and aborting fetuses with similar defects (or executing adults with disabilities).[9] In addition, in the process of testing, embryos are sometimes unintentionally damaged and then are discarded, and this is problematic for the same reason that research that damages the embryo is a problem. In general, research on human beings that is not for their benefit, is done without their consent, and could probably lead to their destruction, should not be allowed in society. Similarly, embryo testing that damages embryos or leads to their being discarded, is morally problematic.

It is understandable that embryo testing for couples at risk for transmitting genetic diseases seems to some a very responsible way of procreating children. Rather than taking their chances with the roll of the genetic dice, they use embryo testing to give them a measure of control and to avoid passing on harmful genes to their child or children. To deny the legitimacy of embryo testing might seem to take away the only responsible way of procreating a genetically related child for couples who have a history of genetic disease. However, the underlying reasoning that justifies embryo testing in this case is a crude form of utilitarianism, in which the ends justify the means, and in which results are more important than ethical principles. As Arthur Dyck demonstrates historically in an earlier chapter in this book, such utilitarian undermining of ethical principles in the genetics arena is extremely dangerous. Though genetic disease, like any disease, can be quite costly in many respects, sacrificing embryonic persons for the sake of having a healthy child is too high a cost for anyone, Christian or otherwise, who recognizes that personhood begins at conception.

BEYOND THE CLINIC

In addition to the clinical concerns about when prenatal genetic testing is legitimate, there are other social concerns about prenatal genetic testing in general. For example, consider its impact on how society views the disabled adult population. Disability advocacy groups are understandably concerned about the abortion assumption inherent in much genetic testing. They fear that the loss of respect for the disabled unborn will translate into less respect for the adult disabled population. A parallel case would seem to justify their concern. Virtually everyone writing on medical ethics condemns abortion for the purpose of gender selection, on the grounds that it makes a powerful statement about the relative value of the female gender. Since most people who contemplate gender selection favour boys, a preference that is overwhelmingly the case in much of the third world and places where there are restrictive population policies, feminist groups are rightly concerned about the devaluing of their gender in society. When it comes to the disabled, however, no such concern is apparent; society has already sanctioned abortion for virtually any disability that testing may uncover.[10]

The landmark President's Commission on Bioethics in the 1980s illustrates this double standard. While the Commission gives approval for genetic testing, it also condemns use of such testing for gender selection. It states, '[gender selection] is incompatible with the attitude of virtually unconditional acceptance that developmental psychologists have found to be essential to successful parenting. For the good of all children, society's efforts should go into promoting the acceptance of each individual – with his or her particular strengths and weaknesses – rather than reinforcing the negative attitudes that lead to rejection.'[11] What holds for gender should also hold for disability. If anything, disabled children, because of their greater degree of vulnerability, may even be owed this acceptance more than healthy children, irrespective of gender.

This unconditional love and acceptance at the heart of all responsible parenthood may also be affected by the cultural ethos produced by widespread genetic screening. Testing can involve a conflict between unconditional love for a child and a parental desire

to have the best for their children. Sociologist Barbara Katz Rothman asks pointedly, 'What does it do to motherhood, to women,
and to men as fathers too, when we make parental acceptance
conditional, pending further testing. We ask the mother and her
family to say in essence, "These are my standards. If you meet these
standards of acceptability, then you are mine and I will love you
and accept you totally. After you pass this (genetic) test." '[12] An
extension of this same mindset is the futuristic scenario in which
parents use testing and genetic engineering to customize their
children by selecting the most desirable traits and gender. Though
trait selection for children is still far in the future, the mentality that
underlies it may already be present.

Though it is legitimate for parents to want every advantage for
their children, seeking such advantage must not come at the expense
of the unconditional acceptance that ultimately gives children their
greatest advantage. To the degree that prenatal testing encourages
a way of thinking that undercuts parental love and acceptance
toward children, society should resist its routine use. For the
Christian, testing should be employed for preparation, not abortion.
Disabled people are already too marginalized, without the added
burden of prenatal testing designed to exclude them from life itself.

NOTES

1. That is not to say that any specific genetic disease is the result of a specific sin
committed by one of the parents of the child in question. On the contrary, genetic diseases
are usually the result of the general presence of sin in the world.

2. The scholarly literature on the subject also makes this presumption. For example,
Kathleen Nolan states that, 'Out of respect for reproductive decision making and genetic
privacy, and to prevent abuses such as attempts at eugenic control, virtually all genetic
counselors espouse the ideals of value-neutral counseling and autonomous decision
making.' 'First Fruits: Genetic Screening', in 'Genetic Grammar: Health, Illness and the
Human Genome Project,' Special Supplement, *Hastings Center Report*, vol. 22 (July-August
1992), pp. S2–4.

3. Though also lamenting the loss of choice for parents who desire to raise a
handicapped child, sociologist Barbara Katz Rothman nevertheless makes this assumption
too when she states that, 'Although some people have discussed the value of being
forewarned of genetic or other diseases even in a pregnancy the woman intends to carry
to term, abortion is an integral part of this new technology [of prenatal testing].' 'The
Products of Conception: The Social Context of Reproductive Choices', *Journal of Medical
Ethics*, vol. 11 (1985), pp. 188–192, at 189.

4. Elizabeth Kristol, 'Picture Perfect: The Politics of Prenatal Testing', *First Things*
(April 1993), pp. 17–24, 18.

5. For further defence of a substance view of a human being, see Mitchell, John A.,
and Rae, Scott B., 'The Moral Status of Fetuses and Embryos', in Stetson, Brad, ed. *The
Silent Subject: Reflections on the Unborn in Society*, (Westport, Connecticut: Praeger 1995),
pp. 19–32.

6. For more detail on this and other justifications for abortion, see Beckwith, Francis

J. *Politically Correct Death: Answering the Arguments for Abortion Rights* (Grand Rapids, Mich. Baker Book House 1992).

7. There is still some debate over the long-term risk of ultrasound imaging. See Kristol, pp. 17–18.

8. One of the tragedies that sometimes occurs with spina bifida is when the parents do not authorize the surgery at birth, choosing not to pursue aggressive treatment. In such situations, the parents take the child home and he or she usually dies at home within the first two years. During that time, the parents become attached to the child and often later regret their decision to refuse the surgery. Discovering that the child has spina bifida through prenatal testing can enable the parents to work through this decision while they have time to do so. Spina bifida is less severe than anencephaly and the surgery does help in most cases. The child with spina bifida is not born with a terminal illness, though the deformities can be severe. Refusing to authorize the surgery for spina bifida would be the moral equivalent of abortion. Though treatment would not have been futile, the child would be allowed to die simply because of his or her anomaly.

9. Even though the NIH panel for embryo research recognized that special moral status should be granted to the embryo, they and many others do not see embryos on the same moral level with fetuses. For example, Professor Andrea Bonnicksen states that, 'Arguably it is morally more acceptable to discard embryos than to abort fetuses.' She further adds that, 'Deliberately discarding faulty embryos is arguably no worse than the constant threat in IVF of embryoloss due to biological fluke.' In the first statement, she apparently assumes that implantation makes a morally significant difference in determining personhood. However, that is only a difference in location, not essence. In the second statement, she ignores the definite difference between accidental death of embryos and intentional discarding of embryos. 'Genetic Diagnosis of Human Embryos', *Hastings Center Report*, vol. 22, Special Supplement, (July-August 1992), pp. S5–11, at 5–6.

10. Kristol, p. 23.

11. Cited in Kristol, p. 23.

12. Rothman, 'The Products of Conception,' p. 190.

Genetic Counselling

Elizabeth Thomson, RN,MA

In a paper published in 1975, the Ad Hoc Committee on Genetic Counseling of the American Society of Human Genetics first formally described the term genetic counselling.[1] Genetic counselling is a relatively new area of health care in which only a small number of health professionals provide services. In the United States, for example, no more than a few thousand health professionals are specialized in genetics and provide direct genetic counselling services. Some are physicians (clinical geneticists) or have Ph.D. degrees in human genetics (medical geneticists), while others are nurses (nurse specialists in genetics) or are master's-prepared genetic counsellors. Currently there are about a hundred programmes in the US designed to include graduate education for geneticists, genetic counsellors, and other health professionals.[2] Almost all of these programmes are less than twenty five years old at this time. This picture, however, is likely to change in the coming years. Whereas the need for more specialists in genetics may continue to exist, some of the genetic counselling that has been provided in the past by specialists will probably be provided by various other health professionals in the future.

Historically, many people who entered the field of genetic counselling did so because of their interest in the field and not because of special training in human genetics. At first most genetic counselling services were provided in pediatric or obstetric departments, almost always at major university or medical settings. Even today, most genetic counsellors work in pre-natal or peri-natal settings, although this is beginning to change. In the future, primary care providers will probably provide some genetic counselling services, and they will do so in more than prenatal and perinatal settings.

It has been just forty years since the actual number of human chromosomes became known. The first chromosome abnormality (Down's syndrome) was described in 1959. In the 1960s, only very limited genetic testing capabilities existed, and the amount of information that tests could reveal was also limited. In those days, chromosomes appeared in laboratory tests as darkly stained bodies, so it was possible to tell only if a person had an extra chromosome

146

or was missing a whole chromosome. It was not until the 1970s that newer technologies made it possible for light and dark banding patterns on the chromosomes to be distinguished, enabling laboratory technicians to look at smaller and smaller pieces of chromosomes. Since the 1970s, genetic testing has changed to molecular testing so that now technicians are actually able to look for missing genes or sequences of DNA, or for altered or additional sequences of DNA. It has become virtually impossible to keep up with what is happening on a day to day basis. The best one can do today is to know what resources exist to answer the questions that may arise.

THE GOALS OF GENETIC COUNSELLING

Against this backdrop, the process of genetic counselling has developed. Genetic counselling can perhaps best be understood in terms of five goals. The initial goal is to help people to comprehend the medical facts. Markie Jackson's experience presented in the opening section of this book is a striking testimony to the need for people to have good information. Geneticists and genetic counsellors through the years have spent a lot of time sitting with the parents of children with genetic diseases and discussing such things as, 'Your child has disease X, and a child with this disease typically will experience these types of problems in the future.' They try to explain the genetic variation and its expected consequences to the parents. Genetic diseases commonly have long, confusing names, e.g., mucopolysaccharidosis, type 3. While many doctors and nurses will know what mucopolysaccharides are, they may not know exactly how the disorder involved will affect the child. So the first part of the genetic specialist's job is to help parents understand the nature of the genetic disease affecting their child. This typically consists of an hour or two spent discussing the child's genetic condition, as well as providing the parents with written information to take home.

The second goal of genetic counselling is to help people understand the genetic contribution to a particular disorder. This part of the counselling process has undergone much change over the years. When I started in genetics some 20 years ago, we did not know the cause of many genetic conditions (e.g., Prader Willi, Angelmann, and Williams syndromes). We believed that they were likely to have some genetic contribution, but we had no idea what that was. Now we do. In some cases, there have been identifiable deletions or other changes discovered in the genetic material. However, there are still many other disorders for which the cause has remained elusive. Individuals or families with such disorders commonly end up in a genetics clinic, because no one has been able to determine what caused their disorders. As a result, genetic counsellors have often talked with individuals or families with such disorders, whether they had a known genetic basis or not. Often such conditions were not thought to be genetic because they did not tend to 'run in the family'; yet we have now learned that in fact many such disorders are genetic. In some cases the genetic change has occurred in an egg or sperm cell involved in the formation of a child. Hence, even where there has been no previous manifestation of the condition in other family members, it may still be genetically based.

The third goal of genetic counselling is to help families understand their reproductive risks and options and make future health care decisions. Counsellors spend a good deal of time talking with people concerned about passing a genetic disorder to future children. Some of those individuals already have a child with a birth defect or genetic disorder; others have a family history of such a condition. Such people commonly ask if the condition about which they are concerned is genetic and if it might occur again in future offspring. Often in the past, such families have been told, 'It won't happen again.' After it happens again, they may then seek genetic counselling. In some cases, counsellors do not see families until after they have their third or fourth affected child. Eventually a family member will say, 'Maybe this is genetic.' Often it is.

The fourth goal of genetic counselling is to enable families in which a genetic disorder exists to choose the courses of action that are best for them, and to make choices while taking into consideration their own values and beliefs in both reproductive decision-making and follow-up care. Whether or not they should have other children, raise their child at home, or place their child in a special school are very important questions. The fifth and final goal of genetic counselling is to help people who have genetic disorders to make the best possible adjustment to the challenges they face.

There is nothing mystical or magical about the practice of genetic counselling. Health professionals engage in various parts of the genetic counselling process every day. Historically, health professionals have not become involved in the part of genetic counselling that focuses on the genetic contribution to the disorder. However, many health professionals are well-qualified to perform other aspects of genetic counselling. So the task is to help professionals learn enough about genetics to be more confident to provide the genetic information that people want to receive. People commonly wonder, 'What caused this? Could it happen again in our family? Is this something my sister should be worried about?' Increasingly, there are resources available to help people answer such questions.

DIAGNOSTIC COUNSELLING

In light of this background information, it is next important to explain the four primary components of genetic counselling. The first component may be called diagnostic counselling. In former days it was not an easy task to establish a definitive diagnosis. Sometimes today this is still not an easy task. In the past, the diagnosis was commonly based on clinical features or symptoms which were observed – e.g., facial features, growth patterns, and developmental patterns. Twenty years ago, there was usually not a test that established a definitive diagnosis. There were some capabilities, such as chromosome tests or biochemical tests, but it was not until relatively recently that molecular genetics tests have become available. Unfortunately, with all the new diagnostic capabilities, we now tend to spend more time on tests and somewhat less time talking with clients about other concerns.

Previously genetics specialists could not avoid extensive personal interactions. In our search for the diagnosis, we sometimes felt as if we were private investigators. We investigated, uncovered, and collected information about the individual or the family. There might have been some vague family history of an aunt's child who died of disease X, but nobody had ever talked about it. So we were commonly involved in extended family discussions to see if we could get information from an aunt, a cousin, or some other relative about the person who had died. In some cases we could offer diagnostic tests. Whenever possible we tried to see the affected person because we sometimes found that an individual had been given an incorrect diagnosis. If one has the incorrect diagnosis to start with, providing genetic counselling about it is not helpful. There are some genetic disorders that look like other genetic disorders, even though the mode of inheritance is quite different. It has always been important, then, to be sure that genetic counselling is based on accurate diagnostic information.

Traditionally, a prenatal history has been a part of the information gathered about a child, to attempt to determine if something might have occurred during the pregnancy that might explain what was going on now in the child. Gathered information has also included results from laboratory tests, x-rays, and consultations with other specialists. For example, there might have been eye conditions, heart conditions, or kidney conditions that together suggest a pattern known to occur in a child who has a particular genetic disorder. One of the long-observable problems in our health care system is that a person typically has one specialist looking at the kidneys, one looking at the eyes, and others looking at other body parts. Those specialists and the other health professionals that they work with do not always talk to one another. So a person can end up with many pieces of information, but no one to explain to them how it all fits together.

In the 1970s a typical couple that would come in for genetic counselling might have included a husband who had two siblings who had died of cystic fibrosis (CF). What could genetic counsellors offer such a couple? They could do a statistical analysis based on the fact that there was a 2 in 3 risk that this young man would be a carrier of CF, a 1 in 25 risk that his spouse would be a carrier of CF, and a 1 in 4 risk of having an affected child if they were both carriers. All factors considered, this couple would be informed that they had about a 1 in 150 risk of having a baby with cystic fibrosis. It did not take long to do the calculation or to communicate this information to the couple. As a result, the counsellor spent more time talking to the couple about their perceptions and experiences with CF, and about what it meant for them to have a 1% risk of having a child with CF. His parents might have thought a 1% risk was far too high to consider having a child. After all, they had watched two of their children die of CF and these had been very painful experiences. This couple, however, might decide that a 1% risk was a risk they were willing to take.

Today if this same couple were to come in, the genetic specialist's assessment would be different. The first goal would be to try to find out whether the affected siblings had detectable genetic mutations. During the last six years, over 600 different mutations have been discovered in the CF gene.[3] So the first step would be to try to locate some tissue from one of the siblings who died. Tissues are commonly stored for many years in pathology labs. It is often possible to obtain these tissues for DNA testing. If a mutation is identified in that tissue, then the individual can be tested and definitive information can be given to the couple.

Obtaining the tissue generally involves getting permission from the parents of the children who died. Doing so can create some difficulties. The young couple may not have even told their parents they were going in for genetic counselling. They may have been afraid to tell their parents because they believed that if they told them they were thinking about having a carrier test or prenatal diagnosis done, it would reflect negatively on their family or their past life with their siblings. They fear they might be perceived as wishing that their siblings had never been born. Such revelations can have a huge impact on the entire family. Even if the tissues can be obtained and the test run, there is no guarantee of gaining more useful information. In about 10% of the cases, mutations will not be found. So while testing can be a rewarding experience in terms of getting more exact information, it can also be very frustrating for families when they go through this process, experience the challenges that may occur, and yet do not get useful information from the testing. This predicament presents a growing challenge for genetic counsellors.

INFORMATIVE COUNSELLING

A second component of genetic counselling – one in which many people can participate – is informative counselling. A tremendous amount of information is available about genetic disorders today. Most people who have a genetic disorder in their family or who are worried about a genetic disorder occurring in their family desire information. They may prefer to receive it gradually over time, but they usually do want information. There is now information on the World Wide Web on just about any known genetic disorder.[4] This is a potentially wonderful resource, although one must be judicious in examining the source of the information. There are also genetic support groups that have much information about various genetic disorders. The Alliance of Genetic Support Groups,[5] located in Chevy Chase, Maryland, is a consortium of about 250 voluntary health organizations that has gathered together a great deal of information. Moreover, there are genetics clinics located all over the US. The American Society of Human Genetics and the American College of Medical Genetics in Bethesda, Maryland can supply the names of geneticists in any part of the country.[6,7] Information on genetic counsellors is available from the National Society of Genetic counsellors[8] and the International Society of Nurses in Genetics.[9]

Informative counselling has traditionally consisted of talking not only with the person affected but also with the person's family. In some cases individuals want to keep the information private, but at times it is appropriate to encourage individuals to open up and share this information with other people in their family who can support them and may also benefit from having it. Sometimes people instead choose a support person who is not a family member. Health professionals, members of the clergy, or others invited by the family are welcome at a genetics clinic to obtain information about the genetic disorder, the genetic basis of it, or what to expect.

Information needs to be practical. For example, parents of babies born with genetic diseases may still need help with feeding their child. When babies come in to a genetics clinic and are 'failing to thrive', it is important to determine whether this is due to the underlying genetic condition or because their basic need for nourishment is not being met. It is important not to focus so much on the genetics of disorder that we forget that there are other basic needs which, if not met, can also result in health problems. Children need to eat, sleep, be warm, and be loved, among other things.

Genetic counselling itself must be based on accurate information. Sometimes people receive information that is not accurate – that is little more than a legend or a self-protecting myth. For instance, a person's relatives may insist that the genetic condition could not be from their side of the family; rather, it must be from the spouse's side of the family. Because many genetic disorders are caused by a mutation inherited from each parent, such claims may well be erroneous. Accurate information is an essential prerequisite of genetic counselling.

People who come in for genetic counselling may also desire information about their reproductive options. This information may not be sought by the couple right away. Many couples who have just had a baby with a genetic disorder may not be interested in having a baby again in the near future. Over time, it may be appropriate to talk with them about whether they are thinking about having other children. A counsellor may need to inform the couple at some point that there is an increased risk of recurrence of the disorder. If such is the case, some reproductive alternatives may be available. While some people will choose to consider such alternatives, other people will choose to take their chances, say their prayers, and hope that the outcome is a good one for their family.

SUPPORTIVE COUNSELLING

Genetic counselling includes a third component, supportive counselling. Supportive counselling involves helping people to work through the impact of a diagnosis of genetic disorder i.e., – the grief process. Even if an affected child does not die, people do commonly go through a grief process resembling that which follows the death of a loved one.[10] This process typically consists of stages of grief including denial, anger, and guilt, which are hopefully followed by some form of resolution. Counsellors and friends need not only to support people through this process, but also to help the family to celebrate the life that they can have with their child. Many families report that their friends did not know what to say to them during this time and therefore stopped talking to them at all. To isolate people because there happens to be a genetic disorder in the family is one of the worst ways one can react to them. At such times, when we do not know what to say, we can just *be there* for them. We do not have to say anything. We need to take our cues from the family as to whether they want us to rejoice with them or they want us to be sad with them for a time.

It is equally important to make people aware of support services available to them. There are early intervention programmes, genetic support groups, and various other parental supports. Becoming aware of the kinds of services that are available is the first step.

One of the greatest needs for supportive counselling is caused by the long-term impact of genetic disorders on families. While some marriages and families get stronger in response to stressful challenges, others fall apart under the stress. Such break-ups present particular problems when there is a child who needs special care – a child with disabilities – and only a single parent remains to take care of the child. Even under the best of circumstances, however, the parents of a child with a genetic disorder will sometimes need a break. In her reflections earlier in this volume, Markie Jackson refers to her experiences as a parent of a child with hemophilia. She felt isolated, and it was hard for her to find a babysitter. It is understandable that most people would be very worried about taking care of a child with hemophilia, because something life-threatening could happen while the child was in their care. Providing such care may not be possible for everyone, but herein lies the strength of the diversity that should be present in any church congregation. There are probably some people in the church who could help care for the child so that the parents could have a much needed break. Parish nurses may be a particularly effective resource in this regard. Those who cannot care for the child directly could consider taking dinner to the family on Saturday night or express their love and support through other such tangible expressions. They could consider joint efforts to help alleviate the extra health care costs, extra educational costs, extra babysitting costs, etc., that may accompany having a child with a disability.

Families who have a child with a genetic disorder may experience what has been termed 'chronic sorrow'. Again, many families cope quite well with having a child with a disability. But there may be periods of time during which the family experiences some form of setback. Parents who initially cope very well with the fact that their child has a genetic disorder may later experience renewed grief, sometimes associated with developmental crisis points. For example, parents who initially accept their child's Down's syndrome may for a time be doing fine. Then their two-year-old child is invited to a birthday party where the other children are all walking and running, and theirs is not. That kind of event can suddenly trigger a new grief, though such grieving is commonly only temporary. Another developmental crisis point occurs when all the other children who are sixteen are getting their drivers' licenses and the parents are confronted with the fact that their child will never drive a car. Parents may experience a similar crisis when all of their child's peers are going off to college and the parents realize that their child will not be going to college – perhaps not even leaving home. At these times, parents realize again that some of the expectations and hopes people usually have for their children will not be fulfilled.

FOLLOW-UP COUNSELLING

A final component of genetic counselling is follow-up counselling. It takes people much time and energy to absorb all of the information they receive. People sometimes misunderstand. Sometimes they receive more information than they can handle. It is vital that counsellors see people from time to time to learn how things are going. Genetic counsellors will commonly see families who have a child with a genetic disorder fairly regularly – every three or six months – for the first two or three years. After this period of time, counsellors typically schedule follow-up visits annually, though families may well later cancel them. At some point families may tell the counsellor that if there is nothing in particular that needs to be addressed, they do not feel the need to come in – everything is going fine. In other words, counselling sessions usually get farther and farther apart as families' needs diminish and other support becomes available. Families may recontact the counsellor at some point because something new has come up and they want another session. However, their ability to deal with the challenges presented by their child's genetic disorder often improves over time.

Embedded in the traditional and important aspects of genetic counselling described here are several concepts that I have personally tried to emphasize in my own genetic counselling. First, I have attempted to provide timely and accurate information to those seeking such information. Markie Jackson is not alone in her frustrations over not having access to or receiving adequate information about her son's hemophilia. This is a theme that emerges quite often. It is not possible for health professionals to know everything there is to know about all genetic conditions. It is possible, however, for them to know where to get the information to share.

Second, in providing genetic counselling services to families, I have tried to support them in processing the information that they receive. Sometimes when families are given 'bad news', my challenge has been to help them work out a way to accept the information, integrate the information into their lives, and move forward with complex decisions about future care and reproductive decisions. Acknowledging individual and family differences in developing their own coping strategies has been crucial.

Third, in my genetic counselling I have tried to provide ongoing care for those who have had no cure, and to provide support to those who have been suffering. I have felt the pain of others in my heart and have sometimes stayed with and prayed with those who were dying. When there is nothing more that can be said or done, I have found that being present is sometimes all I have to offer. Through these past twenty years, I hope that I have, in a small way, lightened some families' burdens, provided support to those in need, shared at least some of their challenges, and given hope to those who may have had little. Genetic counselling can make a substantial difference in people's lives, especially when there is someone (Someone) else there to help lighten their load.

NOTES

1. American Society of Human Genetics, Ad Hoc Committee on Genetic counselling. Genetic counselling, *American Journal of Human Genetics* 27 (2): 240–242 (March 1975).

2. American Society of Human Genetics, 1996–97 Guide to North American Graduates and Postgraduate Training Programs In Human Genetics (1996).

3. See Mutation Database, CF Genetic Analysis Consortium: http:www.genet.sickkids.on.ca/cftr/

4. Online Mendelian Inheritance in Man, OMIM (TM). Center for Medical Genetics, Johns Hopkins University (Baltimore, MD) and National Center for Biotechnology Information, National Library of Medicine (Bethesda, MD), 1996. World Wide Web URL: http:www3.ncbi.nlm.nih.gov/omim/

5. The Alliance of Genetic Support Groups, 35 Wisconsin Circle, Suite 440, Chevy Chase, MD 20815, USA. Telephone: 800 3364363, email: alliance@capaccess.org

6. American Society of Human Genetics, 9650 Rockville Pike, Bethesda, MD 20814-3998, USA. Telephone: (301) 5711825, Fax: (301) 5307079

7. American College of Medical Genetics, 9650 Rockville Pike, Bethesda, MD 20814-3998, USA. Telephone: (301)5307127, Fax: 301 5711895

8. National Society of Genetic counsellors, 233 Canterbury Drive, Wallingford, PA 19086, USA. Telephone: (610) 8727608

9. International Society of Nurses in Genetics, 3020 Javier Rd. Fairfax, VA 22031, USA. Telephone: 703 698 7355.

10. Kubler-Ross, Elisabeth, *On Children and Death* (New York, Collier Books 1985)

13

The Educational Challenge

Martha Newsome, DDS

And the LORD God made all kinds of trees grow out of the ground — trees that were pleasing to the eye and good for food. In the middle of the garden were the tree of life and the tree of the knowledge of good and evil (Gen. 2:9).

> After repeated lapses of memory and loss of coordination leading to several falls, my father made an appointment with a neurologist. Taking a full medical history, the physician was particularly interested in my father's account of his grandfather who had abandoned his evening walks, fearing he would lose his way home. Dad was convinced that he suffered from the same symptoms. The neurologist was quick to recommend genetic testing for Alzheimer's disease. Without consulting the family, my father agreed. Upon learning of this decision, I was anxious about the potential consequences. What if the results were positive for the gene? Future reproductive decisions in our family might be overshadowed with concern for transmitting the Alzheimer's gene. Would Dad's insurance be cancelled? Would each of my siblings seek testing? With no cure available for this late-onset disease, did we really want to know? [1]

Genomic information increases daily as the human genetic code is translated and shared. Researchers promise new technologies that will improve life, and media headlines herald that the age of genetics has arrived. Children suffering from genetic disorders may obtain a cure within their lifetime — cancers may be prevented, and cardiovascular disease reversed. Unfortunately, these bright promises are clouded by an increase in the number of ethical, legal and social quandaries resulting from this knowledge. Genetic testing offers new benefits and creates new risks. Prenatal screening raises the question of therapeutic abortion. Individuals with known genetic disorders or carriers of faulty genes experience discrimination in insurance, employment, and educational opportunities. In a society attempting to minimize discrimination, the potential for stigmatization is expanding in the genetic information age.

Accordingly, a report on the Human Genome Project has observed:

While very challenging issues are raised by genome research, solutions are not simple; defensible rights often exist on both sides of any issue. Further research is needed, as well as activities to promote public awareness and assist in policy development.[2]

In a similar vein, the Committee on Assessing Genetic Risks sponsored by the Institute of Medicine makes the following strong recommendation:

> An informed public is the best societal protection from possible abuses of genetic technology and information in the future. The task, therefore, is to educate the public so that each individual is capable of making an informed decision about seeking or accepting genetic testing and considering personal courses of action . . . This educational imperative is intended to develop a genetically literate public that understands basic biological research, understands elements of the personal and health implications of genetics, and participates effectively in public policy issues involving genetic information.[3]

If the general public is equipped with knowledge about the new genetics, people will gain the capacity to direct the course of the new genetics as well as to make appropriate individual choices regarding genetic testing and procedures. At present, however, the average citizen is far from well-informed.

THE NEED FOR BETTER EDUCATION

By wisdom a house is built, and through understanding it is established (Prov. 24:3).

Most people lack an elementary understanding of genetics and the diverse applications of the new technologies. Education in biology and medicine prior to 1975 included only minimal instruction in molecular genetics, due to the embryonic nature of the field. In the last twenty-five years the rate of technology development has exploded, particularly in the field of genetics. Only one in four Americans, for example, actually 'understand(s) DNA's relationship to inheritance', according to a 1990 study by the National Science Foundation.[4] A March of Dimes' survey confirmed 'that a majority of the respondents knew little or nothing about genetic testing or gene therapy'.[5] Other surveys have revealed that a majority of Americans have little genetics knowledge and yet have firm opinions about genetic technologies:

> Although 85% of those surveyed claimed to have heard or read little or nothing about genetic screening per se, they nevertheless have opinions about genetic testing and appear to sense its potential for misuse: 72% believe the benefits of science generally outweigh any harmful effects, and only 48% think genetic screening will do more good than harm.[6]

Misconceptions regarding the effects of deleterious genes and genetic disorders are common, and these misconceptions can potentially result in the sanctioning of inappropriate practices.

> A 1990 national survey of Americans reported 39 percent said 'every woman who is pregnant *should* be tested to determine if the baby has any serious genetic defects.' Twenty-two percent responded that regardless of what they would want for themselves, 'a woman *should* have an abortion if the baby has a serious genetic defect'.[7]

However, selective screening with therapeutic abortion is only one of many procedures available through the new genetic technologies. Preimplantation diagnosis, genetic testing of minors, DNA banking, and somatic cell therapy are currently available or under serious consideration.

In spite of, perhaps because of, misconceptions about genetics, the demand for such technologies will be great. It is natural to seek these devices to forecast or control one's future or the future of the next generation – spurred on by the fear of the unknown and the possibility of fatal illness. Although hereditary conditions have plagued humankind for centuries, there have been no means available to determine in advance if a particular parent, child or sibling would be stricken with an inherited disease. In the current age of DNA science, remarkable developments allow one to peer ahead to predict probabilities for future affliction. Many diseases, such as infectious disorders, do not have known genetic causation. However, certain deleterious genes are rapidly being discovered that may predispose one to breast cancer, Alzheimer's disease, Huntington's disease, cystic fibrosis and a myriad other disorders. A majority of Americans who will seek after genetic tests and interventions will not comprehend the potential implications due to their lack of knowledge.

Some respond that lay people need not understand the details about genetics as long as the scientists do. David Suzuki in his work, *Genethics*, issues a warning:

> . . . Science seems to lay outside the average person's ability to comprehend and evaluate. 'Leave it to the scientists' is a common sentiment when it comes to determining how new knowledge should be applied . . . [however] the broader social implication of new discoveries generally lie outside the restricted field of vision of active scientists. Those scientists who do step back to consider the broader ramifications of their research too often lose credibility for ceasing research. Thus, a lay public that is subsidizing the scientific enterprise through research grants. . . and that is directly affected by the application of scientific knowledge must be responsible for determining the direction of science and its application.[8]

Accordingly, Ruth Hubbard, biologist and author of *Exploding the Gene Myth*, recommends that each individual become familiar with medical technologies in genetics if confronted with a medical treatment decision. 'We need to be sufficiently well informed to be able to evaluate critically what the "experts" tell us, so that we can make our own judgments about what tests and what information are likely to benefit us.'[9] Robert Cook-Deegan adds that the scientific and medical communities have a special ability and responsibility to foster better understanding [10].

To sum up, there is a pressing need for education and dialogue. Is there a role for the Christian church and for the Christian medical professional, scientist, educator and theologian in educating the general population? How might a Christian setting be provided in which individuals can grapple with these issues?

Ronald Cole-Turner in his work, *The New Genesis*, comments on the statements advanced by specialized commissions of various denominations, the National Council of Churches, and the World Council of Churches. In 1986, the National Council of Churches formulated several statements, concluding that 'the churches can play a significant role in contributing to public understanding of genetic engineering'.[11] The Catholic Church encourages a public discourse with geneticists that 'is necessary if wisdom and humility are to effect enlightened public policy'.[12] The statement of the United Methodist Church made in 1991 offers excellent recommendations 'calling for increased education of "laity and clergy on the issues of genetic science, theology and ethics." Local churches and judicatories are urged "to become centers for dialogue".'[13]

The new genetics challenges Christians to become informed about emerging technologies, gain an awareness of the benefits and burdens, and provide opportunities for dialogue regarding the crucial issues involved. What types of activities can best promote these goals?

POSSIBLE EDUCATIONAL INITIATIVES

You are the light of the world. A city on a hill cannot be hidden. Neither do people light a lamp and put it under a bowl. Instead they put it on its stand, and it gives light to everyone in the house (Matt. 5:14,15).

Among the activities that would elevate the level of understanding in the church about the new genetics are the following:

- Seminaries could offer classroom and clinical instruction that includes the ethical and theological implications of the new genetics, to inform potential ministers about the current technologies and train them to assist those in crisis. Continuing education of the pastorate could also be offered to the same ends.

- Christians could become involved in legislative activities to develop policies preventing abuses of genetic information.
- Christians considering a college major could be encouraged to enter the field of molecular genetics.
- Churches could offer seminars and other such forums to address issues in the new genetics and provide a setting for dialogue.
- Individual churches could also institute bioethics committees with professional and lay membership to support the pastorate and parishioners in difficult decision making.

Christians must not confine their efforts to fellow believers. Numerous other potential initiatives include the following:

- Churches could adopt a mission statement to serve as a caring institution for those who have experienced genetic discrimination (financially, spiritually, mentally, socially, etc.)
- Most importantly, Christians can influence their communities by initiating dialogue on these important topics in both small and large groups. The new genetics has not received nearly the attention devoted to other issues in bioethics such as abortion and physician-assisted suicide.

Many settings are appropriate; but central to them all is the presentation of the ethical, social and theological implications of the new genetic technologies – what some have called genethics. The nature and content of such presentations warrants careful consideration.

THE PRESENTER

Then I heard the voice of the Lord saying, 'Whom shall I send? And who will go for us?' And I said, 'Here am I. Send me!' (Isa. 6:8).

Providing information and promoting dialogue in order to raise public awareness about the benefits and harms of genetic information and intervention is the goal of a genetics presentation. The presentation may be simple or elaborate depending on the abilities of the speaker. If one lacks public speaking skills or background in genetic science, outside speakers may be scheduled, or other media tools such as videos may be effectively employed. The key is to take the initiative – and anyone can do that.

Initiators should consider both Christian and secular audiences. Their own churches and communities are ideal sites to schedule presentations. Groups within the church, e.g., adult education classes, youth groups, and leadership groups, can be specially targeted. Secular groups such as civic organizations within the community who meet on a regular basis and feature speakers are usually willing to schedule genetics presentations as a service to the community. The business leadership within a community are often members of organizations like the Chamber of Commerce and the Rotary Club, and they constitute important audiences for this type of presentation.

THE PRESENTATION

You are the salt of the earth. But if the salt loses its saltiness, how can it be made salty again? It is no longer good for anything, except to be thrown out and trampled by men (Matt. 5:13).

As with any human-created technology, the new genetic technologies have great potential for both benefit and abuse. Christians are to be the salt of the world – preventing the decay which may result from inappropriate uses of the genetic technologies. As preservatives, they must work to prevent the terrors of the Holocaust and historical abuses of eugenics from recurring in this generation.

Accordingly, presentations should include a wide range of information: 1) a brief and uncomplicated introduction to molecular genetics, 2) some information on the variety of emerging technologies including gene therapy for diseases such as ADA deficiency, 3) descriptions of the benefits and harms arising from these new innovations, 4) a Christian assessment of these dilemmas and, 5) a listing of available resources for further study. The amount of information in the presentation will vary, depending on the time constraints. Ideally, more than one session should be scheduled because of the immensity of the topic. Presenters should regulate the content to the level of audience. Simple definitions of terms such as DNA, gene, chromosome, nucleus, cell, and protein synthesis should be given in an interesting manner. Adding interesting facts like the length of DNA in the nucleus, the total number of cells in the human body, etc. can enliven the lecture. Visual aids should be used if possible. Utilizing analogies, such as comparing the base code of DNA to letters in the alphabet, assists in the basic understanding of DNA and its relationship to inheritance. A brief historical survey of genetics can include biblical material from Genesis and can culminate in a discussion of the Human Genome Project. When lecturing to secular groups, it may be difficult to introduce a Christian perspective. Although the Bible has no direct reference to quandaries created by the new genetics, a case study of Mendelian genetics is presented in Genesis 30. In the historical account of Jacob and Laban, Jacob's successful selective breeding increases the number of spotted sheep and goats in his flock – in retrospect a 'manipulation' of recessive genes.

DEBUNKING GENETIC DETERMINISM

What are people that you are mindful of them, or their children that you care for them? You made them a little lower than the heavenly beings and crowned them with glory and honour (Psa. 8:4,5).

When describing the expression of genes, presenters should emphasize the influence of both genetic and environmental components in forming the traits of each individual. It is common to oversimplify the discussion of gene expression and convey the faulty notion that humans are products solely of their genetic code. Consider lung cancer, for example. Individuals with a genetic predisposition to certain types of lung cancer will have an increased likelihood of developing cancer if they are also exposed to environmental toxins, e.g., cigarette smoke. Thus, lung cancer has both genetic and environmental components. Other genetic disorders may have a greater genetic component and lesser environmental component or vice versa. News reports often neglect the interaction between genetics and environment, as illustrated by the following headlines. All but the last appeared in the *Houston Chronicle* during the period of January to June 1996.

> 'Researchers find possible "personality gene"' (*Houston Chronicle*, Jan 1, 1996).
> 'Gene that affects aging is isolated in patients with rare disease' (*Houston Chronicle*, April 12, 1996).
> 'Smart men should thank mothers, geneticist says' (*Houston Chronicle*, June 29, 1996).
> 'Fitness genes: the next breakthrough?' (*Self* magazine, April 1996).

These headlines suggest that intelligence, physical fitness, and personality are 'all in the genes'. Newspapers are not the only misleading influence. Popular science books for lay readers may also contain figurative language that distorts and exaggerates the nature of DNA. Consider the following example.

> DNA's power is global; it has orchestrated the history of life on earth for three and a half billion years. Yet its touch is intimate; it determines your chances of getting cancer, the amount of cholesterol in your father's blood, and color of your daughter's eyes.[14]

Because most individuals gain their science information from the newspaper and other media sources, it is essential to equip people to review this information critically. The notion that most traits and genetic disorders are caused by a single gene through Mendelian inheritance must also be disputed. Intelligence, heart disease, personality and other complex patterns expressed in humans are unlikely to be due to the effect of one gene, but rather multiple sets of genes in interaction with the environment. Moreover, having the gene for a disease like breast cancer does not mean that one will get the disease; one just has a higher likelihood of getting it. Even if one develops a genetic disorder like cystic fibrosis, the condition may have varying levels of severity. A good presentation on genetics will alert people to the great complexity of the topic.

FOSTERING DIALOGUE

Let your conversation be always full of grace, seasoned with salt, so that you may know how to answer everyone (Col. 4:6).

When presenting the various procedures available such as prenatal screening, genetic testing, and genetic therapy, it is effective to use case studies that illustrate the benefits and the risks of genetic technologies. Only a few of these case studies should be presented if time is limited. However, several of them should present the difficulty yet importance of the choices people must make. Media news stories are excellent resources – for example, the April 1995 issue of *Life* magazine entitled 'Living Legacy: Knowing your Medical Family Tree can Save your Life'. Highlighted in the article is a child diagnosed with a fairly aggressive eye cancer called retinoblastoma. He received early treatment because of his genetic history, confirmed by genetic testing. The cancer was treated, did not spread to his brain, and his life was saved.[15] Reports of such preventive treatment compel geneticists like Francis Collins, director of the Human Genome Project, to continue research in a field with ethical land mines (see Collins' chapter in this volume).

Other issues to discuss include whether or not to undergo testing if no treatment is yet available, who should have access to test results, and whether or not to abort genetically disabled fetuses. Unfortunately, medical interventions have not been discovered for most genetic disorders. This lag in development creates a dilemma when a person discovers he or she has a genetic disorder for which there is no cure. Indeed, many have decided to forego genetic testing, fearing the knowledge will be too agonizing to bear. Genetic tests offer only a sad prognosis for late onset diseases such as Huntington's disease and Alzheimer's disease. In addition to this challenge, genetic information may compromise one's privacy. This threat arises when third parties such as schools, future employers and insurance companies gain access to people's genetic information and improperly use the information to discriminate against them.

The abortion controversy only expands in an age of increased genetic information, as early information about fetal disability increases the reasons for considering abortion. The same concerns about abortion arise here as in situations where the reasons for abortion are not genetically related. Abortion of a handicapped fetus seems to contradict medicine's dictum, 'do no harm'. If the fetus is human, then in the words of Francis Beckwith, 'to promote the aborting of the handicapped unborn is tantamount to promoting the execution of handicapped people who are already born'[16]. Yet, while the church appropriately speaks out in behalf of life through its teaching, its support of families with handicapped members, and its public policy advocacy, there is no place for condemning victims who have chosen the route of selective abortion. The role of the body of Christ in such a case is forgiveness and the promotion of healing. Special compassion and counsel is required in extremely difficult cases, e.g., the frightening Lesch-Nyhan syndrome which causes mental retardation and a powerful urge to self mutilate by biting the lips and fingers. Meanwhile, dialogue must address the dangers of relying on therapeutic abortion to escape from genetic problems. James Watson suggests that increasing use of therapeutic abortion may lead to the abandonment of research that fosters the development of effective therapies for genetic disorders.[17]

A CHRISTIAN PERSPECTIVE

So God created humanity in his own image, in the image of God he created humanity; male and female he created them (Gen. 1:27).

It is important to examine the various issues of the new genetics in a Christian context of love and individual worth. After presenting the numerous potentially beneficial and harmful applications of the new genetics, a biblical, Christian response is appropriate. Although the Bible does not address genetics directly, it contains many applicable fundamental principles, such as the Golden Rule, human dignity, and the importance of protecting those who are weakest.

As Roger Shinn and Ronald Cole-Turner have observed, a moral foundation is crucial to guide policy making:

> Society, not technology or science, distinguishes good from bad, progress from problems. It is society, not biology, that turns some genetic characteristics into liabilities. The moral vision of a society determines the ends that its technology serves. . . .Religious faith, in particular, nurtures the sense of purpose that is needed to guide a technologically advanced society. How people respond to the challenges of the moment will depend largely on their interests, their values, their faith. But purposeful action wants to be informed action.[18]

However, many consider contemporary society to be seriously morally deficient. Robert Orr, David Schiedermayer and David

Biebel in their work, *Life and Death Decisions*, compare the outlook common in earlier decades with the relatively recent moral turn in US society. Previously, society was widely acknowledged to be built on the foundation of the existence of a Creator-God who provides guidelines for morality. 'Rightness and wrongness were measured by these standards.' In sharp contrast, present society is rooted in atheism; therefore people are sovereign and can set their own standards, which are the relativistic shifting sands of the builder in the biblical parable. 'In terms of ethics, personal self-determination (autonomy) has become more important than the sanctity of human life.'[19] For Christians, the choice is not easier, simply more firmly rooted in the sanctity of life which is based upon the *imago Dei*, or the creation of man and woman in the image of God (Gen. 1:27).

Another difficulty with the secular view is that it is based on a concept of genetic perfection. Allen Verhey defines the current concept of parenting as, 'making perfect children, then making children perfect'.[20] Humans are image bearers of God regardless of race, gender, anatomy or genetics. Roy J. Enquist comments on the seeming conflict between equality and diversity as follows:

> Theologically considered, human beings are equal before God even as they are diverse by God's design. With respect to the correlation of disorders and capacities in certain population, the moral temptation is to discriminate in the light of genetic differences (sickle-cell anemia; Tay-Sachs disease). Theology can provide a critical service by showing that justice is not grounded in the demonstration of actual equality by subjects, but that a transcendent perspective enables one to affirm a necessary polarity: e.g. limitations of capacities centered in particular populations require rather than invalidate the moral obligation to affirm human equality[21]

When he saw the crowds, he had compassion on them, because they were harassed and helpless, like sheep without a shepherd. Then he said to his disciples, 'The harvest is plentiful but the workers are few. Ask the Lord of the harvest, therefore, to send out workers into his harvest field' (Mat. 9:36–38).

Effective presentations might conclude by reminding people that everyone carries several deleterious genes that may or may not be expressed. We are not able to choose our genes and it is wrong to discriminate against people because of circumstances over which they have no control. Guarding human dignity and upholding the worth of each individual regardless of genetic makeup, should be a priority for Christians. Society needs such commitments as part of the moral 'vision' required to see us through the stormy dilemmas that will confront us in the years ahead.

Presenters would also do well to close by supplying materials to each individual in the group for further research. These should identify World Wide Web sites on genetics, current legislation on privacy issues, and written works on the topics presented. Christians should visit Web sites with ongoing discussions about ethics and genetics to encourage inclusion of a Christian perspective in the dialogue about the issues.

There is a great need to be the hand, heart and words of Jesus in today's maelstrom of opinion and controversy concerning genetic technologies. Genetic screening, gene therapies, bioengineering and other applications can work for the common good, but also cast a dark shadow. Now is the time to foster dialogue and formulate guidelines and regulations, before the shadows become overwhelming.

NOTES

1. This case study is taken from the author's recent experience with her father.

2. 'Ethical, Legal, and Social Issues (ELSI).' July 1, 1996. Available via Internet: http:www.ornl.gov/TechResources/Human_Genome/resource/elsi.html

3. Andrews, Lori B., et al., eds. *Assessing Genetic Risks.* (Washington, D.C.: National Academy Press), p. 195.

4. Ibid. p. 187.

5. Ibid. p. 188.

6. Ibid.

7. U.S. Congress, Office of Technology Assessment, *Cystic Fibrosis and DNA Tests: Implications of Carrier Screening*, Summary, OTA-BA-533 (Washington, DC: U.S. Government Printing Office August 1992), p. 26–7.

8. Suzuki, David and Knudtson, Peter. *Genethics – The Clash Between the New Genetics and Human Values.* Revised ed. (Cambridge [MA], Harvard University Press 1990), pp. 3, 4.

9. Hubbard, Ruth and Wald, Elijah. *Exploding the Gene Myth.* (Boston, Beacon Press 1993), p. 126.

10. Cook-Deegan, Robert. *The Gene Wars – Science, Politics, and the Human Genome.* (New York, W.W. Norton and Company 1994), p. 248.

11. Cole-Turner, Ronald, *The New Genesis. Theology and The Genetic Revolution* (Louisville, Westminster/John Knox Press 1993), p. 74.

12. Ibid. p. 77

13. Ibid. p. 76

14. Levine, Joseph and Suzuki, David. *The Secret of Life. Redesigning the Living World.* (Boston, WGBH Educational Foundation 1993), p. 1.

15. Adato, Allison, 'Living Legacy' *Life Magazine*, (April 1995), pp. 60–64.

16. Beckwith, Francis J., *Politically Correct Death – Answering Arguments for Abortion Rights.* 3rd ed. (Grand Rapids, Baker Books 1993), p. 65.

17. Brown, Michael S., Collins, Francis S., Goldstein, Joseph L., Watson, James D. and Wexler, Nancy S., 'Roundtable: The Human Genome Project,' *Issues in Science and Technology*, (Fall 1993), p. 44.

18. Cole-Turner, p. 69.

19. Orr, Robert D. et al., *Life and Death Decisions – Help in Making Tough Choices about Bioethical Issues.* (Colorado Springs, NAVPRESS 1990), p. 52.

20. Lecture on 'Virtue Ethics' at the Advanced Bioethics Institute of The Center for Bioethics and Human Dignity, Bannockburn, Illinois, USA July 17, 1996.

21. Nelson, J. Robert, *On the New Frontiers of Genetics and Religion*. (Grand Rapids, Eerdmans 1994), p. 157.

PART III

Genetic Intervention

[14]

Genetic Therapy

Frank E Young, MD,PhD

The first record of medicinal treatment of disease dates to the fifth millennium BC in the Middle East. Initially, these therapies consisted of natural products from a variety of plants, animals, and minerals. Since people attributed many illnesses to indwelling demons at that time, treatment made the body as inhospitable as possible in hopes of driving out the demon.[1] In later centuries some people attributed disease to sin. When the disciples of Jesus Christ encountered a man born blind, for example, the question they raised was whether the man himself or his parents had sinned.[2] In the 18th and 19th century, the germ theory of disease emerged. With the advent of chemical and pharmaceutical industries, simple chemicals and vitamins replaced homeopathic modalities in the treatment of specific diseases. The 20th century began the era of potent medicinal treatments including antibiotics and cancer chemotherapy. All of these therapies treated the phenotype (symptoms of the disease) as in the case of the administration of insulin to a diabetic. Usually no genetic change accompanied the therapy (except random mutations in the case of chemotherapy).

Once the medicine was metabolized, its effectiveness was usually over. In stark contrast to all of these temporary treatments, gene therapy entails a manipulation of the code of life with its attendant permanent change in the somatic cells or germ cells of an individual. In the case of somatic cell therapy, the modification is not transmitted to the offspring. However, successful germ line therapy produces an inherited change.

The molecular genetic revolution beginning with the discovery of deoxyribonucleic acid (DNA) as the chemical that encodes hereditary changes, enabled life to be altered randomly in the test tube. The advent of genetic engineering in 1974 ushered in a new era in genetics, potentially enabling precise, directed manipulation of genomes and the exchange of genetic information among 'widely separated' species.

The fundamental advances required for this new technology occurred over decades, beginning with the establishment of the basic principles of genetics by an obscure Austrian monk, Gregor Mendel, in 1863. Basing his work on the inheritance breeding of colours in peas, he was able to determine that the traits were distributed in unique inherited units that were later to be called genes. An immense number of milestones in the 20th century led to the current understanding of molecular genetics. In less than fifty years after the discovery of the chemical basis of heredity, it was possible to isolate, purify, and characterize genetic elements and introduce them into foreign cells. Since the growth of genetic technologies has proceeded at different paces in different countries, the rest of this chapter will focus on the experience of the United States in order to illustrate the most recent developments in genetic therapy.

The realization of the power of this new technology in 1973 led scientists to request that the National Academy of Sciences establish a committee to outline restrictions for this technology. Conversations between the committee and the government (National Institutes of Health and National Science Foundation) resulted in the Asilomar Conference in February 1975. Approximately 150 scientists, physicians, government officials and representatives from the press and law discussed the risks and benefits of this new technology of genetic engineering – specifically, recombinant DNA (rDNA) technology. Temporary safety guidelines recommended a moratorium on some types of experiments and permitted others to go forward in line with appropriate biological and physical safety standards. Subsequently, the National Institutes of Health issued recombinant DNA guidelines that became the model for voluntary regulations of rDNA technology.

The Secretary of the Department of Health, Education and Welfare established the Recombinant DNA Advisory Committee (RAC) under the aegis of the NIH to evaluate the safety and ethics of rDNA. I served as a member of the Asilomar Conference, the RAC, the Interagency Committee that developed the Coordinated Framework for Biotechnology, the National Biotechnology Board, the Biotechnology Working Group of the President's Council on Competitiveness, and the *ad hoc* group of government experts on the Safety and Regulations in Biotechnology of the Organization for Economic Cooperation and Development (OECD) that was charged to harmonize international regulations. My experience and study in the field of genetics have provided ample evidence that one's world view, Christian or naturalistic, significantly influences the ways in which one seeks to apply these new technologies. Consider the following theological, scientific, and societal issues.

THEOLOGICAL CONSIDERATIONS

Throughout most of the early scientific deliberations on genetics, the church was relatively silent. Nevertheless, there was a tension between those guided by a naturalistic world view and those operating out of a Christian world view. The fundamental disagreement between the two world views concerns the origin of life, i.e., whether or not life was created by God. A number of biblical passages establish key principles of a Christian world view:

> Genesis 1:1 In the beginning God created the heavens and the earth. Now the earth was formless and empty, darkness was over the surface of the deep, and the Spirit of God was hovering over the waters.

> Genesis 1:27–28 So God created humanity in his own image, in the image of God he created humanity; male and female he created them. God blessed them and said to them, 'Be fruitful and increase in number, fill the earth and subdue it. Rule over the fish of the sea and the birds of the air and over every living creature that moves on the ground.'

> John 1:1–3 In the beginning was the Word, and the Word was with God, and the Word was God. He was with God in the beginning. Through him all things were made; without him nothing was made that has been made.

This Christian world view is theistic, trinitarian, and relies on God's direct revelation to us of himself and his works. At the heart of Christian ethics is the relationship of humanity as a creature to the Creator, the creation of man and woman in the image of God, the redemption of a sinful world through Christ's incarnation and death on the cross, and people's capacity to pray to God as Father in Christ's name with the guidance of the Holy Spirit. Therefore, the Christian lives as a 'traveller' in a sinful world, but bound for an eternity in the presence of God. The key to life is the complete love of God and one's neighbour as oneself.[3]

In contrast to this world view, the naturalist contends that life evolved over billions of years through a series of small steps to the current diversity of species. This macro evolutionary view, based on the theory of evolution enunciated by Darwin and championed by Huxley, not only influenced the scientific thought of the day but also became an explanation for social conditions via the concept of the survival of the fittest. Although a number of recent publications have challenged the validity of macro evolutionary changes[4,5], the theory of evolution has developed a sacrosanct status. This theory and its ramifications continue to shape scientific and social policy.

Studies in microbial genetics have clearly demonstrated that spontaneous mutations in cell lines do result in micro evolutionary changes within species. A mutation that leads to survival advantage will be passed on and gain dominance. This micro evolution occurs in spurts – periods of rapid change interspersed with periods of stability.[6] Additionally, many molecular geneticists contend that lineage can be traced by genetic sequences of highly conserved genes such as cytochrome c, an enzyme found in mitochondria.[7] This evidence does support theories of micro-evolution – evolution at the cellular level.

However, those holding a creation view reject the assertion that the vast array of complex life forms was produced through macro evolutionary changes from unicellular organisms. Despite these objections, the theory of evolution has moved from the strict definition of 'the frequency of a gene in the population as a function of time' to a theology of the origin of life and the taxonomic relationship of organisms.

SCIENTIFIC AND TECHNOLOGIC ADVANCES

The discovery of DNA by Avery and co-workers[8] led to a rapid determination and manipulation of the physical and chemical structure of DNA (Table 1), the fundamental chemical of the gene.[9] Initially DNA could be broken only in a random fashion. Research advances in the late 60s and 70s enabled DNA to be broken at unique sites, joined in self-replicating elements, and inserted into animal cells, bacterial cells and viruses. These fundamental advances led to the rapid development of recombinant DNA (rDNA) techniques to cleave, purify and clone genes. Subsequently, methodological innovations made it possible to automate the identification of genes' sequences.

TABLE 1
SELECTED MILESTONES IN GENETICS LEADING TO GENE THERAPY

Discovery	Utility
Inheritance of traits in peas	Ability to follow patterns of inheritance
Location of genes on chromosomes	Analysis of inheritance
Transformation of traits in bacteria	Manipulation of genes in a test tube
Identification of DNA as the transforming principle	Ability to correct specific mutations
Elucidation of the three structure dimensional of DNA	Study of the physical,chemical and biological properties of genes
Discovery of enzymes to break DNA at specific sites	Analysis of the genome
Dicovery of enzymes to join DNA fragments	Construction of chimeras
Discovery of self-replicating elements	Ability to introduce a foreign fragment into replicating structures
Methods to introduce DNA into variety of cell lines	Capacity to make cells produce large amounts of self-replicating elements

Perhaps, the most significant development was the Human Genome Project begun under the leadership of Dr. James Watson who, with Dr. Crick, received the Nobel Prize for discovery of the structure of DNA. The Human Genome Project is designed to produce genetic maps, physical maps and a complete nucleotide map of human chromosomes.[10] The rapid development of new methods for sequencing and mapping should establish the sequence of 100,000 genes by 2005. According to Lander, this plethora of comparative genetic information will 'unlock the record of 3.5 billion years of evolutionary experimentation. It will not only reveal the precise branches in the tree of life, but will elucidate the timing and character of major evolutionary innovation.'[11] Recently Shuler et al. have reported that 16,000 genes of the 50,000 to 100,000 human genes have been mapped.[12] This mapping has enabled scientists to determine whether sequences are similar in widely different organisms (and are therefore 'conserved genes'). Two examples of such sequence similarity are: 1) the homology of gene AD3 associated with Alzheimer's Disease and a protein encoded in a nematode, *C. elegans*, and 2) a gene associated with pancreatic carcinoma, DPC4 and a gene in Drosophila implicated in the transforming growth factor pathway. These similarities allow us to study the genes in other organisms and then apply the knowledge gained to humans.

Historically, the initial work in the field of rDNA focused on the production of medicinal compounds such as insulin and human growth hormone in bacteria, yeast, or animal cells. Diagnostic probes to detect genetic abnormalities, pathogens, and specific gene sequences were also produced. These advances led to new medicinal compounds to modify bodily function (phenotypic modification).

TYPES OF THERAPY

Phenotypic modification	Treatment with medicines or surgical intervention
Somatic gene therapy	Introduction of genes by transformation or transfection
Germ line gene therapy	Introduction of genes into germ line cell

The next step was gene therapy,[13] which initially involved changes in somatic cells. In somatic gene therapy, a vector (a self-replicating element) carries the expressible normal gene into the cell and thereby corrects or replaces the function of a defective gene. The following steps occur either *ex vivo* or *in vivo*:

- Detection of the abnormal gene
- Availability of a purified normal gene
- Availability of a suitable delivery system (vector into which the gene can be inserted)
- Use of the vector to incorporate the normal gene into the desired (target) cell
- Acceptance by the host of the modified cell
- Production of the gene product in sufficient quantity in the host.

For example, diabetics currently receive daily injections of animal or cloned human insulin. Theoretically, the diabetic could be treated by gene therapy. Either cells encoding insulin could augment the insufficient supply of insulin or a vector could deliver a foreign 'normal gene' into the defective pancreatic cells, thereby enabling them to produce insulin. Both of these forms of gene therapy produce modifications of the individual only. These changes are not transmitted from generation to generation. Were the gene instead introduced into the germ cells, the defective gene could be replaced and a permanent change could be transmitted from generation to generation. But there are risks. For example, the permanent genetic change could have unanticipated side effects, including transcription of the genome or the production of a product that is not immunologically compatible with the body.

Technological advances, coupled with the development of rapid procedures for the identification of defective genes, have led to a marked increase in the number of Investigational New Drug applications (INDs).[14] Figure 1 illustrates the number of INDs granted from Fiscal Year 1989 to Fiscal Year (FY) 1995. The increase was substantial in the last two years. Most of the increase in FY 1995

INVESTIGATIONAL NEW DRUG APPLICATIONS

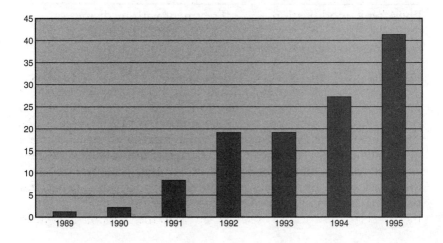

was in the administration of viral vectors (viruses such as retro virus and adenovirus capable of transmission of genes) to patients. Because of the predicted improvement of the technology, it is likely that the viral vectors will become increasingly useful. Accordingly, a marked upswing in gene therapy is predicted within the next four years.

Gene therapy *in utero* is in the formative stages of development. From as early as 1981 until now, postnatal (after birth) bone marrow transplants have been performed to treat inborn errors of metabolism.[15] However, postnatal transplantations have been difficult due to tissue incompatibility and significant organ damage. Advances in the understanding of the fundamental biology of the immune response, increased knowledge of the genetic map of humans, and improved prenatal diagnostic methods have enabled scientists to attempt transplantation with more confidence. They are now ready to try this technique *in utero*. The FDA has received several requests to use bone marrow cells (hematopoetic cells) to treat fetuses *in utero*.

Recent studies cited by Patterson et al.[16] demonstrate that a 'window of time' exists during the development of the human fetus *in utero* estimated at approximately between 12 and 14 weeks, during which the fetus cannot immunologically reject foreign tissue. Thus hematopoetic cells transplanted then would be likely to survive. The goals of such transplantation, summarized by Patterson et al.,[17] include: '(1) establishing normal cellular function before the target organ damage occurs; (2) establishing stable and durable chimerism that will obviate or diminish the need for post natal transplants; and (3) inducing donor-specific tolerance that would permit post-natal transplants with minimal or no preparative immunosuppression'. Theoretically, genes can be introduced into germ-line as well as somatic cells. The implications of this possibility for such questions as when life begins and the rights of the fetus must be carefully considered.

SOCIETAL CONCERNS

Once people appreciated that genes could be mixed from widely divergent sources through rDNA techniques, they called for a moratorium on this type of research and requested that a conference be convened in Asilomar to review the safety considerations. As discussed by Young and Miller,[18] this meeting focused on the unknown consequences of mixing genes from widely divergent organisms. Participants reasoned that if molecular geneticists could devise a system of self regulation, government regulation would not be necessary. Accordingly, following the Asilomar meeting, scientists developed interim guidelines. In 1976 the National Institutes of Health Guidelines[19] replaced these interim guidelines. A Recombinant DNA Advisory Committee reviewed the NIH guidelines annually thereafter, incorporating ethical as well as scientific evaluations. Throughout, there was substantial conflict and uncertainty about the evaluation of the products developed through biotechnology. Eventually the Reagan Administration formed a Domestic Policy Council Working Group on Biotechnology that developed a coordinated framework for regulating biotechnology.[20] The FDA concluded that biotechnology-derived products produced no novel risks and could be regulated in the same fashion as other new drugs and biologicals. As the projected commercial applications of biotechnology became a reality, a number of governmental studies addressed the balance between safety, product quality and commercial interest.[21, 22, 23]

The international community also reviewed safety of rDNA through the Organization for Economic Co-operation and Development (OECD). In a seminal publication,[24] the OECD recognized that 'recombinant DNA techniques have opened up new and promising possibilities in a wide range of applications and can be expected to bring considerable benefits to mankind'. They developed international guidelines for various aspects of rDNA technology as well as procedures for the safe large-scale industrial production of rDNA products.[25, 26, 27, 28] Of particular significance was the policy of substantial equivalence.[29] The product produced by the permanent introduction of genes into animals and plants used for food was to be treated in the same manner as the traditional food or food component if it was found to be substantially equivalent to an existing food or food product.[30] This policy permitted permanent modification of plants and animals by gene therapy or 'controlled genetic manipulation' to be treated in the same fashion as traditional animal or plant husbandry. The international community thereby recognized that products of biotechnology can be evaluated by standard regulatory procedures.

Ethical concerns about these developments have received considerable attention. As early as 1982, the President's Commission for the Study of Ethical Problems in Medicine and Biomedical and Behavioral Research voiced a concern for the ethics of germ-line gene therapy:

> In addition to the technical difficulties involved, genetic manipulation of embryos raises ethical concerns. Altering the human gene pool by eliminating 'bad' traits is a form of eugenics, about which there is strong concern. In 1982, the Council of Europe requested 'explicit recognition in the Human Rights Convention of the right to a genetic inheritance which has not been interfered with, except in accordance with certain principles which are recognized as being fully compatible with respect to human rights'.

Yet the meaning of 'respect for human rights' is vague. Some favor gene therapy in embryos because it offers a treatment other than abortion for genetic defects. But – especially in the early years while the techniques are being perfected – it would probably be standard practice to examine the embryos and either not implant or if already implanted, to abort any found to be abnormal. Not to do so would risk creating offspring who have genetic problems created by the 'therapy' rather than naturally occurring defects.[31]

These ethical concerns remain despite the rapid advance in technological capabilities. The most significant questions currently are: (1) Is it safe permanently to alter the germ line? (There is no way to 'correct' a technological mistake if one considers abortion not to be an option.) (2) Who has the legal capacity to give informed consent for the fetus – the mother alone, the mother and father together, or someone else? (3) Who is legally liable if a mistake occurs resulting in disability or death? (4) Are genetic defects 'disabilities' and as such afforded special legal protection (for example, under the Americans with Disabilities Act in the United States)? (5) Is the fetus truly a 'person' with full rights of personhood at 12–14 weeks when stem cell and other forms of genetic therapy should be instituted? (6) How accurate is prenatal diagnosis (and what difference should the potential for inaccuracy make)? (7) Is genetic therapy cost-effective in view of other pressing public health needs for the population at large?

Throughout the eighties and early nineties, the National Institutes of Health conducted not only a scientific review but also an ethical and safety assessment of the protocols for gene therapy. Then, as the technology matured, the NIH relinquished its special review of the scientific aspects of gene therapy to the FDA.[32] However, the NIH Director proposed to convene three to four conferences per year involving participants 'who possess significant scientific, ethical and legal expertise and/or interest that is directly applicable to a specific recombinant DNA research interest'. At present, germ-line gene therapy is of particular concern in the public arena. Debate often revolves around the issue of sanctity of life, the desire to correct genetic defects in the offspring of couples who carry major harmful genetic loci, the malpractice issues associated with errors, and the cost effectiveness of germ-line therapy in view of the millions of aborted fetuses each year.

A ROLE FOR THE CHURCH

The opposing world views, creationism and naturalism, yield different concepts of human dignity which flow from conflicting understandings of the origin of life. The Judeo-Christian belief in God as the creator and humanity as the creature created in God's image contrasts starkly with the belief that humanity as well as all other life evolved from nothing but raw materials of the earth. Although many Christians would, on reflection, heartily affirm a Christian world view over a macro-evolutionary paradigm, the church needs to articulate this world view more carefully as part of its assessment of recombinant DNA. For example, the church can affirm that humanness is 'the distinctive quality implied by the symbol of "in the image of God," the image in which everyone is created and which is the presupposition of life's meaning; everyone's unique identity is the creation and endowment of God.'[33] Moreover, the church can acknowledge three different aspects of life reflected in three Greek words for life in the New Testament: '*Bios* meaning subsistence or bare survival; *Psuche* meaning enjoyment of the experiences of individual, familial, and social living with more than a minimal degree of health, activity and expectations; and *Zoe* meaning life being fulfilled already through participation in the eternal quality of living as, according to the Christian faith, it is willed and offered by God in Christ Jesus.'[34] The sanctity of life in all these dimensions and hence the dignity of the human being stem from creation in the image of God.

In view of the clash of world views as society struggles for the values to guide this new technology, several church initiatives are in order. First, individuals, congregations, denominations, and other Christian groups must study creation and be able to express a Christian world view clearly and in contrast to a naturalistic world view. The contrast between humanity in a fallen sinful state and the Darwinian concept of gradual improvement in life forms is important in this regard.[35] Second, Christians must understand the limits of technology in addressing the fundamental issues of life. Third, Christians must enter the arena of controversy. Frequently, Christians avoid the conflict between faith in Christ and allegiance to humanistic societal values.

Entering the conflicts requires a deep understanding of Scripture and a thorough knowledge of the scientific and technical issues facing society. Christians must be prepared to bring the truths of God's word into the contemporary technological debates, confident that God is the Creator and the Redeemer. Otherwise, the Christians will be 'missing in action' in one of the more important engagements of the 21st century.

NOTES

1. Boussel, P., Bonnemain, H., Bove, F. J., *History of Pharmacy*, (Paris and Lausanne, Asklepios Press 1982) p.17.

2. See the biblical Gospel of John 9:3–5.

3. Gospel of Luke 10:27.

4. Johnson, P. E., *Darwin on Trial*, (Downers Grove, InterVarsity Press, 1992).

5. Behe, M.J., *Darwin's Black Box*, (NY, Free Press, 1996).

6. Elena, S. E., Cooper, V.S. and Lenski, R., 'Punctuated Evolution Caused by Selection of Rare Beneficial Mutations', *Science* 272:1802–1804, (1996).

7. Ayala, F. J., 'Evolution', In Davis, B.D. (ed.), *The Genetic Revolution*, (Baltimore and London, The Johns Hopkins University Press 1991) p. 183–189.

8. Avery, O.T., Macleod, C.M., and McCarty, M., 'Studies of the Chemical Nature of the Substance Inducing Transformation of Pneumococcal Types', *J. Exp. Med.* 79:137–150.

9. Davis, B.D., 'The issues: Prospects versus perceptions', In *The Genetic Revolution*, ibid p.10–27.

10. Lander, E.S., 'The New Genomics: Global Views of Biology', *Science*, 274: 536–539 (1996).

11. Ibid., p. 537.

12. Schuler, G.D. et al. 'A Genetic Map of the Human Genome', *Science* 274: 540–546,1996.

13. Gene therapy is defined as 'a medical intervention based on modification of the genetic material of living cells. Cells may be modified *ex vivo* for subsequent administration or may be altered *in vivo* by gene therapy products given directly to the subject . . . . The genetic manipulation may be intended to prevent, cure, diagnose or mitigate disease or injuries in humans.' Federal Register 58:53248–53251 (1993).

14. After a potential medicine is discovered, it is tested in animals. The next stage is testing in humans. Before the drug can be tested, the chemical and animal data must be submitted to the Food and Drug Administration in the form of an Investigational New Drug Application (IND). Following the human studies for both safety and efficacy, the corporate sponsor can submit a New Drug Application (NDA). The time of application from an IND to the approval of a NDA is approximately eight years. Most of the time is devoted to the industrial sponsor's tests of the drug's safety and effectiveness. Studies have shown that only twenty percent of the INDs for innovative drugs reach the approval stage, primarily due to the drug failing the safety and/or effectiveness standards.

15. Hoobs, J. R., Smith, H. R., and Parkman, R., 'Bone marrow transplantation for inborn errors of metabolism', *Lancet*, 2:735–739 (1981).

16. Patterson, A. P., Weiss, K.D., Noguchi, P.D., and Fletcher, J. D., '*In Utero* Stem cell Transplantation: Clinical and Ethical Implications', in press.

17. Ibid.

18. Young, F.E., and Miller, H. I., 'Concepts and Safety Principles for Assuring Safety of Biotechnology Products, BioJapan '92', *Symposium Proceedings*,484–496, (1992).

19. National Institutes of Health, Recombinant DNA Research Guidelines, Federal Register 41: 27902 1976.

20. Office of Science and Technology Policy, Coordinated Framework for Regulation of Biotechnology, Federal Register 51: 23302–23393 (1986).

21. Vice President Dan Quale, *The President's Council on Competitiveness* (1991).

22. National Biotechnology Policy Board Report (1992).

23. Biology for the 21st Century, A Report of The Federal Coordinating Council for Science, Engineering and Technology (1992).

24. *Recombinant DNA Safety Considerations*, (Paris, Organization for Economic Cooperation and Development 1986), p. 7–10.

25. *Biotechnology and the Changing Role of Government*, (Paris, Organization for Economic Cooperation and Development 1988).

26. *Biotechnology and Economic and Wider Impacts*, (Paris, Organization for Economic Cooperation and Development 1989).

182 *Genetic Intervention*

27. *Safety Considerations for Biotechnology*, (Paris, Organization for Economic Cooperation and Development 1992).

28. *Field Release of Transgenic Plants*, (Paris, Organization for Economic Cooperation and Development 1993).

29. *Safety Foods Derived by Modern Biotechnology: Concepts and Principles*, (Paris, Organization for Economic Cooperation and Development 1993), p. 13–15.

30. The introduction of genes into the germ line of animals and plants used for food introduced many of the same ethical and scientific concerns as in human gene therapy.

31. 'Splicing Life: The Social and Ethical Issues of Genetic Engineering with Human Beings', *The President's Commission for the Study of Ethical Problems in Medicine and Biomedical and Behavioral Research* (1982) p. 47,48.

32. Recombinant DNA Research: Notice of Intent to Propose Amendments to the National Institutes of Health Guidelines for Research Involving Recombinant DNA Molecules (National Institutes of Health Guidelines) Regarding Oversight of Recombinant DNA Activities, *Federal Register*, 61 :35774–35777 (1996).

33. Nelson, J. Robert, *Human Life: A Biblical Perspective for Bioethics*, (Philadelphia, Westminster 1984), p. 130.

34. Ibid., p. 137.

35. Genesis 3 describes humanity as fallen in sin whereas Darwin postulates steady improvement, as noted in P. Appleman's *Darwin* (Norton Press), p. 123 'It may be said metaphorically that natural selection is daily and hourly scrutinizing, throughout the world, the slightest variations; rejecting those that are bad, preserving and adding up all that are good; silently and insensibly working, whatever and wherever opportunity offers, at the improvement of each organic being in relation to its organic and inorganic conditions of life.'

15

A Theological Basis for Genetic Intervention

John S. Feinberg, PhD

By cracking the human genetic code and through recombinant DNA technology, science and medicine have brought us to the brink of a brave new world. Experiments in human gene therapy have already been conducted which promise to address previously unassailable genetically-controlled diseases. With this technology comes the eventual possibility of designing human beings according to our own taste. Some like Joseph Fletcher welcome the prospects this technology affords:

> We are told that we should 'let nature alone' and 'keep out of the womb' and stop 'tinkering' with the building blocks of human beings because we are getting 'too close to the mystery of life.' How close is too close? Why should we not get so close that like other mysteries the secret of life comes to be no secret at all? Robert Sinsheimer of the California Institute of Technology points out that the opponents of genetic engineering 'aren't among the losers in the chromosomal lottery,' which saddles us with 'four million Americans born with diabetes, or the two hundred fifty thousand children born in the United States every year with genetic diseases, or the fifty million Americans whose I.Q.s are below ninety.' Genetic engineering and fetal control will help enormously.
>
> The accusation that the new biology is trying to create a 'master race' is fair enough if it means that a people with fewer defects and more control over the crippling accidents of 'nature' are better able to master life's ups and downs. Most of us would want to belong to the master race in that sense. Mastery in the sense of good health and inheritance is sanity.[1]

To the objection that so artificially manipulating the components of human life dehumanizes humans, he responds:

> Technology, whether of the 'hard' physical kind or the 'soft' biological kind, is man's creation and man's hallmark. . . . To be civilized is to be artificial, and to object that something is artificial only condemns it in the eyes of subrational nature lovers or natural-law mystics.[2]

Moreover, in a paraphrase of Marx's claim that philosophers have only interpreted the world, whereas the point is to change it, Fletcher observes:

So we might say of genetics and the new birth technologies. The midwifery stage of birth and baby making in the past only tried to understand reproduction, but modern medicine is changing it. The jump from 'taking what you get' by way of random or lottery conceptions to selective genetic and fetal engineering is a big jump indeed. But further than that, postmidwifery obstetrics is still entirely natural and being artificial is supremely human – humanly motivated and humanly manipulated.[3]

On the other hand, there are some dissenters. For a long time Jeremy Rifkin has been speaking out against any use of this new technology to tamper with the human genetic code. For example, notes Rifkin:

> . . . proponents of human genetic engineering argue that the benefits outweigh the risks and that it would be irresponsible not to use this powerful new technology to eliminate serious 'genetic disorders.' The *New York Times* correctly addressed this conventional scientific argument by concluding in a July 22, 1982 editorial that once the scientists are able to repair genetic defects 'it will become much harder to argue against adding genes that confer desired qualities, like better health, looks or brains.' According to the *Times*, 'There is no discernible line to be drawn between making inheritable repairs of genetic defects, and improving the species.'
>
> Once we decide to begin the process of human genetic engineering, there is really no logical place to stop. If diabetes, sickle cell anemia, and cancer are to be cured by altering the genetic make-up of an individual, why not proceed to other 'disorders': myopia, color blindness, left-handedness. Indeed, what is to preclude a society from deciding that a certain skin color is a disorder?[4]

Are Rifkin and the *New York Times* editorialist correct? Is there no way to draw a logical distinction between appropriate and inappropriate uses of recombinant DNA technology? We could examine this question from the standpoint of agriculture, industry, or warfare, but the specific focus of this chapter will be the question of altering the genetic code of human beings. Is there any way to draw a distinction between morally acceptable and unacceptable alterations in that genetic code? Once we establish the principle that it is acceptable to tamper with the genetic code of human beings for some purposes, is there no logical way to exclude tampering with the genetic code for other purposes? If not, then apparently we have opened the door for eugenics in a most extreme form, potentially totally redesigning the human genetic code in whatever way we want.

Most of us would probably want to hold a position somewhere between the extremes of Joseph Fletcher and Jeremy Rifkin on this issue. We are sensitive to the argument that if we allow genetic interventions to accomplish certain ends, it will be difficult to exclude interventions to accomplish other ends. However, we would probably add that there must be a way to draw a logical distinction between morally appropriate and inappropriate uses of genetic technology in human beings.

THE THERAPEUTIC-EUGENIC DISTINCTION

Some people would say that an appropriate distinction can be made between therapeutic and eugenic uses of this technology. They would claim that as long as recombinant DNA technology is used on human beings for therapeutic purposes, it is acceptable. What is unacceptable is using it to design individuals.

Although this distinction may initially sound plausible, it is not adequate. It is based on a valid intuition, but by itself it is not enough. One difficulty is that therapeutic uses of genetic technology can be defined in a number of ways. On the one hand, a therapeutic use of this technology might entail using it to correct a defective gene that produces a fatal genetic disease. On the other hand, certain brown-eyed, black-haired people might think that blonds have more fun, and that their lives and careers would be much happier if they were blond and blue-eyed. Therefore, the fact that they are not blond-haired and blue-eyed is a defect. Even if this 'defect' does not create physical problems, it creates psychological problems. If we would just 'correct' or change the genes for hair and eye colour for these people, we would be engaging in therapeutic intervention. It would be psychological therapy, but as long as therapeutic uses of this technology are acceptable, then the intervention would arguably be appropriate. Distinguishing therapeutic and eugenic interventions, then, may be hard to do in practice.

The simple distinction between therapeutic and eugenic uses of recombinant DNA technology is inadequate in another way as well. Just as defining what counts as therapy is problematic, so is defining eugenics. Eugenics is typically understood to involve trying to create 'the perfect person', as opposed to correcting physical or psychological difficulties in particular people. However, when people talk of creating the perfect person (or of enhancing the overall well-being of an individual), they sometimes have in view an enterprise that includes correcting certain deleterious genes. So, again, the categories are not very distinct in practice.

In light of these various issues, one might initially despair of ever being able to draw satisfactory distinctions between acceptable and unacceptable uses of genetic technology. However, the stakes are too great to abandon the quest, for genetic intervention without limits would be disastrous and not to carry out any genetic intervention would be tragic. What other ways are there to draw a logical distinction between acceptable and unacceptable uses of genetic technology? We may not need to discard the eugenics-therapeutics distinction ultimately, but we need to put it aside temporarily so that we may consider some theological principles.

A BIBLICAL APPROACH

Many would begin by appealing to biblical teaching that we should have compassion on the sick and do what we can to heal them. Although this is a valid concern, it runs into some of the same problems just discussed with regard to what therapy entails. We should indeed be concerned to heal the sick (see James Peterson's chapter later in this volume), but what counts as an 'illness?' The would-be blue-eyed blondes might deem their lack of such traits a bodily problem needing correction – an illness of sorts. The person with an IQ of 135 who would prefer an IQ of 180 might consider their condition an illness. So a simple appeal to the need to heal the sick will not give us a clear distinction between acceptable and unacceptable uses of recombinant DNA technology on human beings.

Instead we must turn to the biblical teaching that we live in a fallen world. Our world was created without sin, but human and angelic beings disobeyed God and sin entered the universe. In Romans 5:12 the apostle Paul says that through the action of one man, Adam, sin entered the human race, and through sin death entered our world. Sin and death passed to all of us because all had sinned in Adam. According to this passage, then, the ultimate reason people die is that there is sin in the world. If people are going to die, they must die of something. Some people die in automobile accidents, others die in plane crashes, and yet others die as a result of human violence. While there are many ways a person might die, most people die as a result of disease. There are many diseases. Some are not life-threatening, but others are. Some diseases are totally related to bacteria or germs of some sort, whereas others result from a genetic defect. If we agree with Scripture that people die ultimately because they have sinned, then one thing they can die of is disease (even a genetically based disease). This is not to say that one person is more guilty of sin than others and that is why they get a horrible disease while others do not. Rather, everyone has sinned and as a result, all of us will undergo physical death. If we are going to die, we will die of something, and one thing we can die of is genetically controlled diseases.[5]

This theological point alone, however, will not allow us to distinguish between morally acceptable and unacceptable uses of recombinant DNA technology. Another biblical-theological consideration is necessary. Scripture teaches that all of us should fight sin and its consequences. One of the ways to do so is by obeying

God's law. Another way to fight sin is to fight its consequences. Surely, this is what God does. God loved us so much that he sent Jesus Christ to die so that even though we have sinned, we do not have to bear all of the consequences of that sin. One consequence of that sin, namely death, fell upon Jesus Christ, and those of us who trust in Christ as our personal saviour allow him to bear the eternal consequences of our sins.[6] As God fights the consequences of sin, so should we who are his followers.[7]

These considerations provide us with a way to begin drawing a line between acceptable and unacceptable uses of genetic technology. Any use of this technology to fight something in human beings that is clearly a result of the consequences of sin and living in a fallen world is morally acceptable. In other words, if there is a condition in a human being (whether physical or psychological) that is clearly traceable to sin and its consequences, and if there is something that genetic technology could do to address that problem, then that use of this technology would be acceptable. In effect, we would be using this technology to fight sin and its consequences. A similar justification should be used in regard to any other medical procedures and technologies used to fight conditions that result from sin and its consequences. For example, consider the morality of heart bypass surgery or heart transplants, which may seem to some to involve too much tampering with a human being. If heart disease is a result of living in a fallen world, using medical procedures to address that disease cannot be ruled out on moral grounds (though there may be practical considerations that make use of them unwise).

THE IMPORTANCE OF GUIDELINES

Needless to say, any way one uses recombinant DNA technology to overcome sin and its consequences is not automatically acceptable. As W. French Anderson notes, if we are going to use gene therapy (whether germ-line or somatic cell), we need to do so in accordance with certain regulations. He proposes that somatic cell therapy should first be tested on animals, and that researchers should look for three things. First, there should be evidence that the curative genes can be directed to specific cells and remain there long enough to be effective. Second, there should be evidence that the DNA genes will express their product in the target cells at a sufficient and appropriate level (i.e., the gene-splicing must make a difference in the organism's health). Finally, no harm should result to the treated or the surrounding cells of the animal or to its offspring.[8]

Anderson also offers three conditions for moving from somatic cell therapy to germ-line therapy. First, there should be considerable experience with somatic cell therapy demonstrating it to be effective and safe. Second, there should be adequate study of germ-line therapy in animals to establish its reliability, reproducibility, and safety. The study should use the same vectors (vehicles) and procedures that would be used in humans; otherwise, one vector might work in animals, but not in humans. Third, there should be public awareness and approval of germ-line therapy before it is used, because of the implications for future generations.[9]

CLARIFYING THE APPROACH

To sum up, then, using recombinant DNA technology to address something in a human being that results from humanity's sin and its consequences is a truly therapeutic and morally acceptable use of this technology so long as it is used within appropriate guidelines.

This way of thinking applies to both somatic cell and germ-line uses of genetic technology. If one is trying to address something that is a result of sin or its consequences, whether one addresses it by somatic cell or germ-line therapy, it is morally acceptable to do so.

Some might object that using this technology even for therapeutic purposes seems to be rejecting God's will. If God controls all things, and someone has a disease, it must be God's will. To fight that disease would be a rejection of God's will. In response, one should note that God's will, in the sense of his precepts, is that there should be no sin. If people had obeyed his preceptive will, there would not be any sin, and there would not be death or diseases. So by attempting to fight conditions that result from sin or its consequences, we are not rejecting God's will in the sense of what he wishes us to do. Rather, we are saying that God does not like sin or its consequences, and he does not want us to like it. He fights against it, and we should as well.

On the other hand, if tampering with the human genetic code through recombinant DNA technology is not done to address something that results from either sin or its consequences, it is not truly therapeutic. Is non-therapeutic use of genetic technology always immoral? If one argues that using this technology to change something like hair colour (not traceable to sin or its effects) is immoral, does that mean that it is immoral to change hair colour by bleaching one's hair? Such questions suggest a need for a way to distinguish moral and immoral eugenic uses of this technology. This distinction can be rooted in the motivation behind such enhancement. Immoral motivations include convictions that certain bodily traits (e.g., some hair or skin colours) are inherently inferior to others, that changing such traits will make one more valuable than before, and that people without valued traits are intrinsically inferior (or even worthless) and should be discriminated against (or even removed from society). If one were convinced on the basis of the alleged superiority of particular traits that all people should be given such traits, that motivation would also seem immoral. It would force on others traits that ultimately are matters of personal taste. To desire change in traits for reasons like those above is to hold implicitly that God has done something wrong in including such diverse traits in the human race. Such a conclusion could be considered blasphemous.

The way to distinguish between morally acceptable and unacceptable uses of genetic technology, then, is first to distinguish between therapy and enhancement. Where therapy is at issue, one intends to address something that stems from sin and its consequences, and doing so is moral. Where enhancement is involved, such intervention is morally wrong if done with improper motives. The definitive issue here is not that genetics is involved. Changing traits like hair colour, whether done through bleaching or genetic intervention, is immoral if done with immoral motivations. Similarly, changing a trait through genetic intervention may be no less moral than doing so by non-genetic means.

Can this way of making the distinction[5] insure that there will be no cases where it is difficult to tell whether or not a proposed genetic intervention is morally acceptable? We cannot possibly guarantee, *a priori*, that there will never be any hard cases. Indeed, there may be some condition or trait whose origin is difficult to discover. It may be unclear whether the trait results from sin or its consequences, or is simply a part of the diversity God put in creation. For example, is an aggressive, high-strung personality the result of sin and its consequences or not? Is such a personality totally a matter of genetics and not at all attributable to environment? Undoubtably, we could find a great difference of opinion on such matters. Hence, deciding whether we should tamper with the genetic code to change such traits is going to be extremely difficult. The hard cases, however, do not invalidate the basic distinction[5] here, nor do they mean that all or even most cases will be hard to assess. There will be plenty of cases like cystic fibrosis, Huntington's disease, and Parkinson's disease where it will not be difficult to decide whether genetic intervention is acceptable. Similarly, most should agree that left-handedness, being black, brown or white skinned, or having black hair are traits that would be extremely hard to trace to the fallenness of our existence.[10]

ADDRESSING THE SECULAR WORLD

Admittedly, not all accept the biblical teaching that people die because we live in a fallen world. But if one does not appeal to some biblical principle(s), how can one find grounds for drawing a line between morally acceptable and unacceptable uses of genetic technology in humans? There are several possibilities, none of which seems adequate. One is Kant's categorical imperative. Kant stated the categorical imperative in several forms, a well-known version of which is 'act only according to that maxim by which you can at the same time will that it should become a universal law'.[11] The 'can' in this imperative refers to what one rationally or reasonably can will. Someone who uses Kant's categorical imperative might say, 'If tampering with the genetic code is going to correct a disease, you could rationally will that we use this technology on every case of this sort. However, when it come to things like changing left-handedness or changing skin colour, one could not reasonably will, for example, that it be a universal law that everybody with those traits have them changed. Therefore, those uses of this technology would be ruled out.'

It might appear, then, that the categorical imperative could work as a principle to differentiate acceptable and unacceptable uses of recombinant DNA technology in humans. Yet such is not the case. While one could reasonably will that all diseases be addressed by this technology, probably everyone would not agree about other uses of it. For example, some people might believe that it is reasonable to will that everybody be right-handed, whereas others would claim that such a desire is unreasonable. This sort of disagreement would arise with many traits. Could one, for example, rationally will that everyone have an IQ of 170 or higher? Some would say yes, but others would disagree. Even though the categorical imperative seems like a sound basis for distinguishing acceptable and unacceptable uses of this technology, when the traits in question are not traceable to something we would normally call a disease, this principle will not always allow us to draw the line between moral and immoral uses of this technology.

Another alternative to a biblical approach is that of situation ethics. According to this approach, we should always calculate what is the most loving thing to do in any situation. If it would be most loving to change someone's eye colour, hair colour, or skin colour, then we should do it; if it is not, we should not. However, doing 'the loving thing' is a hopelessly vague standard in practice. How could one be sure that changing a trait would be the most loving thing to do for someone, even if that person wanted the change very badly? Moreover, might not public policies intended to further the public good turn out to be unjust – even oppressive – for particular individuals?

The two non-biblical approaches just cited are not the only ways that someone who rejects Scripture might evaluate genetic interventions. Nevertheless, these are two major ways, and they appear quite inadequate. It is difficult to derive a non-biblical basis for distinguishing moral from immoral genetic interventions for the same reason that we have trouble deciding which secular ethical theory is to be preferred over other secular ethical theories. Any ethical theory that is purely the result of reasoning processes is likely to be refutable by reason. The ethical theories that are most capable of justification are those that are grounded in some biblical and theological facts.[12] Of course, to give ultimate justification to such a theory (or any other theory), one must offer an overall apologetic for the worldview out of which that theory arises. Our strategic challenge is to identify not only the inadequacies of non-biblical attempts to evaluate genetic interventions, but also the deficiencies of the ethical theories and worldviews from which such attempts flow. Then we must have better, biblically-grounded alternatives ready to offer.

———————

Needless to say, this proposal for distinguishing morally acceptable and unacceptable uses of genetic technology in humans does not cover all ethical questions that can arise in relation to this technology. Even when this technology is used acceptably, its use may create other ethical dilemmas. Let me illustrate from personal experience. My wife has Huntington's disease. If at some point genetic therapy can cure this disease, that would be wonderful. However, in my wife's case there have already been many years of deterioration. Somatic cell genetic therapy would stop further deterioration, but it will not replace brain cells already lost.

At least two further ethical questions arise. First, could her physical and mental abilities ever deteriorate to so low a level that it would be better to let the disease take its course than to stop the decline and maintain her at that level? Second, if it not only becomes possible to stop the disease but also to use tissue transplants from aborted fetuses to restore lost brain cells and thereby regain lost abilities, would that option be morally acceptable? In other words, even if this chapter's analysis of distinguishing appropriate and inappropriate uses of recombinant DNA technology in humans is correct, all ethical dilemmas surrounding this technology are not resolved. Experiments with genetic therapy should continue, but so must ethical reasoning about the use and implications of this technology.

NOTES

1. Fletcher, Joseph, *The Ethics of Genetic Control: Ending Reproductive Roulette* (Buffalo, NY: Prometheus Books 1988), pp. 12–13.

2. Ibid., p. 15.

3. Ibid., p. 36.

4. Rifkin, Jeremy, 'Whom Do We Designate to Play God?' *Engage/Social Action* 11:10 (November 1983):22–28.

5. Would there have been non-life-threatening conditions like the common cold if Adam had never sinned? Presumably not – though the focus here is on life-threatening conditions.

6. Scripture also teaches that someday God will remove all the consequences of sin upon our world (Rom 8:19ff.). Moreover, he will ultimately create a new heaven and a new earth in which righteousness dwells and sin has no place (2 Pet. 3:10–13). God fights sin and its consequences in a variety of ways.

7. That we are to fight the consequences of sin does not mean that we are to be consequentialist in our approach to ethics. Consequentialist ethics justifies actions on the basis of the consequences those actions produce. We are to fight sin and its consequences for a deontological reason – because God has commanded us to do so, following his lead.

8. Anderson, W. French, 'Human Gene Therapy: Scientific and Ethical Considerations', in Chadwick, Ruth, ed., *Ethics, Reproduction and Genetic Control* (London, Routledge 1992), pp. 149–150.

9. Ibid., pp. 157–158.

10. It might be helpful in this context to note Wittgenstein's claims about defining a concept so as to perfectly bound it on all sides. Once Wittgenstein adopted a use theory of meaning, he realized that there is no 'essence' to the meaning of words and concepts. Thus, terms and concepts cannot always be so precisely defined as to have such clear boundaries that we can always tell which cases fit the definition and which do not. Yet, it does not follow that we have no idea of what concepts mean or that we can never tell which cases exemplify the concept and which do not. As Wittgenstein says, it is always possible to point out certain family resemblances between similar cases: 'If I tell someone "Stand roughly here" – may not this explanation work perfectly? And cannot every other one fail too? But isn't it an inexact explanation? – Yes; why shouldn't we call it "inexact"? Only let us understand what "inexact" means. *For it does not mean "unusable"* '(Ludwig Wittgenstein, *Philosophical Investigations* [New York: Macmillan 1968], sec. 88, p. 41e, italics added). The same thing could be said about the distinction I have made. There are family resemblances among therapeutic uses of this technology and family resemblances among non-therapeutic uses. The distinction may not be so perfectly bounded as to forestall all hard cases where it is very difficult to place uses in one category (therapeutic) or another (non-therapeutic). While the distinction may be inexact, however, 'inexact does not mean unusable'. Moreover, as already noted, most instances where one would want to apply the distinction would not be inexact at all.

11. Kant, Immanuel, *Foundations of the Metaphysics of Morals* (Indianapolis, Bobbs-Merrill 1959), p. 39.

12. See my discussion of the justification of ethical theories in Feinberg, John S. and Paul D., *Ethics for a Brave New World* (Wheaton, IL, Crossway 1993), chapter 1.

16

Ethical Standards for Genetic Intervention

James C. Peterson, PhD

The Bedouin in the Negev desert traditionally live in tents and move from place to place with their camels. Some camels can be quite curious. It is not surprising to find a camel sniffing under the edge of a tent, trying to discern what smells so interesting inside. One learns quickly that even if one does not mind a pair of large nostrils snuffling nearby, one needs to strike that muzzle with a sandal or hand directly, lest the whole camel soon be inside the tent. Camels seem much larger inside the tent than outside of it.

A commonly raised concern in discussions of genetics and ethics may be referred to as the 'camel's nose under the tent argument'. Sometimes it is called the slippery slope or the thin edge of the wedge. The concern is that taking certain acceptable steps may lead to a camel in the tent (or a thick end of a wedge, or a bottom of a slope) that one never intended. In terms of human genetic intervention, how do we use it where it serves well, without allowing it where it does not belong? Is there a way that we can consistently distinguish appropriate from inappropriate use?

Consider the case of panic disorder. About two percent of Americans sometimes find their heart suddenly racing. Many first assume that they are having a heart attack. They are overwhelmed with a feeling of utter terror, but without being afraid of anything in particular. In ten to fifty minutes the terror subsides, only to return when people least expected. The attacks are distributed through families in a way that implies inherited susceptibility. Would it not be helpful to diagnose genetically the condition before the first attack, so that people could be warned? Would it not be a positive contribution to limit the attacks by pharmaceutical or someday even genetic intervention, if that could be done without adverse side effects? What would make such treatments fall within or outside appropriate intervention?

A CHRISTIAN CONTEXT

Chapter 25 of the biblical book of Matthew – in which Jesus instructs his disciples on what to do in the time between his resurrection and his return at the last day of judgment – contains several themes directly applicable to our question. Today is still the in-between time about which Jesus spoke. Matthew 25 contains three stories. Each one raises issues that the next one answers. The first story is of ten maidens watching into the night for the coming of the bridegroom. The wait was so long that five of them ran out of oil for their lamps. While they were away buying more, the bridegroom came and they missed the wedding feast. The story reminds us always to be ready for the return of Jesus Christ. It could be before the completion of this sentence. On the other hand, it may be a long time. It has now been almost 2,000 years since Jesus gave people this warning. One must have both the foresight to prepare for the long haul (bringing enough oil) and the perseverance to endure. So what then are we supposed to do in the meantime?

The story that immediately follows answers that question. It tells of a master who left five talents with one servant, two with another, and one with a third, to each according to his ability. When the master returned he was pleased to see that the first and second servants had doubled their talents. The master was outraged, how-ever, to discover that the third servant had simply buried the entrusted resource in order to return exactly what he had received. He had failed in his responsibility to multiply the resources the master had given to him. The first story in Matthew 25 warns that we should always be ready, but we may have to wait some time before the second coming. The second story tells us that the intervening time should be spent wisely in God's service, producing fruit from what he has entrusted to us. We are responsible to employ and multiply our God-given resources. In other words, we are to have our suitcases packed and ready to go, but not merely hang out at the airport.

So how should we put our God given talents to work? What goals would God have us pursue? The next and last story in the chapter answers that question. It is a description of the final day of judgment. Those who belong to God's kingdom are separated from those who are not according to how they treated their neighbours. Those who fed the hungry and clothed the poor, cared for those who were sick and visited those in prison, are welcomed into God's kingdom. Those who did not are cast away. Good works do not earn a place in God's family; rather, they are characteristic of people who are in God's family. Such actions do not achieve salvation, but they do reflect it. In the second chapter of Ephesians we read that we are 'saved by grace through faith, lest anyone should boast'. Sometimes neglected, the next sentence reads 'for we are his workmanship, created in Christ Jesus for good works'. These good works are a result of reconciliation with God, not the cause of salvation. Reconciliation with God is a free gift that, if fully received, will affect how one treats others. If one is being shaped by God as a child of God, one will come to care about what God cares about. God cares deeply about people.

The examples of expressing love for one's neighbour in these biblical passages address meeting physical and social needs such as feeding the hungry and caring for those who are sick. Apparently matter matters. In the first chapter of Genesis, Adam is described as made from the dust yet uniquely inbreathed with God's spirit. We human beings have a special calling, yet are of this earth. Being physical beings is not a bad thing. God created both this material world and our physical form and declared them 'good'. The physical is not our ultimate concern, but we should care about it because it is part of God's creation and our stewardship.

Jesus lived this concern in his incarnation, teaching, and action. In the historic Christian tradition, Jesus is not only God among us but also the perfect example of what human beings are meant to be. Jesus came first and foremost to reconcile us with God, yet he also gave of himself in caring for people's physical concerns, sometimes to the point of utter physical exhaustion. In John he gives the commission that 'as the Father has sent him, so he now sends his disciples'.[1] We should actively care for people's physical concerns as he did.

Moreover, in all three of these sections of Matthew 25, errors of omission (not bringing enough oil, not multiplying talents, not caring for those in need) are treated as seriously as acts of commission. Pride is a serious danger, but so is sloth. Until the Lord returns, we are to do our best here. That includes our best effort to serve others, including addressing their physical needs.

This is only one chapter of the rich biblical tradition, but it is not an isolated one. Its themes are found throughout Scripture. They remind us to ask first, as we should of any potential tool, how human genetic intervention can best serve our neighbours. Asking that question is not trying to be God; it is following God's mandate to be of service.

DRAWING THE LINE

Now remember the camel, which provides a great service to the Bedouin but does not belong in the tent. Usefulness in one context does not insure usefulness in another. Recognizing the potential service of human genetic intervention is not sufficient. We must ask under what circumstances it is possible to intervene without causing great harm. Thinking ahead is part of the mandate required of us, as illustrated in the story of the maidens and lamp oil in Matthew 25. How do we separate appropriate service of human genetic intervention from destructive use? The Parliamentary

Assembly of the Council of Europe, the French National Ethics Committee, Canada's Royal Commission, and others have stated that genetic intervention is acceptable when it affects only the presenting patient. Such is called 'somatic cell therapy'. In contrast, 'germline therapy', a type of intervention which potentially affects future generations, would never be appropriate.[2] Others have argued that somatic therapy is the appropriate stopping point for pragmatic reasons. Germ-line intervention is not ruled out in principle; rather, it is ruled out until it is safe and reliable.[3]

However, the distinction between somatic and germ-line intervention is not the best place to draw the line between acceptable and harmful intervention. While the somatic/germ-line distinction is clear conceptually, in practice some somatic interventions will have germ-line effects. For example, a person who would not otherwise have been able to pass on deleterious gene may be enabled to live to child-bearing age. The distinction misses the mark morally as well. If genetic surgery is safe and beneficial for one person, why not protect his or her children from having to endure the same genetic harm or repetitive somatic therapy?[4] The stakes of a mistake are greater, but so are the potential benefits. It is not possible to obtain informed consent from the future descendants, but neither is it for infants for whom we often act. When a child is born with a cleft palate, a largely inherited condition, we do not wait for the child to reach the age of eighteen for adult permission to do the needed surgery. Nor do we refuse to intervene because God sovereignly designed the child to be that way. We trust that God is pleased to work through us to improve the child's ability to speak and eat. If somatic therapy is warranted in some cases, germ-line extension of that change is probably so as well.[5]

The distinction between cure and enhancement does not provide a much better line.[6] First of all, it is a very difficult line to discern.[7] The distinction seems to fade the more closely it is analysed. All correction involves enhancing capacity. One who was blind is now able to see. One who was crippled is now able to walk. The difference between the two is that correction is limited to achieving 'normal' levels.[8] But what are normal levels?[9] Human characteristics generally fall within a range. Some people's vision is 20/60; others'is 20/10. If we correct to average in that range there will still be people who have better sight than average. With the lower abilities eliminated from the calculation by correction to the average, the average will increase. What was beyond normal will become normal. If we define correction as rescinding disease or disorder, what is disease?[10] Do we define disease as that which produces pain and suffering? If so, then childbirth and teething are diseases, for they are certainly painful. If disease is departure from the statistical norm, red hair and AB blood type would be diseases. If disease is departure from the statistical norm that the individual does not want, personal values would define disease differently from one person to the next. The syndrome of 'Drapetomania' was described in great detail in the *New Orleans Medical and Surgical Journal* in 1851.[11] According to the article's author, physician Samuel A. Cartwright, it is the disease that causes a slave to want to run away.

If we tie correction to today's average, why such loyalty to our current state? If we tie the norm to our pre-sin state, how do we know what that was? How is remove 'the effects of sin' any clearer than remove 'disease' (though see John Feinberg's chapter earlier in this volume)? Even if one could discern our physical pre-fall state, why make that the final standard? To do so would require the assumption that pre-sin Adam was God's final intent for human physical form. Do we actually know that? Why consider Adam the pinnacle and not the starting point? God has created a world where acorns take decades to become fifty foot oaks. It would be a bit disconcerting for squirrels and hikers if acorns sprang to mature size upon first contact with the ground. Our physical and spiritual lives are characterized by birth followed by a lifetime of growth, rather than instant maturity. God has chosen to design a world that works that way. We can never 'out-design' God. Is it not possible that God might sovereignly choose to develop further our design through us? The point is not to try to be God; it is to listen, prayerfully and thoughtfully, to what the one and only God would have us to do.

FIVE STANDARDS

What would our Lord have us to do? It is much easier to raise questions than to make concrete proposals. However, as an alternative to the somatic/germ-line and cure/enhance criteria, I would propose the following five standards for recognizing if an intervention is appropriate. Any genetic intervention should be:

1) INCREMENTAL

Human genetic intervention should be incremental in degree and breadth of implementation. We are finite beings who do not begin to understand the interrelated complexity of our own bodies. The more I learn in genetic labs and clinics, the more I find myself humming the doxology. I am again and again awed at God's design in two senses. First, I wonder at what I do see. One example is the 3,000 million base pairs of DNA in each cell of the human body, which would uncoil and stretch out to about two meters in a straight line. That is the proportional equivalent of stuffing thirty miles of fine fishing line into a plump blueberry, in such a way that the line could be unwound, copied, and restuffed at will. Secondly, I wonder

at what I do not see or understand. At this point we do not even
know what purpose most DNA serves. Only about ten percent of
it is transcribed into mRNA for making proteins. What is the other
ninety percent doing? It may be important for expression, structure,
or some other function. At this point we do not know.

The pattern is consistent in human endeavours: more knowledge
results in more awareness of what we do not know. One can learn
a great deal about Thailand on a two week visit, including some of
its language, history, geography, and culture. Such new knowledge
often reveals questions one would not have even thought of before.
For that reason, growth in knowledge is not only fascinating and
worthwhile. It is also humbling. When people as finite human beings
are absolutely sure about anything, including genetics, they probably
do not fully understand. The ones who most fully understand will
rarely be absolutely sure (or at least so it seems). By pursuing genetic
intervention incrementally, we can minimize the degree and extent
of unexpected harms.

2) CHOICE-EXPANDING

We should also pursue only those interventions that enhance a
person's options by freeing that individual from what is clearly
destructive or by increasing the person's capability. Human development is immensely complex. Genetic intervention will more often
be able to influence formation than determine it. Using that influence to enhance a person's bodily defences against cancer or to
increase incrementally one's aptitude for memorizing vocabulary,
would not predestine the individual to a particular life. It would
contribute to the range of options available for the individual's
pursuit and achievement. In contrast, interventions that would limit
the recipient – attempting to predestine the individual to a narrow
end – would claim an arrogant authority over the recipient and show
a lack of respect for him or her as a person. For example, it would
not be appropriate for deaf parents to choose deafness for their
child even if they preferred deaf culture to hearing culture. Deafness
limits options. C.S. Lewis made this point for entire generations in
The Abolition of Man. He argued that the first generation that would
have the power so deeply to shape the next generation should not
use it in a way to predestine that next generation's choices.[12] Each
generation should be able to further or undo the last generation's
contribution as they learn from its effects.

3) PARENT-DIRECTED

Genetic intervention decisions should be made primarily by the
persons to be affected or, if that is not possible, by their parents.[13]
Decentralizing choice in this way would first of all help to protect
valuable diversity. Second, it would take into account what some

have called the only empirically verifiable doctrine of Christianity, original sin. Only a generation ago the horrible crimes of the Holocaust were committed under the claim and cover of racial hygiene and eugenics. People will abuse any powerful technology if they are not held accountable. When one prefers sight to retinoblastoma, a genetically-based disease involving blindness, one is valuing a particular genetic endowment over another. That judgment is not nefarious. It is better to be able to see than not to be able to see. In contrast, the Nazi Germany claim of eugenics was horrifying on the following two counts, among others. First, the preferred genetic endowment was defined in terms of race – a characteristic which, even if clearly definable, would be irrelevant to well-being.[14] If genetic intervention decisions were made primarily by parents, no racial group would be in a position to use such choices destructively against another. Second, having other than the desired genetic endowment (or politics, or IQ, or health history . . .) was grounds in Nazi Germany for taking that person's life. However, a person's ongoing life and worth does not depend on genetic heritage. Persons should be protected and nurtured from their beginning, regardless of genetic endowment.[15] Parents are central to meeting that need and so are particularly well-suited to make genetic intervention decisions for their children.

4) WITHIN SOCIETAL BOUNDARIES

What if parents intend to make abusive or even simply foolish choices to the detriment of their own children? A fourth standard is that society should set minimal, broad limits for intervention. An example of such a constraint would be the first standard above – that any genetic intervention should be incremental. Living within some minimal societal limits is how we currently deal with education and medical care. Clearly recognized minimums are required of all parents, although they are free to satisfy such minimums in a variety of ways. Parents may home school their child or choose a private or public school, but as parents they are required to provide a basic education for their child. Children may go to a chiropractor or Chinese herbalist, but life-threatening conditions must be addressed or parents will answer to the state. There is no end of conflict at these intersections, but that is the nature of accountability in a sinful world.

5) BY ACCEPTABLE MEANS

Means are often as important as ends. First, the form of genetic intervention should be as non-invasive as possible for all involved.[16] This is a difficult goal to achieve in some cases; making a change that would multiply throughout the body would probably require intervention at the earliest stages of pregnancy. Second, zero risk is impossible. We cannot achieve zero risk at the dentist's or driving to school, but it is reasonable to limit the risks we take to those proportionate to the intended benefits. Such a criterion is as applicable to genetic interventions as to other aspects of life.

While these five standards can help keep the camel's nose out of the tent by providing criteria to distinguish acceptable from unacceptable interventions, another version of the camel's nose or slippery slope argument remains unanswered.[17] Even if there is a clear conceptual difference between acceptable and unacceptable interventions, this conceptual difference may not be honoured in the real world, either in the choices of individuals or in the formation of social guidelines. Once we head in a certain direction we may run roughshod over appropriate stopping points.[18] This danger is exacerbated by the pervasive self-deception and distortion of individual and corporate judgment characteristic of our sinful state. The most powerful motivators for intervention might even be defensive in nature. If countries or individual parents see children other than their own receiving enhancement safely and to their economic advantage – e.g., through improvement in some aspect of intelligence – they will have a strong incentive to intervene similarly in their own children in order to remain competitive.[19]

If a corporation has invested millions in developing a genetic technology, it will promote its use to gain a financial return.[20] A good illustration of this is the recent direct marketing of cystic fibrosis carrier screening on British television.[21] Not only do standards for genetic intervention need to be developed, but also warranted confidence that such standards will be honoured. Otherwise, the long-term results could be more harmful than beneficial.

Genetic intervention will never yield a utopia.[22] Genetics cannot solve all physical concerns, nor is human life only physical. Published hopes that genetic intervention might deliver us from homelessness, alcoholism, criminality, divorce, and more, expect more than physical change can provide by itself.[23] But genetic intervention within the five standards suggested above can make life somewhat better for many people. If such is possible, we are responsible to our Lord as faithful stewards to pursue it. Even some instances of germ-line enhancement – ruled out by some – may fall within that God-honouring mandate. Being 'bright in the corner where we are', doing what we can to serve our neighbors, is part of our God-given commission and responsibility. May we use the developing tool of genetic intervention wisely to that end.

NOTES

1. John 17:18.
2. Parliamentary Assembly of the Council of Europe, 'Recommendation 934 on

genetic engineering,' 1982. French National Ethics Committee, 'Announcement on Gene Therapy,' *Human Gene Therapy* 2 (1991) p.329. Canadian Royal Commission, *Proceed with Care: Final Report of the Royal Commission on New Reproductive Technologies*, excerpted in *Human Gene Therapy* 5(1994) p. 604. Wivel, Nelson A., and Walters, LeRoy, 'Germ-line Gene Modification and Disease Prevention: Some Medical and Ethical Perspectives', *Science* 262 (22 October 1993), pp. 533–538. Fletcher, John C., and Anderson, W. French, 'Germ-line Gene Therapy: A New Stage of Debate', *Law, Medicine & Health Care:* 20:1–2 (1992), pp.26–39.

3.   Neel, James V., 'Germ-Line Gene Therapy: Another View', *Human Gene Therapy* 4 (1993), pp. 127–128.

4.   Munro, Donald W., used the apt description of human genetic intervention as 'microsurgery' in a speech entitled 'Human Genetic Engineering, God's Gift?' at the Kepler Society, Boston, January 26, 1996.

5.   Reichenbach, Bruce R., and Anderson, V. Elving, *On Behalf of God: A Christian Ethic for Biology* (Grand Rapids, Eerdmans 1995), p. 186. Walters, LeRoy, 'The Ethics of Human Germ-Line Genetic Intervention', in *Genes and Human Self-Knowledge: Historical and Philosophical Reflections on Modern Genetics*, edited by Weir Robert F., Lawrence Susan C., and Fales Evan (Iowa City, University of Iowa Press 1994), pp. 220–231.

6.   For a detailed evaluation of the practical use and desirability of this distinction see Peterson, J., *An Ethical Analysis and Proposal for the Direction of Human Genetic Intervention* (Ann Arbor, UMI, 1992), order number 9237575 at 800-521-0600.

7.   Murray, Thomas, 'Assessing Genetic Technologies: Two Ethical Issues', *International Journal of Technology Assessment in Health Care* 10:4 (1994), pp. 573–582. Bouma III, Hessel, Diekma, Douglas, Langerak, Edward, Rottman, Theodore, and Verhey, Allen, *Christian Faith, Health, and Medical Practice* (Grand Rapids, Eerdmans 1989), p. 266.

8.   Anderson, W. French, 'Genetic Engineering and Our Humanness', *Human Gene Therapy* 5(1994), pp. 755–760.

9.   Pettersson, Berg K., Riis, P., Tranoy, K. E., 'Genetics in Democratic Societies', *Clinical Genetics* 48 (1995) p. 202.

10.   Juengst, Eric Thomas, *The Concept of Genetic Disease and Theories of Medical Progress* (Ann Arbor, UMI 1985). Caplan, Arthur L., Engelhardt Jr., H. Tristram, and McCartney, James ed., *Concepts of Health and Disease: Interdisciplinary Perspectives* (Reading, MA Addison-Wesley 1981).

11.   Cartwright, Samuel A., 'Report on the Diseases and Physical Peculiarities of the Negro Race', *The New Orleans Medical and Surgical Journal* 7(May 1851), pp. 707–709.

12.   Lewis, C. S., *The Abolition of Man* (New York, MacMillan 1955).

13.   Resnik, David, 'Debunking the Slippery Slope Argument Against Human Germ-Line Gene Therapy', *The Journal of Medicine and Philosophy* 19 (1994), pp. 35–37.

14.   Hitler, Adolf, *Mein Kampf*, translated by Ludwig Lore (New York, Stackpole 1939), p. 281. Seidelman, William E., 'Mengele Medicus', *The Milbank Quarterly* 66:2 (1988), p. 223. Hohlfeld, Rainer, 'Jenseits von Freiheit und Wurde: Kritische Anmerkungen zur gezielten genetischen Beeinflussung des Menschen', *Reformatio* 32(May 1983), p. 220.

15.   Jones, D. Gareth, and Telfer, Barbara, 'Before I Was an Embryo, I Was a Pre-embryo: Or Was I?' *Bioethics* 9:1 (1995), pp. 32–49.

16.   Kass, Leon, *Toward a More Natural Science: Biology and Human Affairs* (New York, Free Press 1985), p. 109. Ramsey, Paul, *Fabricated Man: The Ethics of Genetic Control* (New Haven, Yale University Press 1970), pp. 89, 132–137.

17.   Childress, James F., 'Wedge Argument, Slippery Slope Argument, etc.' in the *Westminster Dictionary of Christian Ethics*, edited by James F. Childress and John Macquarrie (Philadelphia, Westminster Press 1986), p. 657.

18.   Nelson, Hilde Lindemann, 'Dethroning Choice: Analogy, Personhood, and the New Technologies', *Journal of Law, Medicine & Ethics* 23 (1995), pp. 129–135.

19.   Gardner, William, 'Can Human Genetic Enhancement be Prohibited?' *The Journal of Medicine and Philosophy* 20 (1995), pp. 65–84.

20.   Editorial, 'Capitalizing on the genome', *Nature Genetics* 13:1 (May 1995), pp. 1–5.

21.   Harper, Peter S., 'Direct Marketing of Cystic Fibrosis Carrier Screening: commercial push or population need?' *Journal of Medical Genetics* 32 (1995), pp. 249–250.

22.   Passmore, John, *The Perfectibility of Man* (New York, Charles Scribner's Sons 1970).

23.   Holtzman, Neil A., 'Policy Implications of Genetic Technologies', *International Journal of Technology Assessment* 10:4 (1994), pp. 570–571. Proctor, Robert N., 'Genomics and Eugenics: How Fair is the Comparison?' pp. 76–93 in *Gene Mapping: Using Law and Ethics as Guides*, eds. Annas George J. and Elias Sherman (New York, Oxford University Press 1992).

[17]

The Case of Human Growth Hormone

Dónal P. O'Mathúna, PhD

A major issue in the current debate over genetic intervention is whether or not it is ethical to enhance healthy human beings, as opposed to correcting deficiencies. We need not merely speculate about future scenarios, however. The current development of Human Growth Hormone forces us to confront the key ethical issues. Human Growth Hormone (hGH), also known as somatotropin, is a small protein molecule released by the pituitary gland. It promotes growth in almost all tissues of the body, but its most obvious effect is on bone.[1] Normal secretion of hGH during childhood allows normal height development within the boundaries set by hereditary and environmental factors. However, hGH has many other roles in the body, such as increasing the rate of protein synthesis, increasing energy production from stored fat, and decreasing the use of glucose throughout the body. Athletes and body-builders use it without medical approval for these effects.[2] Accumulating evidence also suggests that hGH plays an important role in the maturing of ovaries and testes during puberty.[3]

Growth Hormone Deficiency (GHD) is a group of conditions characterized by reduced secretion of hGH. Without correction, people with GHD are much shorter than average. Hormone replacement therapy has been available since 1958 using hGH extracted from the pituitary glands of deceased humans.[4] In 1985, hGH made by recombinant DNA technology became available. As one of the first products of the emerging biotechnology industry, it immediately removed two of the major problems with earlier hGH replacement therapy: limited supplies and concerns about purity.

However, unlimited supplies raise new concerns about who should receive treatment. Short stature can be caused by many things other than GHD. In one study, hormone deficiencies were found in only 5% of the children below the 3rd percentile for height who also had a slow growth rate.[5] In contrast, 81% of those children were short because of familial short stature and/or constitutional growth delays.[6] The recombinant form of hGH provided unlimited amounts of hormone to test on children without hormone deficiencies. People soon discovered that hGH increases the rate of growth of any child, provided a sufficient dose is given.[7] The recognition that diagnosis of GHD is imprecise and based on an arbitrarily chosen secretion level only further fuelled greater use of hGH.

Parents of short children often want to help their children grow taller because of the psychosocial problems that short children may experience. Many surveys show that shorter children are frequently teased and bullied, viewed as inferior, and can have greater difficulty being successful in dating relationships, school and career pursuits.[8] Discrimination on the basis of one's height, called heightism, is widespread in America.[9] However, many studies also show that, in spite of heightism, shorter children are as psychologically and socially well-adjusted, and as academically successful, as children of average height.[10]

Parents' desires to help their children avoid hurt and disadvantage are understandable. But should we use powerful drugs to change someone's height? Giving hGH to patients with a deficiency is similar to giving diabetic patients recombinant insulin: it brings the hormone levels back to normal. Few would question the appropriateness of this therapy. But giving hGH to children without deficiencies is using a drug to enhance normal characteristics and give these children an advantage in life. How we respond to this use of hGH will strongly influence our response to genetic therapies with similar goals. Are there important differences between using genetic products to enhance characteristics in healthy children, and preventing or treating an illness?

Christians must critically examine this therapy in light of biblical revelation. While there is no clear biblical command against this type of therapy, Paul reminds us that even when things are lawful, they may not be profitable. We must avoid being mastered by lawful things and ensure that what we do is edifying (1 Cor. 6:12; 10:23). In this light, biblical principles give clear reasons why Christians should willingly forgo enhancement therapy. Doing so will provide opportunities to witness to the hope we have in Christ by being faithful images of God to a fallen, hurting world.

Stewardship of our resources requires that we evaluate the effectiveness of therapies. Particularly when hGH is used for anything other than replacement therapy it should be put through a rigorous risk-benefit analysis like all other drugs.[11] We must evaluate if the therapy does what we desire. We will first focus on the physical aspects of hGH therapy, and then on the psychosocial and theological dimensions.

EFFICACY OF TREATMENT

Giving hGH to any child will speed up his or her growth. However, increases in final adult height have been confirmed only under two conditions, one of which is the presence of GHD. Even in such cases, those treated were still shorter than average as adults. In one study, treatment raised the average height from six standard deviations below the mean to two below.[12] In another, the average height after treatment was 5 feet 2 inches.[13] These authors therefore recommended phrasing the treatment as a way for children to 'not fall further behind', or to 'catch up in height', as opposed to becoming tall.[14]

In only one condition where there are relatively normal hGH levels does increased adult height sometimes result from hGH treatment: a congenital endocrine disorder called Turner's Syndrome. However, some researchers are not convinced of the therapy's effectiveness with this condition and are cautious in their recommendations for its use.[15] The gain in final height is even less than with GHD, and some patients do not respond to therapy at all.[16] For example, girls with Turner's syndrome were predicted to grow to 4 feet 9 inches, but after 6 years of hGH therapy they grew to an average height of 5 feet 0 inches.[17]

In all other conditions with normal hGH levels, there are no conclusive results that the initial increase in growth rate leads to taller adults. Because of the length of time these studies take, 'The question of final height in a comparison of randomized treated and untreated subjects will not be resolved in the near future, . . .'[18] When treatment is initiated in late childhood (11 or 12 years old), recent reports have been 'pessimistic', with gains of around an inch in final height.[19]

Whether starting treatment earlier will demonstrate greater gains in final height 'remains questionable'.[20] A large increase in growth rate occurs during the year therapy is begun, but this falls off in subsequent years. Although growth remains faster than prior to treatment, children without a hormone deficiency are usually given twice the dose GHD children receive. In addition, children must complete the long-term treatment because, according to the National Institutes of Health:

> Stopping growth hormone treatment in children who are not growth hormone deficient before they have reached their adult height may cause them to grow more slowly than they did before treatment. This may occur because taking the extra growth hormone causes the body to temporarily stop making its own growth hormone.[21]

Treatment with hGH may also stop growth earlier than expected through its effect on children's progression through puberty.[22] Children without GHD enter puberty later when given hGH therapy, but progress through puberty more quickly. Since children have a natural growth spurt during puberty, shortening this time period may result in less growth overall. This observation has led the investigators to conclude: 'The gain in height prognosis acquired during prepuberty may therefore be lost during puberty.'[23]

A set of guidelines was published to help physicians discuss hGH treatment with parents of short children. One guideline reads: 'Assure that the family knows that there is no good evidence that GH will make the patient a taller adult, even if short-term acceleration of growth is achieved. Remove taller adult height as an objective of therapy.'[24] According to these guidelines, the goal of therapy should be short-term growth acceleration to help the child socially and psychologically. But this misses the whole point of why parents seek this therapy and results in huge disappointments. The lack of effectiveness is a reflection of the complexity of the human body. Enhancement therapies (genetic or otherwise) entice us with relatively quick and simple solutions to complex problems. In spite of their current ineffectiveness, people will continue to seek them as long as society places so much value on functional traits.

SIDE-EFFECTS OF TREATMENT

In light of the uncertainty of any significant gain in adult height, it is important to evaluate potential risks and side effects of hGH treatment. To date, there appear to be few. A connection between hGH treatment and leukemia is a possibility, but the data are inconclusive.[25] A higher incidence of leukemia seems to exist among children *with* GHD who are treated with hGH. However, this increase may arise from an increased predisposition to leukemia due to the deficiency itself.

While serious side effects are not common, little study has been done on hGH's other metabolic effects. As already mentioned, hGH treatment impacts the progression of puberty. Children treated with hGH show a marked reduction in body fat (up to 76%) and a gain in lean body mass of up to 25% – the types of changes sought after by body builders. 'The children became skinny, with obvious loss of adipose tissue from all areas of the body but especially from the limbs and face. The girls in particular looked inappropriately muscular.'[26]

In addition to these changes, the almost daily injections are painful as well as inconvenient. Recipients consider them to be the most negative aspect of treatment. Nevertheless, 85% of those treated say they would recommend the treatment for others with GHD.[27] They often do not achieve their expected height gain, however. We must take steps to ensure that patients' and parents' expectations are realistic. 'Inflated expectations of ultimate height are rarely realized after growth hormone therapy, leading to disappointment and even clinical depression at the conclusion of therapy. Feelings of anger, pessimism, negativity, and unacceptability are common.'[28] These are also serious side effects.

While the physical side effects have been minimal, 'At the very least, the reports of leukemia provide a cautionary example of the unpredictable side effects of hGH when used for lesser indications in greater numbers of patients.'[29] Vigilance in monitoring these effects is essential, particularly in patients without GHD who need twice the dose of GHD patients. Hypersecretion of hGH leads to acromegaly, raising concerns that 'high doses of GH over many years may induce a gigantism-like metabolism picture'.[30]

Growth hormone is a powerful molecule with systemic effects. As a way of relieving psychological burdens and improving body-image, it belongs to the group of 'relatively drastic procedures'.[31] In many ways it would be similar to giving young girls hormone injections to increase the size of their breasts. Even if studies showed that full-chested women were happier and more successful, many would question the morality of this treatment – particularly in the absence of a clear understanding of long-term side effects.

Treatment with hGH also raises a number of ethical issues. Even were final height to increase, there are still several ethical concerns against giving this treatment to non-GHD children. Biblical principles add weight to these concerns and provide grounds for Christians in particular to forgo such treatment.

THE GOALS OF MEDICINE

Christians have the responsibility to act as faithful images of God – but what does that mean in the genetics arena? Some reject all or many genetic treatments as attempts by people to 'play God' (see Allen Verhey's chapter earlier in this volume). However, every illness raises the troubling question of why God allows it. If God chooses not to cure an illness, why do we? If it is acceptable to try to cure it, are all treatments ethical? We are tempted to solve all our own problems in ways that distract us from trusting God (Jer. 17:5–7). The Israelites were constantly faced with the tension between relying on their weapons and chariots for success in battle, and relying on God (Ps. 44; Isa. 31:1). Yet they still had to go into battle and engage the enemy.

Any argument against Christians participating in a certain treatment must not thereby rule out helpful treatments God intends us to use. For example, to claim that shortness is natural, and that to change it is going against God's will, could also be used as an argument against the treatment of inherited diseases. How can we distinguish between the conditions we should try to change and those we should accept and leave in God's hands? Would Paul have pursued medical treatment for the thorn in his flesh if it had been available (see 2 Cor. 12:7)? In biblical times the usual response to illness was prayer (1 Ki. 8:37–40; 14:1–3; Ps. 35:13–14; Jam. 5:13–

16). Little else was available then. However, faithful people did make use of the medical interventions of the time (2 Ki. 20:1–7; 1 Tim. 5:23; Jam. 5:14). One aspect of Jesus' ministry was to bring physical healing (Lk. 4:18). Jesus also instructed his disciples to heal as part of their ministry (Mk. 6:13; Lk. 9:2; Acts 5:15–16).

In these various cases, people were being restored to health. Something intrinsically wrong or dysfunctional was being corrected. In overcoming the groaning and suffering of this present age, we are imaging God faithfully (2 Cor. 1:3–7). Medicine can be seen as one way to prevent or relieve suffering and disease. Diseases would then be defined as deviations from the biological norms of health.[32] They reflect the corruption of creation in this present age (Rom. 8:18–25). To correct or prevent diseases is to restore some of the original order and beauty to fallen creation.

Human Growth Hormone treatment, then, is appropriate to remedy deficiencies. The intentions underlying this or any other treatment are important. The primary intention behind giving hGH to GHD children is to restore the normal concentration of hormone because of its many important metabolic and anabolic functions. The benefits these children receive from being taller are, in a sense, incidental.

When hGH is given to children who are not hormone deficient, however, height gain for performance enhancement is the primary, if not the sole, intention. Even if psychosocial improvement is the ultimate goal, it is a product of the height gain. It is very questionable if performance enhancement *per se* is a proper goal of medicine.[33]

THE NATURE OF ILLNESS

Some claim it is appropriate to give hGH therapy 'to alleviate the handicap of short stature, rather than the treatment of GH deficiency'.[34] People can be so short that activities like driving a car become very difficult. Reflecting on these difficulties, one man who is 4 feet 4 inches tall observes:

> When I or another little person or a handicapper experiences a problem, we've been encouraged to blame it on ourselves. We've been encouraged to think that there is something wrong with us, with our emotions, with our minds, our bodies. Yet when other people experience the same kinds of problems, they are encouraged to blame it on the environment, and their solutions, of course, focus on the environment.[35]

We should be more concerned about making things accessible to short people than we are about changing the people. This is particularly the case with respect to short children who are not small enough to face physical limitations. These children – who may have to deal with problems like poor self-image, teasing, greater difficulty in relationships, and discrimination – are the focus of the remainder of this chapter.

Calling shortness a handicap is problematic because doing so is based on cultural values and prejudice. 'Short stature is, to some extent, a natural variation and falls within the limits of normality. The associated psychological morbidity results from cultural prejudice. We do not usually call prejudice-induced conditions, which confer social disadvantages but have no intrinsic negative health effects, diseases.'[36] Nor do we put the responsibility for dealing with prejudice on the shoulders of the ones against whom people discriminate. The uncertain benefits and possible risks of hGH treatment put a severe burden on the one already being unfairly treated. Furthermore, by calling shortness a handicap or disease, we imply that other traits that provoke discrimination – nose shape, weight, skin colour, gender – should be labelled similarly. Would we then expect people to take pigmentation therapy to change the colour of their skin because those of their colour experience discrimination?[37]

We can also distinguish shortness from 'diseases' by looking at the effects of a completely successful corrective programme. Giving hGH to the shortest people will not eliminate the problems associated with shortness. If the programme successfully increased height, the treated short people would grow taller than others, who would then become the shortest. 'The paradox of GH therapy is that no policy regarding its use will ever eliminate the 1st percentile.'[38] In all likelihood, those people would be subjected to the same prejudice. On the other hand, if everyone was given hGH, everyone might be taller, but the shortest would still face the same problems.

In this respect, hGH therapy is very different from other treatments such as giving recombinant insulin to diabetes mellitus patients. If all respond as hoped, the illness will be alleviated and no additional people will be subject to the problems faced by diabetics. If genetic technology leads to a better anti-cancer treatment, all will applaud the alleviation of that illness. Other cancer patients will not thereby be put at greater risk of the negative consequences of having cancer. Appropriate forms of therapy prevent or eliminate something intrinsically negative. Shortness does not fall into that category. Shortness is part of our natural variation, not a disease.

RELIEVING PSYCHOSOCIAL PROBLEMS

Growth hormone therapy could still be seen as an appropriate medical intervention to relieve psychosocial problems. Unfortunately, it has not lived up to its promises in this regard either. 'The psychological benefits of hGH therapy in non-GHD short stature have not been documented and remain, on a scientific level, only a presumption.'[39]

Even GHD children who ended up taller because of hGH therapy fail to show major psychosocial improvement. '[I]t is questionable whether children *made* taller enjoy the social advantages of *being* tall'[40] (emphasis original). Self-esteem remains low, and problems persist in social relationships with members of both sexes.[41] Unemployment rates are three times the norm, marriage rates are one-fifth the norm, and many patients are socially isolated.[42] The authors of this last study have called for an urgent review of the goals of hGH therapy, 'since increased height does not necessarily lead to normal social integration in adult life'.[43] Such findings confirm the biblical perspective that solutions to social problems must address people's hearts and spirits, not merely our physical appearances.

In fact, children placed on hGH therapy may experience new psychosocial problems. While parents want what is best for their children, trying to eliminate shortness is not the best option. 'Paradoxically, parents who are most desirous of obtaining GH for their child may confirm by their actions what his classmates' teasing suggests – that he would be a better person if he were taller.'[44] Shortness is so undesirable that the family takes on the painful injections, frequent inconveniences, and huge expense to avoid it. This creates confusion for the short man quoted earlier: 'On the one hand, I'm supposed to feel encouraged to participate fully in society, but on the other hand, I'm supposed to be encouraged not to be here!'[45]

As secular authors have noted, counselling is often a more effective and less expensive way of dealing with the psychological issues raised by shortness.[46] 'The effective physician should respond to concerns about short stature more often with counselling than with injections.'[47] Christians have the added security of knowing that Christ accepts us completely. Our security does not come from our physical appearance or functional abilities, but from our relationship with Christ (Philp. 3:4–10). Our identity is that of adopted children of God (Eph. 1:3–6). We are so valuable that the God of this universe suffered and died so that we could know how much he loves us and wants to spend eternity with us (1 Jn. 4:9–10). This brings true security. We learn to be content in all circumstances, even when we are the shortest, or tallest, or fattest, or ugliest, or slowest, or weakest (Philp. 4:11–12).

God uses the failures, hard knocks, and unfairness of life to teach us the reality of our security in him. Paul went to great lengths to explain to the Corinthians the value of weakness in the eyes of others (1 Cor. 1:26–31; 4:9–16; 12:22–25; 2 Cor. 11:30; 12:5–10;

13:2–9). Through acknowledging our weaknesses we learn to be humble before God. We learn to depend on others. We learn where we are strong and gifted, so we can humbly contribute to the Body of Christ. We also learn to appreciate the gifts and strengths of others, especially as these differ from our own (1 Cor. 12:4–31). Through a spirit of cooperation, we learn to contribute to the whole community (Eph. 4:11–13; Heb. 10:24–25).

In contrast, the pursuit of hGH treatment for shortness refuses to accept the acceptability of short people. Social pressure to conform to a certain height is fuelled by deeply held cultural values. 'In our competitive and individualistic society, we feel compelled to enhance our children's chances for success in relation to everyone else. . . . Performance oriented, we push our children to achieve.'[48] In doing so, however, we end up promoting unbiblical values and character qualities like competitiveness, narcissism, individualism, and self-interest.[49] Enhancement therapies, like hGH for normal children, promote these values because they succeed only when access to the therapy is limited. If all children were treated and all grew taller, there would be no advantage to the therapy.

The view that providing 'therapy' to give one a competitive edge is legitimate must be corrected before genetic technology provides other, more dramatic 'opportunities'. If 'enhancement therapy' gains widespread acceptance, we may not be able to withstand the pressure to permit more invasive genetic enhancement therapies.[50] Consider the related widespread problem of performance-enhancement drugs in competitive sports:

> The pressure to use exists when people *believe* that something confers a competitive advantage, whether or not this is objectively true. There is, then, an *inherent coerciveness* present in these situations: when some choose to do what gives them a competitive edge, others will be pressed to do likewise, or resign themselves to either accepting a competitive disadvantage or leaving the endeavor entirely. While sport is not an adequate metaphor for life in most respects, the phenomenon of inherent coerciveness is almost certainly not limited to sport. It is a general feature of society where competition dominates a number of settings, especially work.[51]

The competitive nature of our world can leave us addicted to the need to succeed. Paul warns us not to be mastered by those things which are lawful for us (1 Cor. 6:12). The pursuit of greater height, if not inherently immoral, may be a symptom of our enslavement to getting ahead. In the words of a parent of one boy predicted to grow to 5 feet 4 inches: 'You want to give your child the edge no matter what. . . . I think you'd do just about anything.'[52]

Unfortunately, there will be disadvantages from not competing in every way that others do. We and our children will experience trials and disappointments. But through these we can show our children that there are more important things than physical appearance and success in this world. Parents may be concerned about how their short children will respond when they learn that hGH therapy is available. Knowledge of the limited effectiveness of the therapy will help. However, Christians can rest in the knowledge that we help our children most when we raise them in the discipline and instruction of the Lord (Eph. 6:4). The best way to deal with difficulties and mistreatment is to turn to the Lord in dependence (1 Pet. 2:23).

Interestingly, many GHD patients and their parents note that being shorter than normal makes children much more compassionate towards themselves and others.[53] Coming to accept ourselves as we are is an important step in learning to accept others with their limitations. 'When you take pride in yourself and pride in your people, whomever you define as your people, it's almost impossible not to make that next step, the most important step, and that is taking pride in all people.'[54]

As parents we must consider when we might be trying to cut ethical corners to remove the very trials by which God wants to shape our children's characters (Rom. 5:3–5). Having to deal with shortness, and the unfortunate limitations and discrimination it may bring, is not an unmitigated evil. It can give children and their parents the opportunity to become better images of God. Through this character transformation we can learn to say confidently, 'The Lord is my Helper, I will not be afraid. What shall people do to me?' (Heb. 13:5–6).

PREJUDICE

Accepting our children's shortness does not mean we should accept the prejudice that underlies heightism. God hates such prejudice and the discrimination that goes with it, and so should those who seek to be his images (Acts 10:34–35; Jam. 2:1–9). Since all people are images of God, all should be regarded equally (Gen. 9:6; Jam. 3:9–10). This standard applies very much to children, who hold a special place in God's heart (Mt. 18:1–6; 19:13–14).

It is possible, as one author claims, that heightism was behind Samuel's choice of Saul as king – for Saul was handsome and 'from his shoulders and up he was taller than any of the people' (1 Sam. 9:2).[55] An examination of the biblical text suggests otherwise. These words are part of a description of Saul. We are not told that he was chosen as king because of his height. On the contrary, a few chapters later God explains to Samuel how he is to select a new king: 'Do not look at his appearance or at the height of his stature, because I have rejected him; for people see not as God sees, for people look at the outward appearance, but the Lord looks at the heart' (1 Sam.

16:7). Similarly, we are not to judge people on the basis of their physical characteristics (Mt. 23:25–28).

Ironically, hGH therapy for children without GHD may even promote heightism by substantiating the belief that shortness is bad. Like other 'illnesses', it is to be eliminated; or, like other 'handicaps', it is a significant limitation to be avoided. 'To perceive short stature as undesirable is unfair to those who are short.'[56] Previously unaware of a problem, short people may now find themselves regarded as handicapped or diseased.

The real problem is not with shortness, but with the person's heart who teases or discriminates against the short person. To 'treat' the shortness is to hide the underlying problem. As God's images, we must be willing to speak up against all forms of discrimination. People often hurt others because they themselves are hurting inside. Truth spoken in love can reveal the real issues, providing us with an opportunity to act as ambassadors of God's message of reconciliation (2 Cor. 5:20–21).

JUSTICE

Many of the preceding issues are matters of justice – a subject addressed frequently in the Bible. Justice is one of the weightier provisions of the law, and we must not neglect it (Mt. 23:23). If hGH therapy worked, it would only further social injustices.[57] Only those who could pay for hGH would have access to it. Therefore, the children of the rich would benefit the most from this therapy. While a similar disparity could be operative with other therapies, the case of hGH is somewhat different. While the rich get taller and thereby richer, the poor remain short and then disproportionately experience the discrimination and prejudice of heightism all the more as the number of short people decreases.[58]

Images of God should plead the cause of the afflicted and needy. This is what it means to know God (Jer. 22:16). As Job reminds us, we should be just in our treatment of every person, including the poor and the needy, because: 'Did not [God] who made me in the womb make them, and the same one fashion us in the womb?' (31:15). Faithful images of God will not act in ways that further oppress the poor and needy.

We are also unjust when we refuse to share our abundance with those less well off (Job 31:13–23; 1 Jn. 3:17). While others perish in need, the unjust put their confidence in wealth (Job 31:24–28). We can reveal God's justice by being good stewards of our resources. The overall cost of hGH therapy is quite large. In the USA alone, expenditures on it during 1993 totalled $300 million. The annual cost to each patient is up to $30,000, and sometimes more, with treatment lasting six to ten years.[59] In one of the Turner's syndrome studies where adult height was increased, the cost was approximately $58,000 per inch.[60] In light of the limited health care resources available and the more pressing health care needs of many members of the population, it is difficult to justify this expense.

Some may respond that since their insurance pays for the treatment, they are not spending their own money. However, insurance payments do not come from a bottomless gold mine. Others in the insurance plan contribute to our expenditures. If it is unjust to spend money from our own pockets on hGH, it is even more unjust to use others' money on it. We should not spend tens of thousands of dollars on the uncertain possibility of making our children a little taller or the even more uncertain possibility that this will make them happier and more successful. While people in the richer nations pursue these goals, millions in the poorer nations die of starvation. Such disparities are an abomination to God (Amos 5:11–12).

———————

God has given us amazing abilities to use our environment for our good. The minds and hands of people have fashioned many ways to prevent or treat illnesses. But there is a limit to what we should try to change. Particularly when we are not intrinsically damaged or dysfunctional, our challenge in some situations will simply be to accept the way God has made us. As Christians we have a powerful perspective to help us endure the teasing and discrimination that may result. Each of us is fearfully and wonderfully made (Ps. 139). God knows us intimately, and treasures us for who we are.

As images of God, we have a great opportunity to tell our friends, family, and physicians why we would not give our short children hGH. We can talk about how the Lord will help our children develop their character to deal with the adversity shortness brings. We can talk about how we refuse to better our children's lives at the expense of other children. We can talk about the injustices in the current distribution of the world's resources. Through these conversations, we can witness to the hope that is in us (1 Pet. 3:15).

Genetic research will lead to new therapies to heal or prevent diseases. However, there will also be more possibilities for enhancement. 'New therapies may be directed not at health maintenance or disease prevention but at the augmentation of health, beauty, or well-being.'[61] Already some are promoting hGH for rejuvenation of older men in spite of evidence that it does not work.[62] We need to draw a line between genuinely restoring well-being and worshipping health and youth.

God helps us to determine which interventions to pursue, and which to let pass. As his images he calls us to correct injustice and bring healing – sometimes even to forgo 'the lawful' in order to do 'the loving'. We carry out such mandates by bringing his truth to bear on the ethical issues of our day and by offering the true healing of a living relationship with God through Jesus Christ. He is the true elixir of life and happiness (Jn. 4:13–14).

NOTES

1.   Guyton, Arthur C., *Textbook of Medical Physiology*, 8th ed. (Philadelphia: W.B.Saunders 1991), pp.822–6.

2.   Kimbrell, Andrew, *The Human Body Shop: The Engineering and Marketing of Life* (San Francisco: Harper 1993), pp.142–4.

3.   DeVile, C.J., Albanese, A., Thomas, B., and Stanhope, R., 'New Challenges in the Growth Field', *Journal of Pediatric Endocrinology*, vol.vi (Jul.-Dec.1993), pp.295–301.

4.   Neely, E.K., and Rosenfeld, R., 'Use and Abuse of Human Growth Hormone', *Annual Review of Medicine*, vol.xlv (1994), p.408.

5.   Lindsay, R., Feldkamp, M., Harris, D., Robertson, J., and Rallison, M., 'Utah Growth Study: Growth Standards and the Prevalence of Growth Hormone Deficiency', *Journal of Pediatrics*, vol.cxxv (Jul.1994), pp.29–35.

6.   Constitutional growth delay is where the child's growth is slower, but lasts longer. Although shorter than their peers as children, they do eventually catch up with them. Diekema, Douglas S., 'Is Taller Really Better? Growth Hormone Therapy in Short Children', *Perspectives in Biology and Medicine*, vol.xxxiv (Aut.1990), p.110.

7.   Brook, C.G.D., 'Who's For Growth Hormone?' *British Medical Journal*, vol. ccciv (Jan.1992), pp.131–2.

8.   Benjamin, M., Muyskens, J., and Saenger, P., 'Short Children, Anxious Parents: Is Growth Hormone the Answer', *Hastings Center Report*, vol.xiv, (Apr.1984), p.8.

9.   Allen, David B., and Fost, Norman C., 'Growth Hormone Therapy for Short Stature: Panacea or Pandora's Box', *Journal of Pediatrics*, vol.cxvii (Jul.1990), p.17.

10.   Stabler, Brian, and Underwood, Louis E., ed. *Slow Grows the Child: Psychosocial Aspects of Growth Delay* (Hillsdale [NJ], Lawrence Erlbaum Associates 1986).

11.   Editorial, 'Little Bigger, Little Better', *Lancet*, vol.cccxliv, (Sep.1994), pp.627–8.

12.   Neely, p.410.

13.   Mitchell, C.M., Joyce, S., Johanson, Ann J., Libber, S., Plotnick, L., Mignon, Claude J., and Blizzard, Robert M., 'A Retrospective Evaluation of Psychosocial Impact of Long-term Growth Hormone Therapy', *Clinical Pediatrics*, vol.xxv (Jan.1986), p.18.

14.   Ibid., p.22.

15.   Neely, p.417; Brook, p.132; Cianfarani, S., Vaccaro, F., and Boscherini, B., 'What is the Rationale for Growth Hormone Therapy in Turner's Syndrome', *Lancet*, vol.cccxliv (Jul.1994), pp.114–5.

16.   Chipman, J.J., 'Study Design for Final Height Determination in Turner Syndrome: Pros and Cons', *Hormone Research*, vol.xxxix (1993), pp.18–22.

17.   DeVile, p.298.

18.   Neely, p.413.

19.   Originally reported as 3 cm; Ibid.

20.   Ibid.

21.   National Institutes of Health Consent Form, paragraph 9, quoted in Kimbrell, p.146.

22.   DeVile, pp.295–301.

23.   Ibid., p.297.

24.   Underwood, Louis E., and Rieser, Patricia A., 'Is it Ethical to Treat Healthy Shirt Children with Growth Hormone?' *Acta Pædiatrica Scandinavica Supplement*, vol.ccclxii (1989), p.21.

25.   Neely, p.409.

26.   Walker, J.M, Bond, S.A., Voss, L.D., Betts, P.R., Wootton, S.A., and Jackson, A.A.,'Treatment of Short Normal Children with Growth Hormone – A Cautionary Tale?' *Lancet*, vol.cccxxxvi (Dec.1990), p.1332.

27.   Mitchell, pp.17–23.

28.   Diekema, p.113.

29.   Neely, p.410.

30.   Cianfarani, p.114.

31.   Hochberg, Z., 'Growth Hormone Therapy: the Ethical Angle', *Acta Pædiatrica Scandinavica Supplement*, vol.ccclxvii (1990), p.2.

32.   Lantos, J., Siegler, M., and Cuttler, L., 'Ethical Issues in Growth Hormone Therapy', *Journal of the American Medical Association*, vol.cclxi(Feb.1989), p.1020.

33.   For a fuller defence of this view, see Kass, Leon R., 'The End of Medicine and the Pursuit of Health', in *Toward a More Natural Science: Biology and Human Affairs* (New York, Free Press 1985), pp.157–86.

34.   Allen, p.17.

35.   Sawisch, Leonard P., 'Psychosocial Aspects of Short Stature: The Day to Day Context', in Stabler, ed. *Slow Grows the Child*, p.52.

36.   Bischofberger, Erwin, and Dahlström, Gunnar, 'Ethical Aspects on Growth Hormone Therapy', *Acta Pædiatrica Scandinavica Supplement*, vol.ccclxii (1989), p.16.

37.   Kimbrell, p.155.

38.   Allen, p.20.

39.   Neely, p.417.

40.   Allen, p.17.

41.   Mitchell, pp.17–23.

42.   Dean, Heather J., McTaggart, Terri L., Fish, David G., and Friesen, Henry G.,'The Educational, Vocational, and Marital Status of Growth Hormone-deficient Adults Treated With Growth Hormone During Childhood', *American Journal of Diseases in Children*, vol.cxxxix (Nov.1985), pp.1105–10.

43.   Ibid., p.1110.

44.   Allen, p.17.

45.   Sawisch, p.48.

46.   Neely, p.417.

47.   Allen, p.20.

48.   Diekema, p.117.

49.   Ibid.

50.   Gardner, William, 'Can Human Genetic Enhancement Be Prohibited?' *Journal of Medicine and Philosophy*, vol.xx (1995), pp.65–84.

51.   Murray, Thomas H., 'The Coercive Power of Drugs in Sports', *Hastings Center Report*, vol.xiii (Aug.1983), p.27.

52.   Oritis, Luisa, quoted in Kimbrell, p.145.

53.   Mitchell, p.22.

54.   Sawisch, p.55.

55.   Hochberg, pp.1–3.

56.   Diekema, p.116.

57.   Ibid.

58. Benjamin, p.9; Lantos, p.1022.

59. Neely, p.416.

60. Calculated from the reported cost of £14,500 per centimeter, in Cianfarani, pp.114–5.

61. Lantos, p.1024.

62. *National Council Against Health Fraud Newsletter*, vol.xix (May/Jun.1996), pp.3–4.

18

Contemporary Christian Responsibility

Charles W. Colson, JD

In his 1987 novel, *The Thanatos Syndrome*, the late Walker Percy makes a compelling case for the sacredness of life. Percy presents a dark vision of the future when 'qualitarian life centers' would spring up across the United States as an eventual result of a Supreme Court ruling. At the qualitarian centres one could conveniently dispose of unwanted young and old alike.

Percy's novel includes two memorable characters: a psychiatrist educated at an Ivy League university and a priest who is slightly mad. In a confrontational scene, the priest is in a fire tower; the psychiatrist is trying to 'talk him down'. The priest looks at the psychiatrist and says, 'You are an able psychiatrist, on the whole a decent, generous, humanitarian person in the abstract sense of the word. You know what is going to happen to you?'

The psychiatrist keeps him talking, and the priest continues: 'You are a member of the first generation of doctors in the history of medicine to turn their backs on the oath of Hippocrates and kill millions of old useless people, unborn children, born malformed children, for the good of mankind – and you do so without a single murmur from one of you. Not a single letter of protest in the August *New England Journal of Medicine*. Do you know what you're going to end up doing?'

At this point the priest grows a little distracted, but then answers his rhetorical question:

'You're going to end up killing Jews.'[1]

Abortion has always been about more than abortion. Paul Johnson, the British historian, says that the issue of the twentieth century was totalitarianism, and the issue of the twenty-first century will be life.[2] Abortion opens the gates to other 'life issues' – cloning, eugenics, controlling life, and eventually to euthanasia, which is not so far down the road. Once we are there, as Percy's priest postulates, we are dangerously close to 'killing Jews'.

Several years ago, on a cross-country flight, a bright-looking young man recognized me and introduced himself. 'Oh, Mr. Colson!' he said. 'I'm delighted to meet you. I appreciate your books . . . I am going to be a missionary, as soon as I finish school.'

'What are you studying?' I asked.

'Molecular biology.'

'Where do you want to be a missionary?'

He said, 'Well, I want to go to South America. My parents were missionaries to South America.'

I wondered if I had understood correctly. 'You are studying molecular biology, and you want to be a missionary in South America?'

He said, 'Oh yes, I want to serve the Lord.'

I probed further: 'Have you ever thought about serving him as a molecular biologist? Not many Christians serve in that field.'

He admitted he had not thought about that and returned to his seat. But before the plane landed, he came back and said, 'Mr. Colson, thank you. Yes, I could be a missionary as a molecular biologist.'

That conversation reminds us that we are called to bring Christian truth to bear on every walk of life and certainly in the medical field, where there are such extraordinary technological advances that need to be understood from a Christian world view.

BRAVE NEW TEMPTATIONS

In *bioethics*, the *bio* stands for the biological endeavours; one might say the biological questions involve what we *can* do. The *ethics* stands for the question of what we *ought* to do, how *ought* we to live. In terms of biological advancements, what ought we to do?

In the 1960s utopians in the US believed they could create a perfect world with social engineering through politics. But they failed. Everybody today, from President Clinton right across the political spectrum, is saying big government has failed to bail out the ghettos and help the poor.

Now scientific advances introduce another utopian possibility: modifying humanity through molecular genetics in an attempt to 'perfect' the human race. The down-side to this dream is seen in the ideas of Francis Crick, who shared the Nobel Prize with James Watson, and who proposed that newborns be examined to see who is fit to live. Creating a substantially improved race, in this view, means weeding out the unfit.[3]

Consider the ramifications of such an approach for criminal justice, a field in which I have worked for many years. In 1985, criminologist James Q. Wilson, then at Harvard, now at the University of California, and the late Harvard professor Richard Herrnstein completed a seminal study on the causes of crime. They identified the critical cause as being the lack of moral training during the morally formative years of childhood. But they did find one possible genetic link: children of criminals, even when they were adopted and not raised by their natural parents, were more likely to become involved in criminal activity than children of non-criminal parents. So Herrnstein and Wilson raised the possibility of a genetic factor in the cause of crime.[4]

Imagine the resultant political pressures if someone said, 'We have identified the crime gene!' Take it a step further, to, 'We have identified the sin gene' – even though society says there is no such thing as sin. 'We have found what causes dysfunction in people's lives. We have found the gene!' It would be difficult to resist the temptation to screen for and exterminate such a gene.

I foresee that pressures will build for facilitating a politically correct lifestyle. One physician asked me to consider the ethical dimensions of the following scenario he had encountered in his practice: A gay couple and a lesbian couple were close friends. Each couple wanted a child. After mixing their sperm, the two men fertilized ova from the women in a Petri dish, resulting in twenty-four embryos. Four of the embryos were implanted in each of the two women. Four were implanted in a third woman – a surrogate – with plans to abort at twenty weeks, so that the adrenal gland could be transplanted to the father of one of the lesbian women. The father, who was paying for the whole process, had Parkinson's disease. Four more embryos were saved as spares. The remaining eight embryos were sent to the United Kingdom for research.

In this scenario, three babies were 'produced'. Two were successfully brought to term; one was aborted, the adrenal gland taken for the man with Parkinson's disease. One gay man married one lesbian woman, so one child could be legally adopted. (The state would not allow adoption except by heterosexual couples.) Once the adoption was finalized, the couple divorced. In the end, the lesbian couple and the gay couple each had a child, one legally adopted. This convoluted scenario illustrates just one issue we face today.

The pressure to relieve suffering of terminally ill patients is another, as reflected in the debates over euthanasia. One side believes we have a constitutionally protected right to be protected from suffering. The pressures are coming – all in the name of mercy – to decide when life is not worthy of breath.

So while genetic research may lead to important medical advances, we must probe the deeper question: What are the restraints? Technological advance may make it *possible* to do something, but *ought* we do it?

At a lecture on embryo manipulation at Green College in Great Britain, Dame Mary Warnock concluded that because there are no 'recognized' moral experts anymore, individuals have to decide for themselves; that is, everyone has a right to sort out and justify one's own feelings on the matter.[5] This outlook is all too characteristic of the ethical reflection in today's world.

ETHICS AND ABSOLUTES

Even as schools seek to teach ethics, they run into trouble. Some years ago a man donated $20 million to Harvard Business School to fund teaching of a refresher course on ethics. After I reviewed the course material, I saw that it was pure pragmatism – utilitarianism: Don't get caught; it is bad for your business. So I wrote some articles claiming that Harvard could not possibly teach ethics. 'Ethics' derives from the Greek word *ethos*, which means an absolute – a resting place, a hiding place. Harvard cannot teach ethics, I said, because the institution today is based on philosophical relativism. Ethics cannot be taught by people who say there is no absolute truth.

My friends with Harvard connections took offence. After some correspondence, Harvard invited me to deliver a distinguished lecture on ethics. After extensive preparation, I addressed an assembly of three hundred and fifty students and faculty to explain why they will not learn ethics at Harvard.

Although I left plenty of time for questions afterwards, no one posed any thoughtful questions. They did not even know the right questions to raise. The same thing happened when I spoke in 1996 on the rule of law at Yale Law School: no tough questions; no challenging debate. Having erased any understanding of truth and objective moral order, the postmodern mind is not interested in debate.

However, a society that cannot think about ethics is unprepared for the forthcoming avalanche of medical breakthroughs. The postmodern spirit cannot provide the kind of moral restraints that would direct medical technology to productive ends. Christians must take a leadership role in helping society to ask the 'ought' question.

The 'ought' question brings us to another issue: By whose or what authority 'ought' we to do or not do something? This question was raised by Arthur Leff, professor at Yale Law School, during a lecture at Duke University. He stated that 'the law' has lost its authority in today's culture. So the issue today is not so much 'the law', but the classic bar-room question, 'the grand sez who'. Nobody today has a compelling answer to that question. So we may claim things ought to be a certain way, but we are trumped by the bar-room question, 'Sez who?'[6]

Lacking an objective standard of truth and any kind of moral authority, the postmodern mind is stymied. Phillip Johnson, a law professor at the University of California at Berkeley, explains the contemporary impasse this way: 'Everyone has a right to live exactly as he or she pleases, but if something goes wrong, some abstraction called "society" is to blame and must pay the bills for the damage.'[7]

The dilemma was illustrated at an editorial briefing for a major newspaper chain to which I was invited. The publisher had brought together editors from around the country. I walked into the meeting carrying my Bible. The publisher leaned over and asked, 'Are you one of those Bible-believing Christians?'

I said, 'I didn't know there was any other kind.'

After we sat down, I talked about the criminal justice crisis in America.

During our discussion, the publisher commented: 'You know, I probably have offended you, but I am responsible for taking the Ten Commandments off the school classroom walls here in our city. Our paper led the campaign to remove them.'

'Why did you do that?' I asked.

'We don't want to offend anybody', he said. 'This is an enlightened era. People should be free from religious interference.'

Conversation continued; later the publisher leaned over to ask if I had read the study that showed that half the kids in US schools are stealing from one another. 'It is terrible, all the theft in our schools. What can we do about it?'

I replied, 'Maybe you can put a sign up on the wall, "You shall not steal." '

Like the publisher, our society does not like an authority like the Ten Commandments prescribing behaviour, and then wonders why children steal.

The crisis of cultural authority, the 'sez who?' that undergirds all the 'ought' questions, turns on a fundamental question. Is there truth? Pilate's question to Jesus still echoes through the centuries: 'What is truth?' Twenty years ago Francis Schaeffer would address an audience and shout, 'The issue is truth! Flaming truth! True truth!' The issue is whether some objective reality really exists, some ultimate point from which all else flows.

Unfortunately the polls suggest that Americans, at least, do not believe in truth. A 1991 George Barna study found that 67 percent of American adults agreed with the statement, 'There is no such thing as absolute truth.' Three years later, Barna asked the general public the same question and 72 percent agreed, 'There is no such thing as absolute truth.'[8]

Surveys of professing Christians do not look much better. In the 1991 study, Barna found that among the broad category of Christians that he called 'born-again Christians' (of which 'evangelicals' were a subset), 52 percent agreed with the statement, 'There is no such thing as absolute truth.' Three years later, the 'born-again Christians' who agreed with his statement on absolute truth jumped to 62 percent.[9]

Truth is at the root of the conflict of world views. The Christian world view sees God as Lord of all; Jesus as Lord of the universe, of all creation; the Christian's job is to take every thought captive in obedience to Christ, and to recognize that a battle is being waged between two distinct and antithetical world views. One is secular, of this age. The other is biblical, eternal. One is naturalistic; nature, that which is observable, is all there is. The other is supernatural. One is utopian. The other acknowledges that humanity is fallen, desperately in need of restraint and the grace of God. One is humanistic, human-centred. The other is theistic, God-centred. One is pragmatistic. The other is idealistic. One is relativistic; the other is founded on absolutes. That is the nature of the battle behind the so-called culture wars in America.

COLLAPSED FIRE WALLS

Sociologist Peter Berger says that America is a country of Indians ruled by Swedes. He is referring to Sweden being the most irreligious nation on earth, and India, the most religious nation. In other words, the United States is a nation of religious people who are ruled by people with no faith. 'The Swedes' have won. They control the centres of thought and influence. The 'sez who?' trumps the 'oughts' in science, in law, in virtually every field. The two restraints that hold a society in check – the fire walls against the raging inferno of sin that is natural to us – have collapsed. One wall is the inner restraint of conscience. The other is the external restraint of the law.

Where are we in terms of conscience? In the 1960s and 1970s America experienced a cultural revolution: find your own way; do your own thing; overcome the nothingness of life by your own heroic individualism was the credo. We thought it was about hippies in long hair and tie-dye shirts. When the 1960s were over, many breathed a sigh of relief. But the kids wearing tie-dyes just changed into pin-striped suits and went to New York to become yuppies. The value-system of radical individualism, the 'pursuit of the unencumbered self', as Michael Sandel calls it, has flourished in America so that today it is almost impossible to say that we genuinely have a community.[10] The soaring crime rates are a sad result of the breakdown of moral values.

We might think that America is safe because it was founded on ordered liberty and the certainty of the rule of law – the second fire wall. America's heritage dates to Samuel Rutherford, the Scottish cleric who wrote *Lex Rex*,[11] which means 'the law is king' – *the law*, not the monarch or the legislature or the judge who interprets the law. This influence was pervasive among the founders; 'the law is king' was integral to the founding documents of the US. For the first hundred years of the nation's life, people believed and practised what those founding documents had preached: American elected officials reigned under the authority of the transcendent law.

But all of that began to change under the influence of the noted jurist Oliver Wendell Holmes, Jr. At Harvard, Holmes formed the metaphysics club along with William James and John Dewey and developed the first American-born philosophy, pragmatism: whatever works is good. As James put it, 'Truth is the cash value of an idea.'[12] Holmes applied pragmatism to law. He essentially divorced law from its basis in transcendent objective reality; law is its own authority, he claimed. To determine what the law should be, we should look not at tradition or natural law, but to scientific disciplines like economics and psychology. It took time for this Holmes perspective to permeate the law in America. But it has now hit it like an avalanche.[13]

His concept of law is particularly reflected in the reasoning behind the 1973 Supreme Court decision *Roe* v. *Wade*. The sexual revolution of the 1960s ultimately led to the Court's decision to develop a legal basis for a woman's 'right to choose'. This was a sociological decision enshrining that sacrament of American life, free sex. Here the Court said the Constitution implies some right of privacy that gives women the right to choose. Contrary to the headlines of the *New York Times* that declared 'Supreme Court settles abortion issue' on that fateful day in January 1973, the decision actually intensified the abortion controversy. Americans aware of a higher law started to protest in the streets, knowing that life is sacred, created in the image of God; they would not accept that decision.

Then in *Casey* v. *Planned Parenthood* (1992), the Court sought to settle the issue again, saying in effect: *You pro-lifers should go away; this issue is settled. We are not going to change our minds.* This time, the Court declared abortion not only legal, but enshrined its 1973 decision into the law as an expressly protected Fourteenth Amendment liberty. Furthermore, the Court articulated a new definition of liberty. 'Liberty', the 1992 decision reads, 'is the right to make intimate and personal choices central to personal dignity and autonomy. It is the right to define one's own concept of existence, of meaning, of the universe, and of the mystery of human life.'[14] According to this decision, every citizen has the right to define for himself the mystery of life!

The lower courts have moved very quickly to apply these concepts to other life and death issues. In *Compassion in Dying* v. *Washington State* (1996), the U.S. Court of Appeals for the Ninth Circuit used the *Casey* language to override a Washington state referendum that had banned assisted suicide. In the eight-to-three decision, the court in effect said that the Washington electorate who passed the referendum did not know what it was doing – because banning assisted suicide violated a constitutionally protected right.

In a reference to those with strong moral or religious convictions, Judge Reinhardt declared: 'They are not free .. to force their views, their religious convictions, or their philosophies on all the other members of a democratic society.'[15]

In this judge's opinion, citizens who are motivated by religious convictions are therefore disqualified from influencing the law because they challenge the notion that individuals can determine for themselves the mystery and meaning of life! Judge Reinhardt even went a step further. The infamous footnote 120 of his decision opens the door to the possibility that, when individuals are not competent to make a decision to terminate their own lives, another party could make it for them. This brings us dangerously close to euthanasia. Who will be the decision maker: a family member with pockets turned up standing by the bedside? a white-coated hospital technician? a well-meaning doctor saying, 'Let's be compassionate and let people gently pass away'? As a colleague of mine pointed out, this was the first court decision that approved Americans killing Americans.

Very shortly after that case, the U.S. Court of Appeals for the Second Circuit decided a similar case. This court also based its arguments on the *Casey* language.[16]

Then came the *coup de grace* that has brought an end to the rule of law in America. In *Romer* v. *Evans* (1996), the Supreme Court overturned a Colorado state constitutional amendment that prohibited local civil rights statutes based on sexual preferences. In the six-to-three decision, Justice Kennedy wrote: 'Laws of the kind before us raise the inevitable inference that the disadvantage imposed is born of animosity towards the class of persons affected. A bare desire to harm a politically unpopular group cannot constitute a legitimate government interest.'[17] Justice Kennedy is claiming that 52 percent of the voters of Colorado were bigoted and biased in ratifying that amendment, even though there was no finding of fact to that effect. That kind of judgment without a finding of fact represents a first for an appellate court. Actually, the facts suggest the opposite. Colorado Governor Romer testified that this was not the purpose of the referendum; Kennedy simply divined it. Like a psychologist uncovering repressed memories, he presumed to know what the people did not even know they were thinking.

The two fire walls are gone. The restraint of conscience is gone because of the radical individualism of our age. The restraint of the rule of law is gone because the Supreme Court has taken it away.

Without these fire walls, who will decide matters of life and death? Who will decide what is legitimate genetic engineering and what is eugenics? Who will decide how far to go in manipulating life to produce a superior species? When the Nazis tried this, they ran into some natural obstacles. In their effort to create a super race, their *lebensborne* experiment coupled men from the SS elite with some attractive women – but they could mate only at the right time of the month, and even then they had little understanding or control of the genetics involved. Now, however, human lives can be produced in a laboratory at any time, in light of rapidly expanding knowledge and control. But who will say we *should not* be doing all that is becoming possible to do?

THE CHALLENGE OF THE CHURCH

While many of the startling strides in biology are frightening if we do not learn how to apply moral restraints, there is never a cause for despair. Recall the first centuries of Christianity. Christians were burned as human torches in the Roman arena, but by A.D. 324, Constantine declared his empire 'Christian'. Then after the Goths and Vandals overran Europe, Christianity retreated to tiny monastic outposts in western Ireland. However, those monks worked at draining the swamps, building roads, and preserving the Word of God; eventually the gospel counter-attack built Christendom. In our own generation, in Eastern Europe and Russia, through intense persecution, the church has remained strong and vibrant. Yes, we face grim prospects, but the church has two vital challenges before it which represent great opportunities.

First, Christians must develop a well-reasoned Christian apologetic on all issues, and of course prominently the issues of bioethics. The apostle Peter said, 'Always be prepared to give an answer to everyone who asks you to give the reason for the hope that you have. But do this with gentleness and respect' (1 Pet. 3:15–16 NIV). Peter challenges us to be able to explain the truth of Christian revelation. This goes deeper than quoting some evangelistic tract. We must be prepared to defend a Christian view of ethics in a world that has disdained it, in a world that always raises the trump 'sez who?' We must be able to give a reasoned answer. We must defend what Scripture teaches and show how that coincides with the moral order of the universe and the absolutes that all civilized societies have affirmed.

Christians believe that Jesus Christ is the truth. All things were made by him, for him, through him, and are held together by him. If we believe these absolutes, we must defend them. Cultures are changed not so much by intellectuals as by ordinary men and women. When we start talking about the modernist impasse in terms our neighbours, colleagues, friends can understand, we can change the culture. Great movements, as John Wesley proved, begin not from the top down but from the bottom up. Christian people with a biblical world view can change their families, their communities, and their professions by articulating the truth that there is an objective moral order. We do not make laws for ourselves; the laws are made by God. There are certain rules. Break a physical law, and certain consequences result. Break a moral law, and just as certainly consequences will result.

Second, Christians must *be* the church, the people of God. Jesus said, 'By this all people will know that you are my disciples, if you love one another' (Jn. 13:35). So the question is: Are we a loving community? Do we radiate the love of Christ? Do people see Christ in us? A yearning for God is deep in every heart. But nonbelievers often see us running around debating theology in public or snidely berating one another. Do they see us as a community of loving believers? The world measures us not so much by what we do, but what we are and who we are, and whether we live in biblical fidelity.

Three years ago I was interviewed by a public television station. Greeting the interviewer, I mentally noted that her heavy make-up could not mask the lines and scars of life; this woman had been through a lot. She nevertheless exuded self-confidence in her willingness to challenge me on a number of issues. Finally, she asked, 'Mr. Colson, how can you be so sure of your faith?'

I replied, 'Well, I know God. I know what he has done in my life.' I then told of my seven months in prison. During that time, I lost my occupation, being disbarred in the state where I had practiced law. I also lost my father. Then I learned that my son was in jail for marijuana possession. It was one of the darkest days of my life.

But a member of my Washington prayer group – Al Quie, then the seventh ranking Republican in the House, later a governor of Minnesota – telephoned me. Al said, 'Chuck, I have an appointment with President Ford tomorrow. I discovered a pre-Civil War statute that allows one man to serve another man's prison sentence. I am going to ask the president if I can serve out your sentence so you can go home.'

As I was relating this on camera, I began to see tears and mascara rolling down the interviewer's face. She said, 'Stop! Stop the cameras!' After some time in the bathroom to freshen up, she returned, her poise intact. 'Now, let's film that part over again.'

I repeated the story and again she started to cry. Later I talked with her off camera. She had attended church as a child but had been turned off. But she said, 'In talking with you, I realize I have got to get back to the church.'

The world would desperately love to know our faith is true – if they could just see us living it. Even as the church defends truth, the church must be the people of God. When the church reaches across divisions and denominational barriers, in love to brothers and sisters, the world can see a loving community.

OUR MOTIVATION

Why should Christians reach out in love and proclaim truth? Three reasons stand out as primary.

Many wonderful things have happened to me in my life. However, the greatest is the most basic: God sent his Son, Jesus Christ, to die on a cross to take away my sins. I could not live with myself unless I knew that Christ had paid that price, taken those sins upon himself and set me free. His work creates what G. K. Chesterton called the 'mother of all virtues': gratitude. Gratitude for what God has done – that is reason number one.

Reason number two comes from an old Jewish tale. An old man would stand outside of the gates of Sodom and Gomorrah, shaking his fist, yelling, 'Stop that debauchery, that abomination before God!'

One day a young man said, 'Save your breath, old man. You can't change them. Stop screaming.' The man answered, 'I know I can't change them, but I am going to keep screaming so they don't change me.'

We need to keep screaming so that the world does not deceive us.

Third, we must remember that in the darkest night, the smallest flame from a match can be seen at a great distance! We serve a great God. He calls us to be faithful, to be a loving community, and to defend what we know to be true. He is sovereign and will do the rest.

NOTES

1.   Percy, Walker, *The Thanatos Syndrome* (New York: Ivy Books 1987), p.139.

2.   Johnson, Paul, *The Quest for God: A Personal Pilgrimage* (New York: HarperCollins 1996), pp. 116–117.

3.   Cited in 'Abortion and Infanticide', *Policy Review* 32 (April 1985):12.

4.   Wilson, James Q. and Herrnstein, Richard J., *Crime and Human Nature: The Definitive Study of the Causes of Crime* (New York: Simon and Schuster 1985).

5.   Warnock, Mary, 'Ethical Challenges in Embryo Manipulation', *British Medical Journal* 304 (1992), p. 1045.

6.   Leff, Arthur, 'Unspeakable Ethics, Unnatural Law', *Duke Law Journal* (1979), p. 1229. Cited by Phillip E. Johnson, *Reason in the Balance: The Case Against Naturalism in Science, Law, and Education* (Downers Grove, [IL]: InterVarsity Press 1995), p. 147.

7.   Johnson, *Reason in the Balance*, p. 148.

8.   Barna, George, *Virtual America* (Ventura, Calif.: Regal Books/Gospel Light 1994), p. 83

9.   Ibid.

10.   Sandel, Michael, *Democracy's Discontents: America in Search of a Public Philosophy* (Cambridge [MA]: Belknap Press/Harvard University Press, 1996).

11.   *The Law and the Prince: A Dispute for the Just Prerogatives of King and People* (1644).

12.   Cited by Sproul, R.C., *Lifeviews: Understanding the Ideas that Shape Society Today* (Old Tappan, [NJ]: Revell, 1986), p. 89.

13. Johnson, *Reason in the Balance*, pp. 139–142.

14. *Casey v. Planned Parenthood*, 112 S. Ct. LEXIS 2791 (1992).

15. *Compassion in Dying v. Washington*, 1996 U.S. App. LEXIS 3944 (9th Cir. March 6, 1996).

16. *Quill v. Vacco*, 1996 U.S. App. LEXIS 6215 (2d Cir. April 2, 1996).

17. *Romer v. Evans*, 116 S. Ct. LEXIS 1620 (1996).

19

The Church and the New Genetics

C. Ben Mitchell, MDiv,PhD (cand.)

The genetic revolution is upon us. What was once thought to be science fiction has rapidly become science fact. Genetic manipulation, gene therapy, genetic screening, genetic fingerprinting, and cloning are now in our cultural and even church vocabulary. New books on genetics are coming off the presses almost weekly. Recent titles include:

- *The Gene Wars: Science, Politics and the Human Genome*[1]
- *The Book of Man: The Human Genome Project and the Quest to Discover Our Genetic Heritage*[2]
- *Double-Edged Sword: The Promises and Risks of the Genetic Revolution*[3]
- *On the New Frontiers of Genetics and Religion*[4]
- *Altered Fates: Gene Therapy and the Retooling of Human Life*[5]
- *Refiguring Life: Metaphors of Twentieth-Century Biology*[6]
- *The Lives to Come: The Genetic Revolution and Human Possibilities*[7]

These are merely the books for popular audiences. Each year since at least 1992, the Department of Energy has been publishing a bibliography of articles on the ethical, legal and social implications of the Human Genome Project. The 1994 supplemental bibliography had no less than 1500 entries. These entries represent articles published in scientific journals such as *Nature, Science, The New Scientist,* and specialized journals such as *American Journal of Medical Genetics, Clinical Obstetrics and Gynecology, Acta Paediatrics Scandinavia, American Journal of Cardiology,* and *American Journal of Diseases of Children.*
Sociologists Dorothy Nelkin and Susan Lindee have recently and persuasively argued that the gene has become a new cultural icon.

> In supermarket tabloids and soap operas, in television sitcoms and talk shows, in women's magazines and parenting advice books, genes appear to explain obesity, criminality, shyness, directional ability, intelligence, political leanings, and preferred styles of dressing. There are selfish genes, pleasure-seeking genes, violence genes, celebrity genes, gay genes, couch-potato genes, depression genes, genes for genius, genes for saving, and even genes for sinning.[8]

We are in the midst of a genetic renaissance in science, law, medicine, and ethics. This renewal can be traced at least to Gregor Mendel's experiments on the inherited traits of pea plants, its most recent manifestation being the Human Genome Project initiated in 1990 by the National Institutes of Health and the Department of Energy.[9] While this project will undoubtedly make amazing contributions to humanity in the years ahead, the iconography of genetics has already taken on a decidedly religious tone. 'In the 1990s geneticists, describing the genome as the "Bible," the "Book of Man," and the "Holy Grail," convey an image of this molecular structure not only as a powerful biological entity but also as a sacred text that can explain the natural and moral order.'[10]

One could argue that the new genetics, for the most part, does not raise any novel moral and ethical issues. That is to say, genetics *per se* only brings a new focus to old issues. What, then, are the foci of this new and burgeoning technology? What challenges must the church face in light of the new genetics as we enter the 21st century? What opportunities are before us? The new genetics is at once a cause for celebration, caution, and outright resistance.

CELEBRATION (PSALM 8; PSALM 139:13–16)

No doubt many of us share a love for the book of Psalms, the sacred hymnbook of the believing community. As David admires God's handiwork and revels in the splendour of the heavens, he is caught up in rapturous delight that the same God who hung the stars in place and hurled the planets in their orbits, is mindful of human beings. He is awestruck that God has crowned human beings with glory and honour (Psalm 8:1–5). Similarly, David celebrates God's handiwork in fashioning the human race when he exults, 'I praise you because I am fearfully and wonderfully made; your works are wonderful, I know that full well' (Ps. 139:14).

Molecular biology helps us appreciate just how fearfully and wonderfully made we are. Who among us does not stand in awe at the fact that within each of the trillions of cells in our bodies there are 23 pairs of chromosomes composed of genes which contain instructions encoded in 3 billion nucleotide base pairs? As one scientist puts it, 'That's like taking 30 miles of gold thread and stuffing it into a cherry pit.'[11] While the received account is that most of the DNA in our cells is so-called 'junk DNA' (because we do not have a clue what it does), I believe in the end we'll find that God does not make junk. Every bit of information is meaningful in relation to the whole. Furthermore, if anyone wants evidence for a supra-intelligent Designer, genetics has unearthed it. The notion that this intricately complex structure and huge catalogue of information emerged from some primordial ooze is simply preposterous. De nihilo nihil (nothing comes from nothing). In fact, the evidence for a Designer is so compelling that a mechanistic naturalist like Francis Crick admits that he has to keep telling himself it is not true: 'Biologists must constantly keep in mind that what they see is not designed, but rather evolved.'[12] What a telling testimony to the veracity of the apostle's observation that individuals 'suppress the truth' (Rom. 1:19). Yet, '. . . since the creation of the world,' Paul declares, 'God's invisible qualities – his eternal power and divine nature – have been clearly seen, being understood from what has been made, so that people are without excuse. For although they knew God, they neither glorified him as God nor gave thanks . . .' (1:20–21a). Rather than being overwhelmed with the obvious, many anesthetize themselves to the discomfort of the evidence. Retreating from the miraculous, they opt for the merely marvellous. Instead, I like the way Francis Collins, Director of the National Center for Human Genome Research, expresses it: '. . . for the scientist who is also a Christian, science is a form of worship. It is an uncovering of the incredible, awesome beauty of God's creation. That is how I feel when I have a chance to glimpse something which no human being previously knew – but God knew all along.'[13] In fact, when he said this, Dr. Collins was echoing the sentiments of one of his predecessors, Nicolas Copernicus.

> To know the mighty works of God, to comprehend His wisdom and majesty and power, to appreciate in degree the wonderful working of His laws, surely all of this must be a pleasing and acceptable mode of worship to the Most High, to whom ignorance cannot be more grateful than knowledge.[14]

Our Lord said that there is a correlation between the obedient presence and good works of believers and the honour of God. '. . . Let your light so shine before people, that they may see your good deeds and praise your Father in heaven' (Matt. 5:16). We might argue that there is reciprocity here. If we praise our Father in heaven, we will be increasingly motivated to good deeds. Celebrating the fearful and wonderful work of God in creating human beings impassions us to use this knowledge for the benefit of those whom God has made. And well it should. If God cares for his own creation and has invested his own image in human beings, how can we do less than show sacrificial compassion and invest ourselves in one another's well-being?

The stated goal of the Human Genome Project is not knowledge for the sake of knowledge (though that is not necessarily a wrong-headed motive), but human healing – not pure science, but science in service to human welfare.[15] The treatment and cure of the 3,000 to 4,000 genetically-linked illnesses is a laudable goal. Molecular medicine is already a tremendous tool for the removal of some of the deleterious physical effects of human falleness.[16] Certainly, this goal is consistent with the ministry, example, and commands of the one who came 'with healing in his wings' (Mal. 4:2), the Lord Jesus Christ. The requirements of neighbour-love (Lk. 10:29ff) demand that we use appropriate means to serve the needs of those who are suffering. Toward that end, the church ought to support, encourage, and celebrate the new genetics.

To meet the challenge of the new genetics, the church must do a better job of education. Many, if not most, of our children are now being taught basic genetics in elementary school. Yet they are not being provided with a theologically-informed Christian worldview through which to see the splendour of God's handiwork. Tracing the contours of a Christian worldview is part of the prophetic ministry of the church.

At present it may be difficult to get church members interested in the ethical implications of genetic science, but increasingly Christians want to learn to integrate their faith with the almost daily news stories about discoveries in genetics. Likewise, Christians are confronted personally by genetic technologies when they see their physicians and find themselves ill equipped to deal with the information learned from genetic tests. They need better instruction on a Christian worldview and its implications for genetics and other aspects of science. However, the church's need for adequate curricular support in this area seems to have eluded Christian publishing houses.

Furthermore, we should encourage our children to pursue the sciences. Not only is this one of the burgeoning academic fields of the new millennium, but biotechnology seems to be a major growth industry for the foreseeable future. We desperately need individuals involved in genetics who have a comprehensive Christian worldview and who are committed to science in service to God and humanity.

CAUTION (GENESIS 1:27; 9:6FF)

As with every technology, however, genetic science holds both promise and risk. As Neil Postman has warned, 'Technology is not a neutral element in the practice of medicine: doctors do not merely use technologies but they are used by them.'[17] Technology seems sometimes to carry its own imperative. If we have the technology, we mistakenly believe we must use it. Preserving the beneficial uses of genetic technology while repudiating its potentially injurious aspects is a difficult challenge.

GNOSTICISM.

The confession of the believing church is that God has made humankind in his own image, after his own likeness (Gen. 1:27). While there is a large body of theological literature on just how to unpack the content of the *imago Dei*, Orthodox and evangelical scholarship, for the most part, has agreed that the *imago* is not defined functionally, as if there were some discrete set of capacities humans possess which, when taken away, makes them less than human. Rather, human beings are, by definition, imagers of God. To be human *is* to image God.[18]

Does the *imago Dei* extend to human DNA? I am not yet certain exactly how to answer that question. This is an important question, since it is the Divine image which distinguishes humans from animal species (Gen. 9:6ff.). It is the Divine image that warrants unique respect for human life. Furthermore, the implications of the answer to this question are critical for genetic research on human subjects, tissues, cell-lines, and genes.

One respected Christian molecular biologist has written,

> To me, it is quite clear that God is crazy about human beings. It is also quite clear to me that God does not feel the same capacity for human tissue. He probably does not grieve as we do not grieve, over the loss of fingernails we just trimmed. He probably does not weep over the disposable products of a haircut. In turn, we do not pray that an amputated arm accept Jesus into its, what, knuckles? before it dies. The conclusion is that there is a distinction between human beings and human tissues. Worth is fused into the one and not the other.[19]

That conclusion causes my theological antennae to twitch. The notion that there is *no* worth in human tissues is a fairly explicit form of molecular-biological gnosticism. And we must exercise great caution here. Most of the believing community has rejected gnosticism as an inaccurate anthropology. Augustine, for instance, taught that the Divine image 'refers to the inner man where his reason and intellect are,' yet he also thought that 'even our body has been so structured that we are superior to the beasts and therefore like God'.[20] Calvin took essentially the same view, even quoting the Roman poet Ovid favourably,

> . . . while mute creation downward bend
> Their sight and to their earthly mother tend,
> Man looks aloft, and with erected eyes
> Beholds his own hereditary skies.[21]

The notion that human flesh has 'no worth' is exceedingly troubling in the light of the biblical witness. There is no support in Scripture for gnosticism. Since human beings exist without a body only temporarily between death and the resurrection, and since the *incarnate* Son of God is both the 'image of the invisible God, the *firstborn* over all creation' (Col. 1:15) and 'the *firstfruits* of those who have fallen asleep' (1 Cor. 15:20), we ought to pause and think carefully about the body's supposed lack of value. In the age of the new genetics the church must exercise extreme caution so as not unwittingly to inhale the vapors of neo-gnosticism.

REDUCTIONISM.

Behind the new genetics occasionally lurks a reductionism that mistakenly assumes that the source of all human ills is genetic in origin.[22] This reductionism leads to extravagant conclusions. For example, some claim that we can cure homelessness through genetics. The argument is developed as follows. We believe that most homeless persons have some form of psychological illness. We further believe that psychological illnesses have genetic causes. Therefore, if we can treat the genetic causes of psychosis, neurosis, and schizophrenia, we can cure homelessness. My intuition is that curing homelessness will not be as easy as developing a gene therapy for schizophrenia. There are many factors which contribute to homelessness, even among those with psychological illnesses.

Furthermore, reductionism has a way of back-firing. Several examples must suffice. First, by assuming that mental retardation is curable merely through genetics, we neglect the most pervasive causes of retardation. There is a need to distinguish carefully between inborn and acquired forms of mental retardation.

> In the lower classes, retardation is often the result of poor prenatal care, denial of sensory stimulation, lead poisoning, or a failure of the schools. In short, it is a social product. But the increasing use of genetic screening and counseling emphasizes only genetic fallibility and therefore highlights only a portion of the problem. If we continue to address retardation solely as a genetic aberration, we will systematically ignore the thousands who suffer the social, not genetic, disability.[23]

Second, when social engineers link up with behavioural geneticists, trouble is bound to follow. For example, the social engineers are busily trying to convince our culture to legitimize and normalize homosexual behaviour. At the same time, some behavioural geneticists are busy trying to prove that homosexuality has a genetic cause. But if six percent of parents say they would abort a child likely to get Alzheimer's disease in old age, and if eleven percent say they would abort a child disposed to obesity,[24] then how many would abort a child if they believed he or she was genetically disposed to homosexuality?

In his recent book, *A Separate Creation: The Search for the Biological Origins of Sexual Orientation*,[25] science writer Chandler Burr recounts attending a meeting at Cold Spring Harbor Laboratory. At the meeting, Dr. Chuck Link, research director for the fledgling Human Gene Therapy Research Institute of Des Moines, Iowa, lectured on human gene therapy. After the meeting, when Burr asked Dr. Link about conducting gene therapy on sexual orientation, Dr. Link replied,

'It's not going to be for a long time.' What's a long time? 'Oh,' he says with a shrug towards a far distant horizon, 'years and years from now.' How many years? Thirty years? He starts, looks slightly offended, and laughs very, very briefly. His eyebrows go up. 'Well, *no*,' he says, 'not that long.'[26]

We are on the threshold of a daunting socio-biological experiment in human sexuality.

Finally, and briefly, genetic screening advocacy wedded to abortion advocacy yields a breath-taking form of self-loathing. Feminist sociologist and abortion advocate Barbara Katz Rothman has said:

> . . . just because someone with whatever genetically produced disability is having a wonderful life, that doesn't mean that any particular woman should have to bear such a child. Some of us are the children of women who should have had abortions because of what was going on in their lives. Some of us are the children of fifteen-year-old kids who didn't want to get pregnant, and if we were counseling such kids, we should tell them that it was okay to end their pregnancy. And we are the children of women who have had an unwanted sixth child. Women who didn't want it, were tired, weren't well, didn't want to have another child. *Even though we may be very glad to be here and breathe the air and everything else, that doesn't mean that our mothers shouldn't have aborted us.*[27]

How foreign these sentiments would be to the psalmist who celebrated: 'For you created my inmost being; you knit me together in my mother's womb. I praise you because I am fearfully and wonderfully made; your works are wonderful, I know that full well' (Ps. 139:13–14).

The church's confession is that the source of all of our problems is sin and its effects on the cosmos. While we desire to find cures for the deleterious physical illnesses which afflict humanity, we must not be distracted from the root cause of illness – the effects of sin on the world. The genetic code is sometimes the locus of our fallenness. But we must be careful not to assume that it always is, or that when it is, immorality is thereby justified. A genetic origin *explains* a trait; it does not morally justify it. Efforts to ignore biblical truth result only in contradiction and paradox. The church will have to be very cautious if it is to celebrate the healing power of genetics without embracing the reductionism endemic to the search for science's holy grail.

To meet the challenge of the new genetics, theologians and ethicists need to probe increasingly the issues at the intersection of genetics, theology, and ethics. Most of the human tragedies which result from new technologies have not been perpetrated by mean people who were trying to do bad things. Rather, many of these tragedies have been the result of unintended consequences beyond human control.

OUTRIGHT RESISTANCE (GENESIS 30:25FF)

In Genesis 30, we have the account of a barter between Jacob and Laban. Jacob, who has labored for Laban for some time asks for a return on his investment of work. He says to Laban,

> 'The little you had before I came has increased greatly, and the Lord has blessed you wherever I have been. But now, when may I do something for my own household?' (vv. 29–30). 'What shall I give you?' asks Laban. 'Don't give me anything,' Jacob replied. 'But if you will do this one thing for me, I will go on tending your flocks and watching over them: Let me go through all your flocks today and remove from them every speckled or spotted sheep, every dark-coloured lamb and every spotted or speckled goat. They will be my wages. And my honesty will testify for me in the future, whenever you check on the wages you have paid me. Any goat in my possession that is not speckled or spotted, or any lamb that is not dark-coloured, will be considered stolen' (vv. 31–33).

Long before Mendel's pea plants, long before Crick and Watson, Jacob understood something about heredity. He might not have known the difference between homozygosity and heterozygosity, or recessivity and expressivity, but he understood that somehow, phenotype was related to genotype and that discriminations could be made based upon them. Now, discrimination takes many forms, some of them appropriate and some of them inappropriate. The believing community does not have a spotless history in this respect, but more often than not, the church has condemned inappropriate discrimination. Genetic discrimination against persons must be strongly resisted.

THE NEW EUGENICS.

The most common application of genetic technology is prenatal screening. Prenatal screening is performed on babies either *in vitro* or *in utero* to diagnose whether they are affected by some genetic anomaly such as Down's Syndrome or spina bifida. At present there are many more anomalies that can be diagnosed than can be treated.

John A. Robertson, Thomas Watt Gregory Professor in the School of Law at the University of Texas at Austin, observes: 'As tests to identify fetal cells in maternal blood are perfected, the genetic condition of every fetus will become a routine part of prenatal care, followed often by pregnancy termination when the test is positive.'[28] Furthermore, says Robertson,

> As advances in genetics grow, persons contemplating procreation will also have more genetic information about potential offspring, including their susceptibility to chronic illness and late-onset diseases as well as the more common autosomal recessive diseases now tested. They may then choose

to procreate, avoid conception, or terminate a pregnancy that has already begun.[29]

In other words, prenatal screening may allow the treatment and cure of some diseases, but it may also allow unborn children to be targeted for abortion. One could argue that the expansive use of prenatal genetic screening casts a shadow of suspicion over every unborn baby. Every pregnancy becomes a 'tentative pregnancy', pending the results of prenatal screening.

Every prospective parent desires a healthy baby. Yet, no one gives birth to a perfect baby. As prenatal screening techniques give us increasingly clearer windows into the womb, who will decide what is a desirable characteristic and what is an undesirable characteristic? Who will define what is a diseased gene and what is normal? It is already the case that some parents, both in the US and in other countries, practise sex-selection abortions. What is to prevent prenatal testing from being a form of 'quality control' and every baby from being subjected to shifting judgments of fitness, worth, and convenience?

In Robertson's view, decisions to abort or not to abort ultimately are informed by what he calls 'procreative liberty'. '. . . In almost all instances an individual or couple's choice to use technology to achieve reproductive goals should be respected as a central aspect of people's freedom to define themselves through reproduction',[30] argues Robertson. Abortion is merely another facet of so-called 'procreative liberty'. Frighteningly, in 1991, Australian philosopher Peter Singer argued in *The New York Review of Books*[31] that it is morally acceptable (even necessary), following prenatal diagnosis, to declare the lives of severely disabled unborn infants not worth living.[32]

Only a robust ethic of the sanctity of every human life will halt the expansion of the new eugenics movement.[33] Only the doctrine of the sacredness of every human life will protect babies judged to have 'lives unworthy of living' from whimsical destruction.

Human babies are not chattels to be disposed of because they do not meet our criteria of normalcy. Every person is made in the image of God (Gen. 1:27) and is, thereby, worthy of protection, love, and respect. Babies do not become imagers of God at birth. They do not become imagers of God at viability. They do not become imagers of God at implantation. Each becomes an imager of God when she or he actually becomes a 'she' or 'he' – i.e., when the chromosomal endowment is passed on from parents to child. In other words, human life is sacred at conception. Furthermore, the quest for genetic perfection of one's offspring diminishes respect for persons with disabilities.[34] Every unborn infant who is tested for fetal anomalies *for which there is no treatment or cure* has the potential for being hunted down by medical detectives for potential destruction. What does this communicate to persons with disabilities? They are being told they have lives not worth living.

Sociologist Marque-Luisa Miringoff offers a sobering warning when she says,

> In the pursuit of good health, we have begun to tread a fine line in 'human selection'. We often choose to rule out certain diseases or, more accurately, certain human beings with those diseases. In some cases, as with Tay-Sachs disease, as of now an invariably fatal illness in early childhood, such a decision may be motivated by compassion. From many viewpoints, there is little quality of life in any sense traditionally understood, and great anguish and tragedy.
>
> Other diseases, however, challenge our logic more severely; our sense of balance between cost and benefit is not as clear. Huntington's chorea is a case in point. Would Woodie Guthrie be born today? Would his parents, as carriers of the disease, bear a child with the known risk? Could we now or would we soon screen him out prenatally? If the pace of genetic intervention continues, such an individual would not be born. Yet I, for one, am glad he lived, although I mourn the anguish of his later life. One wonders, too, whether some perception of his coming illness contributed to the extraordinary creativity of his life.
>
> Clearly, it is a just and meaningful desire to prevent fatal and debilitating diseases. Yet in pursuing this goal, we pay unobserved costs. In eliminating individuals with unwanted diseases, we also create a mind-set that justifies the process of human selection. We thus move into the questionable arena of human worth, and to some degree eugenic thought. We forgo the idea of therapeutic change (i.e., dietary change or other forms of treatment) and opt instead for elimination. Individuals are seen as flawed. It is easier and more desirable to prevent their existence than work for their survival.[35]

Again, it is only a thick version of the ethics of the sanctity of every human life which will preserve respect for persons with disabilities. That is to say, the sanctity of human life must be enriched by and wedded to an understanding of the sovereignty of God. The sovereign God is creator of every individual human life. When Moses offered to God his reasons why he was not suited to tell Pharaoh to free his people, God responded, 'Who gives a man his mouth? Who makes him deaf or mute? Who gives him sight or makes him blind? Is it not I, the Lord?' (Exod. 4:11). The divine potter has power over the clay. How arrogant of us to crush what God has made for his own glory. Medicine may legitimately seek to restore or heal, but it is not within its purview to destroy what God has made.[36]

Finally, as abortion becomes a 'routine procedure' for dealing with untreatable or incurable genetic illnesses, will it be routinized in cases for which there *are* treatments or cures?[37] That is, under the rubric of managed care, scarce resource allocation, and the 'right to choose', if a fetus is diagnosed with a genetic anomaly, and treatment for that anomaly is more expensive than conceiving again, what is to prevent abortion from being used as a 'cost-saving measure'? Children with treatable genetic anomalies might be considered 'tainted goods'. There is nothing, for instance, in John Robertson's normative ethic of 'procreative liberty' to preclude such a scenario. Robertson says,

> . . . there is a presumptive right to procreate because of the great importance to individuals of having biological offspring – personal meaning in one's life, connection with future generations, and the pleasures of child rearing. If a person thought that she would realize those benefits only from a child with particular characteristics, then she should be free to select offspring to have those preferred traits.[38]

Francis Collins has said, 'I see people occasionally in my clinic who have a sort of new car mentality. [The baby's] got to be perfect, and if it isn't you take it back to the lot and get a new one.'[39] Of course, in this case, 'taking it back to the lot' is a euphemism for abortion.

If the church is to meet the challenge of the new genetics, it must provide support and encouragement for those couples who choose either (1) not to undergo prenatal screening or (2) to maintain their pregnancy despite the diagnosis of genetic anomaly. Frankly, many women feel pressure from their doctors, their friends and family, and their own consciences to make sure they do not bring an 'imperfect' baby into the world. Coercion takes many forms, some subtle, some not so subtle. The church must be a supportive community for families of children with disabilities.

GENE-BASED DISCRIMINATION.

The American eugenics movement, the Nazi experience, and the sickle-cell public policy disaster are potent testimonies to ways in which genetic information can be used to discriminate against certain groups in a society.

The new genetics offers the potential, if abused, of using high-technology medicine as a weapon of discrimination. Individuals who are predisposed to Huntington's disease have been unable to secure jobs. In 1988, China passed legislation prohibiting the marriage of mentally retarded persons unless they were sterilized. Nobel laureate and advocate of taking Vitamin C, Linus Pauling, 'suggested that there should be tattooed on the forehead of every young person a symbol showing possession of the sickle-cell gene or whatever other similar gene, such as the gene for phenylketonuria [PKU], that has been found to possess in a single dose. If this were done, two young people carrying the same seriously defective gene in single dose would recognize this situation at first sight, and would refrain from falling in love with one another.'[40] Such stigmatization would be unconscionable.

In light of past abuses of genetic information, Pauling's suggestion no longer seems impossible. Individuals who might be more susceptible to illnesses such as colon cancer, diabetes, or muscular dystrophy are particularly at risk. It may well be the case that they will never develop the disorder, or may be able to prevent its occurrence through changes in diet or lifestyle, yet their genetic profile may be used to discriminate against them throughout life. Persons with disabilities are particularly interested in how the information gained through the Human Genome Project might be used.

A recent study by Lisa N. Geller and colleagues of Harvard Medical School found that of 917 persons who responded to their questionnaire, 455 'asserted that they had been discriminated against after they revealed a genetic diagnosis'.[41] When researchers followed up on these individuals they were given reports of insurers who refused or cancelled policies, adoption agencies that required additional genetic testing, and employees for whom employment was terminated or denied because of an existing or possible treatable genetic condition. In another study done by Georgetown University's Virginia Lapham, 22 percent of those who had a genetic illness in their families reported being denied insurance coverage.[42]

Many bills have been proposed in the US Congress calling for the passage of a genetic privacy act. A number of state legislatures have already passed laws against genetic discrimination.

To meet the challenge of the new genetics, the church must exercise her prophetic voice, calling on both Christians and the larger culture to resist the discriminatory use of genetics. The church must champion the cause of God in Christ and the sanctity of every human life.

The Institute of Religion's 'Summary Reflection Statement' is appropriate:

> A religiously based consensus on the full and equal dignity of all human persons is often contradicted in practice by discriminatory prejudice of one group against another. Ethnic and racial diversities among human beings are due in large part to genetic factors which must never be interpreted as indices of personal or social worth. Neither should the presence of physical or mental disabilities, whether or not they are due to genetic inheritance, detract from one's personal or social value.[43]

WHERE DO WE GO FROM HERE?

Space remains only for a few concluding suggestions. These are certainly not comprehensive, but merely suggestive of the church's opportunities.

First, the church must develop educational resources about genetics. This is not to say that the church must sponsor its own science projects. Rather, Christians must help to interpret the data resulting from genetic advances and demonstrate how those advances fit within a Christian worldview. Advances in genetics offer splendid opportunities for Christian thinkers to explore the ways in which these discoveries and technologies might be used to serve the needs of those with hereditary illnesses. At the same time, these advances provide opportunities for thoughtful ethical reflection about the limits of technology and whether or not certain uses of the technology fly in the face of God's commands, biblical principles, and Christian virtues.

On the whole, the church has not done a very good job of assisting Christians to think Christianly about the biological sciences. More recently Christians have tended to compartmentalize truth and leave the 'physical' to the secular world and focus on the 'spiritual'.

Dichotomizing truth has led to disastrous consequences in both science and public policy. Appropriate curricular materials for children, students, and adults would be a boon to Christian worldview development.

Second, we should continue to lobby for legislation prohibiting sex-selection abortions and restrictions on prenatal screening for untreatable or incurable diseases where screening serves no purpose other than to provide justification for destroying undesirable lives. Since such screening is employed by many today, it will not be easy to restrain. Collaborative initiatives with disability advocacy groups and some feminist groups may be possible. The reminder that prenatal screening targets persons with disabilities and women should be a strong motivation.

Third, congregations must consciously and systematically support parents who have children with disabilities. Undoubtedly, raising children with disabilities presents special challenges. At first, parents may be traumatized by the realization of their child's disability and the implications for the future. Congregational ministry, especially by those who have had similar experiences, can have a stabilizing effect on these parents and their families.

Almost every American has heard of Stephen J. Hawking. Dr. Hawking is now over 50 years old and holds Newton's chair of Mathematics at Cambridge University. Most of us can close our eyes and see his diminutive frame sitting child-like in his wheel-chair. While I cannot agree with all of Dr. Hawking's presuppositions, clearly, my life and the world of science would be the worse were it not for his theoretical musings. His book, *A Brief History of Time*,[44] occupied the *New York Times* best-seller list for a significant period of time. *Astronomy* magazine said, 'When the achievements of the physicists of the twentieth century come to be considered objectively, the work of Stephen Hawking will be writ large in the annals of science.'

Imagine, if Dr. Hawking's parents had had access to prenatal genetic screening technology, the world might have missed one of the great minds of our age. Steven Hawking has been suffering from a genetic illness, Lou Gehrig's disease, for over twenty years.

It is too soon to know whether the information gathered through the Human Genome Project will catapult us into a modern Garden of Eden or into Jurassic Park. However, the church has the wisdom and resources to influence the outcome. It must do all it can to encourage people to welcome the blessings without letting those blessings desensitize them to the need for discernment.

NOTES

1. Cook-Deegan, Robert M., *The Gene Wars: Science, Politics and the Human Genome* (New York, W.W. Norton & Co. 1994).

2. Bodmer, Walter and McKie, Robin, *The Book of Man: The Human Genome Project and the Quest to Discover Our Genetic Heritage* (New York, Charles Scribner 1995).

3. Drlica, Karl A., *Double-Edged Sword: The Promises and Risks of the Genetic Revolution* (Reading, MA, Addison-Wesley Longman 1994).

4. Nelson, J. Robert, *On the New Frontiers of Genetics and Religion* (Grand Rapids, Mich., Wm. B. Eerdmans 1994).

5. Lyon, Jeff and Gorner, Peter, *Altered Fates: Gene Therapy and the Retooling of Human Life* (New York, W.W. Norton & Co. 1995).

6. Fox Keller, Evelyn, *Refiguring Life: Metaphors of Twentieth-Century Biology* (New York, Columbia University Press 1995).

7. Kitcher, Philip, 'The Lives to Come', *The Genetic Revolution and Human Possibilities* (New York, Simon & Schuster Trade 1996).

8. Nelkin, Dorothy and Lindee, M. Susan, *The DNA Mystique: The Gene as a Cultural Icon* (New York, W. H. Freeman and Company 1995), p. 2.

9. See Francis Collins' chapter on the Human Genome Project earlier in this volume.

10. Nelkin and Lindee, p. 39.

11. Medina, John, *The Outer Limits of Life: A Molecular Biologist Looks At Life And The Implications of Genetic Research* (Nashville, Oliver Nelson Books 1991), p. 23.

12. Crick, Francis, *What Mad Pursuit* (New York, Basic Books 1988), p. 138.

13. Collins, Francis, 'The Human Genome Project', in Land, Richard D. and Moore, Louis A., *Life at Risk: The Crises in Medical Ethics* (Nashville, Broadman and Holman 1995), p. 101.

14. Ibid., p.113.

15. *The Human Genome Project: From Maps to Medicine*, U.S. Department of Health and Human Services, Public Health Service, National Institutes of Health (NIH Publication No. 96–3897)

16. See Nigel Cameron's exposition of the goals of medicine in 'The Christian Stake in Bioethics: The State of the Question,' in Kilner, John F., de S. Cameron, Nigel M., and Schiedermayer, David L., (eds), *Bioethics and the Future of Medicine: A Christian Appraisal* (Carlisle, Cumbria, UK/Grand Rapids, MI, Paternoster Press/Wm. B. Eerdmans Publishing Company 1995), pp. 3–13.

17. Postman, Neil, *Technopoly: The Surrender of Culture to Technology* (New York, Alfred A. Knopf 1992), p. 105.

18. O'Mathúna, Dónal, 'The Bible and Abortion: What of "the Image of God"?' in Kilner, John F., de S. Cameron, Nigel M. and Schiedermayer, David L. (eds), *Bioethics and the Future of Medicine: A Christian Appraisal* (Carlisle, Cumbria, UK/Grand Rapids, MI, Paternoster Press/Wm. B. Eerdmans Publishing Company 1995), pp. 199–211.

19. Medina, John, p. 64.

20. Augustine, *On Genesis against the Manicheans* ii.27; cf. *On Various Questions*, Q. 51, cited in Hughes, Philip Edgcumbe, *The True Image: The Origin and Destiny of Man in Christ* (Grand Rapids Wm. B. Eerdmans Publishing Co.), p 11.

21. Ovid, *Metamorphoses*, I.84ff. In Ibid.

22. An important documentation and critique of this reductionism is R. C. Lewontin's, *Biology as Ideology: The Doctrine of DNA* (New York, HarperCollins 1991).

23. Miringoff, Marque-Luisa, *The Social Costs of Genetic Welfare* (New Brunswick, NJ, Rutgers University Press 1991), p. 68.

24. Collins, Francis, 'The Human Genome Project', *Life At Risk: The Crises in Medical Ethics* (Nashville, Broadman & Holman Publishers 1995), p. 112.

25. Burr, Chandler, *A Separate Creation: The Search for the Biological Origins of Sexual Orientation* (New York, Hyperion Press 1996).

26. Ibid., p. 308.

27. Briggs, Laura, 'Gatekeeping at the Gates of Life: An Interview with Barbara Katz Rothman', *Sojourner: The Women's Forum* 20 (January 1995), p. 26. Emphasis added.

28. Robertson, John A., *Children of Choice: Freedom and the New Reproductive Technologies* (Princeton, Princeton University Press 1994), p. 149.

29. Ibid., p. 150.

30. Ibid., p. 18.

31. Singer, Peter, 'On Being Silenced in Germany', *The New York Review of Books* 38, 14 (1991), pp. 34–40.

32. 'If the suggestion is that whenever we seek to avoid having severely disabled children, we are improperly judging one kind of life to be worse than another, we can reply that such judgments are both necessary and proper. To argue otherwise would seem to suggest that if we break a leg, we should not get it mended, because in doing so we judge the lives of those with crippled legs to be less worth living than our own.' Peter Singer, *Practical Ethics*, 2nd ed. (New York, Cambridge University Press 1993), pp. 353–356. For an excellent rebuttal to Singer see, 'Peter Singer and Lives Not Worthy of Living – Comments on a Flawed Argument from Analogy' by Per Sundstrom, *Journal of Medical Ethics* 21 (1995), pp. 35–38.

33. For a superb commentary on this new eugenics movement see, Neuhaus, Richard John (ed), *Guaranteeing the Good Life: Medicine & the Return of Eugenics* (Grand Rapids: Wm. B. Eerdmans Publishing Company 1990).

34. 'Leon Kass, a bioethicist and social philosopher, has observed that a new image of human procreation has been conceived and a new "scientific" obstetrics will usher it into existence. As one obstetrician put it: "the business of obstetrics is to produce *optimum babies.*" ' Leon Kass, 'Making Babies – the New Biology and the Old Morality', *The Public Interest* 26 (Winter 1972), p. 48. Cited in Miringoff, *The Social Costs of Genetic Welfare*, p. 53. John A. Robertson says, on the other hand, 'Freedom to abort a normal pregnancy implies an equal freedom to abort to avoid the special burdens of having a handicapped child. This practice need no more devalue the life of handicapped persons than carrier screening to avoid their birth does, or than aborting a normal fetus devalues children generally',

Children of Choice, p. 159. This is precisely the point; abortion does devalue children and abortion of handicapped children devalues handicapped persons.

35. Miringoff, *The Social Costs of Genetic Welfare*, p. 159–160. I cannot agree with everything in this section of Miringoff's argument, but these paragraphs render an important warning for a culture moving increasingly toward eugenics.

36. For a splendid defence of healing as the goal of medicine, see Leon R. Kass, *Toward a More Natural Science*, pp. 157–186. Says Kass, 'I trust it will shock no one if I say that I am rather inclined to the old-fashioned view that health – or if you prefer, the healthy human being – is the end of the physician's art', p. 159. Similarly, 'I am not suggesting that we cease investigating the causes of these diseases. On the contrary, medicine *should* be interested in preventing these diseases or, failing that, in restoring their victims to as healthy a condition as is possible. But it is precisely because they are causes of *unhealth*, and only secondarily because they are killers, that we should be interested in preventing or combating them' p.162.

37. Again, this is exactly what is argued by John A. Robertson. 'For example, some couples might abort fetuses with cystic fibrosis or phenylketonuria, even though those conditions vary widely in their seriousness or are treatable. Some couples might also abort for reasons of gender or for trivial indications such as disease susceptibility traits. As long as the termination occurs at a stage at which the fetus itself has no interests, such terminations would violate no moral duty to the fetus, and thus be within the moral rights of the woman who does not wish to continue such a pregnancy.' *Children of Choice*, p. 159.

38. Robertson, John A., *Children of Choice*, pp. 152–153.

39. Cowley, Geoffrey, 'Made to Order Babies', *Newsweek* (Winter/Spring 1990), p. 94. Cited in Kimbrell, Andrew, *The Human Body Shop: The Engineering and Marketing of Human Life* (San Francisco, Harper 1993), p. 126.

40. Cited in Duster, Troy, *Backdoor to Eugenics* (New York, Routledge 1990), p. 46.

41. Beardsley, Tim, 'Vital Data', *Scientific American* (March 1996), p. 103.

42. Ibid.

43. Duster, p.46.

44. Hawking, Stephen W., *A Brief History of Time: From Big Bang to Black Holes* (New York, Bantam 1988).

20

The Church as a Welcoming Community

Marsha D. M. Fowler, RN, MDiv, PhD

Kate was a beloved saint in my congregation – a woman of luminous faith, in her mid-seventies, whose life in Christ made me feel repentant. I met her while serving in an older adult enablement ministry. What a wondrous woman she was. Of lively intellect, she read avidly on any topic that she thought required a Christian response or thoughtful reflection for integration into her spiritual life. She worked diligently on workdays at the church, helping to stock the 'deacons closet', delivering meals or flowers to the home-bound, working on the worship bulletins, folding the post, filling envelopes. Whatever it was, Kate was there – early – to help. At every women's gathering, every Circle meeting, Kate was present to share, pray, work, laugh, pour tea, and vote. She was also a faithful participant in Sunday School, which met before worship services. I offered several series of classes and Kate attended every class, took notes, asked hard questions, shared something she might have read, and was a loving, engaging presence. Then one day I noticed that she never attended worship. Oddly, she was at the church for everything *except* worship.

'Kate, why don't you come to worship?'

'Well, I have a daughter . . . ' her voice trailed off.

'Isn't she a Christian?' I asked. Something was not making sense to me.

'Oh yes! She's a member of this church! I don't come to worship because I go home to listen to the service on the radio with Lois.'

Now I was really confused. 'I don't understand, Kate. If she's a Christian and wants to participate in the worship service, why don't you and she attend?'

'Well, Lois has cerebral palsy.'

Shrugging and gesturing her to continue, I was still perplexed and did not understand. 'Okay, but why does that keep you from worship?'

Then, Kate's tragic story unfolds.

'Well, Lois's body makes involuntary twitches and noises, and she drools. When she was a child they thought they could control some of her spastic movements with brain surgery. When they did the surgery, they damaged her speech centre and left her unable to speak. She can walk but only very spastically. We used to sit at the back of the sanctuary, but her body twitched or made noises. People would turn around and stare, then they would roll their eyes or cluck. Eventually they told me I shouldn't bring her back with me. But she's my daughter.'

In the liturgy of the Lord's Supper, Presbyterian tradition begins with an invitation to the Lord's Table. It is this:

> Friends, this is the joyful feast of the people of God! They will come from east and west and from north and south and sit at table in the kingdom of God. According to Luke, when our risen Lord was at table with his disciples, he took the bread, and blessed it and broke it, and gave it to them. Then their eyes were opened and they recognized him. This is the Lord's Table. Our savior invites those who trust in him to share the feast which he has prepared.[1]

This is the Lord's Table; it is not the Presbyterian table, nor the Baptist table nor the Episcopal table. Our Saviour invites; it is not I who invite, nor any other. This is the *Lord's* Table . . . it is our *Saviour* who invites. He invites all those who trust in him.

Therefore, I have to ask forgiveness: For those times when I stood between Lois and our Lord's Table, O Lord, forgive me. For those times when I did not walk with her twitchy, jerking, flailing, tormented body down the aisle to the Table, O Lord, forgive me. For those times when I did not help her spastic hands lift the cup of salvation to her lips, God forgive me.

This, then, is the question that we must ask: 'What kind of community must we be to be a receiving community, faithful to the gospel, that welcomes those with challenges into our midst, and secures for them a place in the very heart of our faith?' Or, more specifically, 'as a community of Christians, what ought we to be for Lois?'

WHAT KIND OF COMMUNITY *OUGHT* WE TO BE?

The genetic sciences and philosophical theology are important, but we also need the glue that makes them cohere as a piece – practical theology, that is, ministry. To ask, 'What kind of community ought we to be for Lois?' is fundamentally to ask a ministry question. The response to this question is sketched here in broad terms; it still must be contextualized distinctly and uniquely in every particular church family.

The premises that underlie this response are these. First, there is no one who is not challenged. We are all challenged by sin, by our brokenness and fallenness, and thus have failed to be loving toward those of our neighbours who are genetically challenged.

Markie Jackson, whose son has hemophilia and is now HIV-positive from a transfusion, poignantly recalls that some of the cruellest experiences of her life have been in churches. She is a Christian, and this cruelty breaks her heart.[2] The words of Jesus present their own challenge at this point: 'I give you a new commandment, that you love one another. Just as I have loved you, you also should love one another. By this everyone will know that you are my disciples, if you have love for one another' (Jn. 13:34–35, NRSV). This is the *is* of our condition.

The second premise is that the grace of God has redeemed us and freed us from what *is*, to be what we would be in obedience to God. This is the *redeemed* in our condition.

The third premise is that in all the ways in which we may have failed, what we *ought* to be we *can* be by the grace of God. The question we must ask is this: 'What kind of community ought we to be in order to be fully loving, embracing, compassionate and enabling of – and where needed to advocate for – those who are genetically challenged?'

In so far as we depend upon the grace of God and the leading of the Holy Spirit, as persons made anew, that *ought* can become our *is*. So what are the characteristics of the ought of our community? The concepts of *health*, *ministry*, and *health ministry* are foundational to a response to this question.

REORIENTING OUR CONCEPTION OF HEALTH

How we define health is critically important. In a sense it is a pre-question as well as a recurring checkpoint. Even where other 'official' definitions are operative, health is often colloquially conceived of as the absence of disease. Such a definition is inadequate, as it limits health to a biological conception rooted in the presence or absence of pathology. With its focus on the physical, such understandings of health lead to treating the 'patient' as nothing more than a body, or as protoplasm gone awry. Health, however, must be conceived of more broadly, as encompassing the totality of our being, in all its varied aspects.

Recognizing the inadequacy of conceiving of health as a biological condition, the World Health Organization in 1946 defined health as 'a state of complete physical, mental, and social well-being, not just the absence of disease or infirmity'.[3] This definition has been embraced in many health professional sectors such as medical and nursing schools and national and specialty associations for health care professionals. While this is a more holistic and a better conception of health, with an underlying (supportive) world political agenda, it is still not adequate for our considerations here. First, 'complete . . . well-being' as used in this definition continues to embrace the absence of physical disease or infirmity as pivotal but adds concepts of the absence of mental affliction or social deprivation. Apart from the unattainablity of *'complete'* biopsychosocial well-being, this definition fails to take realistic account of the frailty of our corporeal existence in the omnipresence of disease or illness, even in 'healthy' individuals.

Second, the definition is focused on the individual, divorced from relationships. It is as if the individual does (or even could) exist apart from a relational web or community, as if health could be defined apart from these relationships, as if health were independent of the health of the community, as if the individual were the sole referent for health. Not only must health not be understood solely in physical terms, but it must not be understood only in individual, or even in communal, terms. Any adequate conception of health for the Christian community must include the physical and more than the physical – the individual as well as the communal – and must bring these aspects together cotemporaneously.

A more adequate, realistic, and useful conception of health can be found in the ancient concept of *shalom. Shalom* is a noun

> . . . having a wide semantic range stressing various meanings of its basic meaning: **totality** or **completeness**. These meanings include fulfillment, completion, maturity, soundness, wholeness (both individual and communal), community, harmony, tranquility, security, well-being, welfare, friendship, agreement, success, prosperity.[4]

To understand health in terms of *shalom* is to keep before us the One who is the author of health, which is both an individual and communal state. In this conception of health, totality or completeness can exist even in the presence of disease or infirmity. Here, totality or completeness, as health, must always be judged both in terms of the individual *and* of the community. The individual is, inseparably, a person-within-community. Health, then, resides in the nexus of person and community. Markie Jackson's health and that of her son depend not exclusively on her emotional well being, or her son's physical health, but upon both those *and* the response of the faith community toward them. Where that response is cruel, there is no health to be found for Markie or her son or their church. Where that response is obedient to Christ and loving, Markie, her son, and the church can find totality or completeness – together – even in the otherwise tragic presence of an HIV-positive test.

RECONSIDERING THE CONCEPT OF MINISTRY

In addition to considering the concept of *health* in our response to persons with genetic or other challenges, we must also consider the concept of *ministry* itself. Simply defined, *ministry* is 'service rendered to God or to the people in God's name'. God equips the people for this service by giving gifts ' . . . that some would be apostles, some prophets, some evangelists, some pastors and teachers, to equip the saints for the work of ministry, for building up the body of Christ . . . ' (Eph. 4:11,12; NRSV). Though the gifts are given to persons-as-individuals, they are for the benefit of the community corporately. While the gifts are to be employed for the benefit of the church, they also bring joy and meaningfulness to the individual as she or he exercises them. Thus, we exercise our gifts for ministry, in ministry, for God's glory, our joy, and our neighbour's good.

There is a dual view of ministry that must be addressed. Ministry may be viewed as the authoritative exercise of the office of shepherd of the people of God, through leadership, teaching, preaching, discipline, spiritual formation and nurture. God has equipped and called specific and limited numbers of people to this priestly office. There is, however, another view of ministry. In this view, the ministry itself must not be confused with the office. A contribution to the church of the 16th century Reformation was the under-standing of the priesthood of all believers, sometimes called the priesthood of the baptized. In Martin Luther's understanding (and that of subsequent reformers), the priesthood of all believers did not refer to an individualized authority for private interpretation of Scripture or the life of faith, or the idea that one served as one's own priest, but rather that the church is a community of saints (*communio sanctorum*). In this community, we are all priests to one another, ministering within and outside the church walls.[5] As the community of saints, we are to intercede for one another, to help one another, to love one another and to bear one another's burdens. We are also to reach out beyond our own family of faith to touch our neighbour. This is what is meant by the priesthood of all believers; this priesthood is the calling of all believers. Herein, as with *shalom*, one is never a solitary, self-sufficient individual but always a person-in-community.

BRINGING *HEALTH* AND *MINISTRY* TOGETHER: HEALTH MINISTRY – A MINISTRY OF *SHALOM*

In bringing health and ministry together in a ministry of health-as-*shalom*, all believers are called to serve, love, help, and intercede for one another and to reach out to our neighbours, embracing and seeking *shalom* – totality or completeness – for all within the reach of our embrace. Health ministry, as such, is not bound to the WHO definition of health. Health ministry is not limited to a few ordained to the office of priest and pastor. Health ministry is not limited to 'our own'.

Health ministry is the nurture of people whom God has created, encompassing the fullness of the human condition as material and

spiritual. It recognizes our embodied existence, even though challenged, as a part of that creation that God called 'good'. It recognizes
our spiritual existence, even though sinful, as bearing the image of
God. It is risky even to speak of such categories, for it is the fallen
world, not the biblical outlook, that divides the person into parts.
Health ministry refuses to engage in a modern gnosticism that
separates the physical and the spiritual and attends to one to the
neglect of the other. Health ministry that is concerned only with
the body is not health ministry. Ministry that is concerned only with
the spirit is not ministry. Health ministry seeks *totality* or *completeness*,
in the fullness of frail human existence, for those within and outside
the community of faith, through the exercise of the gifts given by
God, in obedience to God, for God's glory, our joy, and our
neighbour's good.

We must now return to that overarching question: As a community of challenged people, caring for people with challenges, what
ought we to be? What ought we to be as a community for Lois? Four
attributes of a ministry of *shalom* are particularly important. A
ministry of *shalom* must be incarnational, transfigurative, transformative, and prophetic.

INCARNATION.

A ministry of *shalom* is incarnational in that it embraces the whole
of life, on good days and evil days, in health or in brokenness, and
reclaims a tragic view of life. A tragic view of life recognizes that
there will be suffering on this side of eternity; it is the unavoidable
lot of every mortal. Yet, we are not to deal with suffering as a *problem*,
or as something to be *mastered* (or shunned), but as an *experience*,
wherein we accompany one another. A tragic view of life embraces
life in a ministry of presence in the valley of the shadow of death
(dark shadow), recognizing that there is no way around the valley;
we must walk through it. In a ministry of *shalom* that walk is never
solitary. It is always taken as a person-in-community. We, the family
of faith who embrace those who suffer, are to bring our true selves
and our God into the presence of the one who suffers. We are to
be with one another, not simply by inviting the suffering into our
midst, but by faithfully searching them out and embracing them
and claiming them for our love, making them one of our own.

A ministry of *shalom* is also incarnational in that it thoroughly
recognizes our embodied existence. No one is a disembodied
rationality who experiences the world in dispassionate, disinter-
ested, reasoned ways. A gift that feminist Christian ethics has given
us is to reclaim our experience and ourselves as embodied persons,
subject to the vicissitudes of corporeal frailty, apprehending and
evaluating reality through that embodiedness, and consanguinously
experiencing our co-humanity.

An incarnational ministry must have a proper and lived doctrine of creation. It must encourage us to tell our embodied stories, joyful and tragic, and to share in one another's joys and laments. It must emphasize that we live an embodied spiritual existence (corporeal and spiritual), an existence that was a part of God's good creation. In this we must be present to one another.

TRANSFIGURATION.

Transfiguration is the illumination of our lives that occurs in the encounter with God. It is the shining face of Moses as he descends Mount Sinai having tarried in an encounter with God. In that encounter, confronted by the holiness of God, we find that our lives are fragmented, our priorities are deranged, and our souls are dry. We find that we have stood in the way or failed to help one whom Jesus had called or would call to his Table. We find that we have walked around the man lying beaten on the road to Jericho. We find that we are challenged by sin.

In transfiguration we dip into the living water of the well of God, seeking to restore and renew our lives in accordance with the will of God; and find ourselves washed clean by those waters. Therein lies the abundant life that has been promised us, both for ourselves and for our neighbour. A transfigurative ministry of *shalom* is one that is deeply repentant of the dark sinfulness of our lives (as individuals and as a community); our hearts must be rent. We do not avert our eyes from the horror of our failures to be obedient or loving, but rather seek the light of God's holiness that shows us both who we are and who God is. Herein we are changed inwardly as we are led to be what God would have us be.

TRANSFORMATION.

A ministry of *shalom* must be one that changes us from what we were to what we ought to be, that we may act in accordance with the will of God. It emphasizes stewardship of the body, something we tend to neglect. It emphasizes balance, also something that we tend to neglect. It emphasizes love. Transformation takes our contrition and repentance (*metanoia*, turning around) and sets us in new directions. This is not just for the individual but for the community as well. As we are changed inwardly, we are transformed outwardly as individuals, as congregations, and as a society, as the congregation reaches out into the community to transform it. A ministry of *shalom*, a health ministry, is never a 'stay at home' or self-absorbed ministry. It always picks up the man beaten by thieves on the road to Jericho, binds up his wounds and cares for him. It always meets people with challenges of any sort and welcomes them into the community of faith.

PROPHETIC VOICE.

To be prophetic means to speak or to proclaim in the name of God. What is it that we as a community of *shalom* are to proclaim? It is this: that God seeks for us to be healed, to be whole, as individuals, as congregations, and as societies. Thus the prophetic voice of health ministries denounces that which is destructive of human health or dignity and proclaims that which affirms the *imago dei* and human community. It is an intrinsically social-ethical act.

> Social ethics engages in analysis . . . in order to approve and strengthen those institutions or aspects of a sector of the social system that sustain the moral community, and in order to criticize, transform, or undermine those institutions or aspects of the social system that destroy such possibilities.[6]

In unmasking structures, values, and forms of behaviour that are destructive of human flourishing, a prophetic ministry of *shalom* engages in the three moral functions of social ethics. First, the community exercises a reformist bias that contends for change within the community itself. Here ethics seeks to bring the *is* into conformity with the *ought* within the workings of the congregation itself through critical and repentant self-reflection. Second, the community engages in epidictic discourse. Epidictic discourse

> . . . sets out to increase the intensity of adherence to certain values, which might not be contested when considered on their own, but may nevertheless not prevail against other values that might come into conflict with them.[7]

Epidictic discourse is hortatory in nature, calling us to live the gospel we affirm. The third function of social ethics is to represent the values of the faith community to the larger society. This function argues for change in society itself, unmasking the tyrannies and idolatries of contemporary society.

In reference to the work of the Holy Spirit, the 'Brief Statement of Faith', added to the Presbyterian denominational *Book of Confessions* in 1991, says, in part, that

> the Spirit gives us courage
> to pray without ceasing,
> to witness among all peoples to Christ as Lord and Savior,
> to unmask idolatries in Church and culture,
> to hear the voices of peoples long silenced,
> and to work with others for justice, freedom, and peace.[8]

A prophetic ministry of *shalom* moves within, then outside, its own house to engage in these very activities. It seeks to take the part of those who are challenged, to bring about in society those conditions necessary to human flourishing.

WHAT WILL CHRISTIAN COMMUNITY LOOK LIKE?

Will there be a wheelchair ramp into the chancel so that a physically challenged person might serve as lector? Will there be specially adapted toilet seats in the toilets? Will there be more persons visible with physical challenges? Yes, and there will also be services of healing and wholeness and anointings. There will be a sharing of stories of joy but also of pain. There will be a walking with one another in sorrow and suffering: that is to be incarnational.

Will there be an emphasis on good nutrition, exercise, giving up smoking, and other preventive measures? Will there be classes on prayer or fasting? Will there be retreats? Yes, and there will be a genuine re-ordering of our priorities, perhaps a learning to say 'no', and an increase in prayer. There will be an awareness with repentance of where we have failed in our own self-care, and where we have failed to care for our neighbour: that is to be transfigurative.

Will there be the 'Deacons Relief Closet' or a food chest, or clothing distribution, or bus passes and hotel vouchers as there have always been? Yes, and there will also be a trip to city hall to speak for those with challenges, or a vote for a better health care system, or advocacy for a socially disadvantaged group, or interceding in a hospital or institution that is harming a particular neighbour: that is to be transformative.

Will there be papers and Christian education classes on euthanasia, or abortion, or assisted suicide, or genetic engineering? Yes, and there will be a new ministry of compassion and care of the suffering; an outcry against the unwarranted or unwanted use of technology at the end of life; a unified voice against the poverty that is the single most important source of preventable human misery, including genetic or congenital defect; and an intolerance toward anything within or outside our church walls that harms human dignity: that is to be prophetic.

If the ministries of our faith communities only embrace a WHO definition of health . . . if the ministries of our faith communities are only for the hale . . . if the ministries of our faith communities are only narrowly 'spiritual' . . . if the ministries of our faith communities are only for ourselves . . . we distort the gospel. A ministry of *shalom* as health is rooted and grounded in the gospel of Christ. It is the spiritual nurture of the children of God encompassing the fullness of the human condition as material and spiritual beings. It seeks *shalom,* that is, it seeks *totality* or *completeness.* It is incarnational, it is transfigurative, it is transformative, it is prophetic. It is nothing less than our best service for the glory of God, for our own joy, and for our neighbour's good.

NOTES

1. Presbyterian Church, (USA). *Book of Common Worship* (Louisville, Westminster/John Knox Press 1993) p. 68.

2. See her essay earlier in this volume.

3. World Health Organization. Health. Geneva, Switzerland: author, 1946.

4. Youngblood, R.F., 'Peace', in Bromily, G. (Ed.) *The International Standard Bible Encyclopedia.* Rev. Ed., Vol. 3. (Grand Rapids, W. B. Eerdmans 1986) p. 732.

5. Lehmann, Helmut. T., (General Ed.). *Luther's Works*, Vol. 40. (Philadelphia, Fortress Press 1971), p. 20ff.

6. Stackhouse, Max. 'Ethics: Social and Christian', *Andover Newton Quarterly*, Vol 13 1973, pp. 173–191.

7. Perlman, Ch. & Obrechts – Tyteca, L., *The New Rhetoric: A Treatise on Argumentation.* (Notre Dame, Notre Dame University Press 1969).

8. Presbyterian Church, (USA). A Brief Statement of Faith. *Book of Confessions* (Louisville, KY, PC(USA) 1991) 10.1–6.

Glossary of Genetic Terms

Hessel Bouma III, PhD

Adenine (A):A nitrogenous base which may occur in either DNA or RNA; in DNA, it forms a base pair with thymine (A-T).

Alleles: Alternate forms of a gene or gene locus. For non-sex chromosomes, each person normally has two alleles at each gene position. If the two alleles are the same, the person's genotype is homozygous; if the two alleles differ, the genotype is heterozygous.

Amino acid:A class of 20 organic molecules that function as building blocks for all proteins in living things. Genes code for the assembly of particular amino acids into specific proteins.

Amniocentesis: Fetal test performed between the 14th and 16th week of gestation (as measured from time of fertilization). A needle is inserted through the mother's abdominal wall into the fluid bathing the developing fetus. Approximately 10 ml of amniotic fluid is withdrawn which contains some sloughed off fetal cells. The fetal cells are cultured for several days to several weeks after which they can be subjected to cytogenetic and/or biochemical analysis to determine whether the fetus is a carrier of or affected with a genetic condition (the sex of the fetus can also be determined).

Amplification: An increase in the number of copies of one or more segments of DNA. This may occur inside or outside a living organism and may involve cloning or PCR.

Aneuploidy:A cell with one or more extra or missing chromosomes. Any human somatic cell whose chromosome number is not 46. For example, persons with Trisomy 21 (Down's Syndrome) have 47 chromosomes in each somatic cell, the result of an extra copy of chromosome #21 in each cell.

Autosome:A non-sex chromosome. Autosomes normally occur as pairs in somatic cells, and gene loci on autosomes consist of a pair of alleles. In humans, chromosome pairs #1–22.

Base pair (bp):two nitrogenous bases (adenine-thymine or cytosine-guanine) held together by weak bonds. The human genome consists of approximately 3 billion base pairs distributed on 22 autosomes and 1 pair of sex chromosomes.

Base sequence: The order of nucleotides in a DNA or RNA molecule.

Base sequence analysis: Any method for determining the order of nucleotides in DNA or RNA.

Biotechnology: The alteration of cells or biological molecules for a specific application, e.g. genetic engineering, cell culture.

Blastocyst: An early stage of human development approximately 6–10 days after fertilization when the embryo is a hollow mass of cells about to undergo implantation in the endometrial lining of the uterus. Compare with blastomere and zygote.

Blastomere: Very early stages of human development occurring 1–3 days after fertilization and resulting from the earliest mitotic divisions of the zygote. Fertilization through the 16- or 32-cell blastomere stage can be achieved and maintained *in vitro*; IVF-ET normally transfers human embryos to the woman's uterus at this stage for subsequent implantation.

Carrier: An individual heterozygous (having 2 different alleles) for a recessive trait, these individuals 'carry' the trait, may pass it on to their offspring, but do not express (exhibit) the trait themselves.

cDNA: See complementary DNA.

Centimorgan:A functional map unit used to measure the distance between two gene loci. One centimorgan is equal to a 1% chance that a marker at one gene locus will be seperated from a marker at a second gene locus through crossing over in a single generation. In humans, a centimorgan is approximately one million base pairs.

Centromere: The characteristic constriction in a chromosome which joins sister-chromatids (DNA molecules) and is the site for fibre attachments during mitosis.

Chorionic villus sampling (CVS): Fetal test performed between the 8th and 10th week gestation (as measured from time of fertilization). A needle is inserted through the mother's abdominal wall into the fetal portion of the placenta and several milliliters of extra-embryonic fetal cells are withdrawn. The fetal cells can be immediately subjected to cytogenetic and/or biochemical analysis to determine whether the fetus is a carrier of or affected with a genetic condition (the sex of the fetus can also be determined).

Chromosome:A pair of DNA molecules combined with protein which condenses to become visible on light microscopy during mitosis. Human somatic cells have 23 pairs of chromosomes, 22 pairs are autosomes and 1 pair is the sex chromosome pair; human germ cells have 23 chromosomes.

Clone: Usually a group of genetically-identical cells derived from a common ancestor. May also refer to genetically-identical organisms such as naturally occur with monozygotic twins or may be achieved with embryo splitting.

Cloning: The process of producing genetically identical cells or individuals from a single ancestor. May also refer to process in which multiple copies of one or more segments of DNA are produced – DNA cloning.

Cloning vector:A DNA molecule from a virus, bacterial plasmid, or cell of a higher organism into which a second DNA molecule can be inserted, thereby enabling the second DNA molecule to be copied (cloned) in large quantities. Examples include cosmids (viruses), plasmids (bacteria), and yeast artificial chromosomes.

Codon:a set of three sequential nucleotides whose sequence specifies the assembly of one particular amino acid into a protein.

Complementary DNA (cDNA):DNA which is synthesized from mRNA using reverse transcriptase. Single-stranded cDNA can be made radioactive and used as a probe to detect the presence or absence of matching alleles in cells.

Complementary sequences: Nucleic acid base sequences which form double-stranded structures through base pairs (A pairs with T, C pairs with G). For example:

A-T-C-C-G-A

T-A-G-G-C-T

Consanguinity: The genetic relationship between two individuals sharing a common ancestor, e.g. siblings, cousins. Rare recessive genetic conditions are much more likely to occur in consanguinous matings.

Conserved sequence:A base sequence in DNA or amino acid sequence in proteins which is largely the same from one species to another.

Cosmid: An artificial cloning vector containing the *cos* gene of the *phage* (a kind of virus) lambda. Up to 45 kb fragments of DNA can be inserted into the lambda phage for infection and replication in *E. Coli* hosts. (It would take a minimum of 67,000 of the largest cosmids possible to contain the entire human genome.)

Crossing over:A process during meiosis in which one maternal and one paternal chromosome of a homologous pair break, exchange DNA fragments, then rejoin. Following crossing over, chromosomes are no longer exclusively maternal or paternal in origin, but a blend, thereby dramatically increasing the number of possible genetic combinations occurring in a person's offspring.

Cystic fibrosis: The most common lethal genetic disease in the U.S. affecting one in 2,500 Caucasians, inherited as an autosomal recessive. One in 25 Caucasians is a carrier. Average life expectancy is now in the late 20s. Disease is due to genetic mutations in a large gene whose product is responsible for transporting chloride ions across membranes. The most prevalent mutation is due to the deletion of one codon in the gene which results in one less amino acid in the gene product. Disease causes thick mucus to accumulate which affects the lungs, pancreas, and digestive tract.

Cytogenetics: The study of the number and morphology of chromosomes in an individual and the correlation of chromosomal aberrations with specific genetic conditions.

Cytosine (C):A nitrogenous base which may occur in either DNA or RNA; in DNA, it forms a base pair with guanine (C-G).

Deletion:A mutation in which one or more nucleotides is lost during meiosis. Deletions vary in severity, ranging from harmless if nonsense genetic information is lost to lethal if essential genes are missing from the resulting cells and organism.

Deoxyribonucleotide: See nucleotide.

Diploid:A full set of genetic material consisting of paired chromosomes which normally occurs in nearly all somatic cells (all cells of an organism except the gametes). The normal diploid human genome consists of 46 chromosomes.

Dizygotic: Fraternal (non-identical) twins conceived from two eggs fertilized by separate sperm.

DNA (deoxyribonucleic acid): The molecule which encodes genetic information. DNA is a double-stranded, helical molecule in which the two strands are complementary in sequence and held together by numerous weak bonds. The four nitrogenous bases are adenine (A), cytosine (C), guanine (G), and thymine (T), and form the base pairs, A-T and C-G.

DNA probes: See probe.

DNA replication: The use of one strand or piece of DNA as a template for the synthesis of another strand through complementary base pairing. DNA replication occurs in the nucleus in cells that have nuclei.

DNA sequence: The relative order of nucleotides in DNA.

Dominant: An allele that masks the expression of another allele at the same gene locus or a trait expressed whenever one allele is present (in both the homozygous and heterozygous state).

Double helix: The spiral shape which two complementary strands of DNA assume when bonded together.

Down's Syndrome: Also known as Trisomy 21, this genetic condition is due to the presence of an extra copy of chromosome 21 in a person's cells. The condition affects approximately one in 700 births in the U.S.; the occurrence of Down's Syndrome increases with maternal age, being less than one in 2,500 in children born to women under age 30, rising to one in 40 born to women in their early thirties, and one in 10 born to women in their forties.

Duchenne muscular dystrophy:A sex-linked disorder which affects approximately one in 3,500 males born in the U.S. The disease is characterized by a progressive weakening of muscles and loss of coordination which usually leads to death by the early 20s. Disease is due to the absence of the key muscle protein, dystrophin.

Duplication:A fragment of genetic material lost from one chromosome which joins the homologous chromosome. Duplications vary in severity, from harmless if genetic material is nonsense to severe if the genetic overdose significantly disturbs the normal balance of gene products.

E. coli (Escherichia coli): Small, common bacterium (prokaryote) found in digestive tract of humans and most animals. Its genome is estimated to be 4 million base pairs.

Electrophoresis:A method for separating large molecules or fragments of large molecules of nucleic acids or proteins in an electric field.

ELSI: The Ethical, Legal, and Social Issues component of the Human Genome Project. This segment was included from the inception of the project to address significant issues raised by the newly acquired knowledge. Approximately 5% of the Human Genome Project budget is to be spent on ELSI projects.

Embryo splitting: The process of physically separating multicellular embryos soon after fertilization to create genetically identical clones. For example, this is done to produce identical triplet or quadruplet calves from each embryo derived from the sperm of a bull and the egg of a super-ovulated cow.

Endonuclease: An enzyme which cleaves a nucleic acid at an internal rather than terminal site.

Enzyme:A protein which acts as a catalyst, speeding up the rate at which a specific chemical reaction occurs but not being consumed or altered by the process. Some enzymes catalyze up to 100,000 reactions per second.

Eugenics: The science of improving the quality of a breed or species. Positive eugenics improves the quality by manipulating traits deemed desirable; negative eugenics seeks to improve the quality by preventing traits deemed undesirable from being passed on.

Eukaryote:A cell or organism with membrane-bound compartments (organelles) such as the nucleus within the cell. Such cells or organisms have nuclear DNA packaged as chromosomes. Compare with prokaryote.

Exons: Segments of DNA in eukaryote genes which code for the assembly of amino acids into proteins. Compare with introns.

Expressivity: The extent to which a genetic defect is expressed from one organism to another. For example, variable expressivity is manifested by polydactyly, a dominant condition in which persons may have additional fingers and/or toes. Some have no additional digits, others one, two, or perhaps three digits on one, two, three, or all four limbs.

FISH (fluorescence *in situ* hybridization):A very sensitive technique which utilizes a fluorescent probe which hybridizes to either chromosomes or chromatin to identify the presence and location of specific segments of DNA.

Founder effect: In small populations (due usually to either geographic isolation or religious segregation), an otherwise rare genetic mutation may occur in much higher frequency than in the general population due to the more significant impact one individual may have on the population's gene pool.

Gamete: The mature reproductive cells – eggs of females and the sperm of males – which contain the haploid number of chromosomes (in humans: normally 23).

Gamete intrafallopian tube transfer (GIFT): Assisted reproductive technology in which egg(s) and sperm are transferred to a woman's fallopian tubes where fertilization and subsequent development may proceed naturally. Compare with IVF-ET and ZIFT.

Gene:A functional unit of heredity which determines one trait or characteristic. At the molecular level, the segment of DNA that codes for the protein product which determines the one trait or characteristic. The human genome is believed to consist of 50,000 to 100,000 genes on the 22 autosomes and pair of sex chromosomes.

Gene expression: The process whereby the information in the base sequences in DNA is used to direct the assembly of amino acids into functional proteins.

Gene families: Groups of comparable genes producing similar products. For example, the oxygen-carrying blood protein, hemoglobin, consists of similar proteins designated î-, £-, ¤-, Π-, and ∈-, derived from the 'family' of globin genes.

Gene library: See genomic library.

Gene mapping: Determining the relative positions of gene loci on a DNA molecule and the relative distance between gene loci on the same molecule. The average human chromosome has 4,000 gene loci; a chromosome map reveals the location and sequence of each gene locus on that chromosome.

Gene product: The RNA or protein produced by the expression of a gene.

Genetic code: The sequence of triplet nucleotides in mRNA which dictates the sequence of amino acids assembled into proteins. Since the mRNA sequence is derived from the DNA sequence, the DNA sequence can be used to predict the mRNA sequence which, in turn, can be used to predict the amino acid sequence in the primary gene product.

Genetic map: See linkage map.

Genetic material: The DNA found in all prokaryote and eukaryote cells, and in DNA viruses. Only retroviruses have genetic material which is RNA requiring the special enzyme, reverse transcriptase, to produce DNA from the retroviral RNA genetic material.

Genetic screening: The use of a genetic test to determine whether a particular gene is present or absent. Mandatory genetic screening on human populations is rarely performed unless there is a clear and substantial benefit to the individual being tested, e.g., newborns screened within days of birth for elevated blood phenylalanine levels associated with phenylketonuria.

Genetics: The study of the patterns of inheritance of specific traits.

Genome: The complete complement of an organism's genes. The human genome consists of 50,000–100,000 genes involving approximately 3 billion base pairs.

Genome projects: The mapping and sequencing of some or all of the genome of the human or other organisms including *E. coli*, *C. elegans*, yeast, fruit flies, mice, and *Arabidopsis*.

Genomic imprinting:A rare phenomenon in which there is a parental affect on gene expression. Otherwise identical alleles may have different effects on offspring depending on whether they were inherited from the mother or the father.

Genomic library:A collection of clones possessing overlapping DNA fragments containing the entire genome of an organism. For example, a cosmid library of the human genome would consist of a minimum of 67,000 clones, each containing 45 kb of human DNA.

Genotype: The genetic make-up of one or more genes or the entire genome of an organism.

Germ cells: The reproductive cells of an organism, these cells normally have the haploid number of chromosomes. In humans, eggs are the germ cells of females and sperm are the germ cells of males; human germ cells normally have 23 chromosomes (unpaired).

Guanine (G):A nitrogenous base which may occur in either DNA or RNA; in DNA, it forms a base pair with cytosine (C-G).

Haploid: The single set of chromosomes (non-paired) which occurs in the gametes of organisms – the eggs and sperm of animals and the eggs and pollen of plants.

Hemizygous: Having only one copy of a gene in a diploid cell. Usually used to describe alleles in male somatic cells which have only one X-chromosome.

Hemophilia: Recessive, sex-linked genetic condition in which a person has a defective or absent protein factor necessary for normal blood coagulation. Classical hemophilia, also known as hemophilia A, is due to an absent or defective clotting Factor VIII; Christmas disease, also known as hemophilia B, is due to an absent or defective clotting Factor IX. The genes for both forms of hemophilia are inherited on the X chromosome.

Heterozygous: Having two different alleles at a single gene locus. Compare with homozygous and hemizygous.

Homeobox: Short segments of DNA that regulate patterns of differentiation during the development of an organism.

Homologies: Similarities in either DNA or protein (amino acid) sequences between individuals of the same species or among different species.

Homologous chromosomes:A pair of autosomes containing the same linear gene loci, one paternal and one maternal in origin.

Homozygous: In a diploid cell, having the same allele at both copies of a gene locus. Compare with hemizygous and heterozygous.

Human gene therapy: Insertion of normal DNA into a person's cells to correct a genetic defect. Somatic gene therapy is done on target somatic cells and may correct the defect but only for the individual, not the individual's offspring. Germ cell gene therapy theoretically could be done on fertilized eggs and might correct not only the individual's genetic defect but would be incorporated into their eggs or sperm and affect their offspring.

Human Genome Project (HGP):collaborative 15-year project (1990–2005) to map and sequence all of the approximately 50–100,000 genes consisting of approximately 3 billion base pairs in human cells

Huntington's disease:A rare, lethal, autosomal dominant disease with late age of onset (between ages 35 and 45). The gene occurs at the tip of chromosome #4 and the disease is due to the occurrence of triplet nucleotide repeats (CAG). The disease develops as gradual, progressive mental and motor deterioration which leads inevitably to death over a ten year span.

Hybridization: The process of joining two complementary strands of DNA or one strand of DNA with one of RNA to form a double-stranded molecule. Many very sensitive and accurate genetic diagnostic tests utilize DNA or RNA probes to identify the presence of defective genes through hybridization.

Imprinting: See genomic imprinting.

Informatics: The study of the application of computer and mathematical techniques to the management of information.

***In situ*hybridization:**The use of DNA or RNA probes to detect the presence of complementary DNA in living cells.

Interphase: The period in the cell cycle when cells are not actively dividing. It is during this period that cells grow and the DNA is replicated in the nucleus of eukaryote cells. Compare with mitosis.

Introns:DNA base sequences in eukaryotes which are interspersed with and interrupt the protein-coding DNA base sequences of a gene. These sequences are transcribed into RNA but are cut out before the mRNA moves out of the nucleus and into the cytosol for translation.

In vitro:Occurring outside a living organism.

***In vitro*fertilization – embryo transfer (IVF-ET):**Assisted reproductive technology in which fertilization of eggs by sperm are achieved in a Petri dish. Fertilized eggs are allowed to develop for 1–3 days after which the embryos are transferred to the woman's uterus for subsequent implantation and natural development. Compare with GIFT and ZIFT.

Karyotype:A picture of an individual's complete set of chromosomes arranged in pairs showing the number, size, and shape of each chromosome. Can be used diagnostically to reveal gross chromosomal abnormalities such as Down's Syndrome, Trisomy 13, Trisomy 18, Klinefelter's Syndrome, and Turner's Syndrome as well as major duplications or deletions.

Kilobase (kb):A unit of length for DNA fragments equaling 1,000 nucleotides.

Library:A collection of clones containing different DNA fragments from a particular organism.

Linkage: Two or more gene loci or markers on a chromosome. The closer the two loci are, the more tightly they are linked and less likely to be separated by crossing over during meiosis.

Linkage map:A map of the relative positions of gene loci on each chromosome based upon the frequency with which the loci are inherited together.

Localize: To determine the actual position of a gene or marker on a chromosome.

Locus (pl. loci): The position on a chromosome of a gene and the DNA at that position.

Mapping: See gene map, linkage map, physical map.

Marker: An identifiable physical location on a chromosome, not necessarily a gene, whose inheritance can be followed.

Megabase (Mb):A unit of length for DNA fragments equal to 1 million nucleotides, it is approximately equal to 1 centimorgan (cM). Compare with bp and kb.

Meiosis: The two-stage cell division which must occur in sexually reproducing organisms to produce haploid germ cells. In humans, meiosis occurs in the testes of males to produce sperm and the ovaries of females to produce eggs.

Messenger RNA (mRNA):A type of RNA synthesized from DNA genes which migrates from the nucleus to the cytosol to direct the assembly of amino acids into the protein gene product.

Metaphase: The stage of mitosis in which the sister-chromatids of chromosomes are preparing to separate. Karyotypes are prepared from cells in metaphase.

Mitosis: The process of cell division in eukaryote cells, typically subdivided into the consecutive stages of prophase, metaphase, anaphase, and telophase. This process assures that the daughter cells each receive copies of replicated chromosomes.

Monozygotic: Genetically identical twins conceived from a single egg fertilized by one sperm which, after division into a small mass of cells, subsequently breaks into two masses to become two individuals.

mRNA: See messenger RNA.

Multifactorial disorders or traits: Physical disorders or traits which have genetic components as well as environmental components. For example, atherosclerosis, diabetes, heart disease, and obesity.

Mutation: Any inheritable change in the DNA which is passed on to daughter cells or an organism's offspring.

Nitrogenous base:A nitrogen-containing molecule which is basic (rather than acidic or neutral) in its chemical properties. Nucleotides contain nitrogenous bases in addition to a pentose sugar and a phosphate group.

Nucleic acid:A large molecule composed of a linear sequence of one or two strands of nucleotides. There are two types of nucleic acids, DNA and RNA.

Nucleotide:A basic building block of nucleic acids, each nucleotide contains a nitrogenous base (adenine, cytosine, guanine, thymine and uracil), a pentose sugar (deoxyribose in DNA or ribose in RNA), and a phosphate group. Most genes consist of thousands of nucleotides, most chromosomes have several million nucleotides, and the entire human genome consists of 3 billion nucleotide base pairs.

Nucleus: The membrane-bound part of a cell that contains the genetic material.

Oncogene:A mutated gene which is associated with uncontrolled cell growth, cancer. See proto-oncogene.

PCR: See polymerase chain reaction.

Penetrance: The percentage of individuals inheriting a genotype who exhibit its observable physical trait (phenotype). For most classical genetic conditions (e.g., cystic fibrosis, sickle cell anemia), penetrance is 100%. Polydactyly exhibits incomplete penetrance since some persons have no extra fingers or toes yet their parents and children do.

Phage:A virus whose natural host is a bacterial cell. These viruses may be modified to become vehicles for inserting DNA fragments into bacteria for replication.

Phenotype: The observable physical trait of a genotype.

Phenylketonuria: An autosomal recessive genetic condition, affecting 1 in 14,500 white newborns, in which a missing or defective enzyme results in elevated levels of the amino acid phenylalanine in the blood which, in turn, produces moderate to severe mental impairment. The manifestation of this disease can be prevented and by strictly following a low phenylalanine diet from birth until age 8 (though many geneticists suggest the diet be retained for life), and again for women when pregnant. Mandatory genetic screening of all newborns within days of birth has reduced the effects of this disorder substantially.

Physical map:A map of the locations of sites on DNA including but not limited to gene loci. The linear map distances are measured in base pairs.

Plasmid: Nonessential circular DNA molecules which occur in addition to the regular genome in some but not all bacteria. Plasmids may integrate into the regular genome. Plasmids may be cut by restriction enzymes to allow the incorporation of DNA fragments; these artificial plasmids function as one type of cloning vector.

Pleiotropy: The ability of a gene to affect an organism in many different ways. For example, the gene for albinism (autosomal recessive) not only results in a lack of skin pigmentation but also produces visual disturbances.

Polygenic disorders or traits: Genetic disorders or traits resulting from the inheritance of alleles of more than one gene. Skin pigmentation in humans appears to be due to the additive effect of alleles at three or more gene loci. Compare to single gene disorders and multifactorial disorders.

Polymerase chain reaction (PCR):A rapid and fairly economic method for producing many copies of one or two DNA fragments very quickly (as many as several billion copies can be produced from one or two molecules in several hours). Indeed, a genetic diagnosis can be made from the DNA of a single cell utilizing this technique.

Polymorphism: Differences in DNA sequences among individuals. The A, B, and O blood groups are examples of polymorphisms.

Primer:A short RNA or DNA molecule to which more DNA nucleotides can be added.

Probe: Single-stranded, short molecules of DNA or RNA of specific base sequence, modified to be radioactive or fluorescent, that are used to detect the presence of complementary base sequences in DNA or RNA through hybridization.

Prokaryote: Single-cell organisms (though they may form colonies) such a mycoplasmas, bacteria, and blue-green algae which lack a membrane-bound nucleus and other subcellular organelles have a genome consisting of a single, circular molecule double-helical DNA. Compare with eukaryote.

Promoter:A specific nucleotide sequence in DNA upstream from a gene instructing enzymes to initiate gene transcription and proceed downstream.

Protein:A large molecule comprised of a few to several thousand amino acids joined together. For any particular protein, the number and sequence of amino acids is the same. Proteins are the primary gene products, the sequence of amino acids having been specified by the nucleotide sequence in DNA transcribed into mRNA used to translate the information into the functional protein. A single, linear sequence of amino acids may also be referred to as a polypeptide; a protein may consist of one or more polypeptides.

Proto-oncogene:A normal cellular gene which usually produces growth factors stimulating cellular growth. When mutated, it is an oncogene which stimulates the uncontrolled cell proliferation of cancer.

Purine:A type of organic molecule with a single ring structure which includes the nitrogenous bases of cytosine, thymine, and uracil. In nucleic acids, base pairs normally form between a purine and a pyrimidine.

Pyrimidine:A type of organic molecule with a double ring structure which includes the nitrogenous bases of adenine and cytosine. In nucleic acids, base pairs normally form between a purine and of a pyrimidine.

Recessive: An allele whose expression is masked by the activity of another allele at the same gene locus or a trait expressed only when a pair of such alleles is present (in the homozygous state).

Recombinant DNA:A combination of DNA molecules from different origins.

Recombinant DNA technologies: Procedures utilized to manipulate, replicate, and modify DNA fragments. Under appropriate conditions, modified DNA from the cell of one species can be transferred into the cell of another organism of the same (e.g., human gene therapy)or different species (e.g., bacteria producing human insulin).

Recombination: The process by which offspring inherit a different combination and arrangement of genes than occurred in their parents as a consequence of crossing over during meiosis.

Regulatory regions or sequences: Any DNA segment that controls the expression of one or more genes.

Restriction enzymes:A family of enzymes, derived from bacteria, that recognizes then cuts DNA at highly specific sites.

Restriction enzyme cutting site: The specific DNA nucleotide sequence which is recognized and cut by a particular restriction enzyme.

Restriction fragment length polymorphism (RFLP): Nucleotide sequences in DNA that involve restriction enzyme cutting sites. The absence of a specific cutting site in some individuals will result in their having a larger DNA fragment than other individuals possessing the specific cutting site. The RFLPs are used as markers for physical and genetic maps, may be used in diagnostic tests, and are used in DNA fingerprinting.

Ribonucleic acid (RNA):A large molecule composed of the basic building blocks of nucleotides and found in the nucleus and cytoplasm of eukaryote cells. It occurs in three major different functional types, messenger RNA (mRNA), ribsosomal RNA (rRNA), and transfer RNA (tRNA).

Ribosomal RNA (rRNA):A functional type of RNA that joins with numerous proteins to form ribosomes. See also ribosomes.

Ribosomes: Small, subcellular components composed of ribosomal RNA and ribosomal proteins which function as the site of protein synthesis.

Sequence: See base sequence.

Sequence tagged site (STS):A short, 200–500 base pair DNA sequence of known location and sequence that occurs only once in an organism's genome and can be used as a reference point.

Sequencing: The process of determining the order of nucleotides in DNA or RNA, or the order of amino acids in protein.

Sex chromosomes: The X and the Y chromosome in humans that is the chromosomal basis for sex determination. Females have a pair of X chromosomes, males have one X and one Y chromosome. The X chromosome contains several thousand gene loci but the Y chromosome contains very few loci unpaired with the X. Compare to autosomes.

Sickle cell disease: Most common inherited disease among African-Americans, this disease is due to a single nucleotide mutation in a gene for the £-chain of hemoglobin. Inherited as an autosomal recessive, it affects one in 400 and is carried by one in 10 African-Americans. Average life expectancy of persons with sickle cell anemia is the late 20s.

Single-gene disorder or trait:A hereditary disorder or trait caused by a mutation in the allele of a single gene. Over 4,000 such disorders have been described in humans. Compare with polygenic and multifactorial disorders and traits.

Sister-chromatids: The two identical DNA molecules condensed into the two arms of a chromosome joined at the centromere; the two sister- chromatids of each chromosome go to separate daughter cells during cell division to assure each daughter cell receives one copy of the genetic material of each chromosome.

Somatic cells: In humans, any cell in the body except the gametes and their precursors. Somatic cells almost invariably have the diploid number of chromosomes and replicate exclusively by mitosis.

Southern blotting:A powerful technique for identifying the presence of specific sequence segments of DNA. DNA fragments separated by electrophoresis (in an electric field) are transferred to membrane filters, then detected by radioactive probes through hybridization.

STS: See sequence tagged site.

Tandem repeat sequences: Multiple copies of the same base sequence on a chromosome, these sites serve as a marker for physical maps.

Tay-Sachs disease: Rare lethal genetic disease with disproportionately high incidence in Ashkenazic Jews where it occurs in one in 3,600 births. The normal gene product is a brain enzyme. Inherited as an autosomal recessive, the disease has a defective enzyme which allows toxic brain lipids to accumulate. Manifested a few months after birth, progressive deterioration leads to seizures, blindness, and both motor and mental deterioration with death inevitably by age 6.

Technology transfer: The process of converting breakthrough scientific discoveries in the laboratory into useful products in the commercial sector.

Telomere: The ends of chromosomes, these specialized structures are involved in assuring that the entire DNA molecule in the chromosome is replicated once and only once in each cell cycle.

Thymine (T):A nitrogenous base which occurs only in DNA; in DNA, it forms a base pair with adenine (A-T).

Transcription: The process whereby the genetic information encoded in the DNA base sequence of a gene is utilized to direct the synthesis of multiple copies of complementary base sequence of RNA molecules. Occurs in the nucleus of eukaryotes.

Transfer RNA (tRNA): One of the major types of RNA, these small RNA molecules bind an amino acid at one end and 'read' the codon messages in mRNA to direct the assembly of amino acids into proteins during translation.

Transformation:A process whereby the genome of an organism is altered by the incorporation of foreign DNA.

Transgenic organism:A genetically engineered organism resulting after one or more genes have been inserted into a gamete or the fertilized ovum causing the alteration to appear in every cell of the organism.

Translation: The process in which the instructions in mRNA are utilized to direct the assembly of specific amino acids into proteins.

Translocation: An exchange of DNA segments between nonhomologous chromosomes.

Trisomy 13:A cytogenetic condition in which individual has 47 chromosomes, there being three copies of chromosome #13 instead of two. Associated with severe malformations, significant mental impairments, and average life expectancy of six months.

Trisomy 18:A cytogenetic condition in which individual has 47 chromosomes, there being three copies of chromosome #18 instead of two. Characterized by severe malformations, significant mental impairments, and average life expectancy of six months.

Trisomy 21:see Down's Syndrome

tRNA: See transfer RNA.

Tumor-suppressor gene:A gene whose product normally inhibits cell growth and division, thereby preventing uncontrolled cell growth (cancer). Mutations in this gene may lead to cancer. Compare with oncogene.

Uracil (U):A nitrogenous base which occurs only in RNA.

Vector: See cloning vector.

Virus:A noncellular biological entity, consisting of a protein coat and genetic material which is either DNA or RNA, which can reproduce only in a specific host cell.

Yeast artificial chromosome (YAC):A vector used to clone large DNA fragments (up to 400 kb) in yeast. To contain the entire human genome in a YAC library would require a minimum of 7,500 YAC clones.

Zygote: Occasionally used to refer to any stage of human development from the onset of fertilization until implantation; usually used in a restricted sense to refer to the single cell, fertilized egg before cellular divisions begin. Genetically, the zygote is diploid, having a unique individual genetic identity.

Zygote intrafallopian tube transfer (ZIFT): Assisted reproductive technology in which fertilization of eggs by sperm occurs in a Petri dish whereupon the zygote is transferred to the woman's fallopian tube to complete development naturally.

SOURCES

'Appendix E: Glossary,' *Human Genome, 1991–92 Program Report*, US Department of Energy, June 1992, pp. 230–241.

Campbell, Neil, *Biology, 4th Edition*, (Menlo Park, CA, The Benjamin/Cummings Publishing Company, Inc. 1996), pp. G-1–G-22.

Lewin, Benjamin, *Genes V*, (New York, NY, Oxford University Press 1994), pp. 1235–1257.

Lewis, Ricki, *Beginnings of Life*, (Dubuque, IA, William C. Brown Publishers 1992), pp. G-1–G-8.

Index

ability 97, 108, 125, 159, 210, 214
  intellectual 105, 106, 108
abnormality 56, 139, 140
  chromosome 146
  genetic 129, 139, 141, 175
abortion 8, 14–16, 18, 20, 30, 46, 70,
  126, 128, 133, 136, 139–142,
  144, 158, 160, 163, 164, 179,
  218, 235, 236, 238, 239, 242, 254
  selective 110, 164
  therapeutic 70, 156, 158, 164
abuses 117, 160, 161
  eugenic 30, 34, 161
action 101, 115, 148
  informed 164
  purposeful 164
activity 159, 160
  communal 36
  government 36
ADA deficiency 161
Adam 186, 195, 197
adenine 256
Administration, Reagan 178
adoption 8, 9, 17, 110, 136, 241
advantage 173
  social 210
afflictions 8, 132, 158
AFP blood test 139, 141
agency 241
aggressive 105
aging 162
agreeableness 105
agriculture 184
AIDS 11, 12, 127
alcoholism 80, 84, 200
alleles 257
Alliance for Genetic Support Group
  151
Alzheimer's Disease 78, 86, 156, 158,
  163, 175, 235

American College of Medical
  Genetics 51
American College of Obstetricians
  and Gyneocologists 33
American Eugenics Society 27, 29
American Journal of Human Genetics 29,
  106
American Society of Human
  Genetics 29, 146, 151
Americans with Disabilities Act
  179
amino acid 85, 256
amniocentesis 16, 17, 19, 20, 138,
  142, 256
amplification 256
analysis
  cost-benefit 33
  ethical 108
  laboratory 107
  risk-benefit 204
  statistical 150
anatomy 76
anencephaly 55
aneuploidy 256
animals 116, 119, 171, 178, 187,
  188
  domestic 105
animism 43
Annals of Eugenics 29
Annas, George 130
anomalies 49–53, 55–58
anthropology 81, 234
anxiety 11, 31, 34, 62, 124, 126,
  139
apologetics 63
appearance
  physical 210
Aquinas, Thomas 62
Aristotle 41, 42
Asilomar Conference 172, 177

atheism 165
athletes 203
attitude 80
  hopeful 32
Augustine 234
aunt 100, 149
autonomy 54, 165
autosome 256
Avery 174
awareness 159
  public 157, 160, 188

baby 139, 151, 158, 238
  making of 184
Bacon, Francis 44, 62, 63, 81, 120
bacteria 97, 99, 116, 175, 186
base pairs 97, 256
  nucleotide 85, 231
base sequence 256
  analysis 256
basis 35, 76, 78
  genetic 147, 151
  non-biblical 191
beauty 208, 214
Beckwith, Francis 164
Beecher, Henry 30
Bellah, Robert 40
behaviour 31, 32, 67, 75, 88, 105,
    127, 128
  abnormal 107
  aggressive 107
  human 36, 104
beings
  angelic 186
  humans 35, 42, 61, 76, 78, 80,
      81, 111, 118–120, 142, 165,
      186, 188, 195, 203, 234, 254
  spiritual 254
belief 35, 37, 41, 42, 148
  Judeo-Christian 179
benefit 71, 77, 98, 100, 128, 142,
    156, 157, 159–161, 163, 172,
    178, 196, 200, 208, 209
  psychological 210
Berger, Peter 223
biochemical 78, 84
biochemistry 76, 91
bioengineering 166
bioethics 160, 219
Bioethics in Europe 81

biologist 25, 30, 35, 232
  molecular 76, 78, 81, 104
biology 26, 67, 88, 157, 164, 177
  applied 35
  molecular 76, 219, 231
  new 183
biomedicine 81
biophysical 78
biopsychosocial 88, 249
bios 180
biotechnology 113, 115, 119, 120,
    178, 233, 257
Biotechnology Working Group of
    the Present's Council on
    Competitiveness 172
birth 70, 86, 128, 148, 184, 238
  midwifery stage of 184
birth control 26
Blake, William 46
blastocyst 257
blastomere 133, 257
bleed 7
  nose 9, 10
  traumatic 8
blood 89, 129, 162
  products of 10
blueprint
  genetic 75, 85, 111
Body of Christ 211
body 171, 248, 252
  darkly-stained 146
  human 80
  mortal 33
body-building 203, 206
body-fat 206
body-part 149
Bonhoeffer, Dietrich 61
boundary 41
brain 35, 86, 110, 119, 184, 188
BRCAI 99, 100, 124, 125, 132
breast cancer (see cancer)
breeding
  human 29
  inheritance 171
  selective 161
Brenner, Sidney 77
Britain 27–29
brokenness 53, 56, 81
burden 66, 71, 140, 154, 159, 207,
    209

California 29
California Institute of Technology 183
Calvary 57
Calvin, John 44, 234
Canadian Royal Commission 196
cancer 32, 116, 131, 132, 156, 162, 184, 198, 241
  breast 84, 95, 99, 100, 124–126, 132, 158, 163
  eye 163
  lung 162
  ovarian 100, 124, 125, 132
  pancreatic 175
  prostate 95
capacity 36, 165, 179, 196
  intellectual 108
care 19, 20, 21, 53, 128, 133, 153, 154, 254
  follow-up 148
  health 71
  managed 240
care-giver 88, 130, 185, 204
careless 105, 108
carrier 18, 31, 71, 98, 110, 126, 127, 129, 132, 150, 156, 257
case
  hard 189
Casey v. Planned Parenthood 224, 229
Casti Connubii 28
Caucasian 197
causation
  genetic 158
cDNA (see complimentary DNA)
C. elegans 175
celebration 70, 231–233
cell 85–87, 97, 109, 148, 161, 172, 187, 197, 231
  animal 174, 175
  bacterial 174
  bone-marrow 177
  brain 191
  egg 85, 109, 148, 260
  germ 109, 171, 188, 196
  modification of 109, 176
  pancreatic 176
  somatic 171, 175, 177, 188
  sperm 29, 67, 85, 97, 109, 136, 196, 220
  target 176, 187

cell-line 174, 234
  immortalized 118
centimorgan 257
centromere 257
challenge 101, 102, 140, 141, 148, 150, 154, 156–167, 214, 231, 233, 240, 241, 246–255
Chamber of Commerce 161
change 42, 43, 104, 109, 148, 171, 173, 176, 200
chaplain 3, 12
characteristics 34, 108, 238
  behavioural 106
  genetic 164
  personality 107
  physical 213
  chemicals 171
  brain 107
chemotherapy 171
Cheure Dor Yeshorim program 129
child 8, 9, 10, 137, 139–141, 143, 148, 150, 152–154, 158, 220
  birth of 141
  diseased 29
  formation of 14
children 3, 11, 13, 14, 31, 32, 40, 49, 70, 106, 110, 111, 126, 132, 133, 136, 140, 144, 199, 200, 204–215, 240, 242
  desire for 31
  future 8, 148
chimerism 174, 177
China 240
choice 20, 108, 119, 157, 165, 198
  autonomous 30
  informed 34
  reproductive 138, 238
  voluntary 34
cholesterol 86, 162
chotionic villus sampling 257
chromosome 17–19, 97–99, 146, 147, 161, 174, 175, 231 257
  extra 146
church 12, 13, 15, 16, 20, 43, 54, 56, 89, 101, 102, 140, 159, 160, 164, 172, 179, 180, 226, 227, 231, 233, 236, 240–242, 246, 248, 250
Ciba Symposium 77
circumcision 7
citizen 117

civilization 35, 36
classwork 106
cleaving 174
clergy 151
client 33, 149
clinic 29, 100, 143, 144, 151, 197,
    240
clone 218, 230, 357
cloning 118, 174, 257
clotting factor 7, 8, 11
code 96
    genetic 79, 85, 125, 156, 162, 183,
        184, 187, 190, 236
codon 258
coercion 30, 33, 46, 240
Cohen, Daniel 81
Cole-Turner, Robert 159, 164
college 153
Collins, Francis 137, 163, 232, 240
colour
    of eyes 78, 162, 190
    of hair 78, 188–190
    of skin 184, 188–190, 209
colour-blindness 184
commercial interest 178
committee
    bioethics 160
Committee on Genetic Risks of the
    Institute of Medicine 1994
    157
commodification 121
community 36, 120, 160, 161, 178,
    234, 240, 247, 250, 252–254
    human 34, 37
    medical 30, 159
    religious 20
    scientific 30, 159
compassion 3, 63, 164, 186, 212,
    232, 254
Compassion in Dying v. Washington State
    224, 229
competitiveness 115, 211
complementary sequences 258
completeness 249
component 178, 183
    genetic 95, 96, 162
    environmental 95, 162
compound
    medicinal 175
conception 36, 136, 139, 142, 143,

    184, 238
concern 44, 60, 61, 89, 101, 117, 186
    ethical 120, 178, 179
condition 11, 12, 78, 87, 151, 163,
    189, 201
    genetic 7, 18–20, 31, 70, 89, 127,
        147, 148, 151, 154
    hereditary 148, 158
    human 44, 250
    physical 49, 187
    psychological 187
    social 173
confidentiality 124–135
conflict 131
congregation
    church 14, 153, 180, 242, 252, 253
consanguinity 258
conscientiousness 105, 108
consequence 61, 62, 66–68, 148,
    156
conserved sequence 258
consideration 121, 177
    theological 172–174, 186
constitution
    genetic 95, 147, 148
consultation 149
contamination 10
context 76, 84–92, 107
contribution 96, 193
    genetic 95, 147, 148
control 34, 46, 56, 69, 80, 100, 111,
    165
    over health 80
    over life 80
    over security 80
Coordinated Framework for
    Biotechnology 172
coordination 156
Copernicus, Nicholas, 61, 62, 232
corruption 33, 120
cosmid 258
cost 121, 213, 214
    educational 153
    health-care 89, 153
Council of Europe 178
counselling 10, 11, 19, 33, 77, 130,
    132, 146–155, 210
    diagnostic 148–150
    genetic 29–32, 34, 49, 127,
        146–155

informative 151–152
supportive 152–153
counsellor
genetic 19, 30–33, 47, 89, 138,
146, 147, 150, 154
couple 110, 138, 142, 179, 220,
240
at risk 110, 142
courage 10
cousin 100, 149
creation 43, 49, 50, 56, 64, 66, 69,
120, 165, 173, 180, 189, 195,
232, 251,
beauty of 96, 232
corruption of 208
doctrine of 252
fallen 50, 208
intricacy of 96
creator
God as eternally living 37
creature
humanoid 118
credibility 101
Crick, Francis Dr. 175, 219, 232,
237
criminals 219
Crombie, A.R. 42
crossing over 258
CTT 97
culture 36, 40, 61, 67, 72, 221, 235
culture war 40
cure 19, 21, 31, 32, 97, 98, 154, 156,
163, 196, 207, 236, 238, 239
CVS 14, 18–20, 142
cystic fibrosis 3, 13, 14, 18–20, 95,
97, 98, 110, 111, 128, 129, 132,
149, 150, 158, 163, 189, 258
testing for 13, 98
cytochrome C 173
cytogenetics 258
cytosine 258

danger 40, 47, 80
Darwin, Charles 25, 26, 35, 104, 105,
173
Darwinists
social 26
data 79, 206
database 96
death 3, 4, 6, 20, 21, 30, 40, 44, 53,

70, 97, 141, 150, 152, 179, 186,
188, 234
merciful 28
debate 34, 180
public 115, 117
de Chardin, Teilhard 68
decision-making 61, 113, 115, 160
informed 157
reproductive 34, 148, 156
defect 33, 50
birth 70, 148
genetic 77, 79, 138, 139, 141,
158, 175, 176, 179, 185, 186
deficiency, mental 28, 29
causes of 29
environmental 29
hereditary 29
statistics on 28
dehumanization 80
De Lang's syndrome 52
deletion 147, 258
democracy 36, 37
demon 171
denial 32, 152
denomination 159, 180
deoxyribonucleotide (see nucleo tide)
depression 31, 132,
clinical 206
descendants 111
Descent of Man 104
desertion 31
design
of God 197
desire 190
determinism 76, 77, 162, 163
development 49, 79, 86, 87, 91, 113,
114, 121, 124, 139
embryonic state of 110
height 203
human 26, 198
Dewey, John 224
diabetes 32, 86, 96, 98, 183, 184,
204, 209, 241
diabetic 171, 176, 209
diagnosis 14, 16, 19, 70, 77, 79, 110,
124, 136, 148, 149, 152, 179, 241
clinical 79
genetic 70
preimplantation 110, 158
prenatal 117

dialogue 159, 160, 163, 164, 166
Diamond v. Chakrabarty 113–116, 118
dignity
    human 67, 164, 165, 179, 180, 253
dilemma 100, 102, 161, 163, 191
dinner 153
diploid 258
disability 17, 53, 54, 56, 127, 140,
        141 142, 144, 152, 163, 179,
        209, 213, 238, 240–242
    inherited 108
    persons with 140
disappointment 206
discourse 159
    epidictic 253
discovery 98, 100, 233
discrimination 31, 33, 34, 100, 101,
        104, 126–129, 156, 163, 165,
        204, 209, 212–214, 240, 241,
    genetic 18, 101, 160
discussion 166
    family 149
disease (see also illness) 3, 12, 26, 29,
        31, 33, 52, 76, 86, 95–98, 111,
        115, 124, 125, 128, 133, 156,
        171, 186, 188, 190, 196, 209,
        242, 249
    absence of 248
    causes of 77
    congenital 81
    cure of 25
    genetic 4, 20, 77, 78, 111, 133,
        138, 140, 142, 147, 151, 183
    hereditary 3, 8, 25, 158
    late onset of 156
    life-threatening 186
    prevention of 111, 214
    rare 162
    treatment of 111, 238
disorder 4, 75, 96, 125, 126, 129,
        147, 148, 165, 196, 241
    fatal recessive 97
    genetic 148, 149, 151, 152, 154,
        156, 158, 162–164, 184
    infectious 158
    rare 95
distinction 185, 196
    germline 196
diversity 165, 189, 198
dizygotic 259

DNA 50, 69, 75–77, 79, 85–87, 91,
        96, 99, 157, 161, 171, 174, 187,
        198, 231, 234, 259
    banking of 158
    base pairs of 96, 99, 197
    cleaving of 174
    double helix 259
    human 99
    junk 231
    length of 161
    physical and chemical structure of
        175
    power of 162
    probes (see probes)
    replication 85, 259
    sequence 77, 96, 99, 100, 107,
        147, 161, 259
dog
    breeds of 105
dogma 76
    central 78, 80
Domestic Policy Council Working
    Group on Biotechnology 178
dominant 259
dominion 43, 44, 55, 69
Down's syndrome 15, 52, 53, 71,
        137, 139, 140, 146, 153, 259
DPC4 175
Drosophila 175
drug 44, 98, 119, 204
    performance-enhancement 211
Duchenne muscular dystrophy 259
dualism
    mind-body 76
    mind-matter 76
duplication 259
Duster, Troy 84
duty 43, 44
    Christian 81

earth 64, 66
    God's recreation of 81
earthquake 108
Ecclesiastes 1:18 100
E. coli 259
economics 224
education 11, 28, 106, 108, 157, 160,
        233
effect
    metabolic 206

systemic 207
eggs (see cell)
elelctrophoresis 259
element 172
  self-replicating 174
elite
  intellectual 108
ELSI (Ethical, Legal and Social
    Implications branch of Human
    Genome Project) 100, 259
embodiment 81, 84
embryo 85, 109–111, 118, 133, 136,
    178, 220
  development 78, 85, 86
  preimplantation 109, 142, 143
  splitting 260
  testing 142
emotions 11
employer 33, 34, 101, 126, 128
  future 163
employment 18, 100, 101, 126–128,
    156, 241
encouragement 3, 50, 240
endonuclease 260
energy 85, 203
engineering
  fetal 184
  genetic 81, 85, 111, 113, 117, 118,
      159, 171, 172, 183, 184, 225,
      254
  human genetic 184
England 29
enhancement 86, 111, 189, 196, 214
  genetic 137
  performance 208
Enlightenment, the 61–63
Enquist, Roy 165
environment 9, 86, 87, 95, 96, 104,
    106, 108, 162, 163, 189, 214
  cultural 28
  natural 76
  social 28, 76
enzyme 14, 85, 107, 173, 174,
    260
epistemology 43, 78
Equal Opportunities Employment
    Commission 101
equality 36
  natural 26, 165
eschatology 67, 81

Esiason, Boomer 97
ethicist 3, 47
ethics 30, 67, 81, 88, 101, 159,
    165, 193, 221, 231, 239
  Christian 107, 173, 251
  situation 190
  social 253
eugenics 25–39, 178, 184, 185, 199,
    218, 237–240, 260
  democratically contrived 35
  German 26
  history of 25–30, 37
  in Europe 27
  negative 27, 29, 32, 33
  positive 27
  practices in 26, 27
  purpose of 27
eukaryote 260
euthanasia 30, 218, 220, 254
  programme of 28
  voluntary 28
Euthanasia Legislation Society
    28
evil 50, 51, 120, 212
  knowledge of 36
  natural 108, 112
  proneness to 36
evolution 173
  cultural 36
  genetic 36
  of the brain 35
  theory of 26, 35, 173, 174
existence 251
  human 109
exons 260
experience 5, 10, 86, 105, 150, 153,
    251
expense 210
experimentation 43, 71, 172, 175
  unethical 30
expressivity 260
extraversion 105, 108
ex vivo 175

factor 11, 106, 124, 150
  determining 80
  environmental 85, 86, 104,
      203
  genetic 80, 86, 104, 108, 220
  hereditary 203

faith 6, 10, 41, 49, 63, 101, 104, 108,
        120, 180, 233
    religious 63, 64, 164
faithfulness 4, 72
failure 210, 252
family 3, 4, 7–12, 4, 31, 89, 90, 96,
        104, 110, 124, 126, 128, 130,
        131, 133, 136, 147–154, 164,
        240
    at-risk 111, 126
    extended 9, 107
FDA 177–179
fear 11, 34, 56, 84, 89, 124
feature
    facial 139, 140
feeding 51
fertilization 109, 110
fetus 14, 16, 70, 110, 128, 137, 139,
        142, 163, 177, 179, 240
    aborted 18, 191
    handicapped 164
    human 164
FISH (fluorescence *in situ*
        hybridization) 260
fitness
    physical 162
Fletcher, Joseph 60, 65, 183
flourishing
    human 253
form
    anatomical 165
Fost 34
founder effect 260
Fourteenth Amendment 224
framework 46, 47, 77, 79
    interpretive 80
    meaning-giving 80
    moral 41
French National Ethics Committee
        196
friends 11, 12, 15, 89, 214,
        240
fruit 81
fruit flies 99
function 85, 86, 125
    anabolic 208
    cellular 85, 117
    metabolic 208
future 84, 133, 152, 158, 218

Galton, Sir Francis 25, 26, 29
gamete (see cell)
gamete intrafallopian tube transfer
        260
gender 141, 144, 165, 209
    selection of 144
genes
    AD3 175
    addition 109, 184
    as source of good and evil 77, 80
    CF 97, 98, 110, 150
    conserved 175
    defects (see defect)
    deletrious 142, 158, 165, 185,
        196
    expression 162, 261
    families 261
    fitness 162
    foreign 176
    functioning 109, 110
    library (see genomic library)
    malfunctioning 109, 110
    manipulation of 46
    mapping 261
    missing 19, 147
    normal 175
    personality 162
    potentially lethal 29
    product 261
    purified 176
    recessive 161
    replacement 109
    transfer of 118
Genes of Hope 81
gene-carrier 97
gene pool
    human 178
gene-splicing 187
generations
    future 35, 109–111, 158, 188,
        196
genethics 160
Genethics 158
Genetic Privacy Act 130
geneticist 25, 29, 33, 35, 37, 47, 97,
        147, 159, 163, 231
    behavioural 105, 106, 108, 235
    clinical 146
    molecular 173, 177
Geneticists' Manifesto 29

geneticization 75
  age of 156
  behavioural 88, 104–109
  medical 75–77, 81
  Mendelian 161
  microbial 173
  molecular 77, 157, 160, 161, 172
  new 157, 159, 160, 164, 231, 233,
    240, 241
genome 77, 99, 101, 171, 176
genome projects 261
genomic
  imprinting 261
  library 261
genotype 87, 237
gentleness 4
George, Robert 40
germ cells (see cell)
germ-line 77, 179
Germany 26–29, 33
  Nazi 25, 33, 35, 199
GHD 203–208
gift 211
gland
  pituitary 203
Glass, Bentley 132
glory 50, 53
glucose 203
gnosticism 233–235
goal 99, 232
goats 161
God 5, 6, 10, 11, 15, 20, 41, 50, 51,
    55–58, 107, 108, 121, 133, 138,
    207, 211, 213–215, 222, 233, 252
  Almighty 102, 133
  as Creator 37, 41, 42, 52, 69, 79,
    165, 173, 179, 180, 195, 197,
    231, 239
  as Father 173
  children of 210
  creative work of 173
  grace of 3, 5, 11, 45, 54, 56, 64,
    108, 248
  loved by 33, 35, 37, 210
  personal 35, 37
  providence of 52, 53, 56
  sovereignty of 49–59, 121, 239
  suffering of 210
  will of 42, 188, 252
'God of the gaps' 63–67

Golden Rule 164
good 40, 164, 166
  knowledge of 36
  proneness to 36
gospel 33, 66, 253, 254
government 33, 36, 127
  federal 114
grace (see God)
grandchildren 111
Grand Sez Who 221, 223
Graham, Mrs. Billy 69
Grant, George 45
Greeks 41
grief 139, 153
  process of 152
group 125, 160, 180, 199
  genetic-support 128, 151
guidance 130, 133, 173
guidelines 29, 41, 46, 165, 166, 177,
    178, 206
  rDNA 172
guilt 15, 132, 139, 152,
guanine 262
gynecologist 32

hair
  colour of 78
handicap (see disability)
haploid 262
harm 124, 131, 160, 161, 187, 196,
    198
Harvard 35, 116, 219, 224
Harvard Business School 221
Harvard Medical School 30, 241
Hawking, Stephen 242, 243
healing 44, 70, 95, 164, 232, 254
health 20, 70, 184, 208, 214, 248, 253
  as-Shalom 250–254
  maintenance of 214
  needs 100
  physical 109, 249
  professional 31, 33
  WHO definition of 248, 250,
    254
health care 16, 100, 130
  access to 100, 101
  alternatives 148
  costs of 18, 153, 214
  system 254
heart 210, 213

disease 32, 95 162, 187
heaven 55, 56
  God's recreation of 81
height 204–215
  average 204, 205
  gain 204–206, 208
heightism 204, 212, 213
hemizygous 262
hemophilia 7–12, 147, 153, 154, 248,
  262
heredity 77, 104, 106, 172
heritability 106
Herrnstein, Richard 219, 220
heterozygosity 237
heterozygous 262
HGH therapy 203–217
Hippocrates 124, 126
historian 34, 41, 218
history 41, 42, 45, 76, 120, 133
  family 125, 130, 148, 149
  genetic 163
  human 96
  medical 136
  prenatal 149
Hitler, Adolf 28, 29
HIV 10, 12, 248
  infected 7, 11
  virus 10, 11
Holmes, Jr., Oliver Wendell 224
Holocaust 161, 199
Holy Spirit 173, 248
homeobox 262
homeopathy 171
homologies 262
homologous chromosomes 262
homozygosity 237, 262
homosexuality 80, 235
hope 3, 33, 37, 49, 56, 70, 102, 120, 153
hopelessness 31
hormone 86, 204, 208
  deficency 203, 204
  human growth 175, 203–217
horse 105
host 176
Houston Chronicle 162
humanness 180
human gene therapy (see also
  therapy) 261
Human Genome Project 19, 25, 70,
  71, 75, 84, 95–103, 111, 137,
  138, 156, 161, 163, 175, 230,
  232, 241, 243, 262
Human Rights Convention 178
humanity (see also nature, human)
  61–63, 65–68, 76–78, 91, 104,
  111, 120, 121, 158, 173, 179,
  223, 231, 233
humility 4, 54, 159, 211
Huntington's disease 30–33, 124,
  128, 130, 131, 136, 137, 140,
  158, 163, 189, 191, 262
  test for 30–32, 132, 136, 240
Huntington's Disease Society of
  America 31
Huxley, A. 46, 173
hybridization 114, 262
hybridoma 118
hygiene
  racial 26, 27, 29, 34, 35, 199
hypersecretion 207

identification 98, 174, 176
identity 180, 210
idolatries 253
ignorance 37
illness (see also diseases) 3, 6, 44,
  125, 132, 171, 207,209, 213,
  235, 239, 241
  fatal 158
  medical 102
  nature of 208, 209
  prevention of 131, 204
  treatment of 204
illumination 252
image of God 36, 41–43, 54–56, 165,
  173, 180, 212–214, 233, 234,
  238, 253
image of humanity 76
  Cartesian 76
immunosuppression 177
impact 152
imperative 157
  categorical 190
imprinting (see genomic imprinting)
improvement 180
  psychosocial 208, 210
incentive 113–115, 120, 121
incompatibility 177
inconvenience 210
Indiana, State of 27

Indiana University School of
  Medicine 31
individuals 28, 30, 36, 87, 102, 109,
  110, 125, 129–131, 133,
  147–149, 151, 249, 252, 253
individualism 211
industry 114, 115, 118, 184
  chemical 171
  pharmaceutical 171
inequality 35
  socioeconomic 34
infants
  malformed 56
  newborn 56, 97, 137, 141
Infantile bilateral stratal necrosis 3, 5
infection 11, 97
influence 104, 106, 108, 113, 162
informatics 263
information 31, 99, 101, 106, 126,
  128, 131, 138, 139, 147,
  149–151, 154, 157, 159,
  161–163, 231
  accurate 149, 154
  genetic 26, 34, 71, 81, 101, 106,
    124, 156, 160, 163, 171, 241
  hereditary 76
ingenuity 121
inheritance 26, 104, 106, 157, 161, 174
  genetic 178
  Mendelian 162
  mode of 129, 149
injection 56, 109
  hormone 206, 207, 210
injustice 120, 213, 214
innovation 63, 115, 161, 175
insemination
  artificial 29, 67
insight 79
in situ hybridization 263
instinct 105
Institutional Review Boards 30
insulin 78, 171, 175
  animal 176
  cloned human 176
  recombinant 204, 209
insurance 13, 18, 31, 33, 71, 100,
  101, 126–128, 156, 214, 241
insurers 34, 71, 100, 101, 127, 128
integration 210
intelligence 26, 105, 162

interaction 85, 162
interface 101
interferon 78
interphase 263
intervention 43, 76, 99, 128, 191, 196
  genetic 80, 104, 158, 160, 183–203
  germ-line genetic 104, 109–112
  government 26
  incremental 197, 198
  medical 163, 208
  palliative 77
  surgical 175
  therapeutic 77, 185
introns 263
introversion 105, 108
in utero 137, 139, 142, 177
inventor 113, 116, 118, 119
Investigational New Drug
  Applications (INDs) 176
in vitro fertilization 109, 110, 133,
  136, 142, 263
I.Q. 27, 183, 190, 199
isolation 12, 152, 153, 210
Israelites 207

Jackson, Markie 147, 153, 154, 248
Jacob 161, 237
Jacob, Francois 78
James, William 224
Jesus Christ 3, 171, 210, 222
  as Saviour 187
  cross of 173
  death of 173
  healing ministry of 69, 70, 95, 96,
    233
  incarnation of 173, 195
  name of 173
  resurrection of 37
  return of 193
  the Good Shepherd 4
  trust in 187
Job 37, 213
Johnson, Paul 218
Johnson, Phillip 221
Johnson, Samuel 46
Judaism 36, 50
judgment 64, 65, 79, 140, 159, 193
justice 71, 100, 101, 120, 165,
  213–215
  social 70

justification 44, 139, 191
  moral 124, 131

Kaiser, Christopher 42
Kant 190
karyotype 263
Kennedy, Anthony 225
kidney 149
killing 67
  allowable 28
kilobase 263
kindness 4
knowledge 11, 26, 34, 36, 37, 43, 56,
    61–66, 69, 88, 101, 120, 124,
    133, 156, 163, 175, 177, 198,
    210, 212
  genetic 36, 37, 60
  molecular biological 78
  of evil 36
  of good 36
  scientific 61, 76, 79, 115

Laban 161, 237
laboratory 19, 109, 146, 197, 226
Lander, E.S. 175
Landsberg Prison 29
Lang, Theobald 35
law 30, 42, 71, 101, 107, 119, 120,
    172, 224, 231
  of God 186, 213
  patent 71, 113, 116, 118–121
  universal 190
  written on the heart 36
lawyers 34
Leff, Arthur 221
left-handedness 184, 189, 190
legislation 18, 101, 116, 117, 129,
    166, 223, 240, 242
Lenz, Fritz 29
Lesch-Nyhan syndrome 164
leukemia 206, 207
Lex Rex. 223
liability 33, 164
liberty
  procreative 238, 240
life 5, 10, 20, 32, 37, 40, 56, 68, 70,
    79, 115, 117, 130, 131, 133, 141,
    144, 156, 164
  eternal 37
  human 71, 117, 119

mystery of 183
new in Christ 33
quality of 54, 112, 132, 139
sanctity of human 165, 179, 180,
    218, 238, 239
tragic view of 251
Life magazine 163
Life and Death Decisions 165
life-forms 101, 180
  complex 174
lineage 173
Lincoln, Abraham 113
linkage 126, 263
linkage map 263
limitation 80, 113, 115, 131, 208,
    212, 213
Lindbergh, Charles 121
locus 263
  genetic 179
load
  genetic 29
Lord's Supper 247
lottery 184
  chromosomal 183
  natural 108
love 4, 102, 153, 164, 213, 251
  of God 5, 53
  of neighbour 33, 44, 195, 250
lungs 97, 98
Luther, Martin 44, 55, 56, 250

Macdonald, Mr. & Mrs. 16–21
MacIntyre, Alasdair 47
machine 49
  genetic hormonal information 47
  metaphor of 76, 80
makeup
  genetic 50, 95, 117, 119, 121, 165,
    184
malpractice 179
  medical 33
mammogram 100
manic-depression 78
manipulation 42, 43, 46, 47, 78, 81,
    117, 121, 171, 174, 220
  genetic 115, 161, 178, 230
  of human beings 80
map
  genetic 99
  physical 99, 175, 265

mapping (see also gene map, linkage map, physical map) 25, 175
March of Dimes 157
marker 97, 99, 263
marketing 34
marriage 210
Maryland 151
Marx, Karl 183
mastery 45, 69, 183
materialism
  scientific 35–37
material
  genetic 19, 118, 119, 147
  living 116
meaning 45, 79
means 199, 200
mechanism 79
media 98
  headlines 156
medicine 25, 44, 75, 80, 138, 157, 175, 183, 231, 239, 240
  goals of 207, 208
  modern 76, 77, 80, 184
  molecular 99, 232
megabase(Mb) 263
meiosis 263
memory 156
Mendel, Gregor 105, 171, 237
messenger RNA (mRNA) 264
metabolism
  gigantism-like 207
  inborn error of 177
metanoia 252
metaphase 264
micro-organism 71, 78, 116
Middle East 171
Miller, H.I. 177
millennium 171
mind 35, 43
minister 159
ministry 44, 249–253
  definition of 249–250
  dual view of 250
  educational 108
  health 249–251, 253
Miringoff, Marque-Luisa 239
misspelling 97–99
misuse 157
motochondria 85, 173
mitosis 264

models 76, 80
  abstract 76
modification 109, 171, 176, 178
  phenotypic 175
molecule 125, 207
  protein 203
monoamine oxidase A
  deficiency of 107, 108
monozygotic 264
moratorium 172, 177
morbidity
  psychological 209
mother 162, 179
Mouse, The Harvard 116, 117
mRNA (see also messenger RNA) 198
mucopolysaccharides type 3, 147
mucus 97
multifactorial
  disorders 264
  traits 85, 264
mutation 100, 107, 109, 125, 126, 150, 152, 171, 173
myopia 184

narcissm 211
National Academy of Sciences 114, 172
National Biotechnology Board 172
National Council of Churches 159
National Health Region 29
National Institute of Health 100, 172, 179, 205, 231
National Institute of Health Guidelines 178
National Science Foundation 157, 172
National Socialism 35
National Society of Genetic Counsellors 151
nature 41–46, 61, 63, 65–67, 69, 104, 117
  accident of 183
  human 36, 47, 68, 69
  laws of 115
  products of 115
Nazis 25–29, 34, 36, 37, 225, 240
needs 101, 195
  basic human 151

health care 179
  human 37, 185
negatives
  false 33, 139
negativity 126, 206
neighbours 33, 250
Neue Anthropologie 29
neural tube defect 33
neurologist 4, 31, 156
neuron 86
neuroticism 105
New Atlantis 81
New York Jets 97
New York Times 184, 224
Newton, Isaac 64
Nietzsche 61
Nirenberg, Dr. Marshall 121
nitrogenous base 264
Nobel prize 132, 175, 219, 240
Nordic movement 27
norepinephrine 107
Norm
  biological 208
normality 209
nucleic acid 264
nucleus 96, 161, 264
nucleotide 85, 264
Nuremberg Code 30
Nuremberg Trials 28
nurse 3, 89, 146
  parish 153
nursing home 31
nurture 70, 104, 250, 254

obesity 78, 80, 84, 235
objectivization 75, 76, 79, 80
official
  government 172
offspring 171, 179, 238
  future 29, 32, 148
On Human Nature 35
On The Origin of Species 26
oncogene 264
opinion 166, 189
oppression 120
option 18, 70
  reproductive 152
opportunity 101, 159, 211, 212,
  131
  educational 156

Organization for Economic
  Cooperation and Development
  172, 178
organisms 77–80, 99, 116, 118, 119,
  121, 175
  divergent 177
  health of 187
  taxonomic relationship of 174
  unicellular 174
origin 76, 174
Orr, David 164
ovum (see cell, egg)
oyster
  polyploid 116

pain 3, 4, 6, 57, 119, 154
pantheism 43
Paracelsus 44
Paradise 81
parent 8, 108, 152, 158
parenthood
  responsible 111
parents 8, 49, 70, 108–111, 119,
  126, 131, 141, 144, 148, 150,
  152, 158, 198, 199, 204–206,
  238, 242
  single 152
parishioners 160
Parkinson's disease 189, 220
Parliamentary Assembly of the
  Council of Europe 196
passion 101, 102
pastor 12, 14–16
pastorate 159, 160
Patent Office 115–119
patenting 40, 71, 101, 113–123
pathogen 175
pathology 76
pathway
  transforming growth factor
  175
patient 3, 11, 33, 67, 79, 80, 124,
  126, 127, 129–132, 162, 196,
  207, 210, 220, 248
  diabetes mellitus 204, 209
Patterson, Amy 177
Paul, the apostle 186, 207, 210
Paul, Diane 34, 88
Pauling, Linus 132, 240
PCR (see polymerase chain reaction)

peas 174, 237
pediatrics 16, 17, 19
penetrance 126, 264
Penrose, Lionel 29
perfection
　genetic 165, 238
performance 127
　intellectual 106
person
　affected 198
　as individual 185
　black-haired 185
　blonde 185
　blue-eyed 185
　brown-eyed 185
　short 203–215
　within community 249, 251
personality 105, 108, 162, 189
　aggressive 105, 189
　highly strung 189
personhood 56, 142, 143
perspective 56, 60, 64–68, 71, 87, 120
　Baconian 61–63, 72
　biblical 50, 84, 90, 210
　Christian 164–166
pessimism 206
phage 264
phenomena 76
　physical 115
phenotype 85–87, 171, 237, 264
phenylketonuria 85–87, 171, 237, 265
philosopher 183
philosophy 32, 45, 81
physicians 7, 9, 11, 13, 15, 19, 25,
　　29–35, 44, 75, 80, 81, 127, 129,
　　131, 141, 146, 147, 156, 172,
　　206, 210, 214, 233
　British 28
　Christian 159
　German 28, 37
physics 88
physiology 76
plane crash 186
plant 81, 116
Plant Patent Act 116
Plant Variety Protection Act 1970
　116
plasmid 116, 265
'playing God' 60–74, 207
pleiotropy 265

Ploetz, Alfred 26, 27
pointers 105
polarity 165
　public 25, 34, 159, 164, 240, 242
politician 111
polygenic
　disorders 265
　traits 265
polymerase chain reaction (PCR) 265
polymorphism 125, 265
poor persons 44, 69, 70, 71
Pope Pius XI 28
population 86, 87, 91, 109, 159, 165,
　214
　Jewish 99
positives
　false 33, 139
Postman, Neil 233
postmodernism 45
power 60–64, 66, 67, 114
　value-laden 80
practitioner
　medical 19, 32
Prader Willie syndrome 147
pragmatism 121, 221, 224
prayer 12, 15, 45, 152
predestination 198
predisposition 80, 107, 111, 131,
　133, 137, 162
pregnancy 14, 15, 17, 19, 20, 98,
　136–141, 149, 199
　tentative 238
preimplantation 111
prejudice 209, 212, 213
premiums 101
presentation 160, 161, 163
President's Commission for the
　Study of Ethical Problems in
　Medicine 60–63, 67, 131,
　178
pride 68, 212
priesthood
　of all believers 250
principle 40, 41, 60, 67, 142, 143
　biblical 164, 190, 204, 207
　scientific 115
　theological 185
privacy 130, 163, 166
probe 265
　diagnostic 175

procedures 158, 163, 207, 239
  medical 187
  regulatory 178
process 65, 118
  cognitive 79
  genetical 76
  mental 76
  physiological 76
  reasoning 191
procreation 27, 67, 132, 238
product 176, 178
  genetic 85
  quality of 178
production
  energy 203
profit 71
prognosis 19
programme 25, 114, 209
  government 30
  testing 31
progress 26, 44, 164
prokaryote 265
promise 53
promoter 86, 265
promotion 101
prophetic voice 253
protection 100, 116, 121, 157, 164
  legal 101, 119, 179
proteins 78, 85, 86, 198, 265
  human 78
  synthesis of 77, 78
  translation into 76, 77
protocol 100, 179
proto-oncogene 266
psuche 180
psychopaths
  institution for 107
puberty 205, 206
public 89, 115, 117
  informed 157
  policy 25, 34, 159, 164, 240, 242
Pulitzer prize 35
purine 266
purifying 174
Puritans 56
pyrimidine 266

Quaid, Kimberley 31–33, 38
qualities
  desired 184

mental 105, 125
physical 25
racial 25
quantification 75
quarrelsome 105, 108
Quie, Al 227

Rabelais, Francois 120
race 25–27, 165
  inferiority of 27–28
racism 29, 106
Ramsey, Paul 60, 66
Rattansi, P.M. 44
reality 75, 76, 118
  reduction of 75
reason 10, 102, 191, 196
recessive 129, 266
recognition 79
recombitant DNA (rDNA) 172, 175,
  178, 180, 266
Recombitant DNA Advisory
  Committee 127, 128
reconciliation 195, 213
redemption 50, 55, 57, 66, 173
reductionism 75–92, 235, 236
regulation 166, 172, 187
  government 177
  self 177
regulatory
  regions 266
  sequences 266
Reinhardt, Stephen 225
relationship 75, 210, 215, 249
  physician-patient 80
  social 204, 209, 210
relative 131, 149, 151
religion 35, 36
religiosity 75
repentance 252
'Repository for Germinal Choice'
  29
reproduction 29, 104, 188
research 30, 44, 87, 88, 92, 104–113,
  115, 117, 119, 142, 158, 164,
  174
  biological 78
  genetic 14, 56, 78, 84, 102,
    104–112, 115, 214, 234
  genome 34, 157
  molecular 78

researcher 47, 81, 88, 104–112, 156, 162, 187, 241
resources 71, 90, 91, 100, 133, 161, 193, 204, 214
health care 71, 214
respect 234
responsibility 10, 49, 50, 61, 65, 80, 81, 95, 107, 111, 120, 159, 193, 219–229
diminished moral 107, 108
ethical 104
restriction enzymes 266
restriction fragment length polymorphism (RFLP) 266
retardation 17
mental 28, 108, 235
retinoblastoma 163, 199
retrieving 105
revelation
biblical 173, 204
review
scientific 179
revolution 44, 45, 96
molecular genetic 171, 230
ribonucleic acid (RNA) 77, 266
ribosomes 266
rich 213
Rifkin, Jeremy 184
right
knowledge of 36
right-handedness 190
rightness 165
righteous 101, 120
rights 114, 115
risk 100, 124, 127, 130, 131, 138, 141, 150, 156, 163, 172, 176, 200, 206, 209, 241
increased 125
reproductive 148
social 31
zero 199
Roberts, David 45
Robertson, John 237, 240
Roe v. Wade 224
Romer v. Evans 225
Rotary Club 161
Rothman, Barbara Katz 144
roundworm 99
Rutherford, Samuel 223

safety 177, 188
Safety and Regulations in Biotechnology 172
saints
community of 250
Sanger, Margaret 26, 27
Saul 212
scenarios 110, 125, 130, 139, 144, 203, 220
Frankenstein 47, 102
theoretical 102
Schaeffer, Francis 222
Schiedermayer, David 164
schizophrenia 86, 95, 235
school 148, 163, 204, 222, 233
science 26, 36, 37, 44, 45, 61–63, 65, 76, 79, 81, 120, 157, 158, 164, 183, 231, 232, 242
DNA 158
genetic 26, 34, 101, 159, 160, 233, 247
modern 41, 80
natural 45, 75
scientist 25, 28–30, 34, 44, 75, 80, 92, 96, 97, 104, 158, 159, 172, 184, 232
screening 71, 125–127, 138, 200
alpha-fetoprotein 33
genetic 30, 34, 157, 166, 230, 236
maternal serum 20
prenatal 156, 163, 237, 238, 240, 242
selective 158
Scriptures 50, 53, 57, 58, 64, 186, 195, 234
secretion 203, 204
security 210
selection
negative 35
self-determination 165
self-help 31
self-image 208
self-interest 211
self-knowledge 31
senses 76
sequence (see also base sequence) 78
DNA 77–79, 99–101, 147
genetic 85, 173–175
nucleotide 78
sequence tagged site (STS) 267

sequencing 25, 175, 267
serotonin 107
servant 44
service 44, 49, 72
servitude
  involuntary 118
setback 153
Shalom 13–21
Shinn, Roger 164
shortness 203–206, 208–214
Shuler, G.D. 175
siblings 106, 131, 149, 150, 156, 158
sickle-cell anaemia 78, 165, 184, 240
sickle-cell disease 127, 267
sickness 20, 56
side-effects 98, 176
  physical 206, 207
sin 43, 49, 52, 171, 186, 189, 199, 236
  consequences of 186–189
  human proclivity to 36
man's propensity to 36, 95
sinfulness 36, 252
  effects of 236
Singer, Peter 238
Sinsheimer, Robert 183
sister 148
sister-chromatids 267
slavery 118
slope, slippery 193
smoking 162
sloth 68
social worker 13
society 9, 10, 20, 32, 61, 108, 120,
    121, 140, 164, 165, 180, 221, 253
  contemporary 164
  modern 55
Society for Racial Hygiene 27
Society for the Study of Social
    Biology 29
somatic cells (see also cell) 267
somatropin 203
sorrow 4
  chronic 153
southern blotting 267
specialist 113, 149
  genetic 146, 147, 149, 150
species 36, 171, 173
  human 25, 234
sperm (see cell)
Spina Bifida 139, 141

spirit 210
spirituality 5, 43, 81
sports 8, 9
Sports Illustrated 97
spouse 129, 152
stage 110
  preimplantation 111
  prenatal 111
standard
  relative 165
starvation 214
sterilization 27, 30, 240
  law of 27, 28
  seen as discriminatory 28
steward 69, 91, 213
stewardship 195
stigmitization 18, 31, 32, 241
strength 50, 63, 64, 211
stress 11
  environmental 108
structure 69, 76, 85, 129, 231,
    253
  biochemical 78
  of organs 78
studies 87, 126, 205
  animal 107
  human 107
subject
  randomized treated 205
  randomized untreated 205
suffering 4, 6, 21, 57, 67, 115, 131,
    208, 220, 251
suicide 32, 132, 160, 254
support 3, 153, 164, 240
  service 49, 152
  social 108
supremacy
  Nordic 27
Supreme Court 113, 114, 116, 118,
    225
surgery 100, 141, 196
  heart bypass 187
  morality of 187
surveillance 124, 128
survey 127
survival 36, 991
  of the fittest 26, 173
susceptibility 132
  hereditary 193
Suzuki, David 158

Swift, Jonathan 46
Switzerland 27
symptom 19, 33, 156
  clinical 149
synthesis
  protein 161, 203
system 84, 87, 109, 115
  judicial 115, 117, 120
  theological 108

talent 194
tampering 187–190
tandem repeat sequences 267
Tay Sach's disease 129, 165, 267
Taylor, Charles 47
teasing 204, 208, 210, 213, 214
technician 15
  laboratory 147
techniques 104, 109, 111, 119, 179
  abuse of 111
  gene-replacement 110, 111
technology 41–47, 56, 63, 65, 80,
    115, 120, 136, 141, 142, 147,
    156–159, 164, 171, 176, 180,
    184, 190, 231, 254
  abuses of 157, 199
  eugenic 185
  genetic 34, 40, 41, 75, 80, 138,
    157, 161, 163, 166, 172, 185,
    187, 189, 191, 200, 209, 211,
    233, 237
  human 81
  medical 159
  morally acceptable use of 190, 191
  non-therapeutic 188
  recombinant DNA 78, 114, 174,
    177, 178, 183–185, 187, 190,
    191, 203, 266
  therapeutic 185, 188
  transfer 267
telomere 267
ten commandments 222
tendency 105
  inborn 105, 108
  sinful 36
tests 14, 16, 18, 19, 30, 31, 33, 89,
    158, 159
  chromosome 17, 147, 149
  molecular genetic 147, 149
  neuropsychological 106

prenatal 136–146
presymptomatic 100
testing 8, 18, 19, 34, 125, 126, 156,
    163
  diagnostic 13, 98, 111, 149
  DNA 150
test-tube 171, 174
The Bell Curve 92, 106
The New Genesis 159
The Thanatos Syndrome 218
theodicy, crisis of 20
theologian 41, 47, 108, 159
  Christian 47
theology 35, 104, 107, 131, 159, 165,
    247
theory 76
  ethical 191
  secular ethical 191
therapy 19, 164, 171, 214, 261
  drug 98
  effectiveness of 204, 212
  enhancement 204, 206, 211
  fetal 138, 241
  genetic 4, 85, 89, 98, 110,
    118, 119, 157, 161, 163,
    166, 171–183, 191, 230,
    235
  germ-line 118, 171, 175, 179, 187,
    188, 196
  HGH 203, 204
  pigmentation 209
  somatic-cell gene 111, 158, 171,
    175, 187, 189, 191, 196
Thirteenth Amendment 118
thorn in the flesh 207
thrive
  failure to 151
thymine 268
Time Magazine 75
Timeless Healing 75
tissue 97, 118, 150, 177, 234
  adipose 206
  foreign 177
tolerance
  donor specific 177
totality 249, 250
traits 77–79, 85, 86, 88, 109, 127,
    144, 162, 172, 174, 178, 188,
    190, 209
  origin of 189

personality 104–106
phenotypic 77
physical 188
transcription 176, 268
transfection 175
transfer RNA (tRNA) 268
transformation 175, 268
transgenic organism 119, 268
translation 76, 79, 268
translocation 268
transmission 105, 110
transplant
  bone-marrow 117
  heart 187
  tissue 191
transplantation 119, 177
treatment 16, 20, 32, 96, 98, 110,
  128, 163, 171, 179, 207, 238, 239
  anti-cancer 209
  early 163
  growth hormone 203–217
  medical 86, 159, 171
  morality of medicinal 20
trial 55, 98, 212
Trisomy 13 52, 268
Trisomy 18 15, 18, 19, 52, 268
Trisomy 21 (see Down's syndrome)
tRNA (see transfer RNA)
trust 207
truth 35–37, 45, 56, 213, 221, 236,
  242
  God's 5
  scientifically derived 36
tumor-suppressor gene 110, 268
Turner's syndrome 205, 213, 214
twins 86, 104, 106

ultrasound 15, 16, 139, 141
unborn 4, 20, 71, 238
  handicapped 164
understanding 80, 81, 157, 159
  public 159
  scientific 64
unemployment 210
unfairness 210
unfriendly 105
United Methodist Church 159
United States 26–31, 114, 129, 137,
  146, 151, 172, 179, 183, 204,
  213, 218, 223, 238

United States Congress 113,
  115–117, 241
United States Constitution 113, 118
universe 41–43, 45, 61, 186, 210
unknown
  fear of 158
uracil(U) 268
utility 62, 66
Utopia 81, 200, 219
  as creation of human science
  81

values 4, 36, 45, 148, 180, 253
  cultural 209, 211
  neutral 32
  secular 80
variation 209
  genetic 147
vector (see also cloning vector) 175,
  176, 188
  viral 177
vegetables 81
victims 164
video 160
violence 52, 80, 105, 186
virus 10, 11, 109, 174, 177, 268
  retro 177
vision 56, 164, 196
vitamins 171
voluntarism 42

warfare 184
Warnock, Mary 220
Watson, James 25, 29, 30, 34, 38,
  164, 175, 219, 237
weakness 5, 211
  inherited 108
wealth 100, 213
weight 209
Weimar Republic 27
welfare 120, 232
  biological 25
well-being 34, 63, 66, 185, 214, 248,
  249
Wesley, John 226
Westminster Confession of Faith 50
wheelchair 9
Wilson, E.O. 35–38
Wilson, James 219, 220
wisdom 63, 67, 121, 133, 159

witness 37, 253
womb 56, 136, 138, 139–141, 183, 238
  surrogate 119
woman 128, 144, 173, 242
word-processing 109
world 61
  brave new 183
  fallen 124, 186, 187, 190
  sinful 173
  social (see also society) 9
world-view 35, 41, 46, 172, 179, 191, 222, 223
  Christian 41, 49, 172, 180, 233, 242
  theistic 173
  trinitarian 173
World Council of Churches 159
World Health Organization 248
World War II 29
World Wide Web 151, 166

worship 52, 96, 120, 232, 246
worth 32, 35, 37, 54, 56
  individual 32, 33, 164
wrong 165
  knowledge of 36

X-chromosome 107
X-rays 109

yeast 175
yeast artificial chromosome (YAC) 268
Young, F.F. 177
youth 214

zeal 101
zoe 180
zygote 268
zygote intrafallopian tube transfer (ZIFT) 269